March 2004
For Hermione,
with warm
regards,
Sarah

MODERNISM, MALE FRIENDSHIP, AND THE FIRST WORLD WAR

Sarah Cole examines the rich literary and cultural history of masculine intimacy in the twentieth century. Cole approaches this complex and neglected topic from many perspectives – as a reflection of the exceptional social power wielded by the institutions that housed and structured male bonds; as a matter of closeted and thwarted homoerotics; and as part of the story of the First World War. Cole shows that the terrain of masculine fellowship provides an important context for understanding key literary features of the modernist period. She foregrounds such crucial themes as the over-determined relations between imperial wanderers in Conrad's tales, the broken friendships that permeate Forster's fictions, Lawrence's desperate urge to make culture out of blood brotherhood, and the intense bereavement of the war poet. Cole argues that these dramas of compelling and often tortured male friendship have helped to define a particular spirit and voice within the literary canon.

Sarah Cole is Assistant Professor in the Department of English and Comparative Literature at Columbia University. Her articles have appeared in *Modern Fiction Studies* and *ELH*.

MODERNISM, MALE FRIENDSHIP, AND THE FIRST WORLD WAR

SARAH COLE

Department of English and Comparative Literature
Columbia University

CAMBRIDGE
UNIVERSITY PRESS

PUBLISHED BY THE PRESS SYNDICATE OF THE UNIVERSITY OF CAMBRIDGE
The Pitt Building, Trumpington Street, Cambridge CB2 1RP, United Kingdom

CAMBRIDGE UNIVERSITY PRESS
The Edinburgh Building, Cambridge, CB2 2RU, UK
40 West 20th Street, New York, NY 10011–4211, USA
477 Williamstown Road, Port Melbourne, VIC 3207, Australia
Ruiz de Alarcón 13, 28014 Madrid, Spain
Dock House, The Waterfront, Cape Town 8001, South Africa

http://www.cambridge.org

First published 2003

Printed in the United Kingdom at the University Press, Cambridge

Typeface Adobe Garamond 11/12.5 pt.   *System* LaTeX 2_ε [TB]

A catalogue record for this book is available from the British Library

ISBN 0 521 81923 7 hardback

Contents

Acknowledgments

It is a great pleasure to offer thanks to many institutions and individuals – teachers, colleagues, friends, and family – who have made this book possible. Over the years, I have received a variety of grants and fellowships, and have benefited from the generosity of several foundations and libraries. I would particularly like to thank the Woodrow Wilson Foundation for its three years of support for graduate study, in the form of a Mellon Fellowship in the Humanities. The Rockefeller Foundation Study and Conference Center in Bellagio, Italy, provided me with six marvelous weeks of concentrated writing time. For a summer of intensive work amidst its beautiful gardens, I thank the Huntington Library in Pasadena, California, which awarded me a Mayers Fellowship. I am very grateful to Columbia University Arts and Sciences for funding two summers of invaluable work in London. The Imperial War Museum (IWM) in London has been a superb resource, both for its materials and for its friendly, knowledgeable, professional staff, whom I thank in the warmest terms. I also wish to acknowledge the IWM for its permission to publish the cover photo.

This book began as a dissertation in the English Department at the University of California at Berkeley, a place of exceptional scholarly rigor and easy collegiality. In my years there, I received not only generous fellowship and teaching support, but also intellectual guidance from my professors and many peers. I would like to thank John Bishop, Dori Hale, and Celeste Langan for providing instruction and discussion which had a significant impact on this project. Sheldon Rothblatt in the History Department was a wonderful reader of my dissertation, as well as a limitless reservoir of knowledge about everything to do with British history of the nineteenth and twentieth centuries. Catherine Gallagher, an intellectual mentor from my first days in graduate school, seemed unable to give anything but brilliant advice. Finally, I want to express my gratitude to Elizabeth Abel, a model dissertation director and admirable teacher, who has been a constant source of support in all elements of my professional development.

Many peers have helped me to write this book. From Berkeley, I particularly want to thank Rebecca Steinitz and Catherine Robson, each of whom offered inspiration and wisdom. I also benefited from an engaging and encouraging dissertation group, which provided feedback at critical early moments in the writing process. From later years, I want to make special mention of a number of readers whose insights have made a great difference to my thinking and writing: David Damrosch, Marianne DeKoven, Joseph McLaughlin, Edward Mendelsohn, Victoria Rosner, and Michael Tratner. Jay Winter has provided endless advice and guidance, as well as a virtual encyclopedia of First World War knowledge. Most recently, Vincent Sherry's invaluable stewardship through the final phase of revisions deserves my warmest thanks. I want to thank my research assistants, Emily Wilkinson and Edward Wilson, for their hard work. I am also grateful to Jessica Burstein, Joyce Barlow Dodd, Wayne Dodd, Laura Frost, Stephen Greenblatt, Alison Landsberg, Pericles Lewis, and Vanessa Valkin.

I feel privileged to be publishing my work with Cambridge University Press, whose staff have been nothing but supportive and professional. I particularly want to thank the anonymous readers for their excellent advice; Leigh Mueller, for her patient and meticulous work as copy-editor; and Ray Ryan, who has tirelessly shepherded the book through to publication. Several portions of this book have previously been published in anthology or journal form, and I want to acknowledge the following organizations for granting me permission to publish those sections: Pace University Press, the University of Minnesota (copyright 2003 by the Regents of the University of Minnesota) Press, the editors of *Modern Fiction Studies*, and the editors of *ELH*.

My deepest gratitude goes to several people who have been beacons of inspiration, support, and love through every stage of the book's progress. I cannot adequately express how blessed I feel for Martin Vogelbaum's infinite generosity and for his unwavering faith in this project. Ramie Targoff is a friend and role model for whom no adjectives will suffice. My whole family deserves more thanks than I can offer: Eleanor Swift, for giving everything and demanding nothing, the hallmark of her personality; David Wilson, a source of laughter and wisdom; Ben Glass, who always has a moment to listen and to talk; Felicia Cole, perhaps my oldest friend, who has included me in her wonderful family of Dean Amundson, Abigail Cole, and Talia Cole; and Adam Cole, with whom I have shared so many moments of intellectual companionship. Finally, I want to thank my parents, Belle Louise Cole and Robert Harris Cole, whose peerless example and boundless love make anything and everything possible. I dedicate this book to them.

Introduction

ESTRAGON: How long have we been together all the time now?
VLADIMIR: I don't know. Fifty years maybe.
...
VLADIMIR: We can still part, if you think it would be better.
ESTRAGON: It's not worth while now.
  Silence.
VLADIMIR: No, it's not worth while now.
  Silence.
ESTRAGON: Well, shall we go?
VLADIMIR: Yes, let's go.
  They do not move.[1]

Samuel Beckett, *Waiting for Godot*

ARGUMENT: THE ORGANIZATION OF INTIMACY

In Samuel Beckett's drama, wholly intertwined and wildly dysfunctional pairs of men populate a beleaguered world. Male friendship in *Waiting for Godot* (1954) is what survives the trauma of modernity – war, violence, history itself – and in turns becomes emblematic of such a condition. The two old and ragged friends, who hold an unsteady history in their persons and in their tense interactions, seem all that is left of a faded past. What I shall argue in the forthcoming pages is that this connection between male intimacy and the representation of modernity characterizes many literary works from an earlier moment, when these frameworks were established and tested: the English modernist period. Thus, Beckett – writing in the mid twentieth century, purveying an aura of numbness, desperation, and resilience following the Second World War, embodying a position of complex national affiliation – nevertheless displays in exceptionally sparse and skeletal terms an idea that preoccupied writers of an earlier generation, as they confronted their own historical and national situations. What this book will undertake is to make cultural and literary sense of the movement from an idealized, often utopian notion of male friendship that governed many literary and social conventions in the late nineteenth century, to an image of modernity as reflecting the wreckage of that very ideal. My underlying contention, in essence, is this: that male friendship often occupies a complex position in literary works, that it does more than provide cover for homosexuality or sentimentalize adolescence, and that in the decades surrounding the First World War, the pressures on friendship increased, coming to the fore in a variety of historical contexts and for a variety of reasons. In the cultural settings of late-Victorian and early twentieth-century England, as in many literary works of these years, friendship took on a heightened and intensified importance, even as its place in personal, social, and narrative desire seemed increasingly tenuous. Writers in this period emphasized both the value and the fragility of male ties, developing images of men and masculinity that were at once haunting, beautiful, troubling, desperate, and self-dramatizing.

When *Waiting for Godot* allies its atmosphere of desiccated absurdity with the relational field of male intimacy, it provides something of a culmination for a history of writing about friendship which continually moves in the direction of just this kind of depletion. Like the poor tree at the center of the *Godot* stage, a good deal hangs, symbolically, on the friendship between Vladimir and Estragon, a form of mutual dependency that runs the gamut from the touching to the violent, the grittily convincing to the manifestly impossible. Much can be said of this strange friendship. One might point to the text's homoerotics, represented in both playful and serious terms; to parallels with other relationship models (husband/wife; mentor/student; parent/child; master/slave); to the doubling of doublings engendered by the arrival of Lucky and Pozzo; and to the production of an often lovely poetry *à deux* out of the characters' shared dialogue. Though many of these topics are common to the representations of male friendship that proliferated in the first decades of the twentieth century, what I want to stress here is a more general observation: in *Waiting for Godot*, Beckett stages the simultaneous impoverishment and plenitude of the men's intimacy as a central premise, and this relationship partially embodies the condition of modernity that the play so famously purveys.[2] In Beckett's plays, as in many earlier works that take male friendship as an emblematic and central structure, history's markers are at times obscured, and one question that persistently arises is to what extent the relationship of masculine intimacy comes almost to stand in for history, to set its rather bare outlines in place of a more historically particularized and thick rendering of human relations.

In addition to Beckett's mid-century songs of intimacy, another pared-down and precarious staging of friendship, from a very different tradition, should help to introduce this study. Writing in 1921, the Arctic explorer Apsley Cherry-Garrard (known as "Cherry") chronicled R. F. Scott's disastrous final journey to the South Pole (1910–1913), in a text whose affective power derives from the narrator's relation of comradeship with the lost team. This was Cherry's first and only Arctic voyage, and he writes not solely with future scientists and explorers in mind, but also very much with an eye to the general reader, polar expeditions having become something of a national fascination in England during the era of the Scott and Shackleton journeys. *The Worst Journey in the World* establishes and frames the catastrophe in terms of the concurrent strength and loss of powerful male friendships: "The mutual conquest of difficulties is the cement of friendship, as it is the only lasting cement of matrimony," Cherry writes in his preface, and follows with similar rhetoric: "Talk of ex-soldiers: give me ex-antarcticists, unsoured and with their ideals intact: they could sweep the world ... In a way this book is a sequel to the friendship which there was between Wilson, Bowers [both of whom died with Scott on the expedition], and myself, which, having stood the strain of the Winter Journey, could never have been broken."[3] Cherry had good reason to stress friendship as a theme in his voyage, since the deaths that marred the expedition constituted the central focus of public interest, and since, much to the English explorers' dismay, they attained the South Pole only after the surprise arrival of a Norwegian party. The journey was the "worst," that is, because its signal accomplishments involved traumatic loss and disappointment, and an important element of Cherry's work is to reframe the disaster in more ennobling terms. What Cherry does from the outset is to call up a history of imagining friendship as a vital, masculine counterpart to domestic life, and, equally, to evoke two powerful legacies: heroic Victorian conventions of explorer literature and survival narratives surrounding the First World War. It is remarkable how closely Cherry borrows the terms of friendship from the discourse of war, attempting to associate his state of agonized memory with the losses surrounding combat, at times even competing with the war for the position of most-harrowing trial and most grievous loss of friends. Cherry's text indicates a central point that will ramify widely in the pages that follow: in the early twentieth century, both the power and the potential for bereavement associated with male friendship were typically intertwined with such major cultural narratives as imperialism and war, and the sense of heightened importance that friendship often projected derived from those weighty connections.

For Beckett and Cherry, then, friendship matters in part because it consolidates, in highly personal terms, powerful and complex cultural values. I shall use the phrase "the organization of intimacy" as a kind of shorthand for the process of fixing and structuring male bonds that prevailed among writers in this period, from late-Victorian aesthetes, to imperial explorers, to modernist artist-prophets. One proposition that recurs in many texts (and not only literary texts) is that friendship might function as a bridging structure between individuals and institutions. If the intimacy between individuals comes fraught with vulnerability, what friendship appears to offer is a kind of infrastructure – practices, conventions, a language, a history – that imbues the often shaky relation between man and man with the sanctity of larger, more powerful and sustainable institutions. While writers of the modernist period are often viewed as viscerally hostile to institutions of all sorts, particularly those that serve the imposing will of middle-class respectability, imperialism, mass culture, or literary convention, what an analysis of male friendship shows is a sense of ambivalence around those institutions that underlie interpersonal ties between individuals, and particularly between men. When I repeatedly refer to the "organization" of male intimacy, then, what I shall be emphasizing is this "blessed rage for order," this interest in strengthening and bolstering male friendship, interleaving it into other cultural narratives and practices. Perhaps the biggest mistake one can make in conceptualizing friendship, unfortunately repeated by many critics, is to assume that it is a private, voluntary relation, governed by personal sentiment and easy communion. It is not. Like any complex social relationship, friendship has its own conventions and institutional affinities (schools, universities, social clubs, as well as more rigidly arranged organizations from the Boy Scouts to the military platoon), and it is shot through with social meaning.[4] The anodyne image of an uncomplicated relation – essentially outside of culture – should clearly be rejected. Like the family, against which it is often set as an alternative, friendship will be constructed in such a way as to reflect a culture's positions on sexuality, gender, hierarchy, and power.

The desire to organize male intimacy is not unique to the early twentieth century; what stands out in this period is, first, that this desire seems to increase and self-perpetuate, to preoccupy an array of writers and social critics, and second, that it repeatedly and dramatically fails. Again, Beckett's drama provides a useful template for visualizing this sense of combined intensification and depletion. Beckett used the term "pseudo-couple" for the endlessly combative, dependent, and ineluctable intimacy between men like Vladimir and Estragon, a relationship that functions as a compromise between community and isolation. Frederic Jameson, finding in the pseudo-couple a notable stage in the history of the subject, sees this coupling as a way to ward off the final centrifugal spin into late-capitalist monadism.[5] I would suggest that the pseudo-couple represents something like a last stop on the journey male intimacy makes in the first decades of the twentieth century. If Beckett often characterizes his male partners simultaneously by love and aggressivity, inter-dependence and impoverishment, earnestness and parody, these traits will repeatedly arise in narratives that plot the slow decline of the richly optimistic friendships that populated late-Victorian imaginings. In many of the texts and discourses I shall discuss, the pseudo-couple will stand as a kind of threat – more desirable, it would seem, than the total alienation marked by its final flickering extinction, yet itself a *cul-de-sac*, a harrowing image of the bleak interpersonal structures of modernity.

Of course, the preceding century had its own friendship history, and this legacy marks and delimits the narratives of male intimacy in the modernist period. For the Victorians, friendship had classical, imperial, sentimental, and at times heroic connotations, with the Romantic ideal of the friendship poem and Alfred Lord Tennyson's *In Memoriam* (1850) standing as literary high-water marks, and the milieu of mid-century Oxford representing one of its greatest institutional manifestations. Thomas Carlyle's idealization of monastic community in *Past and Present* (1843), aesthetic movements like the Pre-Raphaelite brotherhood, and the work of such social reformers as Thomas Hill Green at the end of the century present influential examples of a cultural politics organized around idealized male fraternities. Nineteenth-century imperial discourse, too, relied heavily on tropes of male friendship, as did fictions of class reform in much "condition of England" writing. While this varied history cannot easily be schematized, we might generalize enough to argue that the breakdown of the ideological rationale surrounding these well-worn conventions of male comradeship, in many cases, sets off a process of faltering and elapsing male fellowship, a protracted unraveling that emerges most fully in the work of post-Victorian writers.[6] The history of male intimacy is never incidental to the dynamics I will be describing; on the contrary, what makes the tension surrounding friendship at the turn of the century so vivid is precisely the fact that male bonds had been intricately interwoven into many rich traditions of Victorian Britain.

When I began this study, I assumed that some kind of cohesion would be possible between institutions and personal bonds – that, for instance, I would discover a form of productive literary power in the idea of the nation as a brotherhood (along the lines, perhaps, of Walt Whitman's *Leaves of Grass*[7]), or of the university circle as a forum for protecting marginalized sexual identities, or of military service as a rewarding experience of comradeship. What I have found, by striking contrast, is that in all of these cases, and indeed more generally, the urge to organize and structure intimacy becomes an impossible goal to achieve, and this not only for the relatively obvious reason we might predict: that such desires represent a way to secure a safe place for homosexuality, which in the late nineteenth century was increasingly threatened. While the status of unorthodox sexuality will surface repeatedly in this study, it by no means dominates my understanding of how and why friendship fails as a convention with lasting power or as a bridging structure between individuals and institutions. In nearly every case, some conjunction of forces emerges to thwart the establishment of idealized or comforting male relations. Typically, these disruptions come from a combination of internal contradiction (something in the structure of friendship) and external or historical constraint (most notably under the stress of war), which together set in motion a cycle of failure or disappointment. The pressure of the physical body, the loss of ideological cover for imperialist myths, the actual experience of intimacy in war, the disruption wreaked by injury and debility: each of these problems in effect propels the individual out of the safe space of friendship, and each is presented in terms of the "authentic" story of modernity. More than any other event, the cataclysm of war produced gigantic tears in the fabric of friendship and generated a language to account for them.

The First World War represents the pivot of my study, as it has often been perceived by scholars to divide European cultural history into any number of "before and after" sequences. It is here, in the experience of the trenches and in the many retellings of the traumatic years of 1914–1918, that we will find the most direct pressure on the idea (and ideal) of male friendship, and it is here, too, that the story of lost friendship will be most compellingly imagined as a site for the heightened and unmediated experience of modernity. As Cherry's allusions to the war as a highly visible locus of intense and hard-won male loyalty suggest, the war intensified and focused much that had been previously assumed about the role of male friendship in British culture, and the transformations it entailed had lasting consequences for the way intimacy and lost friends were represented in postwar contexts. Combat was not the only forum in which male intimacy was elevated and tested, but it became a kind of standard, as well as a metaphor, for the most resilient, cherished, and vulnerable of bonds. Moreover, given the sense of cataclysmic change that many Britons, both combatants and civilians, associated with the war, the urgency surrounding comradeship in battle seemed to carry an extra charge, to intensify – perhaps to the breaking point – an already loaded cultured signifier.

The war has long been assigned pride of place in the history of modernism. Critics have attributed the formal and thematic shape of such exemplary texts as *The Waste Land* and *To the Lighthouse* in part to the war's myriad effects on the high modernists of the 1920s, and a whole host of familiar features of modernism has been connected with the experience of the war on the Western Front – physical, psychological, epistemological, and ethical. As Paul Fussell writes in his influential study of the war and modernity, "I am saying that there seems to be one dominating form of modern understanding; that it is essentially ironic; and that it originates largely in the application of mind and memory to the events of the Great War."[8] Critics like Sandra Gilbert and Susan Gubar, whose seminal reassessment of modernist gender politics in many ways counters Fussell's agenda, also concede that a particular narrative of modernization is exemplified by the war: "World War I virtually completed the Industrial Revolution's construction of anonymous, dehumanized man, that impotent cipher who is frequently thought to be the twentieth century's most characteristic citizen."[9] At the same time, First World War scholars have continued to refine and nuance their accounts of the war's role in configuring the literary and cultural life of the decades that followed, arguing, for instance, that the war's technologies, psychic effects, and metaphors intervened in diverse spheres of post-war society. Such issues as the politics of class and gender, the commodification of war-related technology, the development of public health, and the treatment of mental disease were fundamentally altered as a consequence of the war, in ways that are often both decisive and surprising.[10] Even if we subscribe to the narrative of war-as-watershed, then, we ought not to assume an easy understanding about how the war codified or undermined fundamental principles, or what the effects would be when civilian writers adopted the war as their own perceptual and epistemological experience.[11] If it was not a straightforward catalyst for one kind of change or development, the war was an incalculably important event in the cultural and literary politics of the period, in setting the tone for many aspects of post-war existence, and in constructing riveting images of modernity. Perhaps most important for our purposes is to recognize that the war produced highly visible reconfigurations of male community and attacked the physical body in terrible new ways, and these powerful features made the war seem to many contemporaries – as to today's critics – like a transformative event in the logic of masculine intimacy.

One subject foregrounded by the war, but implicit in any study of male bonds, involves the physical body. The cultural history of the male body reached a crisis point in the experience of the war, as the clash between technological innovation and physical vulnerability exploded beyond people's wildest pre-war imaginings. The degree and scale of physical decimation, the massiveness of industrial efficacy in killing and maiming, reached an unfathomable apex during these years, and the after-effects can be documented not only as a matter of corpses, but also on the wounded bodies of those who returned from war. Combatants faced the most ghastly forms of bodily dismemberment and loss, and the wider civilian populace, too, was confronted with a scale of injury that challenged fundamental concepts of masculinity, physical integrity, the mind/body divide, and the notion of work. To talk about the body in this period requires that we recognize the terrifying reality of wounded flesh as well as the cultural associations heaped onto the body in war, perhaps its most extreme, over-signifying activity. In this analysis of intimacy, I shall encounter the body in many forms, from the glowing, glistening, vibrant body of aestheticist dreams, to the imperialist body as a repository for ideology, to the smashed and debilitated body at war, and finally to the "broken" body of the post-war years, when the perception of brokenness became a trope for the physical and spiritual state of a war-scarred culture.

To the extent that it makes sense to trace overriding movements, one striking progression involves the body's devolution from idealized whole to broken ruin, from protected and nurtured to torn and abandoned. Such a trajectory might come as something of a surprise, given the general interest, in the years both before and after the war, in notions of revitalization: much attention was paid to health, the clean and powerful physique, the body resplendent and ready for commodification, an answer to the many fears of "degeneration" that haunted the turn of the century.[12] Yet, during the same period, we also see a persistent picture of the body withering and faltering, and not only in the context of the society's failures to revitalize its impoverished urban population. It is often the very paragon of masculinity – soldier, athlete, imperialist – whose physical dissolution becomes a subject of anxiety and/or a metaphor for cultural change. As I chart such movements, I shall suggest homologies with various features of literary modernism (the marginalized physical body an image of modern man; shared mutilation a sign of protest; the broken post-war body a figure for literary self-constructions), and I shall operate on the line between what we might call constructionism and essentialism. If it has become a truism that the body is fashioned, constructed, receptive to cultural shifts, infused and interpolated by intangible power structures, I am also struck by a persistent sense of irreducibility about the body – an irreducibility that I am hesitant to write off as mere mystification.[13] To recognize the body as a product of culture need not require that we lose our sense of its significant and perhaps untranslatable physical qualities: pain, dismemberment, pleasure, detachment from the practices of narrative.[14]

Several models for thinking about male intimacy and the sexual body have received extensive theoretical treatment. The first involves the movements in late nineteenth-century Britain of simultaneous awakening and foreclosure with respect to male desire and homosexual identity. Without entering into the ongoing debate about whether or not homosexuality was "invented" in the last decades of the century, a product of sexological theory and its institutional embodiments, I do want to mention two significant and interconnected developments in England during the period: the availability of languages and theories to depict the homosexual as a coherent ontology and, at the same time, the pursuit and criminalization of homosexual men.[15] Both of these developments transpired with a high degree of spectacle, and thus a pattern emerges of increased publicity in tandem with an ever-greater imperative to closet and encode. Tom Stoppard's play *The Invention of Love* (1998) beautifully captures this double sense. Focusing on the figure of A. E. Housman, the drama is organized around the pronounced – and tragic – contradiction in the late-Victorian period between the romanticization of male love at Oxford, with its rich literary associations, institutional protection, and connection to a host of all-male athletic, intellectual, and social activities, and the harsh new reality of homophobic punishment in the real world, emblematized in the play by London and by the shadowy figure of Oscar Wilde.[16] What Stoppard suggests is that the flowering of a Platonic ideal of male love coincided with (and perhaps helped to ignite) the onset of new medical and legal practices that would effectively crush and closet all possibilities for flexible, homoerotic community. Double talk, canniness, and indirection; the strategic postures of flamboyance and performativity; tragic silencing and psychological trauma; punishment and protest – all of this and more can be understood to follow from the combined opening up and shutting down of a space for homosexuality. Dominant markers in this history include the enactment of the Labouchère Amendment (1885), which criminalized the practice of even private, consensual male homosexual acts in England, and the Wilde trials (1895), with their extreme and lasting public resonance. In short, a basic outline emerges: an increased prominence accorded to male love and desire at many levels – cultural, discursive, medical, aesthetic, and personal;

followed by and/or conjoined with an increasingly stifling and punitive atmosphere; all of this producing diverse literary and cultural consequences, which reverberate not solely in manifestly arch or decadent texts, but in many works that betray this history only indirectly.[17]

Even more of an enabling paradigm for this study, and indeed at the basis of much theoretical work on the subject of male homoerotics, is Eve Kosofsky Sedgwick's *Between Men: English Literature and Male Homosocial Desire*.[18] Sedgwick's essential insight involves what she calls a rupture along the continuum of male relations. Positing and exploring the seemingly inexorable (yet, as she stresses, historically particular) conjunction of patriarchal homosociality with homophobia, Sedgwick traces in English literature a pattern of desire and expulsion with respect to male love that seems virtually omnipresent in such genres as the domestic novel, the adventure quest, and the pastoral (to name just a few). My thinking about how male intimacy was conceived, structured, and challenged in the early twentieth century effectively begins with Sedgwick's observations about the cultural contradictions surrounding male bonding. This influence notwithstanding, it will be helpful, right from the start, to clarify some differences in approach. Most centrally, when I discuss ruptures between individuals and institutions, personal friendship and corporate forms of comradeship, I am pointing to patterns of disjunction that have as much to do, for instance, with imperial or military ideology as with physical desire. What I have found perhaps most remarkable in these investigations is that it is not easy to predict where or why friendship will falter, or a conflict will emerge between personal intimacy and its institutionalization. At times, the importance of sexual desire thwarts smooth narratives of friendship, as one might expect; at other times, sexuality remains marginal to the dislocations that unhinge friendship and propel the male subject out into the bleakness of modernity. In addition to the homosocial/homosexual divide, then, there are other tensions and incompatibilities that provoke a breakdown in the functioning of friendship, and these will matter equally with sexuality in configuring the constraints and limitations on male friendship in the early twentieth century.

Nevertheless, to depict a struggle around male bonds as a central feature animating many works of this period could be said to move in the direction of "queering" the literary. That is, the marginalized position of the male homosexual in this period comes to resonate more broadly, a notable voice in seemingly "straight" texts, and this would seem to contribute to a general adjustment in our rendering of the literary, as challenging new voices assert themselves in strident tones, both discordant and moving.

Such prominence of voice seems promising; and yet, narratives of homosexuality in these years seem persistently to read like narratives of pain. Defeat, despair, lost hope – these conditions will continually come to the fore, as will an often bleak picture of the male body. Many works come burdened with a pressing weight of internal contradiction, as the seemingly legitimizing language of friendship is exposed or rejected, and strategies of empowerment often seem far distant. To argue, as I shall, that something important for literature arises out of this cycle of disappointment – that resonant images and languages of modernity develop out of these movements – is simultaneously to claim a specific queer figure as an agent in the twentieth-century literary imagination and to reiterate an expression of suffering as nearly inevitable for that figure. Still, I would be hesitant to embrace concepts such as abjection or masochism as categories that might productively reorient this focus on loss and isolation. In the wake of influential work on masochistic masculinity (notably Kaja Silverman's *Male Subjectivity at the Margins*), critics have turned to the idea of abjection as a way to theorize the simultaneous release and appropriation of power that accrues to many gestures of masculine self-annihilation.[19] While such a dynamic will often be visible, in the works I am considering, the suffering entailed by the stamping out of friendship remains too closely tied to its (vanishing) institutional history to allow for a real release into a new or desired aesthetic of pain.

DEFINITIONS AND CHOICES: MODERNISM, MODERNITY, LITERARY AUTHORITY

Over the course of this discussion, I will be using three interrelated terms that warrant clarification from the outset: "modernism," "modernity," and "literary authority." Let me begin with literary authority, perhaps the most nebulous of the three. The idea of authority has been attacked in recent years by critics who have looked in detail at the production, dissemination, promotion, and marketing of modernist works and authors.[20] These studies are highly valuable in demonstrating the ways in which authority was, in effect, constructed, and in encouraging a view of modernism that looks skeptically at the pose of artist-prophet and the image of the artist as above the fray of commodity culture, with its attendant self-promotions. My discussion of literary authority, while retaining the spirit of these correctives, will strike a somewhat different note. What I mean to capture in the idea of literary authority is threefold: the way narrators and characters come to speak with a privileged voice, often reflecting a spirit of irony presumed to be shared by the reader (Conrad's Marlow would be an especially direct case); the corresponding power appropriated and represented by the author him/herself, often as a spokesman for some kind of authentic experience; and the way literary history has accorded the privilege of telling the stories of modernity to particular authors, texts, and styles. All three levels present extreme problems of subjectivity, and one should be wary of perpetuating the question-begging entailed by canonicity – who decides what constitutes power, privilege, authority, authenticity? How does one proclaim readerly affiliation? What versions of "modernity" count? Hasn't post-modernism effectively eradicated the idea of authenticity altogether? Despite these serious questions, it seems important to think about the way writers of the modernist period simultaneously offered a challenge to a certain kind of conventional literary authority, represented, for instance, by the realist conventions of the nineteenth-century novel or the egotistical sublime of the Romantic lyric, and vigorously created new forms of language to fill that void.

In particular, I will be concerned with a familiar male voice, characterized not only by its association with irony and disenchantment, but also by its proclamations of solitary struggle and visionary power, a voice that has vigorously – if, once again, ironically – maintained its status as a site of candor and validity in a century marked by doubt, skepticism, and the rejection of the very notion of authentic experience. Manifold cultural projections and historical forces contribute to the production of such an idea as literary authority, at the same time that there often persists what Walter Benjamin might call an "aura" of resonance and perseverance surrounding the literary text. In the case of modernism, that aura involves a sense that these works reckon in especially unmediated ways with some kind of distilled (and often painful) experience, what Woolf calls "life or spirit, truth or reality, this, the essential thing," which takes vivid shape in the context of such events as war, and, more generally, in moments of psychological or physical intensity.[21] The works I am studying, that is, continue to probe and indeed venerate such prospects as authenticity, moral authority, and unmediated experience, at the same time that they do engage the project – which is what we typically associate with them – of deconstructing the edifice of Enlightenment values. As has often been noted, modernism's critique of western culture, history, and literature was never absolute (nor was it meant to be), and it substituted its own beliefs for those it worked to invalidate. The category of "literary authority" represents one such area where un-ironized values tend to cluster in modernist works.

When I speak of "modernity," I hope to gesture towards a spectrum of cultural, technological, and sociological conditions in early twentieth-century Europe, and particularly England, that seemed to galvanize the imagination. In general, modernness in this period often reflected two basic perceptual features: a sense of cultural and technological acceleration, a generalized experience of totalization and/or mechanization, and an uncertainty about the foundations – philosophical, economic, spiritual, and political – of confident, liberal subjectivity.[22] The end of one narrative and the beginning of another; a culture at rest and one dizzyingly and tortuously on the move. What a given writer will understand as constituting modernity is, however, entirely subjective, and the idea of the modern is notoriously elastic and opportunistic – one projects onto the idea of modernity whatever it is one wants to claim as endemic and specific to one's own historical moment. In the early twentieth century, especially, many writers and social critics were quite taken with the idea of modernity as an apt expression of their historical situation, a way of naming what they viewed as the most distinctive and compelling features of the period, and hence deliberate images of modernity have an especially high purchase in the literature of these years. As Rita Felski has it, "the idea of the modern saturates the discourses, images, and narratives of the late nineteenth and early twentieth centuries. It is an era profoundly shaped by logics of periodization."[23] It is an era when the term "modern" often worked as a badge of authenticity and a promise of something both shattering and illuminating. For literary artists of the period, the concept of the modern was often imagined in terms of specific kinds of piercing voices and vibrant forms of narration, rendered with a high degree of personal and psychological urgency. In this study, the voices that speak most loudly tend to do so through the constructs of pain, protest, passivity, disorientation, and alienation.

To talk about both "modernity" (an elastic concept encompassing a range of private and shared experience) and "modernism" (a more narrow literary term) is to assume a continual process of mutual engendering between literature and culture.[24] Modernism, of course, represents an international and interdisciplinary phenomenon, encompassing not only literature, but visual arts, performance, music, and architecture, and the term generally represents a habit of mind as much as a chronological or geographical category. By "modernism" in the limited, literary-historical sense, I mean to suggest a sensibility and a set of forms, themes, and practices attributed most often to highly self-conscious artificers between about 1880 and 1940, who tended to stress the many depletions left in the wake of the Enlightenment's troubled ideals, and to construct for their era what they viewed as challenging new languages, narrative practices, character types, and forms of spiritual authority.[25] While such a characterization – simultaneously too broad and too limiting – has been appropriately critiqued by feminist critics and others on grounds of exclusivity and self-perpetuation, it is not meant to exhaust the period's literary accomplishment, or to circumscribe our sense of what is important or representative in the literature of these years. On the contrary, I am quite interested in the interconnections between the kinds of works that fall just on the borderline of high modernism and those more famously at the center. Many of the works I discuss do not fully belong to the high canon, and yet the familiar landscape of modernism is an important point of reference for this study, primarily because the texts I discuss often construct their versions of lost friendship in ways that rub closely against standard embodiments of modernism. The relationship between canonical modernism and the problem of male intimacy varies considerably – in some cases, it seems that modernism effectively usurps the voice of the scarred friend for its own purposes; at other times, the figure of the lost friend is offered as an emblem of modernity; friendship can stand either as a bulwark against totalizing features of modern culture or as a sad casualty of those processes – but, in each case, to see how familiar elements of modernism intersect with a discourse of male friendship will, I hope, be illuminating for both realms.

My focus is on those writers whose interests and accounts of modernity were most intricately bound up with the idea of male friendship; this focus has led me in the direction of important historical events in the modernist period (such as the war), but often away from the most famous modernist innovations in form. With the exception of Conrad, the major writers in this study (Forster, Lawrence, the war poets) tend to have a slightly equivocal status in modernism – canonical, yet a little off center, in the sense that their texts tend not to perform the kinds of radical experimentation often valorized in and as modernism. Yet this slightly marginal quality is itself notable, since one element that characterizes all these figures is that they invoke with particular urgency the affective and narrative power of Victorian institutions and conventions. If nineteenth-century British culture had allied male friendship with conventional forms of domestic, imperial, and military ideology, these writers, working close to the Victorian threshold (in spirit if not always in time), embraced the concept of male fellowship just as that larger value-system was eroding, when the grip of tradition was loosening, when intimacy – far from providing an entrance into comforting institutions and traditions – was locked in tension with conventional sanctifying forms. These threshold modernists thus offer an especially revealing window into their own authorizing strategies, and they provide interesting foils for more radical modernists who will, at times, appropriate or recast these direct and trenchant depictions of friendship and loss.[26]

The story I tell here is very much a story about men. Why not discuss women's friendships? First and foremost, female friendship has its own specific history, its own tropes and narrative devices, its own literary past.[27] Any attempt to assimilate a feminine story to the model I am developing, with its focus on masculine narratives and institutions, would risk distortion. The late nineteenth and early twentieth centuries saw an especially pronounced flourishing with respect to women's relationships, and women writers explored questions of female community in depth and with nuance, developing themes of friendship and antagonism, alliance and disconnection, possibility and limitation. We can trace in the literature of these decades a number of routes by which women created and sustained powerful networks. In Victorian England, female communities and bonds were often constructed through tactics of indirection, and the project of female authorship in these years – simultaneously such a fraught and successful enterprise – often produced conflict or ambivalence on the subject of rich female relationships.[28] In later decades, the work of major female modernists, like Virginia Woolf, Djuna Barnes, Rebecca West, and Gertrude Stein, reflects a more robust and heightened sense of possibility for female community and mutual empowerment – Chloë liking Olivia for the first time in literary history, as Woolf would have it.[29] Critics have argued that women's bonds in the twentieth century seem to hold potential for voice, embodiment, and narrative promise in an unprecedented sense, and have focused on specific locations where women's partnerships developed and prospered – Paris' Left Bank, the literary salon, new workplace environments.[30] While the flourishing of female intimacies thus forms a central part of the landscape of modernism, alongside the patriarchal stifling that continues to trouble works by women writers of the period, it belongs to a different project to develop links between that narrative and the story of masculine intimacy I pursue here.

STRUCTURE: FOUR SITES OF MASCULINE BONDING

The book is structured – loosely – according to the temporality of the war. The pre-war period is divided into two chapters, according to two major endeavors of these years, classicism and imperialism; a consideration of war writers is at the center; and the final section returns to the domestic arena of post-war England, where the effects of war on masculine community and the male body were extreme and far-reaching. Each chapter begins with a discussion of the cultural and institutional climate surrounding one broad topic (classicism; empire; war; post-war discourses of recovery) and culminates in a detailed interrogation of how major literary figures addressed and reconstituted these problems. In terms of the discussions at the opening of each chapter, I have stressed the kind of historical and textual material that I deemed important for the inquiry at hand, and have also given consideration to the relative familiarity of the narratives. Thus, if the oft-told story of public-school ideology could be made with relative ease (Chapter 1), the final chapter's engagement with a rather neglected area of British cultural politics required more extensive delineation. Similarly, the type of material under consideration varies with each chapter. The first chapter aims at both center and margin with respect to late-Victorian masculinity, by looking at the dominant, tenacious institutions of male education during the period, alongside several erudite and rarefied discourses about male love embedded in aesthetic criticism of the 1870s–1890s; in my discussion of imperial friendship, I rely primarily on literary and other highly visible texts, including the famous travel narratives of the mid nineteenth century, to set up the paradigms I will examine in Conrad; for the war discussion, much of my analysis of non-canonical writers comes from unpublished letters, memoirs, and fiction, or from lesser-known literary works about the war; and when I discuss the post-war period, I shall pay attention to a variety of artifacts, including political speeches, newspaper accounts of soldier activities, commentary from the medical establishment, and public practices of commemoration.

The book's first chapter, "Victorian dreams, modern realities: Forster's classical imagination," offers a reading of the male body in a series of *fin-de-siècle* texts, culminating in an analysis of Forster's work, and ultimately offering a reassessment of Forster's role as a theorizer of modernity. I begin with late-Victorian Hellenism, and particularly with Edward Carpenter, John Addington Symonds, and Walter Pater, all of whom valorize classical Greek traditions for celebrating friendship and aestheticizing the male body. In this discussion, I shall address both the coherence and the incoherence of the late nineteenth-century habit of protecting male desire under the legitimizing sign of Greek comradeship, and will emphasize the institutional location of classical studies in the public schools and universities. With this history in mind, we are in a position to see how Forster explored and critiqued the Hellenic model of male comradeship; for him

the limitations of the discourse ultimately overpowered its liberatory potential. Although Forster remained in a university setting for most of his life
and is remembered as the great champion of male friendship, in works like
The Longest Journey and *Maurice*, he undermines the classicist friendship
ideal by exposing an incompatibility between the body and its containing
narratives. Even Forster's appeal to intimacy in *A Passage to India* – a text
ordinarily read as a hymn to male friendship – ultimately falters on the
incapacity of available institutions, including popular literary tropes of imperial friendship, to organize and stabilize inter-racial male desire and to
combat the force of the colonial machine. Forster's texts often represent
modernity as a form of dislocated and friendless masculinity, as he sets in
motion a transformation of Victorian conventions for safeguarding male
love into disjunctive images of loss and solitude.

In "Conradian alienation and imperial intimacy," I turn to the role male
intimacy played in organizing imperial fictions, and argue that Conrad's
classic modernist accounts of the imperial situation telescope critical
problems of community and epistemology in the over-determined male
encounter. Looking in particular at Henry Morton Stanley's iconic *How
I Found Livingstone*, this chapter sets up the trope of the "imperial encounter" as a basic structural principle sustaining many imperial fictions,
including Conrad's. My argument is that Conrad avidly borrows from
Victorian travel narratives a belief in the connection between imperialism
and friendship, but the fraught male relations he chronicles become disengaged from their ideological underpinnings; this decoupling, in turn, sets
in motion a pattern of increasing alienation, self-scrutiny, and narrative
breakdown. Conrad's anguish over vanishing standards and literary forms,
dramatized in such texts as *Heart of Darkness*, *Lord Jim*, and *Under Western
Eyes*, can thus be seen as a response to a collapse of a series of male worlds,
which had depended upon the alliance of friendship with imperial myths.
In *Romance*, which Conrad wrote collaboratively with Ford Madox Ford,
the construction of a passive, alienated subject is explicitly drawn from
the wreckage of imperialist, homosocial fantasy. For Conrad, alienation
and the condition of modernity map closely onto the failure of friendship
to produce meaning when disengaged from cultural systems that typically
perform such work. At the same time, the authority to speak is generated
out of this very isolation. In the case of Conrad, then, literary authority
(at all three levels outlined above) and masculine intimacy are palpably
intertwined and mutually engendering.

At the core of the book is a discussion of the First World War, the
event we might expect to mark the triumph of complete and cohesive

male community. Indeed, I begin my analysis of war literature, "'My killed friends are with me where I go': friendship and comradeship at war," by suggesting that, during the war, comradeship was offered as a replacement for nearly all other forms of human and social organization. Yet the crucial point is this: although comradeship was consistently hailed as the saving grace of a world in crisis, the precariousness of personal friendship in the face of the war's annihilating power in fact made it the most vulnerable and dislocating of all relations. Rather than functioning as allied principles, intimate friendship and corporate comradeship work against one another, rival forms whose incompatibility produces some of the central disruptions in the soldier poet's language. Male intimacy ultimately becomes the vehicle not for communal strength, but for individual isolation and bereavement, and the embittered voice that rises from the trenches is specifically rendered as the voice of the permanently scarred friend. Thus the poetry of Wilfred Owen and Siegfried Sassoon delineates an especially emphatic and marked trajectory out of Victorian comradeship conventions, through an ideal of intimacy, and into a language of modernity that proclaims an unimpeachable authority. For many, faith in comradeship was undone by war (the opposite of what one would expect), and the fallout from this startling reversal can be found throughout the literature of the period. By way of example, the chapter concludes with readings of several works of post-war civilian modernism, arguing that figures such as Eliot and Woolf appropriated and remade the image of the bereaved friend as an element in their own articulations of modern isolation.

"'The violence of the nightmare': D. H. Lawrence and the aftermath of war" takes us home from the trenches, exploring a panoply of political and social questions troubling Britain as it emerged from war's devastation. In this discussion, I look, for instance, at physical disability, shell shock, practices of memorialization, post-war soldiers' agitation, and at social reform efforts based on ideals of comradeship. This final section traverses a wide span, primarily because the important issues surrounding the return of the soldier were complex and historically unprecedented, and have been all but ignored by literary critics. The organizational umbrella covering my analysis comes from David Lloyd George's famous imperative to create "a fit country for heroes to live in." As millions of men came home from war, many in states of mental and physical distress or debility, civilian contemporaries worked to understand, assimilate, accommodate, rehabilitate, or simply bypass them. A general cultural sense of disjunction between soldiers and their country preoccupied many Britons, and this issue of "fit" had various manifestations – political, aesthetic, social, and personal. A renewed assessment of male comradeship and troubling new spectacles of male bodies were almost ubiquitous features of the post-war scene, and the combined sense of fear and promise surrounding these men – congregated in threatening numbers or desperately isolated – spread in many directions. The problem of "fit" presents a kind of conundrum, as the bodies and minds of former soldiers seem arrested in states of painful stasis, simultaneously demanding and resisting cultural accommodation and change. What I hope to show is that these developments can productively offer a new interpretive lens for modernist literature of the post-war years, and have particular resonance in the case of Lawrence.

For Lawrence, the problem of war's effects helps to crystallize and focus a life-long preoccupation with masculine intimacy and the male body. In work after work, he investigates the possibility of turning brotherhood into a viable cultural and literary form, and, in work after work, he takes stock of the cost of war on men's bodies and souls. Yet Lawrence's presentation of male love hinges, ultimately, on insufficiency rather than completion. With the war as the great event shadowing his work, his texts repeatedly dramatize the promise of organized intimacy devolving into solitary struggle, as the goal of replacing the family with a fraternal paradise yields not plenitude, but impoverishment. Yet for Lawrence, as for others in this study, such failed intimacy paradoxically provides the core of success, as the broken friend comes to proclaim himself a twentieth-century Everyman. After the war, when the crushed and shattered bodies of men populated the landscape, when the promise of friendship as an organizational structure seemed both urgent and exhausted, when the relation of the nation to its citizens seemed to suggest a depressingly poor "fit," Lawrence made the condition of friendless masculinity emblematic of something highly important to his literary enterprise: the narration of modernity.

Overall, I hope that this analysis of male friendship in the early twentieth century will provide new and productive insights into three broad topics. The first is friendship, a relation that tends to evade the kind of rigorous scrutiny directed at such institutions as the family, marriage, and sexuality. As with any important and complex human endeavor, friendship can and should be examined, theorized, and historicized. With such a refined perception in place, we are in a position to recognize the layered history and complex cultural investment underlying many representations of friendship, right up to our own period, whether in fiction, poetry, photography, film, or television. Second, an analysis of the way masculine intimacy operated in the First World War should suggest analogies with other modern wars, where a similar pattern of reliance and devastation with respect to male bonds was often voiced as a central, and crushing, problem. Modern mass wars often rely on a thriving ideal of comradeship, and the tension between such emphasis and the grief associated with combat shaped the response to conflicts throughout the twentieth century. An outpouring of literature and film about the Vietnam War, the memorial landscape that has grown up around many modern calamities, popular rhetoric surrounding the fifty-year anniversary of the Second World War, representations of even such relatively limited conflicts as the Persian Gulf Wars or the American incursion into Somalia – each of these returns to the problems of friendship and comradeship established by writers from the First World War, elaborated here. Finally, I hope that this discussion will have something to teach us about modernism, or, perhaps more accurately, about how particular problems cut across modernist and non-modernist texts. Modernist literature was permeated and affected by the organization of intimacy, and it often dramatizes the failure of friendship in stark terms. At the same time, one thing I want to underscore is how other works from the period, which may operate without the authorizing sign of high modernism, take up the promise and the burden of narrating male friendship: acting almost as modernist shadows, these texts construct the kind of resonant, self-legitimizing voices we often associate with modernism, and stress such themes as alienation, disconsolation, and a desperately troubled relation to the past. What this discussion helps to demonstrate, then, is how intricately modernism shares its topics, preoccupations, and outcomes with the broader culture that surrounded and helped to produce it. Male friendship is one subject whose reverberations ripple across the literary landscape.

CHAPTER I

Victorian dreams, modern realities: Forster's classical imagination

> He was thinking of the irony of friendship – so strong it is, and so fragile. We fly together, like straws in an eddy, to part in the open stream. Nature has no use for us: she has cut her stuff differently. Dutiful sons, loving husbands, responsible fathers – these are what she wants, and if we are friends it must be in our spare time. Abram and Sarai were sorrowful, yet their seed became as sand of the sea, and distracts the politics of Europe at this moment. But a few verses of poetry is all that survives of David and Jonathan.[1]
>
> E. M. Forster, *The Longest Journey*

Forster is often remembered as a modernist who believed in "personal relationships." An acute social critic with a persistent ironic vision, he nevertheless retained a core belief in the enduring power of intimate ties to mitigate against an increasingly authoritarian and mechanized world.[2] At the same time, passages like this one from *The Longest Journey*, which express a sense of pathos about the potential for male love to be articulated and realized, blend Forster's faith in small-scale humanity with his most private desire. If the erotics are shepherded in quietly, they effectively transform the passage from an example of youthful sentiment into a depiction of more empathetic, adult desire. Such saturated language about friendship would seem to proceed directly out of Forster's personal fantasies, to function in part as a sexualization of his humanist ideal. Moreover, when Forster imagines male bonds as a tempting alternative to the confines of the family and its cultural and political authority, he taps into a broader current of turn-of-the-century thought, preoccupied with the rituals that sustain and delimit male relations. To elevate the institutions and traditions of heroic male friendship, while negotiating a space for real intimacy (including, but not limited to, sexual intimacy) – this two-tiered rhetorical strategy had become the hallmark of a certain strain of late nineteenth-century writing, and Forster might be taken as one of its most ardent, if somewhat belated, exponents.

Here, then, is a relatively clean narrative of classics-and-comradeship; but what I want to argue is rather the reverse, that Forster's place in this story is one of disturbance and his language functions as a note of uncomfortable critique. Far from nurturing a decadent fantasy of ascendant friendship, Forster would eventually shatter that gilded image. Although Forster's elegiac tone may seem to suggest that his aim is primarily to protect and elevate homoerotic bonds, his texts in fact expose the futility and tragic inadequacy of such an enterprise. No harmonious movement from personal desire to social practice will be possible in novels such as *The Longest Journey* (1908) and *Maurice* (composed 1913–1914), as troubling elements reside beneath a thinly idealized surface. Even in *A Passage to India* (1924), where balance and artfulness seem triumphant, not to mention a steadfast commitment to male friendship, the text ultimately refuses to champion its own apparent causes, undoing the very edifice of friendship it so elaborately constructs. Thus, where it might be tempting to assert a smooth transition in these texts from desire to its theorization, in effect to see Forster as a celebrator of "gay" (as distinct from "queer") love, I shall argue that the novels posit disruption.[3] Forster's ultimate emphasis on forms of ambiguity, unease, and isolation surrounding his male protagonists, and his substitution of loss for community, follow directly from the disenfranchisement of friendship.

To focus on Forster's disjunctive function is to unsettle several critical commonplaces. The first involves his status as a modernist – or, better, as a theorist of modernity. With his Austenian tone, settings, and plots, and his generally conventional narrative style, Forster is often figured as something of a latter-day Victorian, and the paradigm-shattering developments of high modernism seem far distant. Though Forster might address problems of modern existence with exceptional grace and insight, literary history in general has not found his texts to "force, to dislocate if necessary, language into his meaning," as Eliot, for one, famously demanded of any work that can be considered "really new."[4] More recently, queer theoretical critics have tended to place Forster, whose texts often instantiate a nostalgic *élan* about the passing of a lost era, as a footnote or coda to the historical, literary, and cultural practices of nineteenth-century aestheticism. If Forster garners sympathy and interest, his inability to see beyond the literary and legal constraints of the *fin de siècle* has limited his appeal and status as an important theorist of sexual difference.[5] In sum, though Forster is widely read both as a part of the broad modernist canon and as a (hesitant) voice for homosexual liberation, he is rarely credited with creating a crux within either of these major literary and cultural movements.[6]

This chapter begins to redress Forster's status as a transitional figure, and hence as a marginal voice in both modernism and twentieth-century homosexual discourse, by focusing on the ramifications of his very transitionality. Ultimately, I will suggest that Forster derived his own complex aesthetic out of the failure of decadent erotics, that his place on the threshold between centuries and world-views creates some of his most interesting and overlooked fictional effects. My analysis begins in the 1880s and 1890s, with a discussion of two topics in late-Victorian cultural politics: the role of the public schools and universities as crucial sites of male community and identity; and the ways in which aesthetic critics worked to hallow masculine bonds and the male body through an idealization of friendship. Although the aestheticist ethos contains its own divisions and contradictions, as I shall stress, it nevertheless presented a relatively coherent and institutionally authorized model for understanding erotic male community, a model that Forster seriously and thoroughly considered. However, Forster's faith in nineteenth-century strategies for representing homoerotic desire eventually gave way, and in lieu of an integrated friendship system, he was left with a form of rootless individualism that looks very much at home in the landscape of modernism. At the personal level, Forster had everything to gain from espousing a nineteenth-century paradigm of friendship that he recognized as his inheritance, yet he became a spokesman for its failure, generating a field of isolated figures and an atmosphere of dis-ease, declining the comforts of classicism in favor of ambiguity, ambivalence, and uncertainty. Ultimately, what perpetuates Forster's rejection of Hellenism, a value system that might have offered a rich ground to sanction and celebrate homosexuality, is his refusal to concede that the physical body can be controlled within a transformative or idealizing narrative. In a thoroughly surprising and ironic development, the body comes to thwart decadence itself, and this move yields an image of the individual as caught between historical modes, in a kind of psychic and cultural limbo.

HELLENISM AND THE BEAUTIFUL BODY: CARPENTER, PATER, SYMONDS

The background for Forster's rich masculine cosmos is a nineteenth century of dynamic, complex, and competing male environments. The late Victorians imagined and constructed multiple sites of flourishing male community, locations and languages dedicated to creating a sphere for intimate male ties, which worked in part as "counter-discourses" to the leviathan of bourgeois respectability and to the sovereignty of a domestic ideal.[7] Certainly, private and public became central ordering tropes in nineteenth-century Britain, helping to configure the world according to a basic gendered division; indeed, the division between the sexes at times seemed to reach a psychotic apex in the high Victorian years. Yet, just as certainly, these were not monolithic spheres (male/female, public/private, world/home), nor was power located in an uncomplicated and totalizing way in one arena or the other. Moreover, within the ordinary constructs of gendered existence, intimate male relations occupied a complex position, for their all-male character might easily point in the direction of a vexed homoerotics, at the same time that the very bastions of economic, political, and social power tended to be sites of exclusive masculinity and vaunted bonding. The nineteenth century, that is, constructed venues and institutions that functioned simultaneously as strongholds of patriarchal, middle-class power, and as forms of resistance against the dominance of domestic ideology. These include, for instance, the imperial adventure tradition (to which I shall return in the next chapter), the rise of bachelorhood as a convention, and the world of urban male "clubland," which enjoyed a kind of flowering in the latter quarter of the nineteenth century.[8]

The historical construct that will concern me most directly here, however, is what I shall call "Hellenism."[9] Most broadly, the term refers to the nineteenth-century rediscovery of ancient Greek art and culture, with the acquisition and display of the Elgin Marbles in the expanded British Museum standing as perhaps the signal aesthetic/cultural event.[10] It may seem surprising, today, to recognize how strongly Hellenism impressed many Victorian intellectuals as a viable idea to help combat a sense of cultural deterioration and to compete with dominant values surrounding Christianity, capitalism, and the middle-class family. Without abandoning the framework of the Judeo-Christian tradition, many thinkers across the political spectrum turned to Greece as an avenue for intellectual, aesthetic, and spiritual inspiration. In the face of what many felt to be the dizzying pace of social, technological, and moral change, looking back to Greece seemed to provide a template for a fully realized, highly cultivated, self-confident society, a model and example for the contemporary world. As one scholar explains it, "[w]riting about Greece was in part a way for the Victorians to write about themselves" (*Greek Heritage*, 8). Because the Greeks held tremendous cultural authority, which only increased as the century progressed, at the same time that Greek civilization appeared – literally and figuratively – in fragments, the ancient Hellenes could be infinitely useful as a kind of *tabula rasa* on which to write whatever one wanted.

The mid-Victorian elevation of the Greeks is epitomized by Matthew Arnold's argument in *Culture and Anarchy* (1869) that what British culture required was a shift from "Hebraism" to "Hellenism," from dogma and obedience to "sweetness and light."[11] For Arnold, Hellenism represents above all a habit of mind: "To get rid of one's ignorance, to see things as they are, and by seeing them as they are to see them in their beauty, is the simple and attractive ideal which Hellenism holds out before human nature" (*CA*, 134). Arnold pits what he views as the active consciousness of Hellenism against a Hebraic (i.e., Judeo-Christian) adherence to stasis and submission, stressing not only the need for social regeneration, but also the pleasure of the vigorous mental life. Arnold's emphasis on the value and delight in the mobile mind and his hailing of classical culture, at the expense of middle-class "philistinism," establish him in some ways as the precursor to later Hellenists like Walter Pater and John Addington Symonds. Arnold, of course, wanted classical Greece to become an ordering and stabilizing force, a bulwark against the anarchy he perceived in the masses, and, like his later, more flamboyant followers, he found in the Greeks something persistently relevant to the modern world of industrializing Britain. Overall, Hellenism, as I am using the term, will involve at least three interconnected themes, on top of its generally humanist orientation: a desire to escape the allegedly feminized world created and disseminated by domestic ideology; a cult of male friendship; and a tendency to idealize the youthful male body as object of desire, pathos, and, at times, national sentiment. Reverence for male bonds tended to follow quickly from the infatuation with Greek culture, and usually involved elaborate references to the heroic, canonical friendships of such figures as Achilles and Patroclus, as well as a valorization of the Platonic ideal of male love, as presented in such works as *Symposium*. In turn, this history was often transferred into a glassy-eyed notion of present-day male worlds, understood as both vigorous and intellectual.

Most striking for his conjoining of key Hellenist elements into a coherent political and spiritual ideal is the late-Victorian socialist Edward Carpenter. Reformer, social critic, poet, and open homosexual, Carpenter championed a vision of male intimacy that welcomed homoerotic desire, patterned the idealized relations of national identity on a friendship model, and seamlessly united individual sexuality with broader institutional affiliations. In the 1880s and 1890s, and indeed all the way until the war, Carpenter was widely known for several things: a large production of essays on such topics as vegetarianism, marital reform, socialist principles, and especially sex and gender; the lengthy *Towards Democracy* (1883), a series of mystical lyrics written under the spell of Walt Whitman; and his unconventional life (turning his back on his privileged Cambridge credentials, he established a communal farm with his working-class partner George Merrill, where they entertained and educated a stream of admiring pilgrims). Carpenter's personal and professional accomplishments attracted the notice of a large cohort of the era's literary figures and social radicals. As Forster described the effect:

Carpenter had a prestige which cannot be understood today [1960]. He was a rebel appropriate to his age. He was sentimental and a little sacramental, for he had begun life as a clergyman. He was a socialist who ignored industrialism and a simple-lifer with an independent income and a Whitmannic poet whose nobility exceeded his strength and, finally, he was a believer in the Love of Comrades, whom he sometimes called Uranians. It was this last aspect of him that attracted me in my loneliness. For a short time he seemed to hold the key to every trouble. I approached him... as one approaches a saviour.[12]

In Carpenter's soaringly optimistic model of comradeship, which borrows liberally from Whitman's "Calamus" poems, the anxieties one might expect to accrue to problems of desire, sexuality, and class politics are wiped away in an ecstasy of loving male community. Indeed, Carpenter's utopian view of friendship's possibilities forms an essential part of his appeal.

For Carpenter, male friendship offers a double possibility, providing an escape from what he views as the sterile and hypocritical impasse of Victorian family values, and opening up a vista for personal, social, and political fulfillment that aims at class equality, national solidarity, and individual freedom. The essence of *Towards Democracy*, for example, involves the claim that political and national organization is, or ought to be, entirely interconnected with personal desire. At the center of the poem's erotic economy is the figure of the working-class man, a locus of fierce eroticism, and, in Carpenter's imaginary, something of a mascot for a revitalized English identity. At the formal level, the text moves back and forth between ruminations on democracy (in a general cultural sense, rather than as a matter of political institutions and practices) and sexualized images of human love, with a particular focus on male comrades, whose virile, working-class beauty dominates the text. Thematically, too, Carpenter repeatedly asserts that the personal spirit of comradeship takes political form in the notion of democracy, and that a sexualized democratic ideal provides the best hope for England's future. Such a national agenda is important to Carpenter, who envisions an England modeled on Whitman's muscular, rugged America, equally with Plato's Greece. Images of soldiers fighting for the national cause abound in the poem, and their powerful devotion to one another acquires institutional shape in the military, as they form a new and heroic Theban Band. In addition to combining the personal with the martial, the homoerotic with the institutional, Carpenter's often maudlin language borrows quite liberally from the rhetoric of Christianity. Though Carpenter's mystical vision shares little with conventional religious discourse, he consistently presents his goal in terms of its potential to transform Britain's sterile and immoral institutions into fertile and sacred bonds, and he repeatedly suggests that the ascendancy of the beloved working-class youth marks a kind of second coming, a new spiritual birth for a decrepit and exhausted civilization. Far from embodying the emasculation and degeneration of England, as many of Carpenter's worried contemporaries suggested, the working-class male promises to re-energize the nation. What these lyrics repeatedly produce and reproduce is an image of men whose mutual love and high social purpose merge in the form of specific structures and rituals, a resounding articulation of the organization of intimacy.

Carpenter's essays continue *Toward Democracy*'s project of making same-sex love a pivotal cultural asset. Brimming with scientific and anthropological language, essays such as "The Intermediate Sex" and "The Homogenic Attachment" analyze the nature and social function of what many contemporaries believed to be a new sexual type. Through their freedom from sexual conventionality, Carpenter's "Urnings," masculine women and feminine men who exist precisely on the threshold between the genders, have the power to lead England towards a bright new future. If the Urning resembles the artist, as conventionally conceived in the late nineteenth century – sensitive, intelligent, misunderstood by his contemporaries – he is differentiated by his ability to channel his comradely sentiment into the work of social reform.[13] What distinguishes Carpenter's sexology from many of his contemporaries', then, is that Carpenter wants to locate the crux of his observations less in the personal consequences of sexual difference than in the cultural promise offered by these new and impressive figures of modernity.[14]

Carpenter will always organize his intimacies, often under the rubric of Greek tradition: "Greek custom, at least in the early days of Hellas, not only recognized friendships between elder and younger youths as a national institution of great importance, but laid down very distinct laws or rules concerning the conduct of them...In Crete, for instance, the friendship was entered into in quite a formal and public way."[15] Carpenter bases his system on the smooth conjunction between intimate bonds and larger cultural structures, organized as friendship and oriented towards the reform of both individuals and the body politic. Yet despite Carpenter's spirited defense of the "homogenic attachment," and his bold claims about the leadership position he feels Urnings merit, he repeatedly suggests that the bonds of friendship remain chaste. Using such words as "clean" and "pure" throughout his prose, and regularly citing the imperative for definitive rules and rituals to contain sexual behavior (as in the above description of Greek friendship), Carpenter insists that comradeship be distinguished from homosexuality, even as he proclaims a special social value in homosexuality and an elevated, almost prophetic role for homosexuals in the national arena.

Perhaps more than any other attribute, what makes comradeship so appealing to Carpenter is his belief that the bonds of friendship open the way for bridging class differences. "Eros is a great leveler," he proclaims, arguing that an eroticized ideal of friendship will draw men from different class backgrounds together through mutual affection and, eventually, structured bonds (*IS*, 114). For Carpenter, homoerotic desire offers the best hope for overcoming class antagonism, as the ideal of democratic fraternity replaces a class-stratified society, and men understand themselves both as individual friends and as brothers in a nation: "It is hardly needful in these days when social questions loom so large upon us to emphasize the importance of a bond which by the most passionate and lasting compulsion may draw members of the different classes together" (*IS*, 77). At the same time, Carpenter never entirely rejects organization by class, for he continues to rely upon class difference to create an erotic charge. While Carpenter's ultimate aim is the obliteration of class privilege, that is, the politics of eros call for the continued presence of the class-marked body.

Carpenter's interest in friendship is exemplary for its political and personal sweep, but his work can also be situated within the context of a group of writers and artists who shared his "Uranian" ideals, employed similar tropes, and invoked a shared cultural imaginary. This group, often dubbed "the Uranians," worked in painting and photography, as well as literature, developed a recognized artistic subculture with a coded language of its own (what Wayne Koestenbaum calls a mode of "double talk"), and published their work in specific journals, such as the *Artist*.[16] In lavish prose and verse, they celebrated the beauty of the youthful male body (like Carpenter), often by way of disparaging contrast with women (here marking a difference from Carpenter's feminist politics), and enthusiastically envisioned an Edenic space that would nurture and protect their fantasies. The visual image of the lovely lad was critical to the project, as was an idealized setting, often pastoral. In general, Uranian rhetoric brings together a host of associations about innocence, freshness, and perfection, with an embodied figure of desire, defined by contradictory features – a youth on the threshold of adult manhood, both sexual and unsexual, vigorous yet vulnerable, handsome yet unselfconscious.

When Oscar Wilde at the end of his trials famously characterized the love between men as intellectual and pure, an emblem of perfection, he invoked this same tendency to see purity not in opposition to male desire, but as one of its attributes. With heavy emphasis on Plato's ideal of love refined beyond the mere body, Wilde followed the Uranian mode of simultaneously delighting in male beauty and turning the eyes further afield, towards the abstractions of Beauty, Purity, and so on. Yet, the example of Wilde reminds us that such rhetorical idealism is often at odds with the exceptionally harsh and destructive atmosphere of Britain in the period after the notorious Labouchère Amendment (1885), which criminalized homosexual acts in private as well as public. Even earlier in the century, as Timothy d'Arch Smith chronicles in his thorough study of the Uranians, the group's writerly utopianism, with its ideal of perfect boy worship, often met extreme resistance in the real world. If Carpenter had established friendship as a zone free of conflict and full of potential for social regeneration, the historical realities surrounding Uranian discourse were often punitive and unrelenting.

In the Uranian landscape, it is men who dominate – their bodies and activities, their forms of beauty – often hailed at the direct expense of women. Thus, in a poem by Edwin Emmanuel Bradford, which we may treat as representative, the poet heaps up imagery of desired masculinity, construed as an alternative to an artificial and vulgar femininity:

> Eros is up and away, away!
> Eros is up and away!
> The son of Urania born of the sea,
> The lover of lads and liberty.
> Strong, self-controlled, erect and free,
> He is marching along to-day.
>
> He is calling aloud to the men, the men!
> He is calling aloud to the men –
> "Turn away from the wench, with her powder and paint,
> And follow the Boy, who is fair as a saint":
> And the heart of the lover, long fevered and faint
> Beats bravely and boldly again.[17]

Or, in an 1894 essay published in the *Artist*, Charles Kains-Jackson, a former master at Eton, hailed the shift from "the Old Chivalry, or the exaltation of the youthful feminine ideal," to "the New Chivalry, or the exaltation of the youthful masculine ideal" which he believed could flourish at a time when the imperative to reproduce was waning.[18] Using a vague sociology to lend scientific credence to his point, Kains-Jackson argues that the aesthetic moment for appreciating the beauty of the young male has come into its own. As both of these texts indicate, the presentation of masculinity in Uranian writing does not conform readily to simple gender categories: it is difficult, for instance, to reconcile the emphasis on naturalized, soldierly masculinity with the notion of boy-worship, which one would expect to be tainted by the ubiquitous Victorian fear of effeminacy. As Alan Sinfield has shown, however, in an analysis of the signs surrounding such interrelated terms as effeminacy, homosexuality, decadence, and virility, to assimilate the rugged masculinity of classical athleticism with the scopic economy of the lovely youth was a standard strategy among late-Victorian homoerotic writers.[19]

For Sinfield, it is only after 1895 that the complex and contradictory associations surrounding the image of the effeminate man took definite shape as the homosexual:

The sexologists and the boy-love advocates made the masculine/feminine binary structure even more central and necessary while, at the same time, doing little to clarify its confusions. The Wilde trials exploded in the midst of all of this urgent ideological work. As a consequence, the entire, vaguely disconcerting nexus of effeminacy, leisured idleness, immorality, luxury, insouciance, decadence and aestheticism, which Wilde was perceived as instantiating, was transformed into a brilliantly precise image. (*The Wilde Century*, 118)

According to Sinfield, then, the queer moment arrives as a kind of stunning unveiling, with the spectacle of Wilde permanently altering the valence attached to the image of the boy-lover, as to the dandy. Thus, while Uranian discourse is characterized by a kind of excess that clearly conflicted with dominant middle-class morality, the construct of the beloved young male body was more adaptable in the period before Wilde's trials than would be feasible in later decades. Yet, as Sinfield concedes, even after the spectacle of Wilde's sentencing, the conjoining of athlete and aesthete, of normative and dissident tropes of masculinity, would maintain a fitful existence, though never again carrying the earlier sense of potential completeness, ease, and blitheness.

A final point to note about Uranian rhetoric involves the rendering of history. Carpenter understood the flourishing of the Urning to be a purely contemporaneous development, and so, too, did the Uranians present their project of replacing the female body with the youthful male, and feminine domesticity with the masculine circle, as symptomatic of their historical time, a fruitful coalescing of style, technology, and political progress. Elaine Showalter, among others, has noted the "sexual anarchy" that accompanied the end of the century: such parallel social constructs as the New Woman and the adventure romancer, with their complex sexual and gender meanings, contributed to a sense of possibility in the last decades of the century, a flux which many hoped (and many feared) would herald an irrevocable dismantling of high-Victorian domestic ideology.[20] At the same time, writers like the Uranians invoke the textual authority of classical precedent, supplemented by a select tradition of post-classical works (the Bible, Shakespeare, Montaigne) and in that sense point to a trans-historical phenomenon, a continuous history of male love from Homer to Hopkins. This combination – historicity in tandem with an ideal of historically extensive male community – takes us straight to the organizations which in many ways governed normative ideas of masculinity during the nineteenth century: the public schools and the universities. In the schools and universities, we find highly developed versions of both parts of this conjunction – an elaborate ancestry of masculine fraternity, to be studied and emulated; a specific contemporaneity, or form for expressing, understanding, and promoting male community. During the long span of years between mid-century and the First World War, male intimacy was almost inevitably understood in one or another institutional context, and it was in many ways the conflict over how to institutionalize male bonds that came to crystallize debates about masculinity, male desire, and the mechanics of social power.

The key point to underscore about the public schools and the universities in the nineteenth century is that both types of institution underwent terrific growth and substantive reform, with the public schools showing an especially marked leap in influence and power.[21] In the fifty years that spanned mid-century, the public schools experienced a stunning reconstitution, as the school tie went from an essentially marginal matter to a crucial badge of access for a host of professional and social privileges, a necessary credential for entry into Britain's developing leadership class. The schools expanded internally, with individual schools consistently increasing their enrollments over the course of the nineteenth century, and in numbers, from nine in 1841 to seventy-one in 1873.[22] Inextricably connected with the numerical expansion was a spirit of reform that was nothing short of transformational. It was largely the influence of Thomas Arnold at Rugby that set the tone for change, as the principles of asceticism and athletics that he inaugurated took on a life of their own.

The cultural and political hegemony of the British public schools during the Victorian and Edwardian years can hardly be overstated. The schools,

which increasingly in the nineteenth century became purveyors of an ideological vision that centered on the perpetuation of England's imperial
mission, provided the core training for Britain's ruling elite, creating a
set of norms about how to live and what to believe that touched nearly
all sectors of British life, at home and in the expanding empire. As Forster
has it: "Just as the heart of England is the middle classes, so the heart of
the middle classes is the public school system . . . With its boarding-houses,
its compulsory games, its system of prefects and fagging, its insistence on
good form and on *esprit de corps*, it produces a type whose weight is out
of all proportion to its numbers."[23] Public-school ideology influenced the
English and their imperial subjects through several circuits: directly, as men
were trained in the schools and steeped in their reigning philosophy; indirectly, as the values and perspectives of this powerful group were transmitted
into large-scale educational, political, and cultural practices; and through
specifically organized and targeted programs, such as the Boys' Brigade and
the Boy Scouts, aimed at diffusing public-school morality into the working
classes.

As Forster's description suggests, the public schools prided themselves
on creating character in their boys, an intangible quality that was widely
viewed as the most important element in education. An aristocratic leadership ideal, now available to a broader spectrum of men, was at the core
of their training.[24] In brief, the public-school spirit of the late nineteenth
century consisted primarily in an adherence to two things: "manliness and
loyalty."[25] The belief that there is a smooth succession along the loyalty spectrum from team, to house, to school, to nation is a staple of public-school
thinking, with especially strong connotations for the twin pursuits of war
(the culmination of masculine courage and loyalty) and the management
of empire (a profession that the schools insisted was an equally important
element of patriotic duty). The full force of this ideal was gradually solidified over the course of the nineteenth century in the living conditions at the
schools, with the cult of loyalty, realized primarily through athletic games
and house rituals, reaching an almost psychotic apex. Whereas, in the early
nineteenth century, unstructured intimacy between boys was accepted, and
individual pursuits like walking, collecting, and naturalism were approved –
a sensibility embodied in the character of Martin in Thomas Hughes'
fabulously popular *Tom Brown's Schooldays* (1857) – by the end of the century the emphasis had shifted entirely in the direction of supervision, group
games, and, more generally, rigid organization at nearly every moment of
the day. The increased discipline, extensive archipelago of prefects and punishment, emphasis on organized athletics, and morally ascetic tone of the

schools came to define their character. Moreover, as I shall discuss further in relation to the Great War, the transference of the schools' loyalty ethos into military ideology played an important role in setting the rhetorical and emotional tone of the war years. That young soldiers would kick a football as they headed over the top at the outset of the battle of the Somme, or compose poems in which it was deemed an honor to die in the name of one's school, can only be understood if we recognize the psychic power wielded by the public-school axiom of an interdependence linking school, sport, masculinity, and patriotism.

The construct of "muscular Christianity" is often used to describe the blend of obsession with athleticism and adherence to conventional piety that characterized at least the official ideology of the public schools. Associated most directly with the mid-century novelist and social critic Charles Kingsley,[26] the muscular Christian is the paradigmatic English citizen, whose body and spirit have been hardened, through games and other rites of passage, and whose will is indomitable. At the same time, he is expected to maintain a Christian spirit of compassion for those whom it is his duty to govern. As the phrase so well suggests, the muscular Christian conveniently conjoins in his person conventional morality with masculinism, reassuring pieties with something closer to an ethos of bullying. If muscular Christianity was meant to provide the overarching moral force at the schools, however, the role accorded to serious religious observance definitively shrank as the century progressed. As Thomas Arnold's specific legacy waned, a suspicion of excessive piety, rather than its practice, became the norm (by all accounts, Arnold was a genuinely pious person whose vision for Rugby involved religious study). As Forster beautifully captures it in *A Passage to India*: "Ronny's religion was of the sterilized Public School brand, which never goes bad, even in the tropics. Wherever he entered, mosque, cave, or temple, he retained the spiritual outlook of the Fifth Form, and condemned as 'weakening' any attempt to understand them."[27] Critics have further suggested that in the actual life of the public schools, where hardship and repression were typically the rule, Social Darwinism rather than any kind of Christian spirit, with or without muscles, provided the ideological force dictating the competitive and often brutal atmosphere into which the boys were thrown.[28]

The figure of the old boy, whose fortitude, loyalty to country, and respectability are ensured by his lengthy stay in the school system, even as he retains a marked quality of infinite adolescence, emerges through a variety of texts and conventions. Following *Tom Brown's Schooldays*, public-school novels enjoyed a huge boom that lasted all the way into the 1930s; the official

language of headmasters and school commissioners wended its way across
the political landscape; and even today the memoirs of men who attended
the schools as boys continue to engage a reading public. George Orwell's
"Such, Such Were the Joys . . .," John Addington Symonds' memoirs, Robert
Graves' autobiography, Virginia Woolf's biography of Roger Fry, Forster's
fictional depictions of public-school life, to name just a few prominent
accounts from the early twentieth century, present a world in which intellectual gifts and non-physical pursuits of any variety were crushed under
the heels of suspicious masters and their organizations of student prefects.
Most critics point to a deeply anti-intellectual spirit permeating all aspects
of public-school life, a suspicion of "weedy" intellectuals who were the obverse of the revered athletic "bloods." Descriptions of the public schools
by intellectuals educated there tend to read like catalogues of insensitivity and philistinism, illuminated only by the occasional companionship of
like-minded students or masters.

Finally, though intellectual life at the public schools might have been
discouraged, classical literature remained the core of the curriculum, and,
more to the point, the schools quite effectively appropriated ideals of classical masculinity for their own uses, primarily in the form of athleticism.
Though the schools were harsh and punitive in their treatment of boys,
and physical existence was deliberately harrowing, they also emphasized the
glory and beauty of the physical body in its prime, and this contrast underscores the complexity of the schools' management of the body. In a circular
logic, the schools combined a draconian system of rules and surveillance
with a reverence for the male body, which they then needed continually to
supervise.[29] Commentators tend to stress the omnipresence of homosexuality as a standard element in the public-school experience, even as a tone of
intolerance dominated official rhetoric and infused the boys' anxious psychic development. In his moving autobiographical memoir, for instance,
Symonds describes a system of "bitching" and "fagging," constructed on a
model of hierarchy, brutality, and exploitation, rather than tenderness or
tolerance, which terrorized the young and confused homosexual. Of equal
importance to the complex enabling and policing of homosexual acts was
the proliferation of intimate, romantic friendships between boys. As with
the regulation of the body, the schools' attitude towards intimacy is contradictory: on one hand, the creation of networks and alliances, life-long
old-boy bonds, and the cult of sport-based friendship were central to the
schools' self-concept and mission; on the other hand, many former students
maintain that their closest friendships with other boys actually collided with
the inevitable cult of *esprit de corps*. Robert Graves, for instance, describes

his beloved school friendships as a form of resistance against orthodoxy. "At Charterhouse," he writes, "no friendship was permitted between boys of different houses or of different years beyond a formal acquaintance at work or organized games like cricket and football," and hence Graves' most cherished relationships worked as a rebuttal of school form.[30]

In a similar vein, Virginia Woolf characterizes Roger Fry's school friendships as the only light in a dark world, and his matriculation as a movement out of spiritual and intellectual morbidity:

it meant an end – an end to Sunninghill and its shrivelled pines and dirty heather and Monday morning floggings, and an end to Clifton and its good form, its Christian patriotism, and its servility to established institutions. From his private school he had learnt a horror of all violence, and from his public school a lifelong antagonism to all public schools and their ideals. He seldom spoke of those years, but when he did he spoke of them as the dullest, and save for one friendship, as the most completely wasted of his life.[31]

Woolf depicts the schools as sites of dearth ("shrivelled pines and dirty heather," "wasted ... life"), and suggests that the spirit of real friendship works in its small way against such life-depleting forces. School comradeship is allied with the institutions' hated "ideals," while individual intimacy provides a small haven for the young men who resist school spirit. Indeed, the problem of the schools, even in Woolf's account, is not only that they exclude intellectual growth (not to mention women), but that their official doctrine of male community distorts and destroys real friendship, whose power and desirability remain as forms of underground resistance to dominant orthodoxy. Thus male intimacy, as distinct from authorized male bonds, becomes an antidote to public-school oppressiveness. We should notice, moreover, that Woolf represents the lifelessness of the schools in language that mocks the schools' pretentions of virility: the "shrivelled pines" are an image of failed masculinity at the very institution that promises to create it. The schools might attempt to make men, but in fact real masculinity abides precisely in the relationships that thwart official school policy.

Yet Woolf's withered phalluses also suggest a strange web of ambivalence around the idea of male friendship. Woolf seems unwilling to abandon a certain nostalgic vision of a masculine world, and she turns to the university as an alternative locale for a more positive male community. That is, the desire to rebel against the hegemony of the public schools without entirely surrendering the goal of organizing intimacy leads to a hallowing of collegiate life, even in the work of such an exemplary feminist as

Woolf. We see glimmers of such community in *The Waves*, for instance, surrounding the person of Percival, and especially in *Jacob's Room*, where the masculine is understood as an almost aesthetic quality, a kind of harmony or beauty that grows out of intimacy and intellectual exchange among men:

> Jacob remained standing. But intimacy – the room was full of it, still, deep, like a pool. Without need of movement or speech it rose softly and washed over everything, mollifying, kindling, and coating the mind with the lustre of pearl, so that if you talk of a light, of Cambridge burning, it's not languages only. It's Julian the Apostate.[32]

For those excluded from the light of Cambridge, there is something painfully attractive about this gorgeous male world, an enclosed circle attached to intellectual pursuits. Woolf muses, here, about a form of masculinity that centers on the intimacy developed among men with shared intellectual, spiritual, and aesthetic values. Though this is an intimacy based on personal choice, it nevertheless belongs to an institution with powerful defining traditions and an imposing history of its own, a tradition and history whose exclusivity Woolf condemns in *A Room of One's Own*. Still, Woolf gazes in the window of the college room: her extraordinary empathy towards the pleasure of collegiate friendship is in part a function of her close relations with men who had prospered in such circles, but it also represents a characteristically Woolfian ability to grasp a contemporary phenomenon with both compassion and irony. What Woolf captures here is the way the intellectual and social organization of the university had recast the schools' brutal and confusing male community into a kind of hallowed domestic circle.

It was in the highly erudite world of the university, then – with its residential colleges and its reading societies dedicated to "the pursuit of knowledge for its own sake"[33] – and particularly at Oxford, that an alternative view of male relations oriented around classicism took shape in the middle decades of the nineteenth century, henceforth becoming a fixed element at both major universities. Like the public schools, the universities underwent fundamental and lasting reforms during this period, involving, for instance, the abolition of religious tests for undergraduates at Oxford (1854), and, later, removal of the celibacy requirement for fellows (1877/1884). The gradual shift at the universities to a secular framework from an ostensibly Christian one, a shift that involved both the subject of study and the population of the university, was intimately connected with the increasing curricular importance of classical, and particularly Greek studies. Moreover, a heightened emphasis on the tutorial relationship functioned in various ways to foster this spirit of change, as the close bonds between fellows and students offered a modern-day analogue for the Greek culture at the center of the curriculum. In her study of homosexuality and Victorian Oxford, Linda Dowling describes the reform period at mid-century as "the unique moment of Oxford masculine comradeship, a window or halcyon interval of particularly intense male homosociality which flourished between the first two waves of university reform."[34] Even the Oxford Movement, an apparent challenge to secularist tendencies, grew out of and depended upon the new dispensation. With the tutorial relationship and the intimate circle at its core, the Oxford Movement was a natural outgrowth of the general shift in university culture towards intimacy, fraternity, and a degree of individual preference in constructing the curriculum.

Dowling argues that the kinds of appropriation of the male body that I will be describing in the texts of Pater, Symonds, and ultimately Forster have their origins in the shifting uses made of Greek history by the intelligentsia of the Victorian period:

As regards Victorian Oxford, my argument is that (1) such leading university reformers as Benjamin Jowett were seeking to establish in Hellenism, the systematic study of Greek history and literature and philosophy, a ground of transcendent value alternative to Christian theology – the metaphysical underpinning of Oxford from the Middle Ages through the Tractarian movement. But (2) once they had done so, Pater and Wilde and the Uranian poets could not be denied the means of developing out of this same Hellenism a homosexual counterdiscourse able to justify male love in ideal or transcendental terms: the "spiritual procreancy" associated specifically with Plato's *Symposium* and more generally with ancient Greece itself. (*Hellerism and Homosexuality*, xiii)

At Oxford, the debates about institutional organization and curriculum were interconnected with a wide reconsideration of intellectual and moral values, and at the center of the new ideal was the intimate male relationship, understood as a revival of Plato's Greece. Yet the late-Victorian university did not uniformly and without resistance accept the views of writers like Pater and Symonds, both of whom were affiliated with Oxford for many years. On the contrary, Pater was in constant conflict with members of the university elite because of his shocking views – expressed most notoriously in the "Conclusion" to *The Renaissance* – and both he and Symonds were passed over for the prestigious position of Professor of Poetry at Oxford for reasons that probably had at least something to do with the politics of their sexual lives.[35] The central point is that Pater and Symonds, like others concerned with masculinity and Hellenism during the period, developed their visions of masculine community in a complex relation of reciprocity and competition with the powerful institutions that surrounded them. As we turn to their texts, we can trace a contest over the male body, in which the different models of male fellowship embedded in the public schools and universities competed against one another, creating tension and ambiguity alongside a seemingly harmonious vision of male love.[36]

Walter Pater, the great champion among the late Victorians of aesthetics, classical studies, and male friendship, invites an immediate reckoning with both the abundance and the limitations of organized intimacy. Pater seems, at first glance, to offer a ringing endorsement of male friendship as both ideal and practice, and to admire without restraint the preeminent historical personae associated with masculine love (Plato, Michelangelo, Winckelmann). And it is certainly true that, like Carpenter, Pater offers a complete vision of friendship as a social and aesthetic structure whose merit and power go unchallenged. Yet, an analysis of Pater's approach to friendship yields some surprising results. For Pater, male friendship will never quite be able to reconcile all the contrasts it seems, at some level, to harmonize and fuse; it unsettles as much as it consolidates. At the center of Pater's concept of friendship, as developed in *The Renaissance* (1877), is conflict – the conflict between intimacy and institutions, which might also be understood as a juxtaposition of male love against stabilizing cultural traditions, the couple versus the group. These contrasts underpin the story of Amis and Amile, which inaugurates *The Renaissance* (in its revised and expanded second edition), and which I will use as an exemplary case of Pater's uneven treatment of male friendship in relation to history.[37] It is a tale of richly physical male friendship, but it also indicates that absorbing such an extreme masculine relation into the broader culture will never quite be possible.

Pater portrays the intimacy of Amis and Amile as powerful precisely because it is connected with important institutions, such as the church, the monarchy, and the military. The two protagonists are leaders in their society, governors and symbols of major institutions, images of absolute loyalty not only to one another, but also to the king. As in Woolf's hallowing of university space, Pater attaches the intimacy of Amis and Amile to solid and powerful organizations, stressing the social structure (primarily military) at the basis of their fierce love for one another. The story thus represents for Pater a rare moment "in which the harmony of human interests is still entire," since there appears to be no conflict between personal desire and state or religious duty.[38] Yet this sense of compatibility between male love and institutional sanction is, in fact, illusory, and cannot be sustained by the wider currents of convention detailed in the story. Despite the "harmony of human interests" that the story proclaims, the continuing cycle of the men's friendship contributes to a severe conflict with social norms. Such conflict is most spectacularly illustrated in the (temporary) destruction – violent and shocking – of Amile's family. Out of loyalty to his twin and friend, Amile kills his own children, and, despite his wretched emotional state, the murder is undertaken with gruesome efficiency. Rather than adopt the public-school platitude of a spectrum of loyalties, Pater's story demonstrates that in the face of an intensely valued male friendship, in which identity itself becomes fluid, traditional institutions such as family risk destruction. If Amis and Amile initially look like models of an integrated system of intimacy within culture, the story in fact takes aim at the very idea of organizing friendship, situating its protagonists in the shifting positions of heroes and heretics.

There is a reason why Amis and Amile cannot unambiguously assimilate into culture, for what characterizes such figures across history is a "spirit of rebellion and revolt against the moral and religious ideas of the time" (*Ren*, 16). Pater presents this revolt explicitly as part of a contest over the body and its place in social discourse: "In their search after the pleasures of the senses and the imagination, in their care for beauty, in their worship of the body, people were impelled beyond the bounds of the Christian ideal; and their love became sometimes a strange idolatry, a strange rival religion" (*Ren*, 16). Crucial to Pater's admiration for figures such as Amis and Amile is that their story situates the body as the ground for spiritual and aesthetic value. To locate the human body at the place where important institutions do their work is to propel the worshipper into conflict with those institutions, to create subcultures, subversions, and dissonance. Thus, it is only at rare moments that the personal and the political are harmoniously united; more typically, the devotion to intimacy and the worship of the body sit uncomfortably alongside such daunting structures as Christianity. The Amis and Amile tale constructs a vision of identity that clashes not only with arbitrary institutional loyalty, but with individualism itself, as the histories and bodies of the two men intermingle right up to their deaths, when their decaying bodies refuse to separate into distinct entities for burial and commemoration. For Amis and Amile, identity is a matter of mimesis, and their interiority, like their exterior persons, is an indistinguishable amalgamation: "that curious interest of the *Doppelgänger*, which begins among the stars with the Dioscuri, [is] entwined in and out through all the incidents of the story like an outward token of the inward similitude of their souls" (*Ren*, 6). A sign of doubleness and mimesis, masculinity here refutes both competition and the ascendancy of the self; such an image of the masculine fits only uneasily into its cultural setting.

In *The Renaissance*, Pater unites the disparate values that orient male intimacy and the male body under a common rubric of Hellenism. Rather than juxtapose Christianity with paganism, Pater establishes his own grid, asserting the subterranean existence of a trans-historical "Greek spirit." According to Pater, this Greek spirit has always had its Christian adherents, especially among those early Christians who accentuated male fellowship and the physicality of religious worship. This widely defined (and, one might add, somewhat self-serving) Greek ideal provides Pater with an asset in his long-standing effort to amalgamate and organize divergent texts and historical periods into a unified polemic. In *The Renaissance*'s conclusory essay on the eighteenth-century art critic Winckelmann, as oddly placed in a study of the Italian Renaissance as is its initial story, Pater explicitly connects the friendship ethos of Amis and Amile with his concept of the Greek spirit, and insists that those who study, admire, and understand the Greek image of "supreme beauty," which is "male rather than female," share a special trans-historical sensibility (*Ren*, 123). These men, who live by a creed of friendship and place a male aesthetic at the apex of the critical hierarchy, are the natural inheritors of the Greek mantle.

Pater's extreme valorization of friendship and his lauding of the male body as a centerpiece for a civilized culture reach a pitch when he describes the Greeks themselves, primarily in the lectures and essays that became *Plato and Platonism* (1893) and *Greek Studies* (1895). In *Plato and Platonism*, a broad and poetical (if idiosyncratic) study of Plato's thought, Pater turns his imagination to Sparta, which he presents as a monastic land of brotherhood and male communion. Pater stresses three things about the Spartans: their asceticism; the organization of their lives around the rites of young men; and their reverence for male beauty. These three attributes continually mingle together in institutions and rituals that center around the physical and mental discipline of young men. The image, for instance, of Spartan youths singing together, which Pater imagines to have epitomized all Spartan values, provides a perfect picture of masculine beauty, control, and ceremony, "one of the things in Old Greece one would have liked best to see and hear – youthful beauty and strength in perfect service – a manifestation of the true and genuine Hellenism."[39] This charged fantasy is characteristic of Pater's discussion of the Spartans, whose physical presence gleams throughout the text. The young Spartans are ascetic, restrained, obedient; yet such discipline is not understood as passivity, much less weakness, but as strength in reserve, an aestheticizing of masculinity by holding it still, like a frieze or sculpture. As in an earlier description of Winckelmann's kinetic attraction to sculpture, Pater stresses the carved body as the paradigmatic Greek art-form, a condensation of intangible essences in the flesh, a "struggle...between the palpable and limited human form, and the floating essence it is to contain."[40] Moreover, just as sculpture is a distillation in the human form of older, more indistinct forces, so do the Spartans themselves epitomize the idea of force contained in the human body. Yet these are real bodies, and the beauty that they epitomize by holding power in suspension is, for Pater, quite extraordinary, because, once again, it represents a specifically masculine beauty. "Yes!" he cries, "the beauty of these most beautiful of all people was a male beauty, far remote from feminine tenderness; had the expression of a certain *ascêsis* in it; was like unsweetened wine" (*PP*, 202). Pater is at pains to create an ideal of beauty that banishes femininity, with its panoply of negative associations. He thus relies on the somewhat paradoxical idea that we can be assured of a spirit of virility among Spartan men because their reverence for the male body was understood and institutionalized entirely in rituals of male comradeship. For Pater's Spartans, it is male community, more than heterosexual desire, that creates and substantiates masculinity.

Pater emphasizes, for instance, the lengthy and rigorous educational system endured by Spartan youths. Spartan schools in Pater's hands look quite a bit like English public schools, characterized by obedience, discipline, surveillance, and a system of self-governance. Yet each time that Pater begins to sound like a spokesman for the public schools, extolling their values and structure, he adds an important nuance, by stressing the purely aesthetic angle of Spartan male beauty, and, even more importantly, by endorsing the institutionalization of male friendship for its own sake. That is, unlike the public schools, which clearly understand the comradeship of boys to be in the service of a larger ideological program, Pater's fantasy of Spartan society continually collapses back into a notion of male friendship in service only to itself. Pater imagines that an Athenian visitor to Sparta asks the local to explain the point of their educational system: "An intelligent Spartan might have replied: 'To the end that I myself may be a perfect work of art, issuing thus into the eyes of all Greece'" (*PP*, 211). Although Pater applauds this imagined response, he nevertheless concedes something strange about the ideal he describes. Unlike the monastic student (a reiterated comparison in the text, as elsewhere in Victorian Hellenism), whose reward is clearly spiritual, or the British youth, whose reward for obedience to public-school morality is social and economic, Pater believes that the Spartan's training provides an end in itself – laboring for beauty and perfection in the interest of perfection itself. Pater's vision here is even more self-perpetuating, self-enclosing, and self-justifying than the familiar decadent credo of "art for art's sake," since the art object is the human body: artist, viewer, and object merge into one another in a vision of aesthetic completeness.

In the case of the Spartans, Pater imagines a world so organized around the male body and its rituals, understood as the institutions of friendship, that these become absolute ends in themselves, overshadowing all other values and interests; such also is the conclusion of *Greek Studies*, a series of essays about Greek myth, culture, and art that Pater published in journals over the course of several decades. The collection closes with "The Age of Athletic Prizemen," a discussion of what Pater views as perhaps the most shining of the golden ages of Greek sculpture, a time when the Persian wars had passed. Pater claims that the art of this period is best characterized by its representations of young athletes in pursuit of the honors that accrue to gymnastic accomplishment. Once the spirit of war has subsided, two things are culled from the former statuary and carried forward by the new generation of sculptors: the beauty of youthful bodies at work, and the heroism of male friendship. The new artists represent "youth in its voluntary labours, its habitual and measured discipline, labour for its own sake, or in wholly friendly contest... We are with Pindar, you see, in this athletic age of Greek sculpture" (*GS*, 251). For Pater, the age of prizemen – emphasizing gymnastic rather than war – is the high-point of Greek plastic art because it celebrates what his Spartans epitomized in their persons and their training: the ritualizing of the beautiful male body and the bonds of male friendship into institutions of their own, where value is determined by internal markers. The gorgeousness of the young body and the pathos of friendship themselves become the standards whereby value is measured, and this signals the apex of an ultra-civilized culture.

Pater's intense elevation of friendship is typically read (whether dismissed or valued) primarily as a coded depiction of private fantasies.[41] Without denying the personal dimension of Pater's erotic scenarios, or engaging in hypothetical reasoning about his precise sexual situation, I want to stress that the intimacy project he develops is perhaps undervalued when we focus primarily on homosexual double-talk. Alan Sinfield has suggested that Pater's "importance lies not in a possible covert or submerged homosexuality, but in his articulation of a framework that did not depend on such categories" (*The Wilde Century*, 89), and I would concur that the often contradictory quality of Pater's presentation of the organization of intimacy is precisely what makes it both interesting and representative. Rather than functioning as a straightforward articulation of desire, his portrayal of friendship and its institutions tends to get caught in its own work of heightening and valorizing male bonds. Pater's descriptions are full of Uranian-style desire, the men's beauty is presented as sheer delight, and their eroticized rituals dominate the social space; at the same time, the friendships he describes are "pure" and "chaste," the young men are highly disciplined, and their relationships are rigorously structured. Again, the context of these contradictions matters, in a conflicting valorization of public-school morality versus university intimacy, and Pater's depictions of absorbing masculine communities balance themselves on a series of often precarious and uncertain thresholds. Yet balance he does: what both anticipates later writers like Forster and differentiates Pater from them is that Pater continues to assert harmony as his privileged category, to recruit Hellenic friendship as a system that might threaten to come undone, but never quite does.

Pater was not alone in blending a focus on the "Greek Spirit" with a semi-utopian vision of male community. Symonds, a contemporary of Pater's at Oxford and the author of voluminous essays about Renaissance and Greek art, engaged in a parallel endeavor, with results that are similarly conflicted. If Pater's homosexuality has been debated, Symonds was a self-proclaimed "invert," and his posthumously published memoirs provide a moving account of his life-long struggle to understand, accept, and fulfill what he understood as his nature, within the narratives available during his life.[42] As Symonds stresses in his memoir, the Greek ideal of heroic friendship, especially in its Platonic form, came as a kind of revelation for the young man, offering him a measure of hope for both conceptualizing and realizing his own sexuality. Moreover, whatever one may say about the artistic merit of Uranian literature, Symonds felt exhilarated when he discovered their work, and his writing in turn contributes to the canon of celebratory literature on male love. *A Problem in Greek Ethics* (1883), originally a private text, which was eventually published as an appendix to Havelock Ellis' *Sexual Inversion* (1897), can be read in part as his most straightforward attempt to utilize Hellenism to legitimize and sanction homosexuality in a world that was becoming increasingly intolerant, harsh, and dangerous for "inverts." Adopting a tone of scientific detail, the text examines the representation of boy-love in high Greek literature; at its core is an extended discussion of what Symonds believes to have been a heroic and unsurpassed tradition of male friendship among ancient Greek writers.

Yet it is limiting to understand Symonds' texts uniformly as defenses for homosexuality. In *Greek Ethics*, Symonds plays a complicated game (also demonstrated in his memoir), in which the championing of friendship

is meant to provide a model of social organization that includes homosexuality, but does not depend on it, and, in fact, his writing is wracked
with anxiety and contradiction about the body. Symonds demonstrates real
ambivalence about the place of the sexual in the heroic narratives of friendship that his texts elaborate. Probably most impassioned and tortured on
this issue is *Greek Ethics*, which, even in Symonds' own privately printed
copy, is absolutely explicit in distinguishing "the nobler type of masculine
love developed by the Greeks" which is "almost unique in the history of
the human race," from the "vulgar" form of pederasty which is associated
with the "voluptuousness" of the East, and from which Homer is emphatically and repeatedly dissociated.[43] Thus, "we find two separate forms of
masculine passion clearly marked in early Hellas – a noble and a base, a
spiritual and a sensual" (*SI*, 172). What Symonds chooses to call "Greek
love" is a blend of these two, a form of love which in practice can never
match the ideal as presented by the poets, but which nevertheless remains
"spiritual," "noble," "heroic," and untainted by "vice" or "voluptuousness."
Symonds takes a surprisingly binary approach, in which the cosmos of male
desire is split into positive and negative categories (the latter of which carry
the familiar tokens of "eastern" excess). On one hand, then, there is an
undeniable personal dimension to Symonds' interest in male friendship,
which sanctifies and ennobles passionate intimacy between men. On the
other hand, Symonds, like Pater, turned to male friendship and its rituals
because it offered a wide-ranging space for rethinking the way social and
sexual practices could be understood. Symonds may have internalized some
of his society's denigration of the physical aspect of male love, but, more
importantly, he also recognized that to take on powerful institutions like
the public schools required a broadly conceived model of male relations
that did not constrain friendship or the physical body to be place-holders
for sexuality.

In *Studies of the Greek Poets* (3rd. edn., 1893), an exhaustive discussion
of individual artists and over-arching themes in Greek literature, which is
very similar in places to the more narrowly focused *Greek Ethics*, Symonds
looks longingly and nostalgically at a world that he believes was organized
around male community, a culture that held up the figure of the male
friend as the ultimate citizen. The lengthy text draws to its close on a note
of sadness: "The Greeks had no past: 'no hungry generations trod them
down': whereas the multitudinous associations of immense antiquity en-
velop all our thoughts and feelings."[44] This lament continues, as Symonds
wonders how we, who have "now grown old," can make contact with the
beautiful, innocent culture of the Greeks.[45] Symonds here echoes many of

his contemporaries, who often portrayed the old world of super-civilized England in terms of the life-span of the individual, hence in a kind of twilight or old age. Moreover, although it was something of a common-place among mid-century intellectuals to draw a parallel between Periclean Athens and Victorian Britain (naturally a flattering comparison), perhaps even more compelling was the connection between imperial Britain and imperial Rome, and this presented a more disturbing parallel, pointing as it inevitably did to fall as well as rise, degradation as well as glory.[46] Thus for Symonds to look across the chasm of time at the youthfulness of Greece was to tap into a number of well-established terms for expressing a generalized anxiety about the overall health and vitality of a culture seemingly at the zenith of its power and self-confidence.

Symonds represents the longed-for world of the ancients with a mar-velous image: "Like a young man newly come from the wrestling-ground, anointed, chapleted, and very calm, the genius of the Greeks appears be-fore us. Upon his soul there is no burden of the world's pain . . . nor yet has he felt sin. The pride and the strength of adolescence are his" (*GP*, 362). Like Pater, Symonds imagines Greek society itself as a young male body, glowing and desirable, entirely self-sufficient. One senses that the writer has constructed his image with sculpture in mind: with a twist on the Pygmalian story, Symonds has imaginatively turned a statue of a healthy male athlete into flesh – or text. What is perhaps most striking, though, about the image of Greek genius as a young man is that it places Symonds himself in the position of the desiring older man, longing for friendship with the handsome young athlete, the Uranian pose. The act of aesthetic criticism symbolically performs what it describes: an intimate connection between two men, based on desire and dripping with eros. Yet there re-mains an irreconcilable distance between the spiritually aged man of the nineteenth century and the Greek adolescent. Such contact, even in its ideal form, would be based on an essential disjunction. In Homer, by contrast – and this will provide the key to the text's ultimate self-contradiction – Symonds claims that we find the true model of equality between men, and it is this comradeship that he most unambivalently praises.

For Symonds, heroic friendship between men represents Greek civi-lization at its best. Though he cites many instances of the friendship ideal in Hellenic literature, the greatest example is to be found in *The Iliad*, in the majestic love of Achilles and Patroclus: "The love of Achilles has no softness or effeminacy," Symonds claims, echoing Pater's descrip-tion of Spartan friendship (*GP*, 82). Over and over, Symonds insists that the institutionalization of Greek male friendship, especially in military organization, ensures its powerful virility: "The fruit which friendship bore among the Greeks was courage in the face of danger, indifference to life when honour was at stake, patriotic ardour, the love of liberty, and lion-hearted rivalry in battle. 'Tyrants,' said Plato, 'stand in awe of friends'" (*GP*, 98). To expend one's energy in the love of other men signals a special kind of virility, which Symonds hopes will be seen as even more masculine and hence admirable than any relations involving women. Like Pater, Symonds hopes that the connection of friendship with the state will help to elevate and redeem it in the eyes of a suspicious public, just becoming attuned to the idea of the homosexual. Interestingly, though, Symonds' vision accords more closely to what writers several decades later would stress – his interest in military valor as the apex of male comradeship and love allies him more closely to the First World War generation than does Pater's emphasis on male friendship in service only to itself.

Symonds looks to trace an impressive genealogy of male friendship in part because he believes that the western tradition since the middle ages has ignored friendship as an essential category of human relations and passion. As a corrective, Symonds offers an elaborate comparison between Greek friendship conventions and medieval chivalry. "Nearly all historians of Greece," he says, "have failed to insist upon the fact that fraternity in arms played for the Greek race the same part as the idealization of women for the knighthood of feudal Europe" (*GP*, 97). This point is made repeatedly in Symonds' text, simultaneously redressing an aporia in the historical understanding of the two worlds (Greek and medieval) and borrowing from the early Christians a certain sensual mood, a tone of heightened passion that conjoins romantic love with military fervor (along the lines of Carpenter's texts). Both Pater and Symonds attempt to correct the historical record, and they believe their project has ramifications beyond what might seem the limited realm of aesthetic criticism. If modern norms of gender – including the fetishization of female beauty and virtue, codes of courtesy and manners, separateness of spheres for women and men – are justified partly in terms of an imagined English Christian history dating back to the middle ages, then to resurrect a competing Hellenic tradition has consequences for the way gender is assimilated into culture. By stressing in particular the parallel between Greek traditions of manly love and a Christian warrior ethos, Symonds blends an old-fashioned adherence to ideals of patriotism and heroism with a carefully wrought rewriting of the history of gender.

At the same time that Symonds utilizes a rhetoric of virility and patri-otism that might strike today's reader as conservative, he also insists that male friendship is the province of those who value equality so strongly that they cause fear in the hearts of tyrants, and this ideal of democracy signals a difference between Symonds' commitment to institutionality and the values of the particular institutions with which he contends. For all his adulation of military valor, a trait that seems to require adherence to hierarchy, Symonds' idea is that heroic friendship differs from other relationships because it is based on non-hierarchic conventions and values. Familial, religious, and educational organizations are inevitably structured around strict stratification. By contrast, because friendship in Symonds' rendering is lateral, voluntary, and mutual, it has the potential to be entirely democratic. This spirit of equality works at two levels: it implies equality between men; and, relatedly, it thrives only in political conditions that enable and perpetuate liberty. We might pause for a moment to consider the broader notion that friendship in its idealized form can be viewed as a threat to political systems and other institutions that depend upon fixed class differences. At issue, in part, is the relation of same-sex desire to political constructions of difference. Christopher Newfield has argued, for instance, that homosexuality in nineteenth-century America was often perceived as a challenge to basic American political practices precisely because it seemed to imply equality between men, and to spurn hierarchy. It was thus connected, in the minds of those intent on repressing it, with the mob, and, in turn, with palpable threats to traditional forms of order and power.[47] In the context of Symonds' Greece, this sense that male intimacy runs afoul of arbitrary political power has the advantage of a concrete political history, since, at least in Symonds' rendering, Greek tradition always celebrated both democracy and eroticized masculine fraternity.

And yet, for Symonds, the connection between friendship and equality is actually fundamentally unstable, as the relationships in question continually revert to an organizational model based on structural inequities. *A Problem in Greek Ethics*, which I described earlier as in part a defense of homosexuality, struggles palpably with what the writer feels is a tendency for the type of friendship he admires to be degraded. The point that Symonds makes most strongly and repeatedly in *Greek Ethics* is that the Greek tradition of pederasty, which involves an older man ("inspirer") who loves a beautiful, younger boy ("hearer"), represents a historical corruption of the pure Achilles/Patroclus ideal of perfect lateral friendship. Not only, then, do later Greek practitioners of pederasty succumb to sensuality, vice, and so on, but they also, and perhaps as a result of the former, fall away even from the political ideal of equality. For Symonds, equality relies on sameness: if two lovers are of different ages or stations in life, even if they follow the Platonic requirement of spirituality in love, they nevertheless become trapped by some kind of hierarchy, and their love is thus inevitably only a shadow of the purer Homeric example. Even at their most sublime, texts like *The Symposium* or *The Phaedrus* would thus fall short of what Symonds feels is the real comradeship ethos.

Symonds' difficulties with issues of difference, equality, and hierarchy are at the core of his project, and they signal its self-contradictions. I have said that *Studies of the Greek Poets* is structured around the image of an older man looking longingly back at a glowing youth – partly himself as an adolescent, partly a desirable object. This yearning to cross the unbridgeable gulf to youth is met by the writer's assertion that only sameness can make for equality, and only friendship based on equality has value. Even to want that connection with the younger man is a fall from Homeric grace. Real desire, in this case the longing an older man feels for a younger, cannot conform to the requirements of Symonds' idealized theory of Greek friendship. Moreover, if Symonds asserts throughout his texts that the worship of the beautiful male body and the institutions of friendship go together, that they are two sides of the same coin, nevertheless this conjunction may also involve an act of willful contradiction, since to worship the body – to watch it, study it, sculpt it – requires distance, probably age and experience. What Symonds presents as a natural coexistence of the worship of the body with the structures of friendship may thus present a conflict, because one suggests distance and difference, while the other involves sameness and equality. Again, if what Symonds wants is a smooth continuum from his own desire to its theorization, his texts undercut themselves, since they insist on a qualitative discrepancy between the form of longing the text incorporates and the ideal it describes.

This pattern of desire unraveling into inequality is dramatized in Oscar Wilde's *The Picture of Dorian Gray* (1891), a text whose commentary on issues of sameness and mimesis is dizzyingly intricate. In her brief discussion of Wilde's text in *Epistemology of the Closet*, Eve Sedgwick elaborates the complicated relationship in the novel between same-sex desire and the desire for the same.[48] Sedgwick interprets Dorian's relation with himself as a narrative about the uneven desires surrounding difference, figured not in terms of sex (the Victorian marker of difference, *par excellence*), but of age, health, and beauty, and she suggests that Wilde's cultural commentary about difference is at least as trenchant as his modernist critique of self-worship. What I would stress is that Wilde, in his characteristic way, has managed to pinpoint and dissect a cultural fetish, here the desired Greek youth, as we have seen him idealized in the texts of Pater and Symonds, and to expose some troubling truths about the whole configuration. Despite the difficulty for the critic in disentangling the text's presentation of body-worship, narcissism, sexual deviance, addiction, and degradation, it seems clear that Wilde's portrayal of the Hellenizing project in *Dorian Gray* is undertaken in a spirit of critique. The aptly named Dorian functions as an embodiment of the nineteenth-century idealized Greek lad, desired by older or wiser men like Basil Hallward and Lord Henry Wotton, who use him to fashion their own art and satisfy their own needs. Dorian represents an embodiment of a figure envisioned by nineteenth-century aesthetic criticism, the golden youth whose lovely person provides the anchor for a circle of admiring men. If we read *Dorian Gray* in light of contemporaneous texts by Pater and Symonds, as well as the Uranians, Carpenter, and other Hellenists, it becomes a commentary on them, a demystifying lesson in what happens when a gorgeous young man is made into a work of art, desired by older aesthetes, turned into a kind of institution. When we think about how the novel figures the consequences of its multiple transgressions, that is, we should not lose sight of the fact that Dorian is not only the agent of his extraordinary undoing, but also its victim. He is the object of desire from many quarters, and, more importantly, the cornerstone in an erudite and ultimately self-absorbed mission of cultural regeneration.

The text also forces a confrontation with the equality issue: in Symonds' texts, the idealized friendship of equality continually collapses into longing for the untouchable youth, and here, as well, the atmosphere of male friendship and intimacy is a screen for desires that are never based on real mutuality, but rather on an unspoken assumption of power. Dorian is no Platonic beloved, much less a Patroclus to anyone's Achilles. He never finds himself in the place of the loving male comrade, whose very identity blurs into that of his devoted friend, but culminates as a figure of intense pathos, utterly alone with himself in a world that only values him for the one thing that he must inevitably lose. Dorian embodies a form of modernist catastrophe, then, not simply because the outside world has shattered, leaving him alone with his corrupted reflection, nor solely as a result of the developing legal and medical conceptions of deviance as a punitive category, but also because he has been established as the centerpiece of a new and utopian (or ironized-utopian) community, based on his beauty and the bonds it is supposed to engender among men, which fails absolutely to provide him with any future. If *Dorian Gray* functions in part as a morality play, it is not only because Dorian internalizes society's repressiveness and intolerance, but also because Wilde ruthlessly exposes the contradictions at the heart of the friendship ethos.

Symonds, too, seems aware that his vision is imperiled by its own disruptive self-contradictions. We sense this perception in his palpable struggles to settle the issues of equality and sexuality in the Greek texts. Even more marked for its reckoning with its own almost-hidden repressions is a posthumously published poem that Symonds cherished as a personal and literary monument. Set in the middle ages at a secluded mountain monastery, "Gabriel" (orig. 1878) tells the story of a gorgeous, ethereal lad who arrives at the door of the monastery, apparently from nowhere, and asks to stay among the brothers, sharing their lives and labors. The monastic setting is again mingled with a Hellenic vision of youth, nature, and beauty. In the year he spends among the monks, Gabriel has an extreme effect on them: like Pater's eponymous Denys d'Auxerre in *Imaginary Portraits* (1887), Gabriel's presence brings sunlight, spring flowers all year long, something magical and harmonious. But it also carries torment, in the form of awakened sexuality – strange dreams and desires – among the virgin monks. In the end, confrontation with an all-knowing hermit exposes Gabriel's demonic underside, literally, as his clothes fall from him in a classic Una and Duessa dénouement.[49]

What is most striking about the poem is its literalization of the potential for degradation that Symonds fears might exist alongside his idealization of male friendship. Symonds presents a picture of a mystical brotherhood whose motive force comes to circulate around a beautiful youth, an embodiment of the Greek friendship ideal transferred into a Christian brotherhood. Yet, at the same time, he warns that such a dream may in fact become a demonic nightmare, a self-delusion that Symonds suggests must be challenged, exposing the unexpressed and inchoate dissonance that lurks beneath an idealized surface. Though the particular nature of Gabriel's diabolism is never specified, the poem vividly dramatizes that the fellowship idea contains the seeds of its own destruction. Thus "Gabriel" truncates a series of desires and concerns that also animate Symonds' Greek texts, centering around the problematic incompatibility between two elements that Symonds repeatedly – yet ultimately unsuccessfully – attempts to conjoin: physical desire between men and the idealization of friendship.

THE FALL OF HELLENISM: FORSTER'S MODERN DISAFFECTION

I have been discussing a historical moment, the last quarter of the nineteenth century, when writers in the literary establishment used aesthetic criticism to engage in a wide-ranging debate over masculinity and male relations. To the intelligentsia of this period, the Greeks seemed to offer examples of enduring relevance for the modern world. As they hailed the achievements of Greek artists and philosophers, canny writers like Pater and Symonds could appeal both to a mainstream intellectual audience steeped, for instance, in Arnoldian conceptions of culture, and to an initiated homosexual elite, without seeming either antiquated or overtly transgressive.[50] Reverence for the Greeks provided the late Victorians with a shaping structure that fused highly valued classical traditions with a focus on the athletic male body, under the rubric of the public schools and the universities, and we can thus recognize a kind of coherence and interconnectedness about the classicizing ideal in these years. As we move into the twentieth century, perhaps the first question to ask is whether the language of Hellenism remains relevant, tenable, important. After the cataclysm of the Wilde trials in 1895, the increasing dispersal in England of sexological theory (including Havelock Ellis' important work *Sexual Inversion* in 1897), the arrival onto the literary scene of such aggressively and self-consciously "new" movements as vorticism and imagism, the high visibility of an energized women's suffrage movement, the emergence of women into the professions and into degrees at the university – in the context of such developments, what would it mean to imagine classical ideals of male love and the university circle as viable and desirable forms to organize modern desire and aesthetic values? If writers such as Forster continue to invest in Hellenism on cultural and personal grounds, isn't this move simply a backward glance, a kind of failure to grow up into the modern world of sexuality-as-species, modernity-as-technology, and a public sphere increasingly integrated in terms of gender?

My view is, quite emphatically, that Hellenism does continue to matter, and for several reasons. First, I have already indicated that the idea of the university as an attractive alternative to the brutal public schools became something of a commonplace among many of Forster's contemporaries. When Forster describes this movement into collegiate harmony in *The Longest Journey*, his attitude is more representative than idiosyncratic: in a manner that would be familiar to many, for example, in the Bloomsbury circle, the protagonist Rickie "had crept cold and friendless and ignorant out of a great public school, preparing for a silent and solitary journey, and praying as a highest favour that he might be left alone. Cambridge had not answered his prayer. She had taken and soothed and warmed him" (*LJ*, 6). Second, even after the degrading, terrifying, and above all consolidating spectacle of the Wilde trials in 1895 had seriously undermined aestheticism's relatively sentimental model for representing homoeroticism, the burgeoning field of homosexual commentary continued to rely for legitimization on Hellenism's powerful textual authority. Symonds' *Greek Ethics* began to circulate widely only in 1897 as an appendix to Ellis' *Sexual Inversion*, Pater's work continued to be read (and attacked) as an important statement of a decadent ethos, and Edward Carpenter's utopian writings about homosexuality and culture also experienced delayed publication, to arrive in the first decade of the new century. Third, with interest in archeological developments continuing into the twentieth century, the intrigue of Greek civilization persisted, as did the belief that Greek culture could invigorate and help to make sense of modernity. New scholarly works about pre-Olympian religions by Jane Harrison and the other "Cambridge Classicists" (Gilbert Murry, R. F. Cornford, A. B. Cook), which were published during the first two decades of the twentieth century, were especially influential and provocative, for they suggested a kind of archaic challenge to the high order of the Olympian system; by returning to an earlier moment in ancient history, Harrison and the others seemed to call up a host of rich, repressed elements in the Greek imaginary, and, to a newly Freudian intelligentsia, this represented a stimulating, somewhat radical approach to the Hellenes. Fourth, in the case of gender, one might argue with some justice that to invest in male institutions at this moment functioned as a kind of shoring-up of power, raising ever-higher bulwarks against feared female incursions into the sacred space of educational organizations and professional circles. Such would certainly be true in the case of someone like D. H. Lawrence. Fifth, and perhaps most important, what I want to suggest is that it is precisely the trajectory from continuity to disenchantment with Hellenism that accounts for some of the most haunting effects in Forster's work. By carrying over and transforming the concepts of masculinity and eroticism from the aestheticist ethos, Forster (like Wilde in *Dorian Gray*) constructs his own image of modernness. If T. S. Eliot and others would turn to classicism ten years later, and would stress different values (order, virility, universality) in their appropriation of classical precedent, Forster's engagements with the Greeks provide an interesting bridge. That Forster's novels resonate with the aura of Hellenism does not so much suggest anachronism, then, as his assessment of cultural history; it was, in part, by deconstructing the Hellenist project that Forster came to conceptualize the experience of being caught in modernity.

In both *The Longest Journey* and *Maurice*, Forster scrutinizes the tendency to idealize male friendship as an institution of its own, as proposed by aestheticism; he then gradually exposes the shortcomings and blindspots that had both characterized and made possible the discourse of Greek intimacy. Nearly every one of Forster's novels engages in some way with the

Hellenizing spirit (the Emersons in *A Room with a View*, the Italian and Greek settings in many works, including *Where Angels Fear to Tread*, the classical impulse of the Schlegels in *Howard's End*, to name a few examples), but I shall focus on the texts that most directly work out the promise of Hellenism as a force for organizing male intimacy. Forster recognizes the power and attraction of placing the youthful male body at the center of an imagined social world, providing the centerpiece for a series of intimate friendships that also have important institutional affiliations. Yet he understands the shortcomings of this model all too well: unlike Pater and Symonds, who only hint at the ways in which their vision is imperiled by its own hidden processes, leaning generally towards a celebration of masculine friendship and the glistening body, Forster makes clear that the passionate body is too wild, violent, and uncontrollable to be contained by schemes like the Hellenic friendship ideal. Characters in his fictions break out of the narratives that would make sense of them, insisting instead on the uncomfortable reality of their bodily desires.

The mind and the body are often at odds in Forster's writing, as are forms and styles of masculinity. In exploring the problem of the male body in Forster's work, Joseph Bristow has made the case that Forster's texts almost obsessively recapitulate a pattern of assimilating the weak to the strong, aesthete to athlete, effeminate to hyper-masculine; what this ubiquitous structure suggests is that Forster has internalized his society's harsh vilification of effeminacy. If Forster hopes to construct a more balanced individual, he does so in part by repeatedly denigrating physical weakness in men (which he typically represents as an attribute of intellectuals and the upper classes), and by exhibiting a strange reverence for conventional masculine strength. For Bristow, the famous dictum "only connect" refers above all to a binary structure in the concept of masculinity, and Forster's efforts to heal the divide by creating odd couples may be successful in some cases, but nevertheless capitulate to the culture's devaluation, under the rubric of effeminacy, of the intellectual and aesthetic life.[51] My readings will stress something like the converse of this formula: what I find in Forster's treatment of Hellenism comes closer to the imperative "only disconnect," as we watch a slow disengagement of the physical from the spiritual, the ideal from the brutally real. It is not so much the construction of Hellenism – the effort, in part, to balance public school with university – as its destruction that I shall argue is at the heart of Forster's engagements with the male body. Thus, the language surrounding Stephen Wonham, Rickie Elliot, Alec Scudder, and Maurice Hall consistently indicates that these men exist in precarious positions of alienation and marginality; they seem not only to embody the moment of friendship's failure, but also to highlight the terrific cost potentially to be paid by the object of heroizing narratives when those narratives collapse.

The Longest Journey explores in detail the possibility of actualizing a dream of organized male friendship and tests the protagonist's youthful idealism about Cambridge intimacy against the constraints of an oppressive, intolerant world. *The Longest Journey* functions in many ways as a paean to male friendship, offering the traditions and practices of friendship, both in the university setting and in an unconventional adult version of the collegiate circle, as a substitute for more vicious forms of social interaction. The novel provides a veritable test case for the strategy of pitting the university against the public school, in a restless search for viable forms of permanent male association. It interrogates a range of possible male communities, including the beloved collegiate group; the public school, which represents the worst excesses of Victorian bull-headed intolerance and colludes with the institution of marriage; the intimate pair of friends, often set up as the antithesis of public-school solidarity; and various models of actual and metaphorical brotherhood. As for marriage, the novel describes it as "the dreariest and the longest journey" (*LJ*, 137). It is unremittingly conventional, ugly, and futile, constructed entirely around self-delusion and ideology, rather than love. In the face of the bankruptcy of marriage and the brutality of the public schools, the novel asks for alternative ways to construct both community and the individual around male bonds, a goal that is not only personal, but also aesthetic, social, and political. Yet, despite the text's reverence for ideals of masculine community that combat class oppression and the philistinism of middle-class morality, the closing portion of the novel raises serious questions about both the status of male friendship as a force in the world and the desirability of organizing life around its rituals. The community that will eventually be established around Stephen Wonham, the central figure in the novel's idealizing project, is envisioned as a kind of modern/classical agrarian ideal, located in Wiltshire, where the young men, relieved of oppressive female power, sustain one another in an alternative domesticity. Yet Stephen is too complicated and rebellious to fit neatly into schemes designed to place him in a new social system. Instead, Stephen, who is virtually defined by a thorough hybridity and by a resistance to easy categorization, ultimately forces the text to expose the weaknesses in its own idealizing tendencies.

From the first, Stephen is presented symbolically as a representative of nature, the Greeks, and paganism:

Certain figures of the Greeks, to whom we continually return, suggested him a little. One expected nothing of him – no purity of phrase nor swift edged thought. Yet the conviction grew that he had been back somewhere – back to some table of the gods, spread in a field where there is no noise, and that he belonged for ever to the guests with whom he had eaten. (*LJ*, 230)

Stephen here becomes a figure out of Stewart Ansell's collegiate mythology, a Cambridge idealism that looks to the classics as a venue to understand and revitalize contemporary life. The past-ness is crucial: what makes Stephen unique is his connection with a prelapsarian, lost history. Along similar lines, Mrs. Failing and Rickie wonder if Stephen, who keeps with him a print of Demeter, is not some messenger from the gods, a condensation in his very person of the natural harmony of Hellenic culture. If Mrs. Failing often cruelly manipulates Stephen, whom she tends to view as a failed social experiment, she also sentimentalizes him as a type of classical literary hero come to life, and others in the text, though less coldly dehumanizing, share that tendency. With his healthy physicality and increasing handsomeness, Stephen seems to have stepped out of the pages of Pater or Symonds, some-what transformed by his modern surroundings, a provocative centerpiece for a reformed community.

Thus Stephen, in his person, is akin to Rickie's concept of the symbolic moment, the transfiguring instant that turns banal reality into the aesthetic:

"It seems to me that here and there in life we meet with a person or incident that is symbolical. It's nothing in itself, yet for the moment it stands for some eternal principle. We accept it, at whatever costs, and we have accepted life. But if we are frightened and reject it, the moment, so to speak, passes; the symbol is never offered again." (*LJ*, 147)

For Rickie, these moments of transformative beauty, which are the subject of his stories as well as his life, punctuate and define meaningful existence. Stephen is inevitably connected with the ideal of the eternal moment, in part because Rickie's recognition and acceptance of him come in a series of revelatory moments, in part because Stephen himself remains irredeemably symbolic in the eyes of the other characters in the novel.

Stephen's status as a figure for Greek manhood is inextricably connected with his ambiguous class position. When we first meet Stephen, he shifts from acting as shepherd to reading socialist pamphlets, from standing out of doors for hours in the rain to attending a party in the drawing room, and this structure of oscillation characterizes his unfixed class position throughout the novel. On one hand, Stephen is clever, insightful, idiosyncratically educated, a match for the intellectuals who surround him. He has been reared with a certain access to privilege, and expects some inheritance. On the other hand, his naturalistic, earth-bound tendencies and capacities make him a representative of laboring masculinity, a force of nature that connects the image of Greece with the text's reiterated nostalgia for the romanticized, mythic English countryside. His fertility and health contrast with the inherited lameness of Rickie (a somewhat belabored metaphor, perhaps, for the decline and degeneration of the ascendant middle classes), and his rugged virility promises a future for the nation, in a novel highly interested in the idea of national renewal. We have seen that in Edward Carpenter's vision, the working-class male provided the erotic, physical, and social centerpiece for the promise of national regeneration, and here, too, Stephen's affinity for the material world – his excessively embodied nature – constitutes the very essence of his symbolic resonance for characters and text.

Yet Stephen resists the tendency to become something symbolic, flouting instead his often brutal reality. Indeed, the very attributes that make him available for symbolic treatment, his class-based marks of masculinity, are what prove ungovernable. When Rickie persists in viewing him through a veil of symbolism, Stephen rebels, declaring that Rickie "did not love him, even as he had never hated him. In either passion he had degraded him to be a symbol for the vanished past" (*LJ*, 273). Moving to critique the text's aestheticist tendencies, the narrator suggests that, far from elevating its subject, symbolic representation degrades and does violence to the individual. Stephen entreats Rickie to let go of the need to see people as representatives of some wider, elusive world: "'Come with me as a man,' said Stephen, already out in the mist. 'Not as a brother; who cares what people did years back? We're alive together, and the rest is cant'" (*LJ*, 275). Even brotherhood is no better than a metaphor, an over-weighted idea that creates symbolic value at the expense of direct, inter-personal confrontation and intimacy. Stephen rejects the symbolic, and calls instead on the simple fact of shared masculinity to unite the two young men, suggesting that the culture's contorted logic of masculinity would evaporate in the presence of the thing itself. If the idea of masculinity had for a century been connected both with specific institutions and with an intricate ideological web attached to those institutions, Stephen calls for its divestment from such forms. However, even here, Stephen's placement "in the mist," his positioning on a series of symbolic thresholds, works against his effort to refuse representational status. In a circular logic, Stephen's very courage to resist a certain type of symbolic masculinity recasts him as a new image for the masculine – direct, honest, man-to-man, anti-Hellenist. Thus, the narrative process goes something like this: Forster initially creates what seems to be an instance of the embodied Greek spirit, out of the pages of a nineteenth-century aesthetic handbook, and then questions the ramifications of this very dynamic, pressing us to examine our own collusion in the tendency to view people as representatives, and therefore as narcissistic fetishes, along the lines of the solipsistic Mrs. Failing.[52] In the end, however, Forster establishes yet another image of representative masculinity, which itself threatens to entrap the male individual in its symbolic logic. Stephen seems caught not only in the nets of Hellenists and romantic worshippers of working-class masculinity, but in fiction-making itself, which seems insistently to produce and reproduce its icons of maleness.

Stephen offers the most tangible sign of his palpable existence – his general spirit of resistance – by excessively showcasing his physical power. He stamps his feet and bangs his fists; he throws clods of earth at Ansell when the philosopher ignores his greetings; he knocks people from horses; he breaks windows. Despite Rickie's repeated attempts to idealize Stephen and hallow their relationship of half-brotherhood, the man himself fights against all palliative efforts to deny his often fearsome physicality with softening narratives. Thus the relationship between the two men remains strangely violent. In their initial contacts, the young men demonstrate barely submerged hostility towards one another, and so it continues towards the end of the novel, when a new social organization based on friendship is supposed to be in place. The incidents comprising their final visit to Cadover, for instance, are marked as much by miscommunication, betrayal, and physical discomfort, as by any form of beauty or transformation. Even the lush moment when Stephen creates a spectacular light show on the river – a kind of natural, masculine artistry – is described later as bestial, indicating a continuing undercurrent of hostility in the relationship between Stephen and his Cambridge patrons: "[Rickie] had left Stephen preparing to bathe, and had heard him working up-stream like an animal, splashing in the shallows, breathing heavily as he swam the pools; at times reeds snapped, or clods of earth were pulled in" (*LJ*, 297).

Stephen's outbursts trouble this community, especially when he repeatedly flouts their various agreements and compacts, because the group needs its formal commitments; to break an oath leaves the fragile circle without any recognizable status or stability. Oaths are essential to the community of friends that Rickie, Ansell, and Stephen uneasily erect, an experimental social form that depends for its durability on a certain amount of institutionalization. *The Longest Journey* had begun as a hymn to idealized male friendship, in which Rickie experiences Cambridge as an exalted period of male intimacy, and, in this early stage, the innocent Rickie imagines cementing his friendship with Ansell:

"I wish that we were labelled," said Rickie. He wished that all the confidence and mutual knowledge that is born in such a place as Cambridge could be organized. People went down into the world saying, "We know and like each other; we shan't forget." But they did forget, for man is made that he cannot remember long without a symbol; he wished there was a society, a kind of friendship office, where the marriage of true minds could be registered. (*LJ*, 69)

Such language of course represents an early moment in Rickie's development, yet he and his peers will pursue the idea of creating new social forms for men, with their own symbolic repertoire, into post-Cambridge life. If the university offers a humane and compassionate alternative to the public school, what looms after the men go down is a kind of aporia: the dreariness of marriage, the meaninglessness of many forms of middle-class labor, the slow dissolution of the friendships that alone had been accorded value in the novel. Although Rickie's fantasy of male marriages of the mind is presented with irony, then, it has a certain staying power in the narrative. The sense that close male relationships, as constituted by the elite universities, conflict directly with the other major institutions that dominate middle-class conformity, and that they therefore need their own symbols, rituals, and status in order to compete for possession of the male soul, is held up by the novel as the only hope for salvaging Rickie's increasingly catastrophic life.

In a direct blow to such a model of male community, Stephen demonstrates hostility both to the idea that the life epitomized by Wiltshire is one of male friends united by common intimacy and respect, friend to friend, and to the ceremonies and practices that sustain the ideal. He is, in this sense, in a position similar to Wilde's Dorian Gray, the figure for other men's desires – partly sexual, partly narcissistic – desires that have been given cultural credence as a type of Greek revival. Unlike the aptly named Dorian, who internalizes and absorbs the value-system of the aesthetes who surround him, with tragic consequences, Stephen fights against those who want to make him the centerpiece of their utopian vision. By constantly thrusting forward his often unpleasant physicality, whether in the form of fists or bouts of drunkenness, both of which accentuate the physical body at the expense of the mind, Stephen retains his individuality and resists aestheticization. What gets shattered is not only Rickie's already-weak body, but also his dream of organizing a world around male friendship; and what destroys that dream is not so much the essential adolescence of the idea, nor the power of institutions like marriage or the public schools, though these are formidable foes, but rather the body itself. The physical body, which in texts by Pater and Symonds functions as both the linchpin and the fault-line of a matrix of desire, disrupts the smooth transition from Cambridge, through Sawston (the novel's fictional public school, site of extreme perpetuation of the school ethos), to Wiltshire. Forster seems to want Wiltshire, like those other place-names that denote institutions, to be its own type of institution, with rules and rituals that sustain it, a place where the physicality of men and nature is acknowledged and celebrated. But such a scheme requires the healthy Hellenic body, and Stephen refuses to act the part of Pater's Spartan youths or Symonds' young Athenian athletes. Stephen's body is not only beautiful, healthy, and fertile, but, again, violent, unpredictable, often drunk and out of control. If the discourse of Hellenism had laid claim to the male body as its central object of desire and worship, an impulse that finds its culmination in the solipsistic collapse of Dorian Gray, then *The Longest Journey* shows that such a system is destroyed by the body, its central engine.

In this rupture between the Hellenic notion of male community and the reality of material existence in the novel, we can locate a particular spirit of modernity. Of course, as I have suggested, terms like "modern" or "modernity," or even "modernism," remain irredeemably elastic, and I do not wish to press Forster into the service of a preconceived notion of what the modern must entail. Rather I am interested in teasing out a kind of mood or spirit in the novel, in which certain forms of humanity are crushed between the sense of a lost past and a future that moves in dizzying new directions. Frederic Jameson has demonstrated how a certain incommensurability in *Howard's End*, between the performance of empire and its ostensible center, creates the formal notes of modernism. Here, too, a sensibility of inconsistency between what the protagonist and his peers can imagine and where the novel inevitably moves is central to its representation of the modern. In a text preoccupied with both the ancient past and the vague idea of a national future, the break-up of Hellenism suggests a kind of threshold. The fact that both Rickie and Gerald Dawes die – aesthete and athlete, university man and public-school old-boy – while Stephen survives, reproduces, and in fact "believed that he guided the future of our race," suggests that the old all-male constructs have given way to a new kind of masculinity and a new model of the domestic (*LJ*, 308). And while Stephen's movement into futurity would seem positive, along with his nurturing of a small daughter, the novel's insistence on crushing all the old notions of organized male intimacy intimates that the text's central consciousness is itself cut out of the closing vision. What the physical body effects in *The Longest Journey* is the destruction of Hellenism and the positing, in its place, of an uneasy gesture towards an unknowable future.

The Longest Journey, then, begins the process of transforming the loss of viable constructs of male friendship into an uncertain vision of modernity, and it effects this atmospheric shift without making a direct claim for homosexual desire as the root cause of masculine alienation. In *Maurice*, Forster's only novel to treat homosexuality directly, we will be shown even more startling and problematic consequences of the body's power both to activate and to destroy a friendship ideal, as the text wreaks havoc on a well-established view about male love and its place in public life. The body looms increasingly large in *Maurice*, as it gradually comes to the forefront of the protagonist's consciousness, and all efforts to contain or idealize it are finally discarded, in a sense completing the trajectory begun in *The Longest Journey*. With this acknowledgment of the fierce reality of the physical, Forster rejects the idea of male friendship as a useful and fulfilling concept, especially in its institutional manifestations, and he accordingly discards late-Victorian Hellenism. Forster follows his predecessors in relying heavily on an ideal of male friendship, and when he finally spurns the whole concept, he is left with no replacement that might provide such a complete conjunction of male bodies with institutions and culturally authorizing traditions. The result is an undercurrent of discord, of ominous alienation and the erasure of identity, even despite the happy ending. The novel develops an image of homosexuals as wrenched out of cultural institutions, their modernity in a sense thrust upon them. I offer, then, a view of *Maurice* as helping to construct, out of the failure of Victorian classicism, a modern image of homosexuality, and, more broadly, of masculinity. And I hope this discussion will help to enrich our view of the novel, a text that has generally been taken by critics as straightforward and inartistic, a *roman à clef*, polemic, and shadow text to *The Longest Journey*, even by those who are sympathetic to the text's mission to produce a homosexual *Bildungsroman*.[53]

We can begin to unravel *Maurice*'s adoption and rejection of Hellenism by examining Forster's authorial position in the novel. The narrative voice is less nuanced than is typical in Forster's novels, tending to offer flat, clear interpretations of characters, especially Maurice, who is resolutely presented as average and uncomplicated. Early in the novel, the narrator describes two dreams that had haunted Maurice's boyhood, registering an apparent contempt for Maurice's psychic simplicity: "Where all is obscure and unrealized the best similitude is a dream. Maurice had two dreams at school: they will interpret him."[54] Both tone and content contribute to a sense of flattening and restricting, a closing off of interpretive space.

In the terminal note, appended many years later in a further effort to impose an interpretive scheme on the novel, to tie up loose ends and function as a self-critical coda, Forster explains his choice of simplistic protagonist: "In Maurice I tried to create a character who was completely unlike myself or what I supposed myself to be: someone handsome, healthy, bodily attractive, mentally torpid, not a bad business man and rather a snob." Maurice is a simple English type, Forster maintains, "Maurice is suburbia" (*M*, 250, 251). It is not difficult to understand why Forster insists on Maurice's normality, since one goal of the novel is to demonstrate that homosexuality can be innate in even the most unremarkable Englishman. Yet Maurice's averageness also contributes to the text's tendency to constrain interpretive possibilities, a reduction of scope that contrasts markedly with the imagistic and thematic layering in such novels as *Howard's End* and *A Passage to India*.

Not surprisingly, given the relative simplicity of the characters and the heavy hand of the narrator, critics have tended to follow Forster's interpretive directions, reading the narrative – with varying degrees of sympathy – as a transparent report of homosexual experience. In one especially helpful example along these lines, which documents the key transitions in the novel, Robert Martin describes Maurice's painful movement out of the repressed, intellectual homosexuality of Clive and Cambridge, through a more natural, physical experience that involves bodily desire, until Maurice reaches a full-scale political understanding of his own identity: "The novel thus develops three stages in Maurice's development. In the first, Maurice comes to accept homosexuality as idealized friendship, as the expression of a pure and spiritual love. In the second he moves toward acceptance of lust in the physical expression of homosexuality. In the final stage he begins to accept the social and political consequences of homosexuality."[55] Martin's argument amplifies Forster's instructions to understand Maurice as comprising two sides – one brutal, one ideal – and, following the terminal note, in which Forster details the genesis of the novel in a visit to Edward Carpenter and George Merrill, examines Carpenter's influence on the novel.[56] Joseph Bristow, too, stresses the text's painful merging of opposites, as Forster works within the familiar binary structure of intellectuals meeting athletes, minds meeting bodies, a dualist model which pivots on issues of class. Bristow, like Martin, sees Carpenter as the presiding spirit, his life with Merrill providing a correlative for the text's concluding vision. Taken together, Martin and Bristow provide a thorough and compelling analysis of Forster's agenda in the novel, attuned both to the text's political purpose and to the author's psychological and narrative predilections for constructing new configurations of male love across class lines.

Yet the text partially resists the very reading that it most clearly displays, and it thereby works against a larger social formula for writing about homosexuality. At one level, that is, the novel does tell a three-part story, in which Maurice moves through idealization and then its opposite, to arrive in the end at some kind of fulfillment. Or, to use the terms I have been developing, *Maurice* describes the attractiveness for young men of the Hellenic discourse beloved by aestheticism and fostered in the university, only to demonstrate the ultimate insufficiency of this model. Yet the final movement, which follows the rejection of Hellenism, is fraught with ambivalence and violent rumblings more serious than those in *The Longest Journey*, and seems to culminate in disruption as much as harmony.[57] I believe that the discord and violence that the text associates with male (homo)sexuality overpowers all controlling and containing narratives, including not only Victorian Hellenism, but Forster's own interpretive instructions.

In the first part of the novel, Forster offers a textbook rendition of the Hellenic ideal. An unsophisticated Maurice arrives at Cambridge, where he meets Clive Durham, and the two develop a rich friendship, which they view as both subversive and sacred. Though the precise nature of this intimacy is never articulated, it is clear that, for the most part, the boys are celibate. Like Pater, Symonds, the Uranians, and even Wilde (in the speech at the trials' close), the homoerotics of the Cambridge portion of the text depend on the claim of sexual purity, even as a form of homosexuality is finding its home. Clive supplies Maurice and the reader with the standard Hellenic formula, encouraging Maurice to read Plato's *Symposium* and *Phaedrus*, which contain "a new guide for life" and where he finds spiritual love between men championed and idealized (*M*, 70). The boys thus come to see their intimacy as noble and elevated, if somewhat rebellious, and wholly characterized by the masculine world of classical education. Clive haughtily extols the superiority and purity of male love over heterosexuality: "'I feel to you [Maurice] as Pippa to her fiancé, only far more nobly, far more deeply, body and soul, no starved medievalism of course, only a – a particular harmony of body and soul that I don't think women have even guessed'" (*M*, 90). Clive's smug sense of superiority here is typical: the relationship between the two boys is characterized by a certain adolescent misogyny, in conjunction with an idealization of Greek male friendship and the institutional security of Cambridge. For its part, the college grudgingly fosters the friendship, and the boys understand their relationship to be intrinsically connected with the idyllic institution: "Their love belonged to it, and particularly to their rooms, so that they could not conceive of their meeting anywhere else" (*M*, 80). This period of Cambridge love, which is dominated by the term "friendship" and the dream of a male friend, represents what the text establishes as the ideal side of Maurice's sexual nature.

When Clive abandons Maurice, he inaugurates the second, more violent stage of Maurice's homosexual development. For all of Clive's talk of the hypocrisy of Cambridge dons who abhor "the unspeakable vice of the Greeks," in the end his own conventionality transforms him into a mouthpiece for this very hypocrisy (*M*, 51). And when Clive is discredited, so too is the ideal of male friendship as an all-sufficient category. Here the novel parts company with Hellenism, making explicit what was implied more obliquely by such critics as Pater and Symonds, that sexuality is at odds with a discourse created partly out of its aestheticization. Maurice needs more than "a friend": his body craves satisfaction, and the dream of a physical interaction with a man of the lower classes rises to replace the other, more idealized image. In Martin's reading of the novel, Maurice's agonized search for bodily release, which culminates finally in a harmonious relationship with Alec Scudder the gamekeeper, represents the final stage of this development. By transcending the repressed and bookish ideal of friendship with a full acceptance of homosexuality, both physical and political, Maurice finds a synthetic harmony which, in Forster's words, "was imperative. I shouldn't have bothered to write otherwise. I was determined that in fiction anyway two men should fall in love and remain in it for the ever and ever that fiction allows" (*M*, 250). Thus the rejection of Hellenism forms part of a productive dialectic, one step along the route to a mature homosexual identity.

Yet the fantastic "ever and ever" that Forster imagines as the outcome of his novel is also characterized by brutality, alienation, and discord. It is a product and a representation of the climate of violence and intimidation surrounding homosexuality in Forster's contemporary Britain, and does not easily conform to the positive analysis that Forster seems, at a certain level, to demand. Even in the happy Cambridge days, the narrator reminds us that "[b]ehind Society slumbered the Law" (*M*, 99). When Maurice first begins to recognize that his desire for other men cannot be understood merely, as Clive would have it, in terms of Greek friendship, this self-awareness is characterized by fear:

His feeling for Dickie required a very primitive name. He would have sentimentalized once and called it adoration, but the habit of honesty had grown strong. What a stoat he had been! Poor little Dickie! He saw the boy leaping from his embrace, to smash through the window and break his limbs, or yelling like a maniac until help came. He saw the police –
"Lust." He said the word out loud. (*M*, 150)

For Maurice, the very idea of lust is understood in terms of violence and punishment. Because his desires are legally, morally, and medically categorized as deviant, there is no way for him to internalize them outside of a cycle of terror.

The violence and fear that Maurice and the novel associate with homosexuality characterize even the harmonious moments of sexual passion. That Clive's cry of pain when Maurice grabs his hair for the first time, inaugurating their intimacy ("'Waou, that hurts!'"), is repeated at the moment of their violent break-up ("'Waow, you're hurting my head'" [*M*, 45, 124]) suggests that strife is as inherent in the act of coming together as in splitting apart. We sense such discord when the boys first kiss. When Maurice enters Clive's bed for this initial embrace, he comes in through the window, a wild outsider, tamed only by the peaceful sanctity of a Cambridge room. Inside, Clive sleeps comfortably, while the other figure – outlaw, outcast, wanderer – enters as a violator of the seemingly safe, interior space:

> Then savage, reckless, drenched with the rain, he saw in the first glimmer of dawn the window of Durham's room, and his heart leapt alive and shook him to pieces. It cried "You love and are loved." He looked round the court. It cried "You are strong, he weak and alone," won over his will. Terrified at what he must do, he caught hold of the mullion and sprang.
>
> "Maurice – "
>
> As he alighted his name had been called out of dreams. The violence went out of his heart, and a purity that he had never imagined dwelt there instead. His friend had called him. He stood for a moment entranced, then the new emotion found him words, and laying his hand very gently upon the pillows he answered, "Clive!" (*M*, 66)

Maurice is presented initially as wildly passionate, animalistic, a little like Stephen Wonham. The image of Maurice drenched in rain, savagely haunting the courtyard, contrasts strikingly with the Hellenic narratives that Clive uses to hallow their relationship. It is not so much love that inspires Maurice to enter Clive's room as the thought of his own power over the other who is "weak and alone." Significantly, the idea – and the ideal – of friendship is what dissipates and desexualizes Maurice's hunger. Nevertheless, the sense lingers that Maurice's homosexual passion is characterized less by "purity" and a desire for friendship than by violent emotions and a craving for power, sensations officially alien to the serene world of Cambridge.

This picture of homosexual desire differs as well from the most developed image of homosexuality in the text, embodied by Risley and "his set." As Sinfield has noted, Risley represents the fully realized embodiment of same-sex desire, the Lytton Strachey of the novel, and Maurice's antipathy towards him can be understood in several ways. In part, Maurice's alienation from Risley's world involves his unwillingness to look squarely at his own developing constitution; more centrally, it is a matter of class and style, for the suburban stockbroker-to-be finds no solace in the Wildean figure of liberation through ultra-sophistication. Cambridge supplies Maurice with two models, the Hellenic ideal of rich friendship, embodied by Clive, and the Wildean homosexual, Risley. What I am suggesting is that Forster creates a third: Maurice, the unremarkable youth being transformed into the unassimilable outsider, surrounded by loneliness and characterized in terms that resonate with darkness, fear, and disconsolation.

Although Maurice's relationship with Alec clearly marks an advance from the more adolescent experience with Clive, it too is staged in such a way as to highlight the potential for violence. In fact, beginning with their first night together, Alec comes to embody the wildness that has hitherto surrounded Maurice, in a shifting of class positions and fantasies. This time Maurice inhabits Clive's former place of class privilege – he who awaits the outsider, the haunting image of masculinity – and it is Alec who quietly enters the room through the window. Indeed, the window becomes the sign of homosexuality, in part for the straightforward reason that open entrance into the house was not a realistic option. The novel accurately represents the threat of blackmail and legal punishment that was the reality for British homosexuals in the early decades of the century, staging scenes of near-blackmail, recording characters' terrors of the police, and stressing the alternative routes, primarily through windows, to which the male lovers take recourse. It is no coincidence that Maurice's vision of Dickie's gruesome death involves his leaping from the window, since the problem of belonging and expulsion takes visual and practical form in the liminal space of the window.

Yet when Alec does come through the window, he will not be greeted by idealizing narratives of friendship. Instead, his very presence, and the danger it represents, is conjured up by Maurice's own terrific desires:

as he returned to his bed a little noise sounded, a noise so intimate that it might have arisen inside his own body. He seemed to crackle and burn and saw the ladder's top quivering against the moonlit air. The head and shoulders of a man rose up, paused, a gun was leant against the window sill very carefully, and someone he scarcely knew moved towards him and knelt beside him and whispered, "Sir, was you calling out for me? . . . Sir, I know," and touched him. (*M*, 192)

Alec's gun dominates the scene, protecting the inhabitants from harm as well as representing the potential for violence that is a by-product of Maurice's crackling desires. This is a poignant moment in an often bleak narrative, especially in the tenderness of Alec's address, yet the threat of trouble lingers. That sexual contact between men cannot be imagined solely as a private moment of harmony, outside of time and social space, is epitomized by the smudge of dirt that Alec leaves behind him in Maurice's room, a physical reminder not only of Alec's class position, but also of the impossibility of ensuring secrecy. The uncertainty of what might accrue when fundamental social barriers are crossed remains front and center in all of the harmonious scenes between the men.

This general sense of uneasiness surrounding Alec stems from both class difference and the presence of the law looming in the shadows. For all their mutuality and passion, the relationship between Maurice and Alec is marked by an undertone of anger and resentment, as the two engage in threats of blackmail and abandonment, culminating in a climactic scene at the British Museum – ironically the site of those very sculptures of Greek athletes that had so stimulated the aesthetes of the nineteenth century. Despite his attractiveness and generosity, Alec embodies an aura of unsettling discord. In the terminal note, Forster describes Alec in strange, amorphous terms, almost as masculinity itself:

In the first place he has to be led up to. He must loom upon the reader gradually. He has to be developed from the masculine blur past which Maurice drives into Penge, through the croucher beside the piano and the rejecter of a tip and the haunter of shrubberies and the stealer of apricots into the sharer who gives and takes love. He must loom out of nothing until he is everything. (*M*, 253)

Notwithstanding Alec's ultimate status as "the sharer who gives and takes love," the descriptions of him here are generally ghostly and threatening: croucher, rejecter, haunter, stealer – a shape that haunts the premises. The word "loom," used twice, also suggests something ominous about Alec, who never quite distinguishes himself as an individual from the "masculine blur" that is his origin.

Homosexuality in the novel is thus characterized by a kind of wildness that carries with it a potential for violence and disturbance. The figure of the homosexual is he who enters through the window, he who looms just outside of the social world as a vision of alienation and potential loneliness. Before Alec enters the story, it is Maurice who occupies the outcast position, and this involves powerful images of his solitude and marginality: "beyond the barrier Maurice wandered, the wrong words on his lips and the wrong desires in his heart, and his arms full of air" (*M*, 165). Unlike Alec, who seems to exist outside of any clear and demarcating social limits, including the categories of gender and sexuality, Maurice is tied to social structures, and his ejection from them has real consequences. Because Maurice finds himself entirely cut off from the "beautiful conventions" that welcome heterosexual couples, and because the idealizing narratives of heroic friendship have been exposed as hypocritical and useless, he is left in a kind of no-man's land, outside of institutions as well as personal intimacy (*M*, 165). Even Forster's happy "ever and ever that fiction allows," which enables the two men to disappear together into the greenwood, suggests that, without social connections, individuals lose their palpable existence. I read the final invisibility of Maurice and Alec as a sign not so much of fulfillment and empowerment, but of their almost inevitable eradication as individuals.[58]

This position of marginality, which seems potentially catastrophic, is created and characterized not only by social forces such as the law, but by the passion of the body. The homosexual body is understood by the novel as the object of state punishment, but it is also, in itself, the site of turbulent sensation, of Maurice's own burning desires. Moreover, Forster suggests that once both the possibility of institutional sanction and the belief in a friendship system have been abandoned, all the passions and needs of the body must be controlled by the body itself. For Pater and Symonds, for the schools and the universities, the body was aestheticized, surveyed, adored, sculpted, encircled, and contained. Yet the work that the concept of friendship did for Hellenism cannot be achieved by the desiring body on its own, which threatens to disrupt everything around it. Such disruption appears as early as Maurice's first dream, when a naked garden boy races down a field towards the dreamer, threatening both extreme (if willed) bodily force and its converse, "brutal disappointment" (*M*, 22). The dreamer understands himself to be wiped out by the body of his own fantasies, by his internal irrepressibility. This threat – both courted and feared – never vanishes from a text that continually presents sexuality and hostility in an ongoing mutual struggle. Not only, then, does the novel tell the story of a man learning to understand and accept his physical desires, even when these are powerfully disbarred by social convention, but it also posits the body as a dangerous and volatile thing that cannot easily be contained or refined to conform to palliative narratives. As in *The Longest Journey*, where the reality of Stephen's physical body continually disrupted the schemes of characters, reader, and narrator alike to transform his story into a heroic or Hellenic representation of male camaraderie, so in *Maurice*, physicality in general and homosexuality in particular cannot comfortably be placed into containing narratives.

Alec's position in the text vividly underscores the failure of idealization as a useful strategy for representing male intimacy. Unlike Stephen, who recognizes and refuses the symbolic position that others put him in, Alec seems destined to be a figure for other men's needs, a "well-trained dog," as Maurice thinks (*M*, 197). In the narrator's characterization of him as an embodiment of Maurice's fiery insides, or in the description of him as "the touch on the backside" that Forster received from George Merrill, Alec represents a certain kind of class fantasy, which combines the hope of "sharing" and communion with the desire both to know and to master a man of lower class status (*M*, 252).[59] As in works by both Carpenter and Symonds, and of course in *The Longest Journey*, the working-class man becomes a place-holder for turbulent and difficult emotions that are not easily domesticated. Only if Alec exists as the embodiment of rough masculinity – thus maintaining powerful class stereotypes and perpetuating a key element in Carpenter's system of reverence for the working-class body – can the novel control its dynamics of desire. Because of Alec's class markings, the uncomfortable aspects of the fantasy that created him are partially naturalized.

I have been arguing that in *The Longest Journey* and *Maurice*, Forster uncouples the ideal of heroic friendship from the reality of both physicality and homosexuality, rejecting his own initial attempts to present structures or rituals that might create a new system of human community around male friendship. In this refusal to institutionalize friendship, Forster unleashes a form of energy that seems to fly out in precarious directions. Both novels radiate unease and loss. In *The Longest Journey*, the catalogue of sudden deaths is nearly overwhelming, and the idea that friendship might provide lasting harmony and mutuality is a crucial element in the novel's thin thread of hopefulness. The fact that it consistently disappoints, and this for fundamental reasons, has heavy connotations for the sense of deterioration clouding the narrative's progress. In *Maurice*, the atmosphere of heaviness takes form, as I have tried to show, in the figure of the homosexual, who moves between the twin poles of wildness and invisibility. To lose the wholeness associated with friendship, at least in its university form, is to toss the male characters out into a space that is, in its essence, uncertain and threatening.

Most striking for a complete abandonment of idealization are the stories collected as *The Life to Come* (1972). Taken together, Forster's homosexual stories, written over the course of fifty years, present an uneven picture, in terms of both aesthetic quality and general spirit. Yet I detect at least one unifying feature in these posthumously published works, which Forster says he wrote only "to excite" himself, and which he never expected to publish: all pretense of a positive social or political significance is removed from erotic male relations.[60] In stories such as "The Life to Come" and "The Other Boat," in particular, sexual congress is presented as a violent interaction in which power is more coveted than intimacy, and where class and racial differences are openly exploited.[61] Despite its comic appeal, the imperial myth at the center of "The Life to Come" presents a deeply disturbing tableau of multiple forms of corruption and manipulation, a complete demystification of any notion of harmonious racial interaction. Similarly, "The Other Boat," which dramatizes a dynamic of surface gentility and secret transgression, and figures homosexuality degenerating into power mania and inevitable death, could not be further from the Hellenic idealization of eros-as-friendship. In these stories, as well as most others in the collection, no serious attention is paid to the idea of friendship, and the sexual body finds itself in permanent conflict with all social institutions and accepted conventions. Despite a spirit of irony and, in some cases, rich humor, the collection presents a general tone of firm skepticism with respect to the idealization of male relations in all their myriad, complex configurations. In an analysis to which I shall return in my discussion of *A Passage to India*, Christopher Lane has argued that the stories of *The Life to Come*, with their violence and wild homosexual subversiveness, function as a kind of repressed underside to the more artful and aestheticized fictions for which Forster is famous. Thus Lane stresses a psychic interdependence among the diverse works in Forster's canon, which correlates with what I see as a consistent tendency in Forster's work, in the novels as well as the erotic stories, away from idealization and in the direction of disturbance and dis-ease.

I would argue, then, that Forster's texts characterize homoeroticism in terms of a devolution towards inequality and discord, a tendency seemingly at odds with his much-discussed humanist and aesthetic vision. Forster rejects the notion that idealizing narratives might protect and nurture a utopian male order surrounding the body, because he credits the body both with tremendous importance and with a tragic inability to coerce or motivate cultural institutions. Tragedy, loneliness, fragmentation, loss: these are the qualities I am attributing to the rejection of Hellenism's coherent vision. Yet one might very well query the relentless negativity of these terms. Is it necessary to understand the simultaneous power and intransigence of the desiring body primarily as a source for propelling the individual into isolation? Do we need to associate the refusal to idealize and the ejection from particular cultural practices with heartbreak and the erasure of the individual? Instead, we might adopt an alternative perspective, along the lines suggested by such diverse theorists as Leo Bersani, Judith Butler, and Kaja Silverman, each of whom takes seriously the productive capacity of sexual configurations that are ordinarily marginalized and denigrated, pointing the way towards a consideration of Forster that would embrace, rather than lament, the discord of human sexuality.[62] Such structures as inequality, inauthenticity, and masochism could thus be appropriated and recast, to recircuit the dynamics of devolution in Forster's texts and to produce a genuinely transgressive concept of the self, which lays claim to a particular (post)modernity.

Yet, for all its appeal, this more empowering paradigm is not entirely satisfying as a theorization of Forster's texts. Because Forster follows writers of the late nineteenth century in relying for his social vision on ideals of humanism, aesthetic purity, revered ritual, and other virtues associated with classical studies – a set of principles which insistently situated male love within one or another of the primary masculine institutions of the day – his recognition that sexuality refuses to conform to this vision is a blow of impassable proportions. The texts I have discussed lack any vision of a present or future that might derive new sustaining structures to take account of the body. Without such organization, the individual seems less empowered than effaced. In Forster's institutionally dependent world, the most hopeful scenario to develop is a slip into invisibility; the least, a form of Lukacsian cultural homelessness. It is true that Forster's narrative voice consistently registers an astute grasp of what we might call the cultural constructedness of the body, and this canniness might seem to indicate an access to power. Yet, there is a gulf between Forster's ironized understanding about the way culture creates the individual's experience of himself, on the one hand, and a sense of empowerment for either characters or readers, on the other. His characters cannot be said to perceive the narrator's insight into the way public forms shape intimate relations, nor can they realize any productive capacity that might accrue to such an insight. They are very much at the mercy of all these forces, cultural and physical, and the constraints surrounding them are powerfully determining.

For Forster to elevate hierarchy (much less brutality) in personal bonds would also require that he abandon a fundamental political element – central to earlier writers such as Carpenter and Symonds – in the friendship ideal. As I have suggested, Carpenter, following his idol Whitman, envisioned a smooth trajectory from erotic desire to social harmony and community, refusing to pressure the class assumptions that sustained his visionary language. In important respects, Forster did not want to reject the democratic dream exemplified by such nineteenth-century utopians.

Forster admired Carpenter, not only for his personal courage, but for his ability to imagine comradeship as a genuinely productive personal and political concept. Nevertheless, Forster was unable to follow the route of proclaiming a workable continuum from the revered male body to a political goal. To ask Forster's texts to become vehicles for championing the unequal and the discordant would be significantly to misunderstand his relation to the kind of humanist fantasy expounded by Carpenter, which he admired and partially emulated, even if he could not, in the end, share its optimism. For both Forster and Symonds, the move to valorize the inequalities that constitute desire is a step too far from their essential convictions. Yet Forster is even more elaborate than Symonds in dramatizing the wrenching of the ideal of fraternal bonds from the reality of the material body. Ultimately, neither aestheticist models of male love nor the performance of dissident gender can overcome the disjunction in Forster's texts between institutions and individual desire, a disjunction that creates an intractable problem of isolation and a spirit of incompleteness, uncertainty, and ambivalence.[63] The dreams of masculine friendship belong to the "last moment of the greenwood," and the possibility of some new phoenix rising from its ashes is never offered (*M*, 254). Yet, I would suggest that for Forster, such an in-between state itself constitutes a kind of modernity, as the death of homoerotic hope contributes to an image of the modern individual, thwarted and alone.

A PASSAGE TO INDIA AND THE FAILURE OF INSTITUTIONS

I have been focusing on several of Forster's lesser-read works, yet to mention male intimacy in conjunction with Forster inevitably brings to mind *A Passage to India* (1924), as well as the late essay "What I Believe" (1939), two texts that famously proclaim the power of friendship to confront and transform political realities. The courage to betray one's country for one's friend ("Believe") and the desire to make personal bonds triumph over the processes of colonialism (*Passage*) are the hallmark of these works, which sound a cheer for the beauty and value of personal intimacy. Hence the argument I have developed up to now – that in several early novels, Forster struggles with nineteenth-century concepts of male intimacy, ultimately to reject them in the name of honesty about the force and intransigence of the physical body – would seem inapplicable with respect to these later works, especially *A Passage to India*. It is certainly true that Forster's final novel, composed nearly a decade after *Maurice*, is set in an entirely different world from that of the domestic Edwardian texts, so rooted in England, its classical ethos, its collegiate male circles; and the later novel does appear to make a renewed commitment to the idea of friendship as a crucial shaping structure in both personal and political relations. In *A Passage to India*, male intimacy has been divested from the Hellenist context, at the same time that the narrative's exploration of the power of intimacy to combat immense social forces extends its reach, becoming more exhaustive and elaborate, and engulfing a wider range of characters and situations.

Yet there are continuities. Most centrally, what I want to suggest is that *A Passage to India* follows the earlier works in dramatizing a form of modern disaffection and uncertainty as a product of the failure of friendship to live up to its promises. The novel is terribly concerned about promises and promise-keeping – in general terms, "[India] is not a promise, only an appeal" (*PI*, 136) – and it is friendship that makes the most devastatingly unfulfilled promises in the text. *A Passage to India* engages the issue of the organization of intimacy in resigned, albeit earnest tones. If Stephen Wonham in *The Longest Journey* had thwarted the propensity to make him into the symbolic center of a new friendship system, there is no single agent in the later novel to occupy that resistant position; yet the whole of the text essentially chronicles the unhinging of friendship's promise. *A Passage to India* dramatizes a tremendous pathos accompanying the failure of male friendship to complete its work of racial and spiritual reconstitution, a failure that results directly from the incompatibility of male intimacy with colonial structures. When the strong desire for friendship meets the incapacity of institutions, the result is a formless aura of loss and unfulfilled longing, an atmosphere that represents not only Forster's particular desires and disappointments, but a larger cultural investment in male friendship as a basic organizing relationship for colonialism.

Two important elements set *A Passage to India* apart from texts like *The Longest Journey*. The first, of course, is that instead of Hellenism and the collegiate community, the structures that organize male love must grow out of colonial soil. Whatever one may say about Forster's accession to orientalist patterns, he was appalled by the overall tenets and quality of colonial rule, and he never tired of satirizing the self-serving and hypocritical nature of Britain's global policemen. Given this perspective, as well as his wider liberal humanist vision, nearly all available models for constructing personal ties under the rubric of imperialism will be tainted. The novel asks how men can make, keep, encourage, develop, and extend their intimate ties under the regime of colonization, and whether there are institutions that might protect and stabilize these bonds, to prevent the slow creation of the lost soul we saw in *The Longest Journey* and *Maurice*. Moreover,

Forster's presentation of modernity seems intertwined with this narrative of tenuous friendship. These issues form the basis of my discussion of *A Passage to India*. In elaborating them, I hope also to point towards the next chapter, which will explore Conrad's treatment of the relations among male intimacy, empire, and alienation. Forster's novel, though a chronological follower of Conrad, forms a kind of link, in the sense that it addresses both the Hellenist ideal of aestheticizing male love and the terrific problem of envisioning intimacy under the aegis of imperial domination.

The second change marking *A Passage to India* is that it was completed, and largely composed, after the First World War. The question of how and where the war is manifested in the novel is an especially tricky one, for Forster has gone out of his way to divest his novel of the recognizable historical signifiers of the period, including the war. The novel is set, ambiguously, in the early years of the twentieth century (clearly pre-Amritsar, 1919; and before the rise of Gandhi's Congress Party, 1920s), and most of its dominant historical markers – notably the events of 1857 – largely refer to the imperial history of the subcontinent, rather than to a European history defined by major wars. To the extent that Indian divisions fought in the war (and, indeed, were often accorded a special status as *ur*-warriors in the English imagination), this aspect of India's relation to England does not enter into the novel. Certainly, a sensibility of post-war pessimism can be said to permeate the text, and critics have made connections between elements in the novel's perceptual and ideological landscape and the famous breaks and fissures associated with the war in the British literary imaginary. Equally as provocative as this somewhat general sense of underlying cultural trauma is the notion that Forster was interested in the feverishly patriotic state of mind of the war-time British populace, and that he reflected this problematic phenomenon in the chauvinistic hysteria generated and organized among the Anglo-Indians in the novel.[64] Yet the question of friendship remains uncertain. In later chapters, I shall discuss the widespread treatment of comradeship during and after the war, a rhetorical onslaught with which Forster was certainly familiar, and it is tempting to hypothesize that Forster's extreme investment in the notion of male intimacy as a structure with political currency relies on the war's discourse of comradeship-as-heroism. The increased and expanded role accorded to male friendship in Forster's last novel was perhaps enabled by a widely shared belief that the masculine comradeship of the trenches had fundamentally altered the way male relations might be conceptualized, opening up a new vista of possibility for intimate male ties as a force in public life. To track the rise and fall of friendship in the novel thus allows us to ally the text with other war and post-war writings (notably *Women in Love*, whose final cry of lost friend-ship anticipates the conclusion of *Passage*), to see the failure of friendship in the novel as part of a broader post-war tendency to recognize male ties as sites of loss and grief. Despite a certain speculative quality, this thesis holds appeal, and it seems reasonable to assume some convergences be-tween Forster's post-war approach to male friendship and that of many of his English contemporaries. For the purposes of this discussion, however, I shall stay closer to the novel's explicit framework: since Forster's aim is to work out the ideals and the limitations of friendship in the colonial context, I shall focus my attention there, leaving the war, for the time being, in the background.

One goal of the following analysis is to resurrect several early twentieth-century models for thinking about the relation between friendship and empire, to restore to *A Passage to India* a number of elements in the cultural history of intimacy. In addition to the concept of Hellenism and the con-sistent issue of schools and universities, I want briefly to describe two other areas of interest for the novel, each of which offers insights into contempo-raneous ideas about the way male intimacy was interlocked with empire. First, I offer a brief discussion of the culturally fraught notion of imperial eroticism, a wide-ranging concept that had for years helped to organize western attitudes about eastern sexuality. Less frequently discussed by crit-ics, however, and hence occupying a lengthier discussion here, is the idea that inter-racial male friendship was believed to have a role to play in the promotion of English power. Such a notion is laid out with particular zest in a popular imperial novel of the Edwardian period, which I shall offer as an exemplification of the paradigm.

There is nothing new in observing that the imperial imagination was soaked with eros, that by the time Forster first visited India in 1912, the space of imperial geography was filled with preconceptions about sexual power, exoticism, and rich fantasy. More specifically, the notion that the East provides a site of both real and imagined homosexual possibility for men – whether figured as liberation, conquest, self-abnegation, surprised delight, or a kind of languid tourism – had been firmly established in the orientalist canon by the early decades of the century. Critics have discussed these dynamics in detail. Joseph Boone's exposé, "Vacation Cruises: or, The Homoerotics of Orientalism," to name one particularly succinct example, lays out several strands of male homoerotic fantasy in the Egyptian setting.[65] Boone stresses that by the end of the nineteenth century, the literary trope of the seductive Egyptian boy had become an established feature of the cultural imaginary, as "the act of exploring, writing about, and theorizing an eroticized Near East [was] coterminous with unlocking a Pandora's box of phantasmatic homoerotic desire" ("Vacation Cruises," 93). In addition to providing a space for homoerotic (and pederastic) fantasy, however, Boone stresses that Egypt and North Africa could also offer western men – and he is interested primarily in literary figures like Gide and Forster – the possibility of actual sexual relations with young men or boys, available for consumption at a relatively bargain price, and in an atmosphere that was far more permissive than Europe, not to mention England. As Boone reminds us, the East was figured as a place of erotic danger, of forbidden delight and terror, at the same time that actual homosexual sex could be (and was) rather easily purchased in cities like Tunis, Cairo, and Alexandria.[66] For Forster in particular, whose sexual relations with young, working-class Egyptian men have been well documented, it seems quite clear that Egypt provided both a setting and an economic situation that enabled a degree of sexual fulfillment not easily negotiated in England. Without presuming to judge the personal dynamics of Forster's sexual relations in Egypt, that is, one can point to a set of preconditions that would likely have permeated any such relations: the cultural and economic dominance of the white Englishman; an aura, from the colonialist perspective, of exoticism, which might carry overtones of degradation as well as delight; and of course a high degree of transgression, across categories of sex, race, age, and class.

In India, too, Forster had sexual engagements with young men of the servant class, relations that necessarily relied on both the symbolic and material disparities between England and India. Thus what Sara Suleri has described as "Forster's imperial erotic" can be viewed as a matter of biography as well as a pervasive trope in *A Passage to India* and his other eastern writings.[67] For Suleri and others, the sexual dynamics of Forster's novel, which involve not only the eroticized friendship between Aziz and Fielding (to which I shall return below), but also a nexus of issues surrounding rape and female repression/fantasy, are best conceived in terms of the larger rhetoric of sexual drama interwoven with the English presence in India.[68] In the wake of Adela's accusation of attempted rape, a term never actually used in the novel, the Anglo-Indians invoke a host of assumptions about eastern eroticism – degraded, seductive, aggressive, disruptive, polymorphous. Never far from the surface, this history of ideas about Indian sexuality has terrific symbolic resonance, especially in the context of rebellion against British rule, and, in consolidating its forces, the novel's Anglo-Indian community trades on this rhetorical power.

In general, *A Passage to India* inverts the usual image of white male conquest over the feminized space of the East – in the friendship between Aziz and Fielding, for instance, where the nature of sexual desire is mobile and complex, and in the outcome of the trial, where the structure of racial and sexual myth-making is radically exposed. At the same time, Forster cannot help but evoke the standard formulas, if only by omission or reversal; the desire for the exotic other seems nearly axiomatic in the discourse to which he has recourse. For Suleri, it is Aziz's sexualized body in particular that provides a consistent site of longing in the novel, a moving field of desire that both invites the western gaze and offers a certain resistance. The fact that Aziz is partly modeled on Forster's beloved friend Syed Ross Masood, to whom the novel is dedicated, tends to increase the sense of erotic over-determination permeating his character. Christopher Lane's discussion of *A Passage to India* likewise stresses both the spoken and the elided homo-sexual subtexts underpinning and enabling the novel's movements. Lane's argument about the psychic configurations of Forster's work, in which *The Life to Come* stories provide an outlet for the repressed and aestheticized eros of *A Passage to India*, makes the larger case that the British empire in important ways relied on its own unspoken erotics, that the seductions of empire were not a forbidden consequence but an integral part of the colonial enterprise.[69] Thus, for Lane, *A Passage to India* mirrors the material conditions of British colonialism more broadly, which both promoted and suppressed homoeroticism, a simultaneously integral and banished element in the imperial regime.

If the cultural history of imperial erotics clearly permeates Forster's novel, less obvious is the presence of a related idea: that inter-racial male friend-ship, conceived in terms of the English institutions of masculinity, has a role to play in the management of empire. From as early as the 1830s, when Thomas Macauley issued his famous "minute" dismissing Indian literary culture, the creation of an elite, comprised of English-educated Indian men, formed an essential part of the colonial scheme. Indeed, by the middle of the century, the Indian Civil Service was tightly bound with the major British universities, primarily Oxford and Cambridge, where a select number of ambitious Indian civil servants were educated. The personal relationships developed in the university were clearly as important to the colonial project as the educational and cultural dimensions. Though contemporary theo-rists have stressed that this policy opened the way for various forms of destabilization, we ought not to move too quickly from order to disorder, from consolidation of power to the undermining of hierarchy. Put crudely, the notion is that friendship between Indian and English men, if properly structured and organized, helps to consolidate colonial rule. An essential element in British governing strategy, the development of an Indian elite

relied crucially on access for a privileged few to English educational institutions – public schools and especially universities. Because, as we have
seen, schools and universities traded in their differing ways on an ethos of
friendship, we might expect the colonial connection equally to involve a
stress on male bonds. Indeed, as we consider the notion that an Indian elite
might contribute to British dominion of the subcontinent, the importance
of both individualized friendships and institutional affiliation can hardly
be overstated. A striking exploration of this idea is at the center of A. E. W.
Mason's popular (if largely forgotten) novel *The Broken Road* (1907), and
I shall use the text as a kind of template for analyzing the way contemporaries conceived of both the utility and the drawbacks surrounding
the organization of intimacy as a matter of imperial governance.[70] *The
Broken Road*, which combines a focus on the English educational institutions that foster male friendship with an essentialist portrayal of the savagery
of the Indian man, makes the case that the considerable effectiveness of the
English schools in creating friendship ultimately meets its match in the determinism of race. My reading of *A Passage to India* will rely on the notion
that, though these two novels differ in nearly every respect, and though
The Broken Road represents an earlier moment than does *A Passage to India*
in the development of subcontinental nationalism, the premise at the basis
of Mason's text was a central one for Forster too: that male friendship is
not incidental to colonial relations, but fundamental to their workings,
whether one hopes to solidify or to disrupt British power.

The Broken Road is a difficult text for the modern reader. Racist and
misogynist, the novel allies its romantic fondness for the white men whose
life on "the frontier" is supposed to enable colonial progress with an extreme
invective against Indian savagery and female opportunism. The novel's overall idea involves an assertion that deeply held bonds between English and
Indian men are essential for the management of empire, and its invective
against Indians and women is not incidental to that narrative. *The Broken
Road* tells the story of two men whose intertwined fate is developed even
before their birth, in the friendship of their fathers. In a sense, Charles
Linforth and Shere Ali function like an ill-fated couple in a standard
marriage plot: meant by their parents for one another, they undo that
pre-ordained order, trumped by the realities of character and history. The
men's friendship begins at Eton, where they are deliberately assigned shared
rooms, and continues at Oxford. During this time, a mutual dream of
completing the eponymous broken road, left unfinished by their fathers,
motivates the friendship. However, rivalry over the beautiful Violet Oliver
and the eventual effects on both men of rugged, northern India, where

the action moves, undermine all affection. Shere Ali's "natural" savagery is reasserted in his native land; his passion for the white woman becomes violent; and the two men eventually come to oppose one another in battle. In the end, a victorious Linforth tracks down Shere Ali in a bleak, mountainous wilderness: "'I brought him down . . . into India. I brought him down – along the Road which at Eton we had planned to carry on together. Down that Road we came together – I the captor, he the prisoner.'"[71] Conspicuously, the novel does not end in marriage.

Mason's text documents in stark terms a trajectory out of idealized friendship, created and fostered by Eton and Oxford (both institutions rendered with high nostalgia, and presented as entirely continuous and allied with one another), and into its converse: the Frankensteinian couple, whose endless competition can only cease when one is reduced to a pitiful captive, the other a Pyrrhic victor, abandoned to his own disillusionment. What is surprising in this movement, however, is the dual role of educational institutions. On one hand, friendship develops within their idealized spaces, as the boys move seamlessly from one stage to the next, on their way to a civilized manhood that will be defined by male comradeship. On the other hand, Eton and Oxford are held almost entirely to blame for the tragedy of the novel, because, according to the text's repeated logic, they create out of the Indian youth a hybrid figure who belongs to neither culture. As Shere Ali thinks early in the narrative, "'I am no longer in doubt [about which country is home]. It is neither in England nor in Chiltisan. I am a citizen of no country. I have no place anywhere at all'" (*BR*, 63).[72]

Mason thus would seem to inveigh against the standard colonial practice of creating a "mimic" race, whose cooperative role was viewed as essential to the management of an imperial apparatus on a major scale. Or, more specifically, Mason fears that Homi Bhabha might be right, that such a structure creates and invites the possibility of trouble. Bhabha's analysis of mimicry has highlighted the potential for disruption presented by the not-quite-white double.[73] He stresses that the mimic man opens up a space for resistance, for pockets of disturbance and dissimulation, and that the effects of this subtle transformation might alter the balance of imperial power. Mason's Shere Ali presents an interesting version of Bhabha's mimic man: certainly, his near-whiteness is the core issue for the text, and the persona that emerges out of the cracks in the mimic system is dangerous, rebellious, and anti-imperial. At the same time, Mason's highly conservative novel aims to suture those very fissures by declaiming the entire system that enables simulated whiteness in the first place. Mason acknowledges the threat implicit in the fundamental configuration of racial imitation and assimilation, and his conviction could not be more direct: to tamper with the fixity of race is to invite disaster.

Indeed, for Mason, the core point is that race is absolute; *it will out*, and no amount of manufacturing of elites can change that essential fact. Race presents the only sure marker of human potential, and it finally undermines the work of all institutions. In the words of one Englishman, whose sentiments are repeatedly echoed in the text's many voices:

"England overlaid the real man with a pretty varnish... That's all it ever does. And the varnish peels off easily when the man comes back to an Indian sun. There's not one of these people from the hills but has in him the makings of a fanatic. It's a question of circumstances whether the fanaticism comes to the top or not. Given the circumstances, neither Eton, nor Oxford, nor all the schools and universities rolled into one would hinder the relapse." (*BR*, 108)

As this passage suggests, *The Broken Road* is excessively concerned with the problematic relation between surface and depth. Not surprisingly, the text insists that skin is a marker of that which inheres in the person's deepest reaches. As the layers of cultural "varnish" inevitably peel away, the truth of racial identity is revealed. The text has a clear message about the efficacy of institutions: they are too powerful to be treated lightly, yet ineffective when compared with the extreme determinism of blood. Moreover, Eton and Oxford are important not only because they fail to complete the task of racial transformation, but because their particular failure is experienced as the demise of friendship. The basic conceit of the novel – completion of the road – involves a generational continuation of cross-racial male fellowship, as the ritualized bonds of friendship are passed along from father to son, and that relation in turn ensures the continuity of British rule. Even when the boys are young, Linforth recognizes that friendship is his most potent tool for assuring Ali's cooperation in later life, and he sets about utilizing its rituals according to his needs: "Linforth had quietly put forth his powers to make Shere Ali his friend, to force him to see with his eyes, and to believe what he believed. And Shere Ali had been easily persuaded" (*BR*, 36).

The text's assertion that friendship represents the primary relation underpinning the colonial order is matched by a deep suspicion of women. Shere Ali consistently (mis)understands his animosity for Linforth as rivalry over Violet Oliver, and both men view heterosexual entanglement as the death-blow to homosocial male desire: "There was nothing left of the friendship which through many years had played so large a part in his life. A woman had intervened, and Linforth had shut the door upon it, had sealed his mind against its memories, and his heart against its claims"

(*BR*, 118). Yet the text's animosity towards Violet for breaking up the friendship does not dissipate the intensity of male relations. Rather, in a textbook Sedgwickian development, Linforth and Shere Ali perform their ostensible heterosexual heroics in the theater of male rivalry. The men become almost archetypal enemies, pursuing one another over wide geographical spaces, and the trajectory of their mutual intimacy and enmity is meant to tell a larger story of political order and disorder. The failure of English educational institutions represents the transformation from an ideal of male cooperation and sympathy into a vision of colonial fracture, where British rule is assured only by force, and where the intensity of male discord becomes the dominant personal and political mode. That the novel is set in the northern regions of India, where the contest over rule was, in a very real sense, undecided, only heightens the sense of threat posed to imperial consolidation by the breakdown in the men's relationship.

The transition from friendship to animosity is understood as a product of the movement from boyhood into manhood, a threshold with which Mason's novel is preoccupied. The title itself suggests the problem of broken development, and the narrative repeatedly stages the apparent onset of manhood for both Linforth and Shere Ali. If educational establishments are given the task of turning boys into men – as Victorian rhetoric so consistently asserted – the novel worries that the development of masculinity might transpire outside these safe spaces, and will thus be fraught with conflict, as sexual and political desires disrupt an otherwise simple and self-sufficient universe of boys. Eton and Oxford are both credited and blamed for shielding boys from the racial and sexual drama that constitutes masculinity and political reality in the text. Ultimately, the novel posits a fundamental conflict between an institutionalized model of male friendship, which seems to thrive at the moment of transition from youth to manhood, and a matrix of uncontrollable passions, desires, and hard truths, which the novel figures as the reward for achieving masculinity.

The Broken Road indicates that, for all its institutional structuring, friendship will inevitably break down when confronted with the absolute essence that, for Mason, constitutes racial difference. Moreover, the colonial situation demands that if male bonds are not functioning to uphold British dominion, then they must be reconstituted as male rivalry, enabling the white man to (re)exert control. The novel is deeply wistful for an always-already-lost time when organized male intimacy properly directed the growth and management of empire, a time before England came to rely on its schooling institutions to create a mimic elite. Despite its racist assumptions and simplistic morality, the novel's stance about the central role of male bonds in the functioning of the Raj offers an interesting connection to *A Passage to India*, Forster's liberal humanist masterpiece. Forster imagines a colonial situation in which male friendship provides the groundwork not for British domination, as in Mason's text, but for harmony, equality, and a new social foundation. Yet his text also showcases the demise of male friendship, and it, too, will assert that the institutions of intimacy operate as the pivot on which the personal dimension of the colonial project turns.

In *A Passage to India*, friendship dominates as both subject and organizing trope. Friendship between individuals as an analogy for the relations between races; the transcendence of intimate moments of friendship in a harsh and unforgiving setting; political brotherhood and/or nationalism conceived as friendship; the churning imperial homoerotic concealed beneath the orderly concept of male friendship; the friend as the God; Mrs. Moore, the friend of India; friendship across gender and age differences; friendship inside and outside of recognized institutions, zigzagging and cutting across them – the elasticity of the idea of friendship reaches a zenith with *A Passage to India*, as sexuality, politics, religion, spirituality, and vaguer impulses that are posited as beyond the purview of language, all coalesce under its rubric. The narrative opens with a group of Indian men discussing whether it is possible to be friends with the English, and although they do not arrive at a definitive answer, the text avidly takes up the problem of colonial fellowship, right up to its concluding lines, when Fielding's plea "Why can't we be friends now?" is repudiated: "No, not yet...No, not there" (*PI*, 322). Forster's celebrated creed of personal relations, his humanist belief that intimate contact can bring what he elsewhere calls "a little order to the contemporary chaos," is expressed repeatedly in the novel.[74] Mrs. Moore might thus be taken as an exemplary voice, when she thinks, "One touch of regret – not the canny substitute but the true regret from the heart – would have made him a different man, and the British Empire a different institution" (*PI*, 51). Yet even if the novel pleads for human connection as the best hope for change, as it wanders through the many chambers of the house of friendship, it rebuffs easy solutions, relentlessly demonstrating the enormity of the colonial machine, and insisting on the final incapacity of people to overcome the destructive processes of imperialism through their tiny half-embraces.

Almost since the book's publication, critics have discussed this oscillation between the novel's humanist faith in such ideas as friendship and its ultimate skepticism about the ability of individuals to triumph over the impersonal monolith of imperial power.[75] In this analysis, I do not propose to weigh in on the optimism/pessimism debate, nor on the issue of

Forster's degree of orientalist collusion.[76] Instead, I want to point to what I see as two intersecting elements in the text's idea of friendship, each of which, in turn, points back to the contexts I have offered in framing this discussion: the use of friendship as a stabilizing concept to capture and control an excess of desire circulating and eddying in the text; and the suggestion that male friendship provides the linchpin in making a mimic race, with real consequences for the British position in India – only with a twist. Friendship in this novel is supposed to characterize, nurture, and perpetuate potentially transgressive desires, at the same time that it provides structures or rituals to contain and socialize those impulses. Forster hopes to use the rituals of friendship and the gestures of the male body to create some form of permanence or lasting beauty in the world, in a pattern that harks back to his Hellenist texts, and to Pater and Symonds before him. What the over-determined friendship between Aziz and Fielding will finally yield, however, is a concession of disaffection and unfulfilled hopes, as the ambitious idea of making friendship into the catalyst for racial harmony collapses under the weight of imperial difference.

A Passage to India palpitates with desires that are not fully articulated, many of which take shape around the idea of friendship. Early in the novel, the Hindu holy man Godbole sings a song addressed to Krishna, the god understood as the Friend, in which Krishna is implored – always with futility – to approach the singer. Mrs. Moore, for one, is confused by the god's refusal: "'But He comes in some other song, I hope?'" she asks; "'Oh no, he refuses to come,' repeated Godbole, perhaps not understanding the question. 'I say to Him, Come, come, come, come, come, come. He neglects to come'" (*PI*, 80). Forster uses the Hindu trope of supplication, of unfulfilled sexual and spiritual desire, as a kind of catch-all to express a host of yearnings, more and less vague, that preoccupy the narrative voice. Figured as "our need for the Friend who never comes yet is not entirely disproved," this purportedly shared quality is characterized as axiomatic: "In vain did each item in [the countryside] call out, 'Come, come.' There was not enough god to go around" (*PI*, 106, 87–88). Given that the India of the novel's imaginary is marked by its inevitable and extravagant failure to deliver, by its false dawns where "virtue ... fail[s] in the celestial fount," this dynamic of unfulfilled desire becomes part of the landscape, an inhospitable setting whose very soil is "hostile," repelling the foot's pressure (*PI*, 136, 18). At a broader level, the catastrophe at the center of the novel's plot can be read as a feminization of this same dynamic of disappointment, as Adela imagines an assault that never occurred, in a fantasy that never gets articulated.

Indeed, we might go further, to argue that Forster in effect "queers" the entire field of desire in the novel, as he theorizes longing in general – across space and time, gender and race – according to the conditions of his own homosexuality. Desire is imagined as inevitably foreclosed, a kind of beckoning or seduction that cannot be entirely realized, in a continual dance of invitation and disappointment. The text's economy of desire functions according to this generalizing pattern; images of beauty are offered as universal, in a shared eroticism as overarching as the dome of the sky, which "settles everything... because it is so strong and so enormous" (*PI*, 9). The general structure recalls Symonds and Wilde, as the gaze of an older man, aesthetically oriented, is turned on the beautiful and unreachable young male. The most spectacular moment along these lines comes at the opening of the courtroom scene, when Adela draws the reader's attention to an exceptionally eroticized figure:

the first person Adela noticed... was the humblest of all who were present, a person who had no bearing officially upon the trial: the man who pulled the punkah. Almost naked, and splendidly formed, he sat on a raised platform near the back, in the middle of the central gangway, and he caught her attention as she came in, and he seemed to control the proceedings. He had the strength and beauty that sometimes come to flower in Indians of low birth. When that strange race nears the dust and is condemned as untouchable, then nature remembers the physical perfection that she accomplished elsewhere, and throws out a god – not many, but one here and there, to prove to society how little its categories impress her. This man would have been notable anywhere: among the thin-hammed, flat-chested mediocrities of Chandrapore he stood out as divine, yet he was of the city, its garbage had nourished him, he would end on its rubbish heaps. Pulling the rope towards him, relaxing it rhythmically, sending swirls of air over others, receiving none himself, he seemed apart from human destinies, a male fate, a winnower of souls... he scarcely knew that he existed and did not understand why the Court was fuller than usual, indeed he did not know that it was fuller than usual, didn't even know that he worked a fan, though he thought he pulled a rope. (*PI*, 217–218)

This sequence is often noted for its homoerotic and orientalizing flamboyance.[77] The racial configuration forms the crux of the passage: when Forster refers to "that strange race," he seems to sweep all readers into the space behind Adela's and his own eyes, as Europeans looking into a scene of oriental male beauty. Indeed the perspectival slippage in this scene calls attention to the way the text more broadly goes about universalizing a very specific form of desire. The lovely, godlike figure is appreciated by one and all, just as the friend is posited as an image for totalizing desire, unfulfilled and infinite. Yet perhaps the most striking feature in this astonishing description is its manifest impossibility: the idea that the punkah wallah scarcely understands that he exists, does not register his surroundings at all, does not even know that he works a fan, indicates a level of pure fantasy. He embodies an image for the western visitor of a gorgeousness whose only function is to please, an unconscious, involuntary movement that neither demands nor desires the admiration that the aesthetic eye nevertheless cannot help but proffer. The punkah wallah, like the naked Indian man who listens open-mouthed and rapt, "his lips parted with delight," to Godbole's song, and, in Suleri's view, like Aziz himself, provides an extravagant example of free-floating, racialized desire, in a form the text seeks to generalize (*PI*, 78).

Another figure who epitomizes a certain shared need, yet of a specifically non-sexual variety, is Mrs. Moore. The "Indianization" of Mrs. Moore – her transformation first into "Esmiss Esmoore" and subsequently into a figure merged with Indian landscape and legend – functions, again, as an abstraction of the ubiquitous textual desire for the friend, that elusive being who augurs and repudiates such complex goals as sexual satisfaction, racial unification, and spiritual peace (*PI*, 225). That Mrs. Moore's claim to the status of India's friend might be undeserved is suggested by Fielding ("'the old lady never did anything for you at all'" [*PI*, 254]), yet the text refuses to allow rational discourse to undermine the communal energy, even hysteria, that elevates her to a demigod, and Aziz will continue to protest that Mrs. Moore is "my best friend in all the world" (*PI*, 312). Nevertheless, *A Passage to India* throbs with erotic energy, and Mrs. Moore is repeatedly characterized by her lack of sexuality. Her insufficiency as friend-god is thus a product not only of her severe limitations as a person, exposed and exaggerated by the hellish epiphany of the caves, but also of her distance from the imperial erotics at the heart of the novel.

In an alternate course from the Esmiss Esmoore trajectory, the novel suggests that men might fulfill amorphous longings by formalizing and ritualizing the gestures of the male body in a circle of friendship. Here we return to the sensibility of such works as *The Longest Journey*, and the image of peaceful male fraternity replacing the brutality of the public schools. In *A Passage to India*, of course, the public-school ethos is embodied by the ever-adolescent Ronny, whose personality is entirely of the fifth form, and the viciousness of the Anglo-Indians at their worst represents the nadir of human decency, "the unspeakable limit of cynicism, untouched since 1857" (*PI*, 187). As in his Hellenist works, Forster looks in *A Passage to India* for a university-like model of male community as an alternative to the conformity, exclusivity, hatefulness, and philistinism of Anglo-India, something like Woolf's vision of the Cambridge room, and he finds it in the circle of Indian men that continually forms and re-forms around Aziz. Aziz, for his part, shines brightly in these moments of community. Highly attuned to the presence of good will, to the loveliness of poetry as an agent for capturing a unifying spirit among male friends, he creates magical bits of space and time – and not only with Fielding and the intimate male group, but also with his other friend, Mrs. Moore, with her son Ralph, and in mixed company such as the tea party. Conversely, Aziz understands his anger at Anglo-Indians in terms of their perversion of proper civility, and his frustrated hope is "[t]o escape from the net and be back among manners and gestures that he knew" (*PI*, 18). Throughout the text, Forster suggests that communities are a product of their formal languages; without visible, understandable, shared rituals – physical as well as linguistic – there is no hope for harmony among people or for bridges across the divided landscape.

To create community out of a kind of gestural performance is to achieve social, spiritual, and political grace, as in the following exceptional moment of strength and serenity:

Civilization strays about like a ghost here, revisiting the ruins of empire, and is to be found not in great works of art or mighty deeds, but in the gestures well-bred Indians make when they sit or lie down. Fielding, who had dressed up in native costume, learnt from his excessive awkwardness in it that all his motions were makeshifts, whereas when the Nawab Bahudur stretched out his hand for food or Nureddin applauded a song, something beautiful had been accomplished which needed no development. This restfulness of gesture – it is the Peace that passeth Understanding, after all, it is the social equivalent of Yoga. When the whirring of action ceases, it becomes visible, and reveals a civilization which the West can disturb but will never acquire. The hand stretches out forever, the lifted knee has the eternity though not the sadness of the grave. (*PI*, 251–252)

Front and center here is the body, in movement or at rest, conscious or unconscious, eternal in its very mortality. We might recall Pater's Spartan youths here, or his idea of the Greek Spirit, or Forster's own reflections on the symbolic moment. What is perhaps most striking in the passage is the emphasis on "civilization," as the male body essentially comprises culture, bringing together the small-scale intimacy of friends with an aesthetic sensibility that reaches outwards in space and backwards in time. These are gestures that do not come naturally to the westerner; only the eastern man can create eternity out of simple physical movements. Like the punkah wallah whose rhythmic movements fill the room with comfort and the narrator with desire, the Indian man here has an integrity of body powerful enough to withstand western colonial incursions, even if the somewhat elevated nature of this reverie recalls familiar orientalist rhetoric, as the beautiful ritual is viewed and articulated by the sympathetic outsider.

Aziz always resides at the center of such a circle; he epitomizes in the flesh the European ideal of Indian male intimacy, and his relationship with Fielding is the centerpiece of the novel's friendship theme. It is Aziz's warmth that initiates and sustains the friendship, and it is he who consistently crosses the social boundaries whose collapse sets in motion the terrible events of "Caves." When he wrenches off his collar stud and inserts it into Fielding's shirt (perhaps the high-water mark of the text's homosexual iconography), when he displays his wife's photograph to Fielding, in a transaction dense with symbolic capital (as I shall discuss below), or when he slowly eliminates the honorifics of naming, first shedding the "Mr." and eventually the "Fielding" itself – in each of these cases, what makes the relationship possible is the quality of instinctive human understanding that the text, as well as Aziz himself, characterizes as "oriental." Given Aziz's unique ability to cross the thresholds separating English and Indians, not to mention his western education, cultivation, and profession, critics have suggested that Aziz, like his biographical inspiration Syed Ross Masood, conforms to the model of the mimic man. There is some accuracy in this notion, and the rifts Aziz produces in the colonial machinery would accord with Bhabha's sense of the ambivalence inherent in the mimicry position.

Yet what I want to suggest is that it is actually *Fielding* who occupies the role of potential mimic, and that this reversal constitutes an essential element in Forster's subversive appropriation of the standard narrative of friendship and empire. If the creation of the racially other double, via friendship, was at the core of the imperial system in works like *The Broken Road*, Forster ponders what might happen if this model is turned on its head, with the white man amalgamated into the position of almost-Indian, and with a goal not of solidifying, but of undermining, the imperial order. In general, Fielding's combination of independence with respect to institutions and flexibility with respect to allies is his most distinguishing feature. From the first, Fielding is characterized by an aloofness towards British institutions and conventions, and the "gulf between himself and his countrymen" only "widen[s] distressingly" during his time in Chrandapore (*PI*, 61). His great aspiration, as he says, is to "travel light," to "slink through India unlabelled," to resist categorization and affiliation (*PI*, 121, 175). Towards his fellow English, he has "no racial feeling," and his treatment of concepts sacrosanct to the English verges on the blasphemous. Even when it comes to Aziz, Fielding maintains a certain distance, viewing him initially as a bit of an abstraction, an example of a certain type: "Fielding was not surprised at the rapidity of their intimacy. With so emotional a people it was apt to come at once or never" and "he was often struck with the liveliness with which the younger generation handled a foreign tongue" (*PI*, 65). In the period after the trial, Fielding's ability, once again, to think "along independent lines" sets the stage for the fatal rifts in his friendship with Aziz (*PI*, 244).

For the most part, however, Fielding's adaptability and lack of affiliation provide the basic qualifications for being assimilated to Indian culture, and his genuine affection for Aziz is what compels his gradual movement in that direction. After an initial welcoming at Aziz's sick-bed, much of Fielding's acculturation into Indian civilization happens essentially off-stage, yet there are several memorable tableaus, when we watch intimacy develop through a process of cultural absorption, or when we see him already embedded in settings rich in social meaning. The first such moment functions as the seal in Aziz and Fielding's friendship, when the two men come together over a photograph of Aziz's dead wife. Aziz's gesture of showing Fielding his late wife's picture immediately enfolds Fielding into a space of comfortable Indian masculinity, and into the brotherhood of Aziz's own symbolic family. By figuratively admitting Fielding behind the purdah, Aziz solidifies a relation of intimacy and reciprocity with the other man, under the aegis of Muslim convention and family practice. In this tender scene, the traffic-in-women paradigm works exactly according to form: "But they were friends, brothers. That part was settled, their compact had been subscribed by the photograph, they trusted one another, affection had triumphed for once in a way" (*PI*, 122). Despite the language of personal connection and small-scale graciousness – the accomplishment and pleasure of which I do not wish to diminish – the creation of intimacy between the two men nevertheless works according to the rules of patriarchal convention, it uses the language of ritualized male bonding, and it taps into a ready history of male negotiation in female bodies.

A second moment of interest, with respect to Fielding's gradual induction to Indian culture, comes in the courtroom, when we get a glimpse of him (through Adela's eyes, as in the case of the punkah wallah), with "an Indian child perched on his knee" (*PI*, 222). This image of Fielding as part of a family functions as a continuation of what began with the photograph; once inside the Indian household, he has become a part of it. The Anglo-Indians, of course, view Fielding as a traitor, his refusal to "toe the line" constituting a form of switched allegiance that, for the battle-mad English, is unforgivable (*PI*, 171). In the Anglo-Indian view, Fielding has essentially "gone native," and they are right, in a sense. The difference, however, between the conventional notion of "going native," along the lines of Kurtz and scores of nineteenth-century precursors, is that Forster presents the shift not as a matter of forfeiting civilization, but as its attainment. If "going native" always implied a loss of ego, a psychic and sexual degradation, a succumbing to the primitive (as McBryde suggests, when he articulates the mid-Victorian, Burton-esque view that "the darker races are physically attracted to the fairer, but not *vice versa*" [*PI*, 218–219]), here we have the reverse, as Fielding's ability to learn the ways of a highly cultivated society is presented as both a moral and intellectual accomplishment. What the novel is exploring is not so much the ultra-conventional notion of "going native," then, but instead the quite shocking idea of the white man being slowly welded to eastern tradition and culture, through institutions like the family and the elevated male circle, just as selected colonials were meant to learn equivalent English manners and forms.

Perhaps the most striking moment, in terms of Fielding's shifting relation to Indian culture, comes in the scene of the men at leisure, quoted above. We might recall that for all the calm beauty of the scene, Fielding, "in native costume, learnt from his excessive awkwardness in it that all his motions were makeshifts" (*PI*, 251). Included and invited by his friends, Fielding remains excluded at the level of the body. What this illuminating moment shows is that culture can go only so far before, as Fielding later learns, "something racial intrude[s]" (*PI*, 260). On one hand, Fielding's involvement in these moments of casual community, his long evening spent with the victorious forces on the roof after the post-trial celebrations, his familiarity with a widening circle of men – all of this suggests that Fielding has become, in a sense, civilized by them. On the other hand, there are impassable barriers, which Forster, like Mason before him, attributes to race. If we return to Mason's conventional model of mimicry, we might say that Fielding has been schooled to become a member of an Indian elite, a kind of collaborationist whose role will be to serve the interests of that culture, or at any rate to embrace it on its own terms. Yet, like Shere Ali in *The Broken Road*, Fielding finds himself in a kind of no-man's-land, thwarted by his very body, and resistant to the idea of remaining in a position halfway between the divided races and cultures. Both Fielding and Aziz recognize the availability of such a model, and its clear inequity is what bars them from bringing it to fruition:

Aziz was friendly and domineering. He wanted Fielding to "give in to the East," as he called it, and live in a condition of affectionate dependence upon it. "You can trust me, Cyril." No question of that, and Fielding had no roots among his own people. Yet he really couldn't become a sort of Mohammed Latif [Aziz's dependent relative]. When they argued about it something racial intruded . . . (*PI*, 260)

There are, in other words, important structural reasons for the failure of Aziz and Fielding's friendship, but how shall we characterize that "something racial" which obstructs their friendship, and with it the symbolic promise of healing across racial and imperial lines? As was clear in the scene with the photograph, if the relation between the men is to succeed, it will need to be organized, bound by the kinds of rituals and traditions that enable the circle of Indian men to perpetuate their own aestheticized community. In this novel, as in Forster's Hellenist texts, there is always a palpable order behind the apparent spontaneity of word and gesture. Yet this emphasis on institutionalization presents something of an irony, since friendship in *A Passage to India* – as in the contemporary rhetoric about classicism and education that preoccupied Forster and his peers – is attractive precisely because it seems an antidote to entrenched institutions like the public schools. Individuals in the novel turn to friendship because it appears antithetical to the harsh and rigid organization of the political world, and is directed against such structures as national anthems and bridge parties. Yet for all this, the novel follows Forster's other work in insisting that human relations need to be structured, and friendship in particular involves a balance between individual choice and institutional cover. Given the paucity of inter-racial precedents, and the moral bankruptcy of all British institutions in India, the novel seems unable to come up with any other organizing precept that might function as a forum for real intimacy, cultural accommodation, and political change. What is missing, in effect, is the university model, and it should come as no surprise that when the men in the opening dialogue find an exception to the rule of antipathy across race, it involves Hamidullah's years at Cambridge.

In the oft-discussed last paragraphs of the text, when the urge and the resistance to friendship are most directly articulated, the problem of failed institutions reaches an impassable level. At the novel's close, Forster describes a renewed relationship between the two men in language that is both sexual and violent. Conjoining the text's sexual dynamics – an erotic economy that generalizes desire and subsumes different perspectives into its orientalist gaze – with its stance that male friendship is a guiding principle in imperial hegemony, Aziz cries, "'we shall drive every blasted Englishman into the sea, and then' – he rode against him furiously – 'and then,' he concluded, half kissing him, 'you and I shall be friends'" (*PI*, 322). After the politics of nations have been sorted out, Aziz suggests, friendship will triumph in its most saturated form. Yet there is something unique here: the kind of post-colonial friendship that Aziz imagines has no precedent, even in the text's imaginary. Up to now, the men have worked on the model of

mimicry and acculturation, with the friendship relying on Fielding's gradual inclusion in a Muslim friendship circle along the lines of a university
community. Though that model provocatively turns the ordinary stance
of friendship-as-power upside down, it nevertheless relies on the idea that
one race or culture must subsume the other. Here, in the violent desire of
man for man, we have something akin to Stephen Wonham's call for a form
of masculine intimacy that would rebut categories and allegiances, setting
the men's intimacy in effect outside of culture, a stance which *The Longest
Journey*, like the later novel, cannot fully realize.

When we combine the text's investment in friendship as a defining category for both human contact and amorphous desire with its uncompromising recognition that intimacy can only function when organized, we are
left with a landscape of partial satisfaction, unfulfilled desires, friendship
turned to division:

> But the horses didn't want it – they swerved apart; the earth didn't want it,
> sending up rocks through which riders must pass single file; the temples, the tank,
> the jail, the palace, the birds, the carrion, the Guest House, that came into view as
> they issued from the gap and saw Mau beneath: they didn't want it, they said in
> their hundred voices, "No, not yet," and the sky said, "No, not there." (*PI*, 322)

It seems that the novel's inquiry into friendship essentially concludes where
it began: with a qualified, regretful "no." Friendship is asked to carry a
heavy cultural weight in the text, it fails (thus far in tune with *The Broken
Road*, albeit in a vastly different spirit) and the novel then poses the uneasy
question of what might replace it. Over the course of the narrative, various
possibilities have been suggested, each with its own limitations. Aziz, for
one, periodically tests the idea that nationalism, which he thinks of as a
kind of "universal brotherhood," might provide a social and conceptual
structure with real affinities to his sentiments about friendship (*PI*, 145).
The idea of the nation as an extension of the kind of symbolic brotherhood
Aziz and Fielding develop through the photograph appeals to Aziz for both
sentimental and political reasons. Yet Aziz has always operated on the scale
of the small circle and the symbolic moment, and his notion of nationalism would require a kind of de-personalization that he can never quite
admit, even as textual events increasingly expose the inadequacy of his cherished image of individual friendship. Another alternative is offered through
the avenue of Godbole's magnificent religious apotheosis in "Temple,"
an exhilarating scene which carries heightened significance in the novel,
not least because of its key place in the text's tripartite, dialectical structure. However, the ceremony, which creates "a beauty in which there was

nothing personal," remains a form of momentary ecstasy, with little relation to the daily needs of individuals in complex social and personal negotiations, who "revert to individual clods" once the moment has passed (*PI*, 284). The "Temple" portion of the novel may include visions of complete community, but it also focuses squarely on religious and cultural discord, on the inescapability of individuality, difference, and fragmentation. In an important sense, the text never moves beyond friendship as the most desirable organizing relation for all kinds of human endeavors and bonds. In both nationalized brotherhood and Godbole's Hinduism, friendship provides the central metaphor for community (the nation as a collection of brothers; the god as the Friend).

Another way to think about the closure of the novel, with its rejection of what we might call the text's desire ("'Why can't we be friends now...Its what I want. It's what you want,'" as Fielding has it), is that the novel's close simply depicts the end of male intimacy, full stop (*PI*, 322). The friendship between the men has operated throughout the text in a double way: first as a figuration for the excessive and often orientalist desire that the novel does not so much repress as universalize, and second, as a reversed version of the friendship-as-amalgamation concept, where Fielding is "civilized" into an eastern culture, creating a mimicry or pairing which, though fragile, might have pointed towards a partial undoing of imperial power. With the deterioration in the men's friendship, and the text's final articulation of its indefinite suspension, perhaps the point is that the condition of colonial modernity *is* that suspension. Even Mason's racist and histrionic narrative of friendship-turned-to-hatred suggested a parallel development: the powerful rupture in the workings of homosociality, which poses a serious threat to empire and requires a new regime of force, indicates that the glory days of friendship as an imperial asset have been firmly put to rest. In *A Passage to India*, imagery of uneasiness and discomfort is so prevalent as to represent almost an ontology, and, at the end of the text, human efforts to forge community and improve the world through the idea of friendship take us to the very place of dislocation and uncertainty towards which the text has consistently gestured. If Forster's earlier texts had generated an isolated and threatened individual out of the failure of Hellenism's promise, here the quality of modernness is less a matter of individuality than an aura – generalized in the novel, like desire itself – of rupture and endless deferral. For Forster, friendlessness represents a kind of modern condition, whether at home or abroad.

CHAPTER 2

Conradian alienation and imperial intimacy

A Passage to India raised two broad questions: what does empire do to male friendship, and what can male friendship do for empire? In both cases, the text was skeptical, even worried – imperialism exposes basic drawbacks in the promise of male intimacy, and the power of friendship is seriously compromised by the even greater force of racial division. What develops is a sense of being stalled: friendship may have worked in some imagined past – or may work in some imagined future – as a structure to ground and mediate colonial relations, but the present is defined by a host of retreats, including the retreat from the safe spaces under friendship's umbrella. The idea that characters, perhaps history itself, have somehow been caught by the impasse of failed male fellowship is an arresting one in Forster's fictions, and provocative, too, for considering the earlier imperial moment epitomized by Joseph Conrad's tales. To recognize that the history of the British Empire is intertwined with institutions and conventions of male bonding provides an opening premise for an analysis of Conrad's texts, which thoroughly investigate the moral uncertainties surrounding not only imperialism, but the masculine relations that take shape in its troubled spaces. For Conrad, as for Forster, it is abundantly clear that male intimacy has always mattered in the British imperial project, and its fate in the waning nineteenth century preoccupies his work.

Of the major modernists in Britain, Conrad's reputation has perhaps shifted most dramatically over the last several decades. As the language and logic of imperialism have increasingly been subjected to critical investigation, Conrad's texts have come to mark an important moment in a literary tradition defined not by its heroic break with bourgeois conventionality, as the modernists themselves might have it, but by its adherence to a masculine, European, global hegemony. Badly shaken by an assessment of the racial and gender assumptions underpinning his tales, Conrad's status as archetypal early modernist – whose fractured, convulsed narratives represent the turmoil of a literary practice at war with its past – has lost its heroic associations.[1] Although literary critics on the whole have not adopted Chinua Achebe's famously bracing denunciation of Conrad as a "bloody racist," or his recommendation that we expel *Heart of Darkness* from the curriculum, they nevertheless have revalued Conrad's work in the context of a literary economy that functions in both overt and subtle ways to justify imperialism and racial hierarchy.[2] Conrad's voice, it seems, has become something of a test case for the intransigence of a troubled and troubling racial consciousness.

Conversely, when Conrad is read sympathetically today, it is typically because of his modernist innovation and consequent refusal to conform systematically to any single or simple ideology. In a study of Conrad's place in the adventure tradition, for instance, Andrea White concedes Conrad's problematic accession to the idea of an "imperial subject," but suggests that his use of Marlow and other distancing formal devices prevents him from succumbing to a straightforward and repellent racialism.[3] Even Edward Said argues that Conrad's innovative formal strategies create a radical ambiguity around imperialism, an elliptical attitude that enables Conrad to gesture outside of imperial discourse: "Conrad's tales and novels in one sense reproduce the aggressive contours of the high imperialist undertaking, but in another sense they are infected with the easily recognizable, ironic awareness of the post-realist modernist sensibility."[4] As these examples suggest, criticism tends to set off Conrad's imperialist complicity against his modernism: if he is not condemned for ascribing to popular notions of racial supremacy and difference, it is because his guilt is mitigated by his formal commitment to ambiguity, fragmentation, linguistic indeterminacy, and other strategies typically understood as modernist.

What is overlooked by both of these approaches is the important way in which Conrad's modernism grows directly out of his conflicted relation to imperialism and its formal tropes. Both of the critical positions I have outlined, that is, fail to take into account the complete interdependence of Conrad's reliance on Victorian imperial literature and the thematic and formal constructs of modernity he develops. What I shall propose in this discussion is that Conrad's particular renderings of modernity – above all, his creation of an alienated masculine voice – derive in important ways from his simultaneous rejection of and dependence upon traditions of imperial narration, and particularly traditions of imperial comradeship. Conrad's texts circulate endlessly around over-determined male relations in the spaces of empire: Marlow and Kurtz; Marlow and Jim; Jim and Gentleman Brown; the secret sharer and his double, to name just a few. The highly charged male encounter becomes for Conrad a palpable sign of a shift within imperial consciousness, a movement out of comfortable narratives of western domination into the dislocations meant to exemplify a new psychic and cultural mode. Conrad inherits from Victorian adventure narratives a sense of the fundamental connection between imperialism and male friendship, but the intense masculine relations he chronicles become disengaged from nineteenth-century super-structures. And this separation of male community from imperial ideology creates powerful images of alienation in his texts, not only as social relationships collapse into solitary struggles, but also as language disintegrates as a bearer of truth. When Conrad revises Victorian conventions of imperial heroics, then, he invests intimacy with a new urgency and initiates a trajectory that leads, perhaps paradoxically, to social and linguistic solipsism (a paradox because intimacy would seem to promise the very antithesis to solipsism). However, for Conrad to reject a world-view in which domestic ideology is neatly linked with homo-social male institutions, and to replace such a system with an iconography of alienation, is not without its own significance. What emerges from Conrad's (hopeless) struggle to retain and invigorate male intimacy is not only alienation, but also a resplendent – if battle-scarred – masculine individual who speaks with a special kind of literary authority.

FRIENDSHIP'S DRAMATIC DEMISE: *HEART OF DARKNESS* AND *UNDER WESTERN EYES*

The creation of empire is inevitably connected with narrative. As a multitude of literary, cultural, and historical scholars have shown, particularly since the publication of Edward Said's *Orientalism* in 1978,[5] English writers of the nineteenth and early twentieth centuries produced a tremendous array of literature, including fiction, poetry, exploratory narratives, polemics, journals, and official texts of imperial policy, that helped to rationalize Britain's global domination. Narratives about empire, and about racial difference more generally, were not isolated to a remote sphere out beyond the reference of the English populace, but reinforced many of the entrenched myths that naturalized and cemented the governing hierarchies of Victorian life. Writing about empire, that is, almost inevitably meant writing about class and gender, encoding into the imperial drama a host of social, political, and psychic relationships at the core of British culture, at home and abroad.[6] Thus the over-determined male bonds at the center of much imperial literature have strings attached: to domestic ideology, to notions of national dominance and identity, to the idea of masculinity, to British self-definition in a broad sense.

The two genres of imperial writing that best situate Conrad's particular investment in male intimacy are the travel narrative and the adventure quest, both of which flourished from the middle of the nineteenth century through the First World War. The boundaries separating these two types of sensational exploratory text are often blurred, as fictional narratives come laden with maps, tables, and layers of truth claims, while travel tales often utilize fictional tropes and styles to increase their popular appeal. Adventure novels by such writers as G. A. Henty, R. L. Stevenson, Rider Haggard, and Rudyard Kipling, and exotic travel tales by explorers such as Richard Burton, J. H. Speke, and H. M. Stanley acquired huge readerships, and spoke very effectively to the English public, especially its young males.[7] As one critic neatly explains it:

the adventure tales that formed the light reading of Englishmen for two hundred years and more after *Robinson Crusoe* were, in fact, the energizing myth of English imperialism. They were, collectively, the story England told itself as it went to sleep at night; and, in the form of its dreams, they charged England's will with the energy to go out into the world and explore, conquer, and rule.[8]

An essential part of this tradition involved the conjoining of heroic exploration with the creation of male community, both within the stories and in their narrative frames. The texts were organized around uncomplicated male relationships, solidified by race and the tradition of conquest. In both novels and non-fictional accounts of exploration, one finds dedicatory and prefatory material harkening backward and outward to predecessors and peers, to the larger imperial community; and in plots, one often finds a "buddy" or comradeship system as a central feature, whether in tales of the sea (from which Conrad's narratives naturally drew), fictional dramas of men and boys facing the myriad trials imaginatively associated with imperial endeavor, or sagas of exploration across the vast array of geographical and political landscapes traversed by nineteenth-century Europeans. The names of Burton and Speke, for instance, were almost inevitably conjoined, as a result of their famous 1857 expedition in search of the source of the Nile, and they seemed to epitomize the idea of exploration as a shared endeavor, even though their actual relationship became one of extreme personal animosity. Half a century later, Cherry's tragic tale of the doomed Scott expedition taps into this convention of linking daring exploration with masculine comradeship. Moreover, the association of travel writing and romance novels with the public schools, male adolescent journals such as *Boys' Own Paper*, and organizations like the Boy Scouts contributed to the atmosphere of masculine community surrounding the literature. This was, in many ways, a tradition of writing by, for, and about men and boys; it included uncomplicated male bonding in its plots; and it attempted to reproduce itself by passing along its rituals to an avid, young readership.

Within this rich field of rhetorical activity, one might delineate a variety of forms of masculine community, a set of repeated motifs and structures that cuts across otherwise divergent texts. One such structure is what I shall call the "imperial encounter." As I have suggested, I find broad resonance in Jameson's rendering of the "pseudo-couple," which he depicts as a kind of half-way point on the consciousness spectrum, a moment of psychic dependency in which the human landscape is swept nearly clean, leaving a narcissistic and solipsistic couple as a kind of eternal, if haunting, remnant of community. Such an image, which will be useful in relation to the psychic structures of war, provides an interesting endpoint as well for Conrad's vexed trajectories of male identification. The world, that is, often seems to reduce itself in Conrad's work to a kind of skeletal frame holding up a mirror for the male protagonist, and one goal of the present analysis is to trace both the legacy and the consequences of that particular configuration. But the imperial encounter in its Victorian context does not presuppose such harrowing outcomes. Victorian texts staged a variety of imperial encounters, and to varying ends: between men of different races, between older and younger selves (to cite just one famous example, Haggard's *King Solomon's Mines* opens with the older retired man looking back on the younger adventurer self), and of course among white imperialists. Typically, imperial literature stages dramatic meetings between men, often at climactic points in the narrative, against brightly canvassed exotic backgrounds. These face-offs can involve a multitude of interpersonal and political configurations. They traverse racial difference and racial sameness, otherness and mimesis. They might function primarily to shore up European dominance, or, alternatively, generate "ambivalence," a moment of disturbance and destabilization in the imperial management of racial difference.[9] Gender will operate in complex ways, as the male face-off calls up everything from homoeroticism to violent homophobia, trafficking in women to the extreme exclusion of all things feminine. Most important, however, is that the imperial encounter typically enacts something important, it *works* for the text as a central psychological, narrative, or ideological event – whether transformative, climactic, reversing, destabilizing, cathartic, or destructive.

Conrad relished the imperial encounter, his texts enact its dramas in ever-elaborating forms, and I shall argue that its fate is centrally tied to his particular exposition of modernity; the fact that this structure was equally tied to the high Victorian account of imperial work will be central to my argument. Victorian adventure writers were fond of the imperial encounter as an organizing principle, and the relations between white imperialists most often functioned to shore up the sense of inevitable western power. More complex and subversive than the norm, however, was Conrad's contemporary Kipling, who also drew on the conventions of the imperial encounter. "The Man who would be King," to take a rather intricate instance, can be seen as a dark, gothic account of a variety of imperial narrative conventions, including the notion of friendship as a tool for imperial rule.[10] "The Man who would be King" tells the story of two ne'er-do-well loafers who succeed, albeit temporarily, in violently assuming control over several villages in the high terrain of Afghanistan. The men, whose governance holds the equivalent moral and theoretical stature of Conrad's Eldorado Exploring Expedition in *Heart of Darkness*, rule as a pair, in a kind of grotesque comedy of homosocial bonding. The turning point in the story, the moment that ensures the white men's ultimate and spectacular demise, comes when one of the men who would be king breaks an oath of celibacy and demands a wife. The structure of homosocial self-sufficiency, linchpin of white rule in Kipling's account, dissolves with the advent of heterosexual sexuality, and the violence that follows (this time against the white male body) is presented in melodramatic, gruesome detail. The would-be rulers of Kipling's story – vulgar, stupid, morally bankrupt – present parodic distortions of what Kipling recognized as a trope of proper white governance, and their reliance on a model of rule-by-friendship is equally exaggerated and obscene.

Perhaps the most influential elaboration of the imperial encounter – an exemplary instance of Victorian travel writing, a work which resonates for Conrad's texts, and an especially useful template for analyzing *Heart of Darkness* – is Henry Morton Stanley's *How I Found Livingstone*, which achieved the status of cultural icon in both England and America. Stanley's work compellingly illuminates *Heart of Darkness*'s complex investment in imperial friendship because, despite Stanley's extreme personal, political, and stylistic dissimilarity from Conrad, the two texts in many ways tell the same story. Originally published in 1872, at a time when narratives of African exploration were extremely popular, in a prelude to the political "scramble for Africa" soon to take off in earnest, Stanley's narrative provides a detailed account of his much-publicized journey through central Africa to find David Livingstone.[11] The journey, which Conrad once denigrated as a "prosaic newspaper 'stunt'" because of its financing by an American newspaper publisher, enacts and narrates a near-archetypal story of white exploration, ethnographical exposition, and self-promotion.[12] Metaphors of darkness and primitivism abound in the description of Africa, which is presented conventionally, as a savage land in comparison with the civilized West, and yet a land that white men can come to know and subdue through the intellectual tools of observation and classification, and the physical tools of western power, primarily the gun.[13] Stanley represents himself as a path-breaking adventurer moving across an awesome landscape of "streams rushing northward, swollen by the rains, and grand primeval forests, in whose twilight shade no white man ever walked before."[14] His is a journey into the world's primal history, where the category of whiteness is all-important and racial ties overwhelm national or class difference: thus when he gazes at a ship with American and English flags hoisted side-by-side, he thinks "I cannot look at them without feeling a certain pride that the two Anglo-Saxon nations are represented this day on this great inland sea, in the face of wild nature and barbarism" (*Livingstone*, 566). In Stanley's value-system, there is no substitute for the physical fact of exploring, no race so fit as the Anglo-Saxon for the task, no man so committed to these values as H. M. Stanley.

The meeting of Stanley and Livingstone – perhaps *the* paradigmatic instance in nineteenth-century writing of the imperial encounter between white explorers – defines the climax of the text, and Stanley creates out of the high-pitched excitement of the face-off a larger message about male friendship in the imperial context. In a trajectory that is both structural and rhetorical, the narrative moves magnetically towards the meeting of the two men, as Stanley closes in on his oft-repeated goal "To find Livingstone" (*Livingstone*, 421). Surprisingly – given the stoicism with which Stanley ordinarily represents himself – at the climactic meeting, he self-consciously lifts a veil to reveal an emotional interior, demonstrating first the depth of his feelings, almost a savagery of his own, and then its inevitable conquering:

And I – what would I not have given for a bit of friendly wilderness, where, unseen, I might vent my joy in some mad freak, such as idiotically biting my hand, turning a somersault, or slashing at trees, in order to allay those excited feelings that were well-nigh uncontrollable. My heart beats fast, but I must not let my face betray my emotions lest it shall detract from the dignity of a white man appearing under such extraordinary circumstances.

So I did that which I thought was most dignified . . . I would have run to him, only I was a coward in the presence of such a mob – would have embraced him, only, he being an Englishman, I did not know how he would receive me – so I did what cowardice and false pride suggested was the best thing – walked deliberately up to him, took off my hat, and said:

"Dr. Livingstone, I presume?" (*Livingstone*, 411–412)

Stanley's exposure of his own momentary enthusiasm (and his suggestion of the variability of national characters, even among the "civilized"
white peoples) is particularly interesting here at the iconic moment of the
text, the scene for which he and Livingstone are typically remembered.
The creation of this tableau, which relies also on the famous accompanying drawing in which the men lift their hats to one another, achieves
several aims at once, all of which involve a larger goal of fostering a myth
of masculinity and male community in the imperial context. In the above
passage, Stanley indicates that western masculinity consists first in feeling
and then in mastering emotion, a lesson that his text reiterates on other
occasions. For instance, at his parting from Livingstone, Stanley is nearly
undone by his fondness for the doctor: "I had to tear myself away before I
unmanned myself," Stanley confesses, and in the end "I betrayed myself"
with tears. Control is only regained when he returns to the task of ruling
over his native team: "'MARCH! Why do you stop? Go on! Are you not
going home?' And my people were driven before me. No more weakness"
(*Livingstone*, 627). The explorer here appropriates conventional aspects of
Victorian femininity – emotion and its careful tempering – as well as exposing homoerotic attachments, even at the moment when he most publicly
performs the role of proper white masculinity (exerting power over the
African subordinates). Far from challenging ordinary gender assumptions,
Stanley's utilization of femininity suggests a certain nostalgia for the strong
gender binaries that mark Victorian narratives of domestic life. If Africa
is conventionally gendered by analogy (the continent is like a woman; its
people are like children; explorers are figures for patriarchal order), Stanley's
text incorporates the image of domestic femininity into the new geography
by internalizing some of its elements.

In the climactic scene with Livingstone, Stanley spotlights the moment
that for him involves the highest stakes: the super-charged meeting of two
white men, against a backdrop of native exoticism. The meeting functions
as a moment of racial consolidation, and it establishes a comradeship that
Stanley implicates in a firm literary and historical tradition. After the initial meeting, Stanley remains for four months with the doctor, a period
that he repeatedly characterizes as a time of joyful and sustaining comradeship. He recites a maudlin poem about friendship – "'And this makes
friends such *wonders* here, below'" (*Livingstone*, 421, emphasis in original);
he admonishes the reader to value such ties, especially in the context of
exploration – "God grant that if you ever take to traveling in Africa you
will get as noble and true a man for your companion as David Livingstone"
(627); and, above all, he stresses the domestic intimacy that the two men

develop over their months together. Repeatedly characterizing Livingstone as a near-heroic figure, whose moral rectitude matches his physical and psychological fortitude, Stanley not only lavishes praise on his new friend, but also concentrates on their close, intimate, domestic life together. All of this reaches a kind of emotional crescendo when the men part, a structural counterpoint to the famous initial meeting, which leaves Stanley saddened, if re-invigorated, for his journey back to the coast.

But the relation with Livingstone is not simply a matter of two men esteeming one another, for Stanley contextualizes their friendship within a deliberately constructed tradition of male adventuring. The creation of such a community actually begins on the frontispiece, where Stanley dedicates his book to James Gordon Bennett Jr., editor of the *New York Herald* (son of its proprietor) and instigator of the journey, presented throughout the narrative as a man of indomitable will. Livingstone, too, is drawn into the circle of Bennett's admirers, as Stanley includes in the text a letter in which the doctor pays homage to the American patron. Financier, entrepreneur, and explorer/missionary are subtly united in a common mission, as the text enfolds Bennett in its community of powerful men, bent on the conquest and "civilizing" of Africa through interlocking connections with one another. In addition to Bennett, Stanley weaves the famous explorers of the past into his masculine mosaic, recalling a tradition of great men in whose steps he follows, as he, in turn, should be followed by others. At one representative moment, not long before the encounter with Livingstone, Stanley looks down upon the lake towards which he has traveled and he thinks of his predecessors, Burton and Speke. Characteristically, Stanley's thoughts turn at this moment to a companion who had retreated exhausted some time earlier, an instance of failed masculinity: "How much would Shaw be willing to give to be in my place now? Who is happiest – he, revelling in...luxuries..., or I, standing on the summit of this mountain, looking down with glad eyes and proud heart on the Tanganyika?" (*Livingstone*, 407). The image of Stanley as surveyor resonates broadly, the scopic power of the explorer strongly contrasting with the feminized former partner, the eagle eyes an emblem of imperial might, the promise of such success an invitation for future travelers.

Stanley's creation of a masculine exploratory alliance is structured in such a way as to involve the (implicitly male) reader in the heroic tradition and in the ideology of exploration. At one point on the return journey, Stanley indicates the form in which the tradition is passed along, as he assumes the allegiance of "Readers of Livingstone's first book, 'South Africa,' without which no boy should be" (*Livingstone*, 601); he also repeatedly refers to his own earlier writings and to other explorers' words. This is a textual community, created and perpetuated by boys and men who read the stories of their heroic predecessors, and pass along their own tales to imagined protégés. Under the protective eyes of Bennett the publisher, the textuality of the enterprise is complete. The omnipresence of news and newspapers in the text reflects not only the journalistic enterprise at the basis of Stanley's journey, but also Stanley's wider emphasis on the creation and dissemination of imperial ideology through the power of textuality. At the same time, the narrative stresses the importance of the physical facts and hardships associated with actual exploration, and mere fiction-making (along with "easy-chair geograph[y]") is attacked: "It is a disease, a mania with some people, that they never can relate the positive, literal, exact truth. Traveling in Africa is adventurous enough as it is, without any fiction" (Stanley, 467, 583). In Stanley's textual community, only true men are entitled to a voice, and their masculinity is developed through the harrowing trials of adventure. Their consolation, in addition to the pleasure of conquest itself, comes in the form of friendship with like-minded men who form a self-perpetuating and mutually sustaining community.

The system of male camaraderie and imperialist justification that emerges from narratives such as Stanley's is the framework sustaining Conrad's work, and its partial breakdown helps to account for many of the social and literary disruptions Conrad registers. *Heart of Darkness* (1899), to begin with the most canonical of Conrad's works, stages the imperial encounter repeatedly, as it adopts, reshapes, and yearns for the traditions of male heroism and comradeship epitomized by Stanley's writing (though not by his life), and the text's core of hollowness and anguish – often theorized as an abstractly epistemological crisis – results from the failure of these moments of male communion to complete the process of social and ideological consolidation.[15] Along the way, Conrad gestures towards an alternative value system that, paradoxically, places the alienated male voice at the center of textual and moral authority.

Heart of Darkness originally appeared in a commemorative edition of *Blackwood's Magazine*, and for all its withering criticism of imperial hypocrisy, the novella is not as ill-placed in the patriotic and imperialist "Maga" as it might seem, in the sense that its commitment to the superconventional genre of Victorian travel writing is critical to its message. Conrad's text relies upon a number of standard features of the Victorian travel narrative, both formal and thematic, many of which involve an interest in masculine intimacy.[16] The text's persistent image of the adventurer moving (anti)heroically across a hostile landscape, struggling against the intransigence of the natural world and interacting with a community comprised of other western male wanderers, represents a direct legacy of nineteenth-century literary forms. Moreover, as many critics have noted, *Heart of Darkness* revels in standard "orientalist" contrasts between civilized and savage, light and dark, European and African.[17] Though critics continue to debate Conrad's position on race and imperialism, it seems undeniable that the evocative and metaphoric force of the story (what one early reviewer termed the text's "atmospherics"[18]) relies on a series of contrasts that are repeatedly undermined and re-erected, confused with one another, entangled. Conrad's deconstructive project depends upon the existence of seemingly fixed differences between Europe and Africa, and upon the charge created when these boundaries become unstable. The notion that "Africa [is] a metaphysical battlefield devoid of all recognizable humanity, into which the wandering European enters at his peril," to use Achebe's language, is a premise and a fascination for *Heart of Darkness*, which purveys the "desire – one might indeed say the need – in Western psychology to set Africa up as a foil in Europe, a place of negations at once remote and vaguely familiar in comparison with which Europe's own state of spiritual grace will be manifest" ("An Image of Africa," 788, 793).

In addition to these much-discussed imagistic and ideological similarities, Conrad's tale borrows structural aspects from his Victorian predecessors, which bear directly on his enthrallment with the masculine encounter. The story is organized, through its frame narrative, as a tale passed along from man to man. The initial narrator claims a kinship with the other men who listen to Marlow's yarn that goes beyond the momentary spell cast by their position on the *Nellie*: "Between us there was, as I have already said somewhere [i.e., in the opening tableau of "Youth"], the bond of the sea," a professional and spiritual bond that also includes the explorers of England's past, "from Sir Francis Drake to Sir John Franklin, knights all, titled and untitled – the great knights-errant of the sea."[19] Marlow, of course, will wreak havoc on many of the narrator's premises. Nevertheless the novella's surrounding apparatus – including the narrative structure, the evocation of England's history of exploration and conquest, and the sense of strong male community – elicits assumptions about the connection between friendship and imperialism that had been codified by texts such as Stanley's.

Like *How I Found Livingstone*, *Heart of Darkness* is a rescue narrative, and it shares that genre's structural orientation around men meeting in the wilderness. It seems almost obvious to note that the super-charged, if painfully slow, journey in the direction of Kurtz provides the structural and emotional climax towards which the novella moves. Though Marlow launches his journey in the name of exploration, that is, he quickly turns towards Kurtz as the practical and psychological goal towards which he travels, stressing that his search for Kurtz is connected with his own "'destiny in life'" (*HD*, 48). And like Stanley before him, for whom friendship with Livingstone was the primary achievement (in the context of a larger community of successful explorers), Marlow treasures his laboriously attained, albeit ambiguous, intimacy with Kurtz. What often gets lost in the critical literature, surprisingly, is this basic feature of Conrad's novella: that the trajectory towards Kurtz represents a movement in search of a specific kind of male intimacy, and its outcome can be understood, at least in part, in terms of the history of such intimacies.

If Conrad follows the Stanley model in presenting a saturated encounter between the men as a foundational and transformative moment in the narrative, the scene when the two men face one another also demonstrates the particular departure of Conrad's text from its predecessors. The meeting is framed by conventional adventure trappings, as horned figures loom in the firelight behind the protective Marlow's back, and it is thus not surprising that when the two finally come face to face, Marlow elevates the encounter as an important moment in his saga. Despite Kurtz's position of utter isolation, Marlow presents his own arrival as the opening salvo in a new male partnership: "'I did say the right thing, though indeed he could not have been more irretrievably lost than he was at this very moment, when the foundations of our intimacy were being laid – to endure – to endure – even to the end – even beyond'" (*HD*, 65). What differentiates Marlow's narrative from the conventional model of men forging their mutual ties against a wilderness backdrop is that his text becomes inconclusive and broken precisely at the moment when he proclaims unbroken and eternal friendship. Marlow's very sentence disintegrates here, and his voice trails off into a vague motion towards the future (what might be "beyond" the "end" remains characteristically vague), suggesting, even as the intimacy is ostensibly being cemented, that the foundations may be as insubstantial as the withered, hollow, and "irretrievably lost" body of Kurtz himself, "'that Shadow'" (*HD*, 65). It is no coincidence, I want to suggest, that Marlow makes one of his famous pronouncements about the inadequacy of language in the context of this unfulfilled friendship: "'I've been telling you what we said – repeating the phrases we pronounced – but what's the good? They were common everyday words – the familiar, vague sounds exchanged on every waking day of life. But what of that?'" (*HD*, 65). This moment of linguistic saturation and indeterminacy – so basic to Conrad's representation of modern dislocation – is brought on by the inefficacy and incompleteness of the over-charged imperial encounter between Marlow and Kurtz.

This scene of disappointed imperial encounter represents only one of several problematic meetings between the male protagonists. In fact, instead of an exciting moment of connection, the text offers us a series of deferred meetings, so that the long-awaited climax is experienced as something of an anti-climax. The scene in the forest transpires at a point in the narrative only after an initial meeting in the ship's cabin, which is described almost in passing. What does receive extensive description is Marlow's first view through his field glasses of the dramatically open-mouthed Kurtz, where the theatrical nature of the spectacle places Marlow in the position of audience rather than actor – the very antithesis of Stanley, who had self-consciously staged himself in the center of the scene with Livingstone. Marlow, by contrast, finds himself in the position of surveyor, still on board his ship, a kind of voyeur into Kurtz's domestic dominion, or a scout in preparation for invasion (more like Stanley surveying the source of the Nile than meeting his future friend).

Moreover, what Marlow sees in his initial scan of the hillside is not a fellow traveler, but shriveled heads on stakes. Instead of two white men creating out of their coming together an affirmation of masculinity and friendship, the text offers one man's encounter with a "'black, dried, sunken...head that seemed to sleep at the top of that pole'" (*HD*, 57). The revelation marks the parodic distortion of the old pattern, a possibility of communion transformed into grim and revolting difference. Where Stanley's narrative repeatedly affirmed that friendship restored life, here the expected moment of visual contact is replaced by death, the destructiveness of imperial rule, and a strong image of African emasculation. The head also reveals the glue that holds together an imperial system of male bonds, as white explorers solidify their power through the death of native people. For all the necromantic and melodramatic appeal of such a spectacle, Marlow's reaction of a backwards jolt is perhaps shared by the reader, trained to expect magnetism between the white men. Although Conrad is fascinated by the imperial encounter and its institutions, he refuses to allow the reader to enjoy its consolations, forcing us, like Marlow, to confront a dead African in the space once occupied by the white explorer *par excellence*.

The formula linking male intimacy with the assurance of an imperial system breaks down in large part because *Heart of Darkness* presents men as profoundly and irredeemably isolated from one another: "'We live, as we dream – alone'" (*HD*, 30). Of course, the isolation of individuals from one another and from a meaningful sense of communal values represents one of the novella's hallmarks, with a symbolic iconography of its own. The blinding white fog that envelops Marlow's steamer, creating a sense of absolute self-enclosure, is perhaps the most striking image of this alienated condition. Kurtz, especially, is presented as a man heroically confronting his own solitude: "'how can you imagine what particular region of the first ages a man's untrammeled feet may take him into by the way of solitude – utter solitude without a policeman – by the way of silence – utter silence, where no warning voice of a kind neighbor can be heard whispering of public opinion?'" (*HD*, 49). Marlow's curious characterization of solitude as a state in which individuals are unpoliced, and his understanding of neighborly community as a regulatory apparatus, helps to clarify what he and this text mean by isolation. This is an isolation from social institutions – not ontological so much as historical. The state, with its policing power, helps to create human interdependence, just as the unwritten rules that govern smaller groups place people in knowable positions relative to one another.

At the same time, in a circular logic, it is the inconclusiveness of crucial moments of communion – the imperial encounters that both structure and disappoint the narrative – that creates isolation. The circularity of this paradigm of loss and more loss is typical of a text that continually locates the origins of its crises in its own discursive ineffectuality. Thus the text both records and perpetuates the problem of alienation as a function of inadequate male institutions. Such a condition of solitude and linguistic failure derives from the loss of stable, reliable relations of male camaraderie, and all attempts to reaffirm the traditional formulas for male community are undermined by the moral collapse of the institutions that traditionally bolster those ties. With the realization that only the frame of this elaborate edifice remains, that the paradigm is hollow to the core, the text works to recreate those connections through the old channels: passing along the traditions of exploration in the form of narrative. This effort occurs not only generically and in the novella's frame, but also at the level of characters in the story. Even Kurtz, who resists the role of heroic Christian explorer, convulsively grasps at conventions of textual and oral communication among men, passing along his experience and (bankrupt) idealism to adoring men like the Russian harlequin, before ultimately disavowing traditional modes of discursive reproduction.

Nevertheless, the tireless Marlow attempts to reaffirm aspects of an evaporating imperial ideology, and he does so by emphasizing male bonds. At one level, Marlow's "idea" that is meant to redeem imperialism comprises such things as efficiency, work, and devotion to one's cause, virtues that are organized around the individual and stem from a long tradition of individualism in English liberal thought (*HD*, 10).[20] At the same time, however, Marlow suggests that his journey is important primarily because it involves the creation of intimacy with Kurtz. As I have already indicated, the troubled effort to establish intimacy between the men can itself be understood, without recourse to a purely epistemological narrative, as one important element in the text's movement into solipsism. Alienation is not an already-existing and fully formed condition in this novel, for we can trace the deterioration of community in the text itself, as Conrad depicts the breakdown of sustaining male networks and friendships. As Avrom Fleishman has argued, a consistent value in Conrad's work is the commitment to a tradition of "organic community," where group well-being is valued over individual heroics: "In a rough generalization, the individualist man projected by Liberal theory becomes in the tropics a conqueror, while the social man idealized by the organicist tradition becomes in action a colonist."[21] Fleishman shows that Conrad admires a self-sacrificing and communal spirit in the colonizer (epitomized by such characters as Lord Jim), but abhors the exploitative machismo of the lone imperialist (such as Kurtz). To depart somewhat from Fleishman's view, we might say that *Heart of Darkness* presents a world in which community is desired but is reduced at best to the thwarted male couple, in effect the pseudo-couple. Characters in the novella periodically attempt to return to friendships that follow the Stanley model, which involves both intimacy between men and a wider economy of male alliances, but what inevitably prevails is an impoverished reduction of partnership. Thus Marlow describes his relation with Kurtz not as a part of a system of male bonds, but in antagonism against the rest of the western establishment, an "unforeseen partnership, this choice of nightmares forced upon me" (*HD*, 67). This image of dislocation from the group – suggested also in the last lines of the novella, when the frame narrator remarks that Marlow "sat apart, indistinct and silent" – is a far cry from the intricately connected, mutually supportive male matrix envisioned by Stanley (*HD*, 76). In Conrad's rendering, the underpinnings of Stanley's value-system have eroded, but the inter-personal geography remains. Conrad focuses intensely on the status and meaning of imperial intimacy when the larger network of male bonds no longer functions to situate and sanctify the friendship.[22]

Up to now, we might say that *Heart of Darkness* has exposed two primary forms for the experience of alienation, both of which are directly related to the diminishing power of Victorian conventions of male fellowship: as a problem of intimacy, whereby men struggle hopelessly to create bonds and connections; and as a crisis in language, such that the endless pursuit of narrative proclaims its own inability to convey meaning or truth, despite echoes of confident traditions for reproducing narrative. Implicit in this discussion has been a third mode, which involves a fundamental gulf between men and women, where domesticity and femininity are banished to their own sphere, embodied by two spectral women.[23] It should be clear that the social structures whose absence so troubles the narrative are largely the province of men, since Marlow believes that women have always existed in their own world, and this status generates no sense of dislocation or crisis: "'It's queer how out of touch with truth women are. They live in a world of their own, and there had never been anything like it, and never can be'" (*HD*, 16). The disjunction between the sexes reaches a culmination in the final pages of the text, where failed male intimacy and the problem of alienation become nearly interchangeable conditions.

Marlow depicts his visit to Kurtz's "Intended" in exceptionally high-pitched language, even by Conrad's generally dense narrative standards. The common feature uniting the symbolic threads of the last scene is Marlow's determination to assert intimacy with Kurtz: his declaration that Kurtz is present in his absence ("'He lived then before me; he lived as much as he had ever lived ...'" [*HD*, 72]) and his distancing of the "Intended" by depicting her as a repository for light, against the men's ties with "darkness," suggest an alliance between the men that Marlow is at pains to capture and to fix. Indeed, the scene represents Marlow's final effort to reinstate a way of understanding male intimacy – his intimacy with Kurtz – that he hopes will ward off the ominous, threatening slide into self-enclosure. Yet this very effort not only dramatizes its own futility, but also, in an increasingly complex cycle, demonstrates that the failure to create intimacy might offer real power – the power of textual authority – to the man who speaks out of such an isolated, distanced position. Clearly, Marlow and the mourning woman compete for Kurtz's memory (as when Marlow usurps her sensation of immediacy – "'for me, too, he seemed to have died only yesterday, nay, this very minute'" [*HD*, 73]) and Marlow's decision to lie to her is very much in his own interest. More importantly, the dialogue directly addresses the sensations of intimacy and distance that permeate Marlow's narrative language. The words exchanged indicate that, notwithstanding a powerful urge to restore friendship, the realization of male fellowship is elusive and its inaccessibility is debilitating.

In response to questioning by the "Intended," Marlow is forced to confront and articulate a problem that has motivated his entire narrative.

Characteristically, he depicts his friendship with Kurtz in ambiguous language: "'Intimacy grows quickly out there...I knew him as well as it is possible for one man to know another'" (*HD*, 73). These words are heavily ironic: at one level, Marlow attempts to make a strong statement about the (masculine) intimacy that defines his memory of the Congo, to clarify his status as friend of Kurtz. Yet his words also cut in the opposite direction, suggesting that it is not possible for men to know one another, that if the ambiguous and tortured partnership between Marlow and Kurtz is the best that can be achieved, then something has gone seriously awry with male relations. After all, the reader knows that Kurtz's vision of the horror was experienced not as a shared moment with an intimate partner, but rather as a terrifying instance of self-dialogue, which Marlow essentially overhears. To know Kurtz has meant, above all, to understand the man's palpable solipsism.

However, if Marlow's comment is both over-determined and inadequate, the woman's response is even further from the mark: "'You were his friend...His friend...You must have been if he had given you this, and sent you to me'" (*HD*, 73). Her language bespeaks an adherence to a conception of friendship and gender that has disintegrated in Conrad's hands. As Sedgwick has demonstrated, the history of male friendship has often been written within a matrix of romantic love; the two institutions are mutually sustaining, and the traditional language of friendship would suggest that Marlow ought to be in a position to inherit the "Intended" from his dead friend, as part of a triangular structure. Yet Conrad depicts the failure of this system, and the consequences within this textual universe are extreme, as each individual drifts menacingly into solitary reverie. Conrad's rejection of domestic ideology in *Heart of Darkness* is intimately connected with the textual urgency to protect and elevate the idea of male friendship, even as he demonstrates that friendship's institutions have lost their viability.

Ultimately, the narrative logic expressed by the "Intended," which is the logic not only of Victorian imperial tales, but of nineteenth-century domestic ideology more generally, is not valid for *Heart of Darkness*. At the same time, its order lingers as a structural trace organizing and motivating the narrative. The confluence and the contrast between the woman's words and Marlow's thus capture a fundamental cleavage of *Heart of Darkness*. If male friendship is an institution connected with the history of imperialism, then its rituals cannot survive the ideological break with imperialism. The text responds to this movement out of a matrix of male friendships by grasping desperately at the remaining possibilities for deep intimacy and partnership, but this extensive attempt to foster communion is equally untenable, and what remains of the elaborate effort is less an assertion of a new contract among men than a final cry in the dark: "'I knew him as well as it is possible for one man to know another'" – that is, as an unreachable, isolated shadow. Marlow proclaims himself Kurtz's friend, which is to say, he is cut off from Kurtz. Nevertheless, he who can utter this solipsistic cry is in a position to inherit a powerful literary and ethical legacy, and to speak, in a sense, for modernity. This status of hard-won friendlessness recalls the close of *A Passage to India*, a novel which, as we have seen, implied that the losses associated with friendship's eclipse have something to do with the experience of living in a historical frame of pause or uncertainty. Even more concretely than Forster's last novel, *Heart of Darkness* replaces an array of inter-connected ideas about gender, empire, and narrative with an ideological and epistemological system in which male intimacy and alienation become dominant markers for literary authority, and in which the dissatisfactions of modernity, including those of disappointed male encounters, seem to offer as their compensation a certain saliency of voice. It would not be true to assert that this voice is entirely a product of the disenfranchisement of imperial intimacy, but it would be accurate to say that the two phenomena are presented as allied, intertwined, and parallel, two forms for expressing a sentiment of what it means to live in modernity.

Heart of Darkness – its content, atmosphere, message, and metaphorics – relies heavily on its imperial setting. Yet I want to consider, for a moment, another landscape that seems far off, but in fact finds a small entry into the African novella: Russia. The Russian character in *Heart of Darkness*, the harlequin who attends Kurtz, plays an interesting role – simultaneously shifty, pivotal, and comic, and his Russianness is not incidental to this equivocality. In a persuasive study, Christopher Gogwilt has argued that Conrad's "double mapping" of empire and Europe involves the positioning of Russia as a limit against which "the West" invents itself.[24] In Conrad's hands, that is, Russia begins its inevitable slide eastward, as this location of imperial power comes to be defined in opposition (rather than parallelism) with what we now almost instinctively call "the West." Russia becomes, with near axiomatic regularity, a location of instability for Conrad, a place whose "easternness" sits uncomfortably aside its power, its location within Europe, and its glorious literary history (Conrad was particularly affected by Dostoevsky, whose plots and characters find many analogies in Conrad's fiction). Critics have long noted the uncertain positioning of eastern and central Europe in Conrad's work, and have connected such issues as national identity, loyalty, protest, and memory with Conrad's own ambivalent national status.[25] The imperial power in nineteenth-century Poland, Russia naturally occupies a problematic space in that story.

In *Heart of Darkness*, a text whose plot and narrative conclusions hinge on issues of male intimacy, the Russian harlequin represents with particular intensity both the longing for and the loss of male comradeship. His obsessive and unreciprocated devotion to Kurtz represents a caricature of the idealized friendships among adventurers that traditional travel tales had valued. He embodies the novella's basic dynamic of friendship unmoored from imperial ideology at the same time that he functions to ironize the very conventions of imperial friendship the text so assiduously maintains. Indeed, the Russian's liminality, symbolized by his patchwork costume and illegible physiognomy, as well as by his national status, makes him a particularly suitable representative of the simultaneous continuity and absurdity of the intimacy ideal. Marlow responds immediately to what he sees as the man's "'destitution, his loneliness, the essential desolation of his futile wanderings,'" an isolation that leads the Russian to worship Kurtz and to hallow their relationship as sublime friendship (*HD*, 55).

Even more striking is the way the Russian adheres to the model of textual community that an earlier generation had assumed. His sentiments about Towson's *An Inquiry into Some Points of Seamanship* are not as extravagant as Marlow suggests, since the book, with its "'singleness of intention, an honest concern for the right way of going to work,'" embodies a type of narrative that in the past was supposed to create community among men (*HD*, 39). When the Russian prepares for "'a renewed encounter with the wilderness'" armed only with tobacco, cartridges, and the book, he in fact carries with him a symbolic repertoire of adventure literature, since the combination of textual community suggested by Towson and the capacity for real power epitomized by the bullets situate him, albeit in caricature, in the landscape of Stanley and his readers (*HD*, 63). Although Marlow seems to miss the point, just as he mistakes the Russian's notes for cipher, he nevertheless responds instinctively to the text's claims on male community: "'I assure you to leave off reading was like tearing myself away from the shelter of an old and solid friendship'"(*HD*, 40). As a representative of Victorian exploratory alliances, the Russian cuts a strange figure, partially eluding the traditional categories and boundaries that sustain the system, and thus demonstrating its cracks and fissures as powerfully as its continued appeal. The Russian harlequin seems to have arrived on the imperial scene simultaneously too late and too early: unable to participate in a Victorian matrix of male explorers, he is equally unsuited to the anguished landscape inhabited by Conrad's more self-consciously modern protagonists.

In *Heart of Darkness*, Russia functions in part to illuminate the vulnerable aspects of a western self-definition that relies on masculine connections to sustain it; even more insistently, Conrad's most deliberately Russian tale, *Under Western Eyes* (1911), circulates around the problem of depleted masculine bonds. *Under Western Eyes* generates a social and personal tragedy out of the shards of failed male friendship. Where *Heart of Darkness* closed by positing the deterioration of romantic triangulation, the later novel meticulously traces the ways in which both domestic ideology and heroic masculinity are casualties of the failure of friendship to produce personal or cultural coherence. As Conrad transplants the action from a geography of imperialist exploration, where we witness the collapse of friendship conventions, to a more ambiguously constructed East–West division, the breakdown of male fellowship is presented as a *fait accompli*, and the text focuses on the powerful and wide-ranging ramifications of this breakdown. Thus, *Under Western Eyes* acts as a legacy to *Heart of Darkness'* traumatic wrenching of friendship from its imperial bed-rock. The novel presents a social, political, and psychic situation in which the collapse of structured masculine intimacy helps to construct both a desperately alienated male protagonist and a rupture in the ordinary functions of gender. As in *Heart of Darkness*, this dual effect opens up a space for a literary voice that derives its authority precisely from its own disconnection.

Under Western Eyes tells the story of one man's betrayal of another man's proposed friendship, and the psychological, social, and literary ramifications of this treason. The protagonist Razumov is taken into the confidence of a fellow-student, Victor Haldin, who confesses to an act of revolutionary violence. Filled with confused rage, Razumov betrays Haldin to the authorities, and the revolutionist is promptly hanged. Subsequently, Razumov meets Victor's sister Natalia, and the two are drawn together by their connection to the brother/alleged friend. At the climactic moment of union, Razumov reveals his true role in Victor's tragedy, and the relationship is destroyed. The rest of the novel moves swiftly to its close, as a mortified Razumov removes himself entirely from the social world. The tale, which takes place variously in Russia and Geneva, is framed and conveyed through the voice of an English professor of languages, whose eponymous eyes meticulously study the characters.[26] This brief plot summary should convey that *Under Western Eyes* pivots on the utter depletion of the structures governing male friendship. Even more spectacularly than in *Heart of Darkness*, we witness the breakdown of the conventional triangular model of friendship, in which a powerful and homoerotic male relationship is conducted through mutual regard and the possession of a woman. The story enacts an ironic reversal of the expected friendship topos, resulting not in marriage, but in hatred, betrayal, and a love story that collapses at its climax.

Conrad connects the vanishing of classic rituals of male friendship and heterosexual romance with a corresponding erosion in literary expectations. This linkage is revealed most strongly through the conceit of the novel's title, as the professor's devouring western eyes witness the rise and fall of conventional romance:

> they seemed brought out from the confused immensity of the Eastern borders to be exposed cruelly to the observation of my Western eyes. And I observed them … And I thought to myself that, of course, they had to come together, the sister and the friend of that dead man. The ideas, the hopes, the aspirations, the cause of Freedom, expressed in their common affection for Victor Haldin, the moral victim of autocracy – all this must draw them to each other fatally.[27]

The professor's sense of imperative – "had to," "must" – derives from the absolute familiarity of this narrative: all three young people inhabit fixed positions in a readily understandable love story, as does the professor, who contextualizes and interprets the histories of the sister, the friend, and the dead man. When the professor lists in elevated language the shared values that he believes make the union between Razumov and Natalia inevitable, he might add the western literary tradition itself, which seems to demand the creation of a couple out of the dead man's friend and sister.[28]

When the result of the climactic scene is not the expected consolidation and cementing of ties, but instead a chaos of dissolution and bewilderment, the secure place within the textual community of a particular literary inheritance is imperiled. The end of the novel conveys a sense that familiar literary consolations have been lost, perhaps never to be recuperated. Razumov ends his life in semi-isolation, a deaf and emasculated recipient of charity; Natalia, whose moral and physical beauty had seemed to mark her out for a life of Victorian motherhood, instead dedicates herself to public works – a Saint Theresa rather than a Dorothea Brooke. Although contemporary readers might applaud this outcome – and, certainly, the unloosing of Natalia from her literary straitjacket seems a silver lining to this textual cloud – Natalia's unmarried situation at the end of the novel, a result of the fissures that surround the primary male relationships in the text, signals the breakdown of literary expectations and commonplaces, a dissolution that cannot quite be naturalized by the professor's repeated allusions to the mystery of the eastern mind.

What intensifies this sense of literary disruption is the fact that it results not from the events in the story, but rather from the conditions under which the story is told. The hatred that led to Razumov's betrayal of Haldin is never explained. In a gesture whose consequences are extreme, but whose cause remains obscure, Razumov simply refuses to be drawn towards Haldin in friendship, rejecting outright the usual framework for male comradeship. Razumov recognizes that for a man with no understandable place in the world, male fellowship holds the best potential for a satisfying return to community, yet he is incapable of sustaining the impulse towards intimacy, and allows the moment of his desire to pass:

[Razumov] embraced for a whole minute the delirious purpose of rushing to his lodgings and flinging himself on his knees by the side of the bed with the dark figure stretched on it; to pour out a full confession in passionate words that would stir the whole being of that man to its innermost depths; that would end in embraces and tears; in an incredible fellowship of souls – such as the world had never seen. It was sublime! (*UWE*, 83)

Even in this vision of sublime and spiritual friendship, Razumov understands himself as a perpetual outsider and outcast, who cannot simply be recruited into a relational model designed to reproduce the nuclear family and its moral values. In frustration, he explains to Haldin, "'You are a son, a brother, a nephew, a cousin – I don't know what – to no end of people. I am just a man'" (*UWE*, 100). At the end of the novel, when the expected unions have been thwarted and traditional gender roles are correspondingly at risk, Razumov's state of disconnection has dispersed itself across the novel's landscape. Razumov becomes a representative of modernity in the text, the rootless outcast, whose isolated status is determined and crystallized by his (unexplained) sabotage of male friendship.

Under Western Eyes posits chaos across a range of relations. The disruption of social forms, which is also registered as a problem for literary conventions, results from the basic and inexplicable absence of friendship in the initial male relationship that opens the narrative.[29] Yet it seems that Razumov's accomplishment of a narrative voice depends on his extreme position of disconnection and his rejection of male intimacy. We cannot, that is, separate Razumov's placement at the end of a comradeship system, like Marlow's before him, from his imperative to articulate his story. Although we read Razumov's words through a series of filters, the novel makes much out of Razumov's compulsion to narrate his tale; his strong desire to confess leads him to self-immolate before the anarchists and also drives him to write the manuscript that becomes the basis of the professor's text. Indeed, if Marlow embodies the desire to recuperate through language a set of institutions that had codified male intimacy – and whose loss has empowered and authorized the male voice – Razumov's literary impulse also derives (in a more attenuated, if desperate, trajectory) from the collapse of male ties. In both *Heart of Darkness* and *Under Western Eyes*, intimacy is superseded by isolation, and an ethos that privileges the endless narration of the tortured life comes to replace an imagined history that relied for its security on the comfortable conventions of male fellowship.

FROM SYSTEM TO SOLIPSISM: *LORD JIM*

Though *Under Western Eyes* transplants the problem of male intimacy onto a European grid, Conrad's texts more typically inhabit the regions of empire, and the imperial encounter is the device that most palpably organizes his treatment of male relations, masculinity, and literary voice.[30] Two basic patterns emerge in the work immediately following *Heart of Darkness*, both of which can be read within the rubric of failed friendship and imperial relations that I have been outlining. One pattern, of which *Romance* is the best exemplar, uses the generic framework of the adventure quest to give form to a chaos of competing intimacies and antagonisms. The intimate encounter between two men expands outward, proliferating into wider and more complicated alliances. I shall discuss *Romance* by way of conclusion. The second pattern functions as the near inverse of the former: here Conrad traces a movement away from standard models of male community, through an encounter with the double, and finally into solitude.[31]

In *Lord Jim* (1900), a fraught and painful movement out of male community into smaller and smaller spaces, culminating in an anguished partnership and then isolation, is presented as part of a larger upheaval in ethical, communal, and literary traditions. After the novel has chronicled the cultural and literary disruption caused by the fracture of one type of male community, it offers a competing system also based on bonds between men, but these are of a qualitatively different sort; even the text's final tragic movement is motivated and structured according to a problem of male intimacy. Thus we can trace three stages of organized male intimacy in the novel, corresponding to an increasing ritualization of relationships and a reduction in scope. The text moves away from an intertwined network of male alliances connected with a particular literary and social past; into an aestheticized system of equal friendships governed by the rules of romance; and finally into a claustrophobic space dominated by the anguished partnerships-in-solitude that also dominated *Heart of Darkness*. The plot of male intimacy – which moves from generalized fellowship (the "bond of the sea," to recall the well-worn phrase) to overdetermined mimesis – in essence becomes the plot of modernity, and this trajectory is constructed in part as a matter of genre.

Lord Jim has typically been read, both thematically and formally, as an echoing statement of modernist anguish over the loss of traditional norms governing thought and behavior. The first four chapters of the novel epitomize the old ideal, rendered nostalgically by an omniscient narrator, as a time when "[a] marvellous stillness pervaded the world, and the stars, together with the serenity of their rays, seemed to shed upon the earth the assurance of everlasting security."[32] Jim's corresponding state of dreamy confidence, fostered by "light holiday literature," will soon be permanently jolted by his failure to live up to the fictional standard (*LJ*, 11). In this classic reading, the new state of dislocation is mirrored by the endlessly intrusive and self-referential voice of Marlow. Marlow's narrative, that is, both represents and describes the breakdown of institutions that perpetuate shared professional values among men, the very basis of stable community. (Whether the style of narration creates or merely reflects the new precariousness is not under discussion here.) So great is Jim's transgression in disrupting a community of like-minded men that even the statuesque and stalwart Captain Brierly loses his will to participate, and hence to live. Although Marlow ruminates extensively on the loss of a "fixed standard of conduct," which had provided the foundation for an economic and social system of sea-faring, he avoids directly addressing underlying economic and political motivations, limiting his presentation of loss and modernity to a vaguely defined ethos about values (*LJ*, 43). Marlow's oft-repeated claim that Jim is "one of us" presents the core of the problem: Jim's crime is important to Marlow because he is "clean-limbed, clean-faced, firm on his feet, as promising a boy as the sun ever shone on" (*LJ*, 36). At the same time, Marlow's need repeatedly to assert Jim's social, racial, and political belonging suggests an anxiety about the stability of the very system that might coherently absorb Jim into its fold. Critics have seized upon Marlow's phrase, which also closes Conrad's 1917 preface to the novel, as a kind of shorthand for describing a system of masculine camaraderie, all-male institutions, and patriarchal values that continued to hold social and psychological power in England at the turn of the century and whose disturbance presents the crux of the novel's tribulations.[33] Yet *Lord Jim* goes further in its exploration of male relationships than merely lamenting the loss of traditional standards of masculine fellowship. The text repeatedly shifts its ground, as the configuration of male relations changes and develops, and this development marks Conrad's increasingly anxious exploration of forms for the organization of intimacy. The dialectic of male relations in the novel is complex and urgent, as Conrad intimates a connection between formal instability and the demise of friendship's structures, and thus between the text's accounts of modernity and its analysis of male intimacy. How, then, does the phrase "one of us" adjust itself in the novel? In what ways do ideals of male community jostle and move?

It is clear that masculine fellowship provides the cohesive glue that holds together the vanishing system whose status is threatened by Jim's failure; more specifically, the male world of the novel's opening is made up of interlocking relations that follow a father/son model.[34] The most direct such coupling is Marlow with Jim, although Marlow also fondly recalls that he has engaged in many other such pairings in his long career. The text is suffused with a nostalgia for an avuncular or paternal presence – a firm hand on the young shoulder – guiding and enabling powerful male relations.[35] This unequal but mutually sustaining tie creates powerful attachments that in turn perpetuate the socio-economic system:

"He was a youngster of the sort you like to see about you; of the sort you like to imagine yourself to have been; of the sort whose appearance claims the fellowship of these illusions you had thought gone out, extinct, cold...

...What wonder that when some heavy prod gets home the bond is found to be close; that besides the fellowship of the craft there is felt the strength of a wider feeling – the feeling that binds a man to a child." (*LJ*, 99)

The language of community is strong here: "fellowship" (used twice), "bond," "close," "wider feeling," "binds." It is the fact of paternalism, rather than a lateral or fraternal ideal, that creates this atmosphere of attachment. Likewise, when Marlow later describes a moment of "'real and profound intimacy'" with Jim, the sensation is produced because the men finally acknowledge their difference in age and status, "'as though his risk set off against my years had made us more equal in age and in feeling'" (*LJ*, 180). The kinds of fellowship and "equal...feeling" that the text so tortuously demands are the product of difference, of an old-fashioned patriarchal system of mentorship and succession. The fact that these are of course not real fathers and sons – this is a model of surrogacy, of metaphor – only strengthens the productive viability of the system, because such surrogates are endlessly reproducible, geographically flexible, fertile and self-perpetuating. We should note, too, the perceptible erotics of such phrases as "some heavy prod g[oing] home," a sexual layering for which Marlow does not quite account.

Despite the intimacy permeating Marlow's descriptions, there is something generalized, or universalized, about the relationships, the actual individuals becoming interchangeable. It is the organization of the relationships into particular shapes that produces powerful bonds and emotions. This is why Jim's appearance remains so important to Marlow, for Jim's look can be described as representative. He creates a sense of similitude (rather than particularity) that stimulates Marlow's attachment to him. Instead of tending towards personalized intimacy, such a communal system generates a proliferation of connections in a potentially limitless chain, a form of continuity suggested by Marlow's allusion to familial reproduction. The problem posed by Jim, then, is precisely that he threatens to block this otherwise infinite extension of ties. The many metaphors of breakage, disruption, and ellipsis that pervade the text in part represent Jim's severing of the chain of continuing and expanding male intimacies that characterized the world before he leapt from the *Patna*.

When this break becomes unpalatable, Marlow and Stein together engineer a shift in relational and plot structures that will rescue Jim without renouncing male intimacy. The new model is organized under the guise of romance. When Stein enters the text and pronounces Jim a romantic, the formal quality of the narrative takes up his suggestion, and offers a tale of love, heroism, and tragedy that is much closer to the generic model of adventure romance than was the chronicle of disappointment that had preceded it. Yet male relations continue to dominate: rather than shifting cleanly from a male world of sea-faring to a romantic one of heterosexual love, the novel retains its commitment to an organizational model that stands or falls on the strength of its intimate male encounters. Unlike the preceding system, which relied on a potentially limitless extension of paternal/filial bonds, however, the new structure is meant to create an inclusive domestic space, whose sanctity is ensured by a regulating system of equalized male partnerships.

Even before Jim leaves for Patusan, the story of Stein's romantic past sets the stage for the ritualized male comradeship that Jim will embrace. Stein's intimate history is best summarized by his own concise, and aptly ordered, description: "'Friend, wife, child'" (*LJ*, 158). The ideal that Stein's past consolidates has been generated by fervent male friendships, cemented by the ties of war; these in turn enable heterosexual love, family, and power. A formidable capitalist, Stein has utilized individual friendships to perpetuate his dominance over a wide trading region. If Stein's initial placement had been ensured through a formal rite of inheritance from his mentor, the position is safeguarded by the practices of friendship, a system comprised of forms, gestures, and a language which create an inclusive whole. Doramin, to give just one instance, is repeatedly characterized as a "'war-comrade,'" and this terminology resonates for its intertwining of military, sentimental, and adventure tropes (*LJ*, 174). Stein's ring provides the most palpable symbol for this ritualized system of male relations, and it swiftly becomes the chief talisman in Jim's Patusan life. The ring had been the central fetish in Stein's adventure past, and he is able to pass on its psychic (not to mention economic) power to his chosen disciple: "That chap Doramin had given him the ring. They had exchanged presents when they parted for the last time. Sort of promising eternal friendship... The ring was a sort of credential – ('It's like something you read of in books,' he threw in appreciatively)" (*LJ*, 174). All of this is self-consciously literary, ceremonial, aestheticized, a world of abstract and beautiful signs, in service of very clear economic and political benefits. Like the marriage ceremony that the ring-exchange resembles, the male rituals idealized here schematize and glorify a relational structure that reaches into many aspects of personal and community life that are never explicitly mentioned in the text.[36]

Jim immediately recognizes and absorbs the ritualism of this friendship world. Further, we can connect Jim's enthusiasm for the literary quality of the system with his youthful adherence to popular adventure tales, which are themselves highly formulaic. Jim's adolescent dreams of becoming a hero along fictional lines are revived: just as the ring is overtly symbolic, so too will Jim transform himself into a recognizable hero/actor. Jim understands intuitively that the whole system depends on friendship, arranged and conceptualized according to an aesthetic model: "I probably didn't realize, he said with naïve gravity, how much importance he attached to that token. It meant a friend; and it is a good thing to have a friend" (*LJ*, 175). Though Marlow adopts an ironic posture towards Jim's enthusiasm, we should not be fooled into thinking Jim excessively naïve. On the contrary, what Jim recognizes is that, having failed in the patriarchal system of the sea, which depends upon a commitment to specific values within an ordered male community, his only chance for success is to submit himself to a different framework of masculine relations, this time organized by romantic practices of lateral fellowship.

Jim's friendship with Dain Waris is the result. The text presents the relationship in highly sentimental language, "like something you read of in books," as Jim might say. The men become friends because they are a match. Their relationship has a structural basis, and, once again, is sealed by the tokens of romance. When describing the young men, for instance, Marlow becomes exceptionally idealistic: "I seemed to behold the very origin of friendship. If Jim took the lead, the other had captivated his leader. In fact, Jim the leader was a captive in every sense. The land, the people, the friendship, the love, were like the jealous guardians of his body" (*LJ*, 195). It might seem odd, given his enthusiastic tone, that Marlow finds the "very origin of friendship" in structures of power and captivity. It is as if his language indicates a truth about these ritualized bonds that the speaker recognizes only unconsciously: under the aegis of a beautiful equality, serious discrepancies in social and political status are masked.

This aestheticizing of inequality is at the heart of Jim and Dain's friendship. Hence the oft-quoted description of Dain Waris' attained whiteness:

Dain Waris, the distinguished youth, was the first to believe in him; theirs was one of those strange, profound, rare friendships between brown and white, in which the very difference of race seems to draw two human beings closer by some mystic element of sympathy. Of Dain Waris, his own people said with pride that he knew how to fight like a white man. This was true; he had that sort of courage – the courage in the open, I may say – but he had also a European mind. You meet them sometimes like that. (*LJ*, 195)

As in *The Broken Road*, the text here flirts with the idea of disrupted mimesis: almost white, but not quite. Dain Waris and Jim function as mirror images of one another; their gestures are often described as parallels, as when Jim leans on his elbow to listen to Tamb' Itam, "just as Dain Waris had done," and this structure of parallelism recalls a history of young male analogues with echoes as far back as Homer (*LJ*, 301). Yet for the two men to be united, a "mystic element" must be asserted, as if to suggest that even such near-equivalence cannot quite overcome the text's discomfort with a friendship that flouts both geography and race. What most effectively joins the two is class, as Jim and Dain Waris share class-based qualities that naturalize and justify leadership. Yet Jim's shining whiteness make him "tuan," even with reference to his almost-equal, and this organized inequality creates a potential fault-line in the relationship. Apparently unshaken, the text handles the tenuousness of cross-racial sympathy by relying on a staged, romantic style that transforms any sense of individuality into a kind of gestural dance, thus limiting the threat of disruption that might result from Dain Waris' uncomfortable nearness.

The difference between the mimetic, troubled partnerships that dominated *Heart of Darkness* and the idealized sympathy between Dain Waris and Jim is that the latter is governed by the literary rules of romance. The text returns, for a time, to a belief in the power of male friendships to help organize a set of social relations that are stable because hierarchies of race, gender, and inheritance are contained. As in *Under Western Eyes*, where the functioning of male friendship and the status of literary traditions were allied, so here, the novel connects an imagined literary past with a social order that idealizes friendship. Although the new system still relies on comradeship, it looks markedly different from the "fixed standard of conduct" that had organized Marlow's world. I have said that the paternal/filial structure that creates "fellowship" is meant to extend infinitely in a chain of substitutable relations. Here the model becomes domestic: fraternally understood bonds between men mask fundamental racial differences, and this aestheticized relation safeguards a self-enclosed family unit, which banishes the rest of the world to the outer edges of its strict, if penetrable, borders. The Patusan section of the novel is replete with metaphors of isolation, exclusion, walls, lines, boundaries, enclosures, and it also offers the interesting figure of Cornelius, whose emphatically marginal status highlights the structure of borderlines that governs Patusan life.

I have been describing a transition in *Lord Jim* that points to a larger problematic in Conrad's work. An inherited masculine culture has been placed at risk; both the problem of its eclipse and the hope for renewal are connected with the creation of viable forms of male community. In *Lord Jim*, the trouble begins when a masculine economic and social system is threatened. The endlessness of its connections, from (metaphoric) father to son *ad infinitum*, is ruptured, and the practice of narration changes accordingly. The text then shifts into a contracted domestic space, which is nevertheless based on a ritualized system of male interactions. Heterosexual love and its appropriate fictional forms can only develop in the context of masculine relationships oriented around shared class and scripted roles. The text insists that Jim's ample shoulders should carry the weight of a woman's happiness, a larger domestic unit, and beyond that the organization of an entire community: all of this, in turn, depends upon the proper functioning of aestheticized male friendship.

Not surprisingly, the demise of the Patusan romance is precipitated by an imperial encounter and signaled by the death of the friend. The relationship between Jim and Gentleman Brown, like the latter's class prefix, offers a caricature of the mimetic male order I have been describing. The ragged and ruthless Brown is presented, like Dain Waris, as Jim's double. As with the earlier relationship, this new one takes place in a theatrical and symbolic setting. With the stream running between them, the two men face one another, and, in a classic imperial encounter, they find that their similarities to one another become magnified by the difference of the orientalized landscape around them. Jim's relation to Dain Waris had been based on an idealized (in)equality, where racial and political hierarchy were masked by an imagined class compatibility. When Brown enters the scene, the impulse towards sameness becomes irresistible, as Jim is drawn almost instinctively towards his distorted mirror image: "And there ran through the rough talk a vein of subtle reference to their common blood, an assumption of common experience; a sickening suggestion of common guilt, of secret knowledge that was like a bond of their minds and of their hearts" (*LJ*, 286). The call of race becomes all-powerful, and Marlow's phrase, "one of us," seems to ring and resonate in the background, with a newly disturbing valence.

The Gentleman Brown episode dramatizes two critical points. First, it marks the culmination of a movement into smaller and smaller spaces of male community. If cohesiveness and group loyalty were always at the heart of sea-fellowship, nevertheless the world before *Patna* was characterized by extensiveness, an endless chain of fellows. This system breaks down, but the music of romance is available to orchestrate a renewed pattern of male relations, this time organized around a (nearly) enclosed domestic space. The natural end-point of this trajectory is a solipsistic partnership, where two slips imperceptibly into one: the classic modern image of the isolated soul – Jim as "a speck, a tiny white speck, that seemed to catch all the light left in a darkening world" – thus comes to predict a slow movement through succeeding forms of male intimacy (*LJ*, 249). There is an irony here: at each stage, the friendships are based on greater degrees of sameness, until Brown arrives as Jim's virtual double. This increasing parity would seem to offer a view of intimacy, if not harmony, yet the reverse is true, as the increasing sameness or narcissism leads to internally directed violence. The movement out of filial organization towards lateral, fraternal bonds, which would seem to promise increased equality, in fact creates partnerships that collapse into self-dialogue. The old system of paternal/filial relations ensured its own reproduction; these new models are destined for implosion. Hierarchy, it seems, leads to reproduction, equality to self-destruction.

The second trajectory that finds its culmination in the Brown encounter is the Stanley/Livingstone prototype. We have seen that in the high Victorian tradition, the climactic meeting of the explorers was understood as the centerpiece of a wider matrix of male friendships, disseminated through texts. Here that encounter is staged, but, as in *Heart of Darkness*, it is a parody of the former trope, an exposé of the ugliness and brutality that underlies the relation between men whose connections are formed by imperial adventure. Rather than cementing ties of masculine community, it destroys the fragile peace that Jim's friendship with Dain Waris had enabled. The ever-symbolic ring, having been removed from Dain Waris' dead finger and dropped on the floor, now comes to represent the collapse of the whole system. At the level of genre, what is happening is that the romance is being de-coupled from the imperial travel tale. Rather than forming a cohesive whole, bringing together the delights of romance with the ideology of empire, and thus sustaining an embedded structure of male homosociality, the two generic types come to represent opposing world-views (though both depend on male friendship) which cannot co-exist. The framework of the imperial encounter loses its cover, and its racial underpinnings are exposed as utterly destructive, if irresistible. The call of race destroys – rather than upholds – a system of love, friendship, family, and colonial power. Gentleman Brown's sputtering and desperate narrative, endured with disgust by Marlow, appropriately represents the new style of imperial textuality.

HOMOEROTIC HEROICS, DOMESTIC DISCIPLINE: CONRAD AND FORD'S *ROMANCE*

Lord Jim and *Heart of Darkness* would seem to indicate a tight relation between the problem of viable male community and what we might call imperial modernity. Conrad's works continually return, in varying configurations, to the notion that a self-consciously modern sensibility might grow out of failed imperial friendships, and to the problem of the depleted structure of adventure romance. A collaborative novel with Ford Madox Ford (then Hueffer) presents perhaps the most spectacular instance. *Romance* (1903), as its title suggests, deliberately places itself within the formal and thematic universe of the popular adventure fiction of the nineteenth century, and is correspondingly replete with over-determined, often sensationalized, male relationships.[37] Two different narrative tendencies direct the action – one involving the lure of male interactions in the colonies, the other involving the strictures of the domestic love plot – and, by tracing them, I hope to demonstrate that there is a constitutive relation in *Romance* between the end of imperial homoerotics and the beginning of a new and harrowing condition of modernity. Out of the death of the nineteenth-century romance hero, this nostalgic and generically self-conscious novel starkly depicts the emergence of a modern, urban subject. In *Heart of Darkness* and *Lord Jim*, Conrad laments the loss of institutions of masculine fellowship; in *Romance*, the urban establishments of justice, whose power and ruthlessness are daunting, replace the longed-for spaces of male social organization with their own rigid and alienating processes. It is in *Romance*, then – a collaborative effort, and one of Conrad's and Ford's least-read novels – that the excavation of modernity out of lost male comradeship becomes most stark, direct, and uncompromising.

In *Lord Jim*, the usage of romantic conventions seemed almost axiomatically to invoke highly ritualized forms of male friendship, and, along similar lines, for Conrad and Ford to entitle their novel *Romance* was immediately to conjure up a myriad of charged possibilities across the homosocial spectrum. I have been focusing on friendship conventions in the (anti)heroic explorer mode, epitomized by imperial encounters between white, patriarchal men, engaged in the morally suspect project of imperial conquest. But the exoticism of the East, broadly and loosely defined, is of course highly elastic. As we have seen in the context of Forster's representations of the embodied and sexualized Orient, by the end of the nineteenth century, life in the "contact zone," to borrow Mary Louise Pratt's suggestive phrase, presented European readers with a seething site of complex erotic possibilities among men.[38] The notion of romance unites the promise of a masculine adventure tale, whose antics might be expected to cover the familiar homoerotic terrain of late-century orientalism, with a chivalric love story, embedded in the quest tradition. Indeed, generically self-conscious from first to last, *Romance* delivers a dizzying array of heterosexual romantic tropes within a fantastical homoerotics of the high seas. The text teems with masculine desire, intrigue, and rivalry, all the while enacting a ritualistic love story, according to highly formalized outlines. A reader today, armed with insights from both queer theory and masculinity studies, might find in this overlooked novel rich evidence of late-Victorian Britain's penchant for imagining masculine eroticism under the legitimizing sign of imperial geography.

Yet what differentiates *Romance* from other narratives that produce familiar imperialist, homosocial effects is the brutal directness and self-consciousness with which Conrad and Ford chart a trajectory away from the relative comfort of exotic male adventure into a harrowing form of modernity. I have pointed towards such a pattern in a variety of Conradian texts; in *Romance*, the movement becomes starker, more elemental, a product of politico-economic forces. As it looks back to a lost literary and social past, whose disappearance is presented as a casualty of a dawning twentieth-century capitalism, the novel imagines and indicts the global reach of a new economic and national order. In starkly depicting the emergence of a modern, urban subject out of the death of the nineteenth-century romance hero, this apparently backward-glancing novel helps to demonstrate how the idea of the modern was created and theorized by practitioners of modernism. If *Romance* steers clear of the formal experimentation associated with both of its authors, it engages directly with the problem of the individual's helplessness, passivity, dejection, and alienation under the regime of twentieth-century Englishness.

Perhaps the most peculiar element in *Romance*'s fantasy is its elaborate reverence for the feudal past. Beginning with simple matters of plot, the text's own romance involves an imaginative return to a moment when a decidedly pre-modern economic and social system held dominion. The novel's narrator and protagonist is John Kemp, grandson of an earl, who finds himself connected through his sister's marriage with an aristocratic Spanish family. It is Kemp's seduction into the Riego family's drama of decline, as the family's status as a great economic power in Cuba comes under increasing threat, that engenders the narrative of his adventures. Kemp will eventually carry off and marry the heiress Seraphina Riego, last survivor of the old clan, after rollicking escapades involving pirates, kidnappings, incarcerations, near-starvation, and over-determined male enmities. Seraphina provides the necessary link, the object of exchange that enables the British Kemp to inherit not only the family's fortune, but its symbolic power.[39] The novel goes to great lengths to highlight the conventional paradigm whereby men who love one another marry the appropriate sisters or cousins, thus perpetuating international kinship networks and consolidating power within the old families. The Sedgwickian structure of exchange is showcased here, conjoining marital ties with baldly economic motives. As critics have abundantly demonstrated, the imperial location of such forms of desire serves to naturalize excess in general and masculine eroticism in particular. In his study of male literary collaboration and homosexual "double talk," Wayne Koestenbaum offers a reading of *Romance* that stresses the compatibility of homoerotics with the imperial imagination: "Although Conrad and Ford depict empire as morally murky," Koestenbaum writes, "[t]he 'Romance' that so sways [the protagonist] and his authors is a homosexual love affair, a literary genre, and a nimbus of attractive degeneracy surrounding fantasies of English power."[40]

Far from masking the process of woman-exchange that fuels the system, *Romance* extravagantly stages it, drawing attention to its ancient and ritualistic quality, as well as its glittery homoerotics. Most striking for its display of both homoeroticism and economic anachronism is a resonant scene at the death-bed of Seraphina's cousin Carlos, in a fabulous Cuban palace under siege. Although in this scene Kemp technically takes an oath with Seraphina, at her cousin's behest, symbolically it is the men who are joined. Carlos, whose "unearthly fineness" casts an aura over the hushed and darkened room, places an arm around Kemp's neck and Kemp pledges his honor.[41] In the text's symbolic universe, Carlos has always represented the exotic, his appeal heightened by a sense of continuity with the feudal past, and the staging of him in his bed exaggerates both his aristocratic status and his effeminate beauty:

You might well have imagined he was a descendant of the Cid Campeador, only to look at him lying there without a quiver of a feature, his face stainlessly white, a little bluish in extreme lack of blood, with all the nobility of death upon it, like an alabaster effigy of an old knight in a cathedral. On the red-velvet hangings of the bed was an immense coat-of-arms. (*R*, 129)

If Carlos embodies romance and exoticism in Kemp's imagination, such otherness is partially elided by the whitening and disembodying effects of his illness, which draw the two men together not only erotically but racially. Even more importantly, racial difference in the men's relationship is bridged by a class-based ideal of chivalry and honor, an exaggerated form of the class linkage that also united Jim and Dain Waris, revealed at the death-bed exchange in all its formality.

The novel's infatuation with an idealized and theatricalized aristocracy is bolstered by a vitriolic animosity, on the part of Kemp, towards work. Given Conrad's habitual investment in "efficiency," the era's watchword for productive labor, such a violent stance against work comes as something of a surprise. Even before Kemp reaches Cuba, the text associates romance with escape from the drudgery of ordinary labor, presented as both futile and emasculating. These sentiments in no way accord either with the standard work ethic associated with late nineteenth-century Britain, or with the conventional Victorian representation of colonial labor as an elided province that invisibly produces wealth: "I was tired; Romance had departed. [The planters] represented all the laborious insects of the world; all the ants who are forever hauling immensely heavy and immensely unimportant burdens up weary hillocks, down steep places, getting nowhere and doing nothing" (*R*, 51). The young Kemp's invective against labor in part illustrates his surly adolescence, but it also establishes what will become one of the text's primary concerns: a condemnation (albeit in a tone of resignation) of the relentless dehumanization produced by capitalism. Even in these early pages, Kemp intuits capitalism as a system in which workers become insects, labor is despised, and the individual's psyche is fundamentally shaped by his alienation from his own productivity.[42] By contrast, the Riego family, with its enormous contingent of slaves and servants, embodies an ideal of inherited power, sheltered from the body's labors, just as the palace presents a site of calm tranquillity in the midst of chaos and political upheaval. Indeed, as the description of Carlos' death-bed suggests, an aura of somber quiet pervades the giant house, as if movement itself has been suspended, the body rendered nearly obsolete.

If an aristocratic world order is the object of Kemp's and the novel's rueful desire, such a goal is naturally defined by its unattainability. For all the family's fading splendor, death and loss – loss of power, prestige,

relevance – are the order of the day at Casa Riego. Not only are the old patriarch and his heir dying before our eyes, but the extreme anachronism of
the entire establishment trumpets its status as relic. For Kemp, the problem
of loss is attached, above all, to the great dream of romance, and the text
repeatedly characterizes romance as that which one constantly desires but
can never realize. "Journeying in search of romance," Kemp theorizes, "is
much like trying to catch the horizon" (*R*, 62). More interesting than this
repeated lament over romance's intangibility is the text's conflation of such
nostalgia with a sense of mourning over an idealized masculine body. As
Koestenbaum argues, the spaces of romantic adventure in *Romance* teem
with male beauty and physicality, in vivid contrast to an England of emasculated and ineffectual men. Yet even at the very site of such seemingly
virile masculinity, the space itself signifies its own death, and indeed functions less as a thriving alternative to the dilapidation of Europe than as a
hardened fossil: "The general effect of the place was of vitality exhausted,
of a body calcined, of romance turned into stone. The still air, the hot
sunshine, the white beach curving around the deserted sheet of water, the
sombre green of the hills, had the motionlessness of things petrified, the
vividness of things painted, the sadness of things abandoned, desecrated"
(*R*, 157). The state of romance is connected with the physical health of the
body, suggesting that masculine enervation results when romance and its
literary forms have declined. If the shining male body is the centerpiece of
the romantic experience, and if the genre of adventure worships at its altar,
then the "now" of the narrative (Kemp's writing as well as the authors')
recognizes the inevitable failure and "desecration" of that ethos.

Even more than the deserted beaches of Rio Medio, where the Riego
family holds its diminishing court, the city of Havana symbolizes for Kemp
an imaginary, lost past of heroic and venerable masculinity:

I penetrated into the heart of the city.
　　And directly, it seemed to me, I had stepped back three hundred years. I had
never seen anything so old; this was the abandoned inheritance of an adventurous
race, that seemed to have thrown all its might, all its vigour, and all its enthusiasm
into one supreme effort of valour and greed...With what a fury of heroism and
faith had this whole people flung itself upon the opulent mystery of the New
World. Never had a nation clasped closer to its heart its dream of greatness, of
glory, and of romance. (*R*, 455–456)

Kemp creates out of Havana a location to embody his exact idea of romance,
where the "fury" of passionate men discovers a goal that lives up to their
desires, a form of work that engages, rather than erases, their manliness.[43]

Yet, as standard orientalist tropes demand, such a Havana is firmly "past and gone below the horizon," and the contemporary city is presented as a pale shadow of its former self (*R*, 456). Nevertheless, if the present fails to achieve the standard set by the romantic past, the city does offer thrills of masculine community and antagonism notable even in this already steamy male saga. In Havana, Kemp's adventures reach a fevered pitch of homo-erotic and homosocial complexity, as he moves from the crowded streets where men ogle, jostle, and combat one another, to an especially sexualized and over-determined prison term. In contrast to London, where the tale will conclude, the urban nature of Havana is inextricably bound both with its atavism and with its fostering of homoerotic delights.

Romance then, thrives specifically as fantasy. Or, more accurately, in order for Kemp and the novel to perpetuate the mystique of romance, they must consistently repress the facts of history. Thus the novel enacts a kind of competition, in which romance consistently works to obliterate important political, economic, and social realities. On one hand, the text sketches a complex political situation, involving conflicts among English colonialists over slavery in Jamaica, the relation of Spain and Mexico to England, and, perhaps most central, the claims of Ireland against imperial England. On the other hand, Kemp repeatedly distances himself from these political disturbances, insisting that the politics of empire hold only minimal interest for his story. Indeed, Kemp's goal seems to be to divest the entire field of imperial difference and inequality of any reality, aestheticizing and generalizing all such troubling relations. Here, for example, is Kemp's rumination on the contact between the aged patriarch of the Riego family and his life-long slave:

At times he bent towards his master's ear. Don Balthasar answered with a murmur: and those two faces brought close together, one like a noble ivory carving, the other black with the mute pathos of the African faces, seemed to commune in a fellowship of age, of things far off, remembered, lived through together. There was something mysterious and touching in this violent contrast, toned down by the near approach to the tomb – the brotherhood of master and slave. (*R*, 143)

While such language may seem absurd to the point of parody – and I shall take up the larger question of parody a little later – Kemp's willful desire to make all relations among men into forms of aestheticized "fellowship" or "brotherhood" characterizes his entire narration. We can hear the familiar attributes of romance in the evocation of "things far off, remembered, lived through together," as if slavery itself has become the stuff of romance, one more dying form, sadly consigned to the retreating past.

Most central in the text's aestheticizing mission is the relation between Kemp and his arch-rival, Patrick O'Brien. In a text that valorizes a fading aristocracy, the centrality of O'Brien's national and class identity can hardly be overstated, setting him off in stark outlines. He represents a new and hated form of power, achieved through piracy, ruthlessness, and deceit, rather than inheritance, and symbolized by the rag-tag horde that does his bidding. Yet, for all his villainy, O'Brien makes a compelling case for his actions on political and national grounds. Proclaiming himself a rebel and a victim of English injustice, O'Brien defiantly challenges Kemp and his associates in the name of national revenge: "'I would die happy,'" he asserts, "'if I knew I had helped to detach from you one island – one little island of all the earth you have filched away, stolen, taken by force, got by lying…'" (*R*, 196, ellipsis in original). O'Brien's trenchant critique of the hypocrisy of imperialism would seem to position him as a spokesman for uncomfortable truths, perhaps for history itself. However, in keeping with its overall movement, the text, through Kemp's voice, insists on reframing O'Brien's claims as part of the larger romantic picture. His words are depleted of their specificity, de-historicized and generalized in a way that weakens any sense of England's imperial culpability. Thus Kemp stresses eternal categories of difference, insisting that "we were cat and dog – Celt and Saxon, as it was in the beginning" (*R*, 89), or again, "There we were, Irish and English, face to face, as it had been ever since we had met in the narrow way of the world that had never been big enough for the tribes, the nations, the races of man" (*R*, 196).

When the text transforms the enmity between the two men from a specific instance of colonizer and colonized into a historically generalized encounter between "the races of man," it not only weakens the ideological impact of O'Brien's revolt, but also re-invigorates the category of the homoerotic, which thrives, in this text, in the realm of fantasy rather than history. As in the "brotherhood of master and slave," the conflict between the men revives at the moment when moral complexity is eradicated (Kemp is once again the hero, O'Brien the villain). In a movement that recalls the shift from friendship to solipsism in *Lord Jim*, the antagonistic relation between Kemp and O'Brien comes to represent the successor to Kemp's formalized and heavily eroticized bond with Carlos, and the men's rivalry over Seraphina replaces the smooth exchange enacted earlier at Carlos' death-bed. Not surprisingly, given O'Brien's status as Carlos' replacement, Kemp's immediate response to his enemy's death is an instinctive cry of loss, couched in the language of morality: "I almost wished him alive again – I wanted to have him again, rather than that I should have been relieved of him by that atrocious murder" (*R*, 492). Kemp's visceral desire to re-vive his tormenter represents an essential feature of their ongoing enmity. His consistent and irrational proclivity to save O'Brien's life (an other-wise puzzling feature of the narrative) is not so much a plot-generating device as a token of the text's driving impulse to generate homoerotic pas-sions and homosocial rivalries. Suppressing history brings the homoerotic to life, and the elusive, ever-disappearing sphere of romance provides the setting.

Moreover, it is not only the text's primary rivals who are featured in such a structure; a whole host of intertwined masculine relations, too numerous and complex to recount here, flourish under these romantic conditions. Among the many male ties that swarm around the novel's central oppo-sition, however, one figure holds particular interest for this inquiry: the faithful servant Tomas Castro. This enigmatic, dour Spaniard, bandit-like in appearance but defined by his overwhelming loyalty, comes to serve Kemp as a kind of bodyguard. As he resignedly explains, "These [were] Don Carlos' orders. 'Serve him, Castro, when I am dead, as if my soul had passed into his body'" (*R*, 208). In this rich transfusion of male loyalty from one body to the next is presented the epitome of a system of masculine ties that has no clear counterpart outside the sphere of romance. At the same time, Castro's fidelity in no way compromises his masculinity, embodied with symbolic resonance by the knife blade that lodges permanently in the place of his lost hand. To have the phallic Castro as companion is to exist at the apex of a fellowship-obsessed world, where the politics of loy-alty and leadership are understood entirely in terms of contested masculine relations, essentially unmoored from other social structures. Men in this system occupy near-archetypal roles – friend, rival, servant – and inhabit specific sites or institutions where their bonds are formally organized.

Yet the position of Castro, whose style is as exaggerated and histrionic as his dagger-hand, inescapably brings up the question of parody. How serious, we might well ask, is any of this? Isn't the whole sphere of wildly homoerotic intrigue a kind of mock-romance, and isn't our naïve narrator an object of satire, rather than the mouthpiece for his sophisticated authors? Certainly, the text repeatedly veers towards the absurd in its characteriza-tion of the homoerotics of adventure romance, moving even further than *Lord Jim*, which had painted in ironic colors Jim's credulity towards Stein's scripted romanticism. Most obvious as parody is the depiction of Kemp's stay in the Havana prison, where the ludicrous and the homoerotic join hands. In the inner sanctum, among the prison's elite, the caricature of aristocratic ceremoniousness combined with homoerotic rhetoric reaches a fevered pitch, under the direction of a fanatical and theatrical prisoner, who repeatedly invokes his fellow inmates as "'a band of brothers'" and "'kindred spirits'" (*R*, 484). Even the sentimental Kemp recognizes the extreme incongruity of the man's outsized formality, since "his gestures, made for large, grave men, were comic in him. They reduced Spanish manners to absurdity" (*R*, 484). Traditional homosocial rituals of the sort elaborated in the novel up to now (lavishly homoerotic and deliberately formulaic) are here conjoined with an aping of elevated gestures, suggesting perhaps that the whole fantasmatic of the text has likewise been parodic.

I would argue, however, that while the authors display an ironic sensibility through much of the narrative, and while at times they point the finger at Kemp for his *naïveté* in adhering to a youthful notion of romance, nevertheless the text ultimately takes seriously the sense of nostalgia that Kemp repeatedly expresses for a past of homoerotic, aestheticized fantasy. Conrad and Ford quite self-consciously engage the issue of genre, beginning with their choice of title, and the end of the novel – indeed its literal last word – continues to hail "Romance" (*R*, 541). Their idea seems to be to produce a form they simultaneously parody and embody, a familiar modernist move. While a level of debunking remains part and parcel of this strategy, the text also generates pleasure out of its own excess, seeming to revel in its very anachronism. Biographically, we might also note that Conrad, in desperate financial straits at the time of *Romance*'s production, saw the novel as a potentially lucrative endeavor, given the continued popularity of the adventure story at the turn of the century.[44]

More important than genre, however, in assessing the text's seriousness about its own thematics, is the increasingly desperate tone of the novel in the final section, which stages a marked shift from the depiction of imperial geography to the characterization of England as a stifling place of modern repression. Ultimately, Kemp is returned to England under compulsion, in a solitary confinement that contrasts with the sociality of the Cuban prison and prefigures his eventual treatment at Newgate. There are, in other words, two types of narrative logic at work in the text, which ultimately conflict with one another. The first is governed by Kemp's romantic desires, which I have argued involve homoerotic infatuation and the fantasy of an aristocratic escape from both work and history. This paradigm relies upon a tendency to recast colonial power relations into an abstract, aestheticized, narrative of masculine competition, and at times points towards the parodic. The second and oppositional logic involves the development of a textually satisfying love plot. Kemp and Seraphina must emerge as a new and dazzling couple, the product of chivalric endeavor. This second plot-line, which provides the culmination and conclusion of the text, eviscerates any sense of play or parody, functioning instead as a chastening reprimand, a repudiation of the many fantastical possibilities presented by the notion of romance.

Throughout the Caribbean portion of the novel, Kemp's romantic saga has held in balance two structures, a homoerotic set of entanglements and a heterosexual love story, each of which involves its own sedimented traditions. If the homoerotic fantasy depends upon the notion of aestheticized and temporal romance, for the Seraphina story, Conrad and Ford resuscitate an even more fatigued set of literary conventions: Kemp the knight must rescue the princess Seraphina; the two young lovers are like Adam and Eve; the exotic southern woman is brought to the safety and stability of England. Kemp himself frequently and overtly conjures up this literary history. "She was the first woman to me," he intones early in their story, "a strange new being, a marvel as great as Eve herself to Adam's wondering awakening" (*R*, 158). In conventional fashion, Kemp asserts that his specific passion in fact surpasses its literary forebears, since Seraphina "was more to me than any princess to any knight" (*R*, 251). Finally, despite much talk of wonder and marvel, it is England that represents the ultimate home for lovers, the place where young romance can come to fruition. In Carlos' words to Kemp, "'I would like best to see you marry my cousin. Once before a woman of our race had married an Englishman. She had been happy. English things last forever – English peace, English power, English fidelity. It is a country of much serenity, of order, of stable affection...'" (*R*, 150, ellipsis in original).

Yet there are two key features that differentiate the conventional love plot from its masculine counterpart. First, Kemp is finally unwilling to give up the latter in favor of the former, requiring a form of force to tear him away from the terrain of romance. For all his protestations of desire for an English life with Seraphina, he continually thwarts that possibility, prolonging his time abroad and repeatedly sabotaging his own success. And second, while the homoerotics of empire remain fundamentally at odds with the life of home, the heterosexual, chivalric story finds an appropriate counterpart in the text's closing image of the domesticated couple. Or, to put it slightly differently, what *Romance* shows is that the onset of twentieth-century modernity forces the logic of homosocial adventure into conflict with the very narrative it is supposed to engender – the love story – and, when this rupture emerges, the romance hero must be compelled to grow up into a hetero-normative, passive, English subject.

Hence Kemp is returned to England a prisoner in irons, stripped of his identity, and deposited in a miserable, solitary cell in Newgate. The contrast with colonial prison life could not be more striking. In his Caribbean adventure, Kemp's imprisonments form part of a rich fantasmatic experience, but back at home, a modern form of subjectivity is required, and it finds its institutional setting at Newgate:

the whole of the outer world, as far as it affected me, came suddenly in upon me – that was what I meant to the great city that lay all round, the world, in the centre of which was my cell. To the great mass, I was matter for a sensation . . .

All those people had their eyes on me, and they were about the only ones who knew of my existence. That was the end of my Romance! Romance! The broad-sheet sellers would see to it afterwards with a "Dying confession." (*R*, 511)

Kemp's understanding of his own place in a national, cosmopolitan, mass culture resembles Benedict Anderson's influential model of national identity as constituted by the anonymity and homogeneity of print culture.[45] Kemp senses that he is being transformed by the twin operations of textuality and incarceration, and his efforts to resist such manipulation are infused with a sense of futility.

Such a shift in the concept of national identity comes in the context of a sustained loss of paternal authority. As Koestenbaum notes, paternal power in *Romance* is in dire straits: Kemp's ineffectual, weak, and ultimately irrelevant father symbolizes a large-scale failure in the structure of familial power. In the Caribbean portion of the novel, young men battle among themselves for the *de facto* leadership of an empire whose dying patriarch retires increasingly into the background. In England, it is the impersonal apparatus of the state – the British naval authorities in Cuba, the prison and its guards, the magistrates' court – that re-affirms the power of patriarchy despite the loss of paternal viability. Thus the novel stages a movement out of inherited models of filiality (which recalls, in a sense, the opening setting of *Lord Jim*), through a moment of delightfully excessive fraternal animosity and desire (suggested also in Patusan), and finally into a system whereby the overwhelming power of the state triumphs not only over men in their competitive activities, but over the very notion of individuality (something new and unprecedented in the Conradian texts I have discussed up to now).[46]

Even before the final section of the novel, ominously entitled "The Lot of Man," there have been suggestions that what is finally at stake for the text is the nature of power itself, the fate of the individual at a moment when fundamental structures of economic, military, and political power are in flux. For instance, the text begins – and the romance plot gets underway – with a rather confusing depiction of the competition between an established cadre of smugglers (provocatively called "Free Traders") and the king's runners, the official organs of the state. Here in County Kent in the early decades of the nineteenth century, the novel suggests, the question of power has not yet firmly been decided in favor of the state, as highly organized, underground systems of economic and social order battle directly with the king's representatives. Though "of late the smugglers themselves had become demoralized" (*R*, 12), and though at the time of writing the authors can take for granted the eventual triumph of the imperial state, nevertheless the novel begins with a look backward to a moment when the totality of unified national control might still have been resisted, in fantasy at any rate. Thus, if the novel cannot be said to perform a rigorous analysis of politico-economic development over the course of the century, it nevertheless presents in bold strokes the increasingly visible and formidable nature of consolidated power at century's end, an unprecedented system of global order that promises to remain both fearsome and totalizing.

The contest over fundamental structures of social and economic order is not confined to England itself, as suggested by the novel's preoccupation with the problem of piracy, the text's central crime. O'Brien and his pirates wreak havoc on the Admiralty's ships and men, and Kemp's indictment, for which he is nearly hanged, involves the confusion of his identity with that of a notorious pirate. Piracy provides a particularly appropriate form of outlawry for this novel, since it conjoins conventional romantic imagery with a serious consideration of the developing hegemony of the British Empire abroad and the English government (firmly committed to hanging all convicted pirates) at home. Indeed piracy – with its direct assault against England's central imperial weapon, the navy – offers an interesting form of stubborn resistance against the hardening structures of imperial organization across the globe. Like romance itself, piracy is presented here as a disappearing form of rebellion against the utter dominance of the English nation state.[47]

Such dominance makes itself known, once and for all, through the institution of the magistrates' court. The isolated and alienated prisoner faces an impersonal institution whose primary function is to uphold ideological and practical principles for safeguarding colonial trade.[48] In the face of such impersonality and capitalist motivation, Kemp turns to the central form through which the individual traditionally constitutes himself: language. "If there were to be any possibility of saving my life," he recognizes, "I had to tell what I had been through – and to tell it vividly – I had to narrate the story of my life; and my whole life came into my mind"

(*R*, 532). Language and the power of individuality – celebrated icons in liberal thinking, and of course in the history of the novel – contest directly against the official embodiment of state power. What goes on trial with Kemp in the final pages of the novel is both the viability of the homoerotic romantic self and the notion of individual protest. Gender, too, enters the court in complex symbolic shapes, as Kemp confronts figures who embody a variety of contemporary gender stereotypes. Indeed, we might say that the liberal subject itself, gendered and textualized, is on trial, posed against a state whose driving motive has become unabashedly economic.[49]

During the trial, Kemp's mangled and bloody hands provide the most resonant symbol of his over-determined struggle to assert both individual integrity and some form of viable masculinity. His torn body offers a palpable sign of his emasculation, of the damage perpetrated by the massive cultural forces against him, including, at one desperate moment, himself: "I smashed my hand upon the spikes of the rail in front of me, and although I saw hands move impulsively towards me all over the court, I did not know that my arm was impaled and the blood running down" (*R*, 530). Despite a certain resemblance to Christ in the ripped hands, Kemp's increasingly restricted and damaged physical body becomes primarily a token of his feeble protest, of his vulnerable and pitiful stature in relation to the massiveness of the state's power. Further, the spike on which Kemp impales himself recalls Castro's spiked hand – the sign, I have argued, of the phallic power accompanying male companionship in a world organized by intertwined relations of comradeship and enmity – and the shift is significant: far from controlling fidelity and male fellowship, Kemp has been forcefully removed from that promise, sacrificed to the demands of a particular legal and literary logic. Indeed, his release from prison results not from his narrative of self-exoneration, but rather from the timely production of formal validation, submitted to the court by a naval officer. Far from elevating his status, Kemp's resonant performance at the trial showcases his isolated and caged position, his mutilation and impotence in the hands of a power structure that enforces its own formula for individuality and identity.

The magistrate's final words indicate what such a concept of Englishness entails: "'You have suffered much, as it seems, but suffering is the lot of us men. Rejoice now that your character is cleared; that here in this public place you have received the verdict of your countrymen'" (*R*, 540). In the magistrate's world, official procedure, national identity, gender differentiation, and a Christian narrative of obedience unite to constitute an idea of the self that will not be over-ruled. To be a man is not so much to range heroically over colonial geography, nor to narrate the self in compelling language, but to suffer complacently at the hands of the state, and to receive the stamp of masculine individuality through a ritual of public recognition. Perhaps most striking is how immediately and entirely Kemp comes to accept and internalize the court's position, notwithstanding his fitful efforts at rebellion and protest. Thus, in the last pages of the novel, Kemp echoes the magistrate, proclaiming that "suffering is the lot of man...suffering, the mark of manhood, which bears within its pain a hope of felicity like a jewel set in iron..." (*R*, 541, first ellipsis added). Masculinity becomes a matter of endurance rather than an aestheticized contest among men; even the metaphoric jewel is imprisoned in iron, an image that recalls Kemp in shackles aboard the military ship.

If Kemp's theatrical performance had seemed to represent an effort to combat the hegemony of a court bent on flaunting its power, such performativity is now rendered as obsolete as romance itself:

I remember the intense bitterness of that feeling and the oddity of it all; of the one "I" that felt like that [resignation and despair], of the other that was raving in front of a lot of open-eyed idiots, three old judges, and a young girl. And, in a queer way, the thoughts of the one "I" floated through into the words of the other, that seemed to be waving its hands in its final struggle, a little way in front of me. (*R*, 533)

As in Kemp's earlier depiction of his Newgate cell at the center of modern culture, here he offers a somewhat distanced and objective assessment of the modern self as a new product, a being whose emergence is as inevitable as it is painful. The modern "I" to emerge out of the old forms will no longer attempt to protest against its placement in the power structure that has constructed it. It welcomes its imprisonment, its passivity, even its own death.

The counterpart for the new Kemp is quite clearly a domestic Seraphina. The last paragraphs of the novel, which describe the reunion and happiness of the pair in their comfortable English life, are rife with images of death, strangulation, and lassitude, and thus dramatize both Kemp's unacknowledged regret for lost homoeroticism and his complete internalization of the lessons taught by the court. Seraphina herself is characterized by a tendency to suffocate:

The whole world, the whole of life, with her return, had changed all around me; it enveloped me, it enfolded me so lightly as not to be felt, so suddenly as not to be believed in, so completely that that whole meeting was an embrace, so softly that at last it lapsed into a sense of rest that was like the fall of a beneficent and welcome death. (*R*, 541)

Heterosexual life embraces Kemp into death; its processes are silent and soporific, its future absolute. With its direct recollection of the earlier depiction of Newgate, the language here establishes an unbroken continuum from the debilitating imprisonment of mass culture to the strangulation of modern domesticity. Kemp complacently understands this continuity in stasis as "the little heap of dust that is life" (*R*, 541).

One striking feature of Seraphina's position at the end of the novel is how smoothly it has been created out of her earlier role as conventional romantic heroine. Unlike Kemp, who must be forcibly transformed from anachronistic romancer into modern subject, Seraphina's status within domestic ideology is presented as a natural outgrowth from her earlier scripted role. No doubt such continuity derives from her consistent position as object – of exchange, desire, rivalry. As we have seen, the novel follows two oppositional directives, neither of which takes much account of Seraphina as an individual in her own right. The first directive involves a masculine world of adventure, characterized by the fantasy of a lateral matrix of male connections and a nostalgically rendered feudal world order. The second substitutes state power and its institutional apparatus for the fantasy of self-made male communities, and insists on a rigid form of national, anti-individualist, heterosexual identity that conveniently supports an expanding capitalist economy based on trade. Although the love plot ultimately requires that the adventure romance be abandoned and the male hero returned home, Seraphina herself is strangely absent from all of these movements; she neither colludes with nor resists the cultural systems in which she exists. Indeed, as romance heroine she had essentially been acted upon, and, perhaps because of this conventionally passive position, her transformation into a modern domestic woman is rather uneventful, a change of scene but not of subjectivity.

In *Romance*, the connection between lost worlds of male fellowship and twentieth-century alienation is binding. *Romance* fantasizes about an imagined past in which masculine relations of friendship, rivalry, and desire helped to shape the social order, and it posits an image of modernity in which the male individual is escorted firmly out of such a world, to be deposited instead in a national culture that makes no place for male intimacy and has no tolerance for resistance against global capitalism. Both of these modes – the homoerotic romantic as well as the alienated modern – remain entirely male, dependent on gender differentiation and the occlusion of any sense of female subjectivity. Despite its apparent focus on the past, *Romance* fundamentally asks what it means to be modern, how to conceptualize essential categories of identity and desire under an intractable system of totalizing culture. The answer seems to imply that to be modern is to assert the masculine self paradoxically as lost, dying, anachronistic. And inevitably, the narrative logic and authority that accrue to such a para-doxical masculinity fall under the rubric of irony. It is irony then – the irony of constructing masculinity out of disempowerment, status out of depletion – that provides the only form of viable narrative authority under the bleak conditions of urban modernity.

In what sense does *Romance*'s treatment of lost worlds of male fellowship provide an appropriate culmination for the Conradian tradition I have been discussing? In *Heart of Darkness*, *Under Western Eyes*, and *Lord Jim*, Conrad suggests that the breakdown of male friendship as a cultural and literary convention contributes to a revitalization of literary authority, but also to a resounding sense of isolation; yet these images of alienation and ineffec-tuality have been relatively disconnected from the operations of industrial modernity. In *Romance*, by contrast, an urban judicial machine – the very embodiment of nationalized modernity – becomes the central agent pro-pelling the shift out of masculine fraternal bonds into isolated, domestic lethargy. At a formal level, however, *Romance* would surely be called the least innovative, the least modernist, of the texts in question. Representa-tions of modernity and the construction of literary modernism would thus seem to be moving in opposite directions, as a deliberately anachronistic novel offers up a harrowing vision of the way its own obsolescence generates a new and terrible condition. Or, to put it another way, we might say that those texts which work to engender the literary fractures associated with modernist authority do so, at least in part, with a spirit of ambivalence, documenting, for instance, the movement from male groups to isolated men, yet still in a sense holding on to the resonance of the conventions whose eclipse they dramatize. The literary authority that continues to at-tach to figures like Marlow and Conrad himself might be said to derive, in part, from this continued connection with a visibly vanishing past. In *Romance*, there is a good deal of nostalgia, but the reverberating power of imperial or domestic narratives of male love seems long departed, and the figure for modern masculinity that emerges at the novel's close is utterly passive and unprepossessing, a figure not for literary or narrative power, but for literary and narrative erasure.

CHAPTER 3

"My killed friends are with me where I go": friendship and comradeship at war

In the West, the story of war is almost always a story of male bonds. Whatever war may mean for a culture, whatever terrible losses it may entail and whatever troubling instincts it may invoke, it nevertheless is fought and lived as a matter of male relationships, and these powerful ties are often highly valorized, both by the participants themselves and by the home culture that will be responsible for interpreting and assimilating the war's legacy. An emphasis on comradeship seems nearly axiomatic in the European and American imaginary about war, and has been registered in many media – painting, sculpture, fiction, poetry, film – in the context of the twentieth century's major conflicts. As Paul Baümer in *All Quiet on the Western Front* expresses it, "They are more to me than life, these voices, they are more than motherliness and more than fear; they are the strongest, most comforting thing there is anywhere: they are the voices of my comrades."[1] The huge conscripted armies of modern war seem particularly to invite an emphasis on intense masculine friendship, in part because those armies, with their enormous scale and their capacity both to inflict and to suffer extreme violence, present a challenge to the self-concept of the societies they are meant to represent and protect. The friendships associated with combat become important because they humanize and temper the terrible ferocity of war, injecting into mass warfare a hint of the culture's values: loyalty, love, community, sacrifice, valor.

For the British, the First World War brought the issue of war's masculine intimacies quite urgently into focus, and, with respect to the cultural history of male friendship I have been tracing, the years of combat and its aftermath represent a culminating point. Culmination in two senses: first, the dreams and drawbacks about male community that marked both imperial and classical traditions found new life in the experience of the war, where the fantasy of organizing sociality around male bonds became the reality of lived existence, and hence its status, legitimacy, and resolution acquired an unprecedented importance. Because the prospect of a masculine world, with its own structures and rituals, now dominated the actual existence of millions of men, both the redemptive and the destructive aspects of such a model became central problems to absorb, contest, dismantle, protect, and, of course, narrate.[2] These projects took many years to unfold, as the culture wrote and rewrote the experience of combat, and hence the literature that attends the problem of war-time comradeship was produced and published not only from 1914 to 1918, but also over the course of the following two decades.[3] Culmination, too, in the sense that the male bonds that had dominated during the war seemed to promise trouble for the post-war civilian scene. As I shall discuss in the next chapter, the combination of heightened expectations about comradeship in the trenches and the massive physical injury to emerge from the conflict eventually forced a reckoning with some basic issues about intimacy, fellowship, and the body.

I shall make two central points in this discussion, both of which aim to unsettle the most recalcitrant commonplaces about war and male friendship.[4] First, in unraveling the complex knot of ideas that surrounded male relations during the war, I hope to demonstrate that comradeship did *not* function as the culture demanded, and that this failure generated a particularly resonant form of anger and bewilderment. In the official language of the war, comradeship was meant to sustain the soldier, to provide the possibility for heroic action, to redeem the horrific suffering that the war endlessly inflicted. Yet one of the basic facts of the war was that it destroyed friendship. Thus the bracing imperative to organize and stabilize masculine intimacy became a futile enterprise, desperate and debilitating. The crushing problem of male intimacy functioned to coalesce a number of discourses surrounding masculinity and the male body in the war period, but it could not ultimately resolve the contradictions inherent in the different visions of male unity that the war generated. It is this tragic paradox about the impossible demands for intimacy during the war that fueled both popular and canonical writers and continued to engage the post-war imagination. Accordingly, my second overarching point is that the figure of the bereaved male friend – whose persona is, in a sense, constituted by the loss of war mates – becomes a representative of the war *par excellence*, and that post-war disconnection and disillusion is often articulated specifically in terms of the creation and loss of powerful friendships. War writers created an icon who ceaselessly asserts, in Sassoon's words, "my killed friends are with me where I go," and this voice will continue to haunt the literary scene during the years of high modernism, and will hold broad resonance for a half-century of writers and critics.[5]

As in other cases where the organization of intimacy is invoked, the conception of friendship I shall develop here neither banishes nor reduces to the homosexual. The war's urgent language about male love presents a complex set of personal, social, and institutional conflicts, where the homosexual body is linked with other forms of masculine vulnerability and protest, and I shall resist the temptation to isolate homosexuality from this thicket of male bonds. If homoerotic desire flourishes in the war's settings, and if war literature is rife with contradictions about the status of physical intimacy, this is not to say that such desire perforce functions to subvert or challenge dominant gender forms. While there may be theoretical appeal, that is, in arguing that the war's flamboyant all-male theatrics trouble the smooth narrative of (hetero)normativity, I find that the protean shapes of male relations during the war do not conform to a structure of gender deviance.[6] Ultimately, the homoerotic in this discussion will become almost an institution of its own, as war writers imagine forms of intimacy that thwart civilian definitions and categories.[7] The imperative to express extreme and challenging forms of male communion motivates a variety of war texts, as writers develop rich strategies to transform the culturally fraught idea of friendship into a unifying social structure that will have the power to protect male bonds, even as those bonds are relentlessly threatened by the realities of war. It is precisely this saturated, over-determined, and impermeable quality that impels friendship both to withstand the war and to scar the men who proclaim themselves its representatives.

WAR DISCOURSE: FRIENDSHIP AND COMRADESHIP

Now, the war, at any rate on the Western Front, was waged by Battalions, not by individuals, by bands of men who, if the spirit were right, lived in such intimacy that they became part of one another. The familiar phrase, "a happy Battalion," has a deep meaning, for it symbolises that fellowship of the trenches which was such a unique and unforgettable experience for all who ever shared in it, redeeming the sordidness and stupidity of war by a quickening of the sense of interdependence and sympathy. (B. H. Liddell Hart, 1933)[8]

In these exemplary lines, a First World War officer and influential military historian elaborates the widely held view that during the war, male friendship provided the stable anchoring point for a world in crisis. If there is anything to be salvaged from the wreck of trench warfare, surely it is to be found in the powerful comradeship of the troops. For Liddell Hart, fellowship redeems the "sordidness and stupidity" of war, transforming an obscene expense of human life and material resources into a spiritual rebirth.[9] The intimate relations between men are imbued with a religious ethos, and comradeship absorbs the transcendence traditionally associated with Christian self-sacrifice and patriotic duty. In accordance with the dominant morality of the public schools and other such institutions, Liddell Hart privileges corporate identity over individuality, assigning the highest value to "interdependence," "sympathy," and the gradual intermingling of men who become "part of one another." Further, embedded in Liddell Hart's assumption about the positive implications of a world organized around the male group is the belief that comradeship in war functions as the primary replacement for such traditional locales of social order as the school, the church, and the family. So self-sustaining are these "bands of men," and so mutually intertwined, that their community seems to trump the ordinary civilian structures and hierarchies. Yet, Liddell Hart is careful to present this shift as a function of the extremity of war, rather than a sign of social deterioration: friendship does not so much threaten the family and civilian society as improve them, providing a moral guide-post for an implicitly inferior home culture. Liddell Hart's assertion that masculine comradeship provides the only sustaining relation in a time of moral and physical degradation seems blithely to sweep aside tensions that ordinarily inhere in such relations – tensions involving the body, the individual's conflict with the group, the troubled relation of tradition to modernity. Yet despite these important internal conflicts, this image of a devastating war redeemed by the intimacy nourished among its combatants became something of an accepted truth during and after the war.

Many war writers shared the conviction that comradeship provides the moral uplift demanded not only by a horrific and gruesome front-line experience, but also by a damaged and beleaguered culture, and they praised war's bonds in warm and heart-felt terms. The memoirist Sidney Rogerson, for instance, elaborates in *Twelve Days* (1933) the suggestion that comradeship in war provides an exemplary relation on which the imperfect ties of peace might be based: "In spite of all differences in rank, we were comrades, brothers dwelling together in unity. We were privileged to see in each other that inner, ennobled self which in the grim, commercial struggle of peace-time is all too often atrophied."[10] Rogerson creates an idealized picture of social organization within the battalion, invoking the concept of comradeship as the catalyst for a cross-class harmony that civilian life palpably lacks. Lauding the power of comradeship to overpower and contain class conflict, Rogerson elides the complex social differences and hierarchies that in fact marked army existence.[11] Where peace-time culture involves exploitation and the worst kinds of inequality, Rogerson believes that the fellowship of war is based on the higher capacities of men to value one another for their "inner, ennobled" qualities, transcending the impediments of class stratification, individual personality, and what Rogerson reckons to be the selfishness of the capitalist psyche.

This transcendental emotional connection comes with a strong pedigree, as Rogerson's language taps into a ready ancestry of masculine fraternity, aligning the war's friendships with great and revered historical precedents. He praises the "absolute trust" of men for their officers, and admires "the love passing the love of women of one 'pal' for his 'half-section'" (*Twelve Days*, 60). The use of working-class argot here interestingly intersects with the elevating Biblical sanctity of the David and Jonathan narrative, suggesting a modern updating. The reference to the love between Jonathan and David, so common in war literature as to be almost a *cliché*, quite clearly sanitizes and elevates male bonds, and of course helps to shut women out of the emotional universe of war, since a wide range of emotional responses to love and death is captured in the all-male reference. Moreover, Rogerson circumscribes any potential for such a highly valued and eroticized form of male intimacy to disrupt other kinds of loyalties, by allying soldiers' homoerotic love with a list of conventional and sentimentalized middle-class values. To this end, he compares war-time male bonds with the men's "filial devotion" to their "aged mother[s] back in the slums," their "kindliness" towards "wretched mangy French dogs," and finally their respect for "the German wounded and prisoners" (60). The men's capacity for traditional attributes of pity, their potential for civilian leadership, is heightened here in relation to a list of almost parodically powerless objects: old women, starving dogs, and subdued enemies. For Rogerson as for Liddell Hart, comradeship occupies a double position with respect to culture: it provides the sole possibility for transcendence in the grinding existence of soldiers, and it makes these relations the fulcrum for an enhanced and improved civilian value system.

In such writing, a central precept is that the memory of war-time male unity will survive the war, and this further demarcates the special power of comradeship, especially for those reconsidering the war many years later. In an unpublished memoir entitled "Wheels of Darkness," composed as late as the 1980s, R. G. Dixon maintains that comradeship provided the core value of the war years, which are otherwise depicted as "a hell of all-pervading corruption, of terrible and soul-appalling futility."[12] For Dixon, the tragedy is that the transcendence of comradeship has gradually evaporated with the passage of time: "I know for myself that I have known no such comradeship as those old years gave to us who fought on the old

Western Front. As the years go by... there are fewer and fewer of us left who knew that comradeship... [which] implied a faithfulness even unto death to one's fellows, and this is no empty thing" ("Wheels of Darkness," 88). In a memoir characterized by riveting language that forces the past into a present immediacy, these lines stand out for their insistence that comradeship is consigned irrevocably to the past, to an uncapturable, by-gone era. One senses that comradeship belongs to the realm of nostalgia; its status is protected, safely embalmed. The notion that war fellowship cannot properly be conveyed to a new generation pervades this language, and Dixon would seem to regret that the power of comradeship was not more effectively incorporated into post-war culture.

This emphasis on the ineffable quality of the war's loyalties touches a primary creed in war literature, from rough diary notes to canonical poetry: the inexpressibility of war experience, the impossibility, and at times also the undesirability, of conveying the exact quality of the war to non-combatants.[13] If the central problem for war literature is to find a language adequate to the horror, unfamiliarity, and incommensurability of the front lines, such a challenge certainly characterizes the effort to represent war's intimacies. War friendship thus resurrects the kind of double-talk that marked much homoerotic literature in Victorian and Edwardian Britain.[14] In both cases, the impossibility of speaking about male intimacy requires the writer to create a new and cryptic language, often by invoking the historical and literary antecedents that had typically sanctified "the love that dare not speak its name." During the war, the familiar tradition of using elevated language (whether Biblical or Hellenic) to suggest the in-expressibility of connections between men became increasingly common, providing a shared vocabulary for widely divergent texts, where the precise nature of male love remained blurred. Yet there are important differences between the kind of inexpressibility described by writers like Dixon, and the aestheticist, Paterian conventions enumerated in Chapter 1. If decadent critics of the *fin de siècle* had invoked both classicism and the trope of purity beyond words in order to negotiate a space within a punitive culture, war writers experienced the problem of inexpressibility as part of an extreme and ubiquitous failure in language. As the standard critical narrative has it, war writers had to contend with intense and disorienting conditions across the perceptual and epistemological spectrum, a kind of erasure of recognizable signification. In the case of personal relations, the problem of inadequate language is registered by a sense that it is impossible to translate into civilian terms the richness and precariousness of these new ties. For Dixon, what gets lost in the shift to language (a shift in time as well as space) is not the sexual content of male intimacy, but what he views as its spiritual transcendence and its incompatibility with peace-time notions of male love. Memoirists like Dixon insist that war friendship cannot be described because there is no non-combatant language adequate to its particularity, its sanctity, and its compelling memorial persistence.

Such a conflation of ideas about the bonds of war – elevated, powerful, yet almost outside of language – became connected during the years of combat with poetry, often the preferred form for rendering trench experience, and, more broadly, with a self-satisfied attitude about England's mission.[15] In an introduction to a successful 1917 anthology of war poems, E. B. Osborn characterizes comradeship in terms of both inexpressibility and transcendence, and suggests that the verse in his collection will touch the private experience of intimacy as well as a larger national spirit. For Osborn, friendship not only redeems war, but wins it: "In the new sense of comradeship, which is the secret of our victorious warfare, and is an underlying motive of many of these poems, and explicit in but a few (being almost too sacred for an Englishman to write about) rests our best hope for the England that is to be."[16] Friendship, nationalism, purity: these constitute three intertwined features of a war-time ethos to be elaborated in verse. Despite the awkwardness of Osborn's claims about the simultaneous presence and absence of the language of fellowship, his introduction stresses the compatibility of male intimacy with the projects of war, empire, and family. These poems are designed to contribute to the war effort, to offer solace and to revive a sense of national purpose; friendship here falls squarely on the side of the war. More specifically, one reason that writers like Osborn can place comradeship in an uncomplicated hierarchy with other social and personal relations is that such texts do not allow for conflict between individual intimacy and group solidarity. In the example with which I began, Liddell Hart's celebration of the fellowship inherent in war's organization, the writer moves comfortably between images of the personalized intimacy of individuals and the corporate identity of a "happy battalion."

Yet such an easy continuum from the personal to the public generally runs into trouble in First World War literature, as a tension between these two distinct types of loyalty often creates the central problem or crux in war texts. In other words, the relation of private friendship to the structure of the group is vastly more complex than some war writers would have us believe. I want to focus more closely on this distinction, to define and name a phenomenon of disruption that has gone unnoticed by critics. Although nearly all war writers and current critics use the terms "comradeship" and "friendship" synonymously, it will be helpful, in order to put pressure on these concepts, to set up a distinction: I shall use the term "friendship" to apply to individualized relations of amity or love between men and "comradeship" to refer to a corporate or group commitment, a relation particular to war and typically described in elevated language. In his war novel *Her Privates We* (1930), Frederic Manning provides a useful demarcation of the differences between these notions of friendship and comradeship:

"No," he said finally. "I don't suppose I have anyone whom I can call a friend. I like the men, on the whole, and I think they like me...I have one or two particular chums, of course, and in some ways, you know, good comradeship takes the place of friendship. It is different: it has its own loyalties and affections; and I am not so sure that it does not rise on occasion to an intensity of feeling which friendship never touches. It may be less in itself, I don't know, but its opportunity is greater. Friendship implies rather more stable conditions, don't you think? You have time to choose. Here you can't choose...At one moment a particular man may be nothing at all to you, and the next minute you will go through hell for him. No, it is not friendship. The man doesn't matter so much; it's a kind of impersonal emotion, a kind of enthusiasm, in the old sense of the word."[17]

Where many writers either unconsciously or deliberately confuse the personal with the impersonal, Manning takes great pains to expose them as separate and conflicting. For Manning, voluntary choice remains the defining feature of friendship. In contrast, comradeship is attached to the endless substitution of one man for another, to the individual's loss of power over his environment, and ultimately to the horrors of mass conscription and modern warfare. Although in the passage Manning presents the reproducibility of comradeship in terms of its connection with heroism – a positive attribute of the war – the threat of interchangeability troubles his novel, as it does many war texts. The distinction between friendship and comradeship signals the difference between a world that valorizes the individual and one in which human beings become fodder for a voracious war machine.

In the case of Manning's novel, the conflict between the experience of personal intimacy and the reproducibility of comradeship provokes the text's central dilemma. The plot traces the narrator's bond with two men; over the course of the war, each of them is lost (one to injury, the other to death), and, at the end of the novel, a new man steps in heroically to save the narrator's life, instigating a new cycle of friendship. The novel finds itself torn between two ways of understanding this process of producing intimacy. On one hand, Manning honors the capacity of men to retain faith in human relations and to act selflessly, even amidst the devastating grief, continual hardship, and mechanistic nightmare of the war. On the other hand, the fact that the mere structure of men's mutual relations can create new bonds and intimacies disturbs a text that remains fundamentally committed to the ideal of transcendent individuality. If friendship is supposed to mark the site of a personal, emotional investment on the part of soldiers, then its applicability to all men who inhabit a particular structural position indicates that the very concept has lost its viability.

Taking seriously Manning's distinctions regarding the fundamental difference between friendship and comradeship, the question becomes, what is the relationship in war discourse between these two modes of male connection? Does First World War literature address Manning's fear that, with the loss of individuality, intimate friendship degenerates into mass-produced comradeship? In the texts discussed thus far, with the exception of *Her Privates We*, friendship and comradeship have seemed mutually sustaining. But in much war writing, such a concept of complementary friendship and comradeship cannot be imagined or sustained. Different forms of male loyalty may promise to bolster one another, creating a coherent system of interlocked identifications, but in practice one model supersedes the other, and the consequences of this conflict can be far-reaching. Indeed, the war's literature insistently points towards a disjunction among different forms of male bonds, and this rupture will often be responsible, at least in part, for the bereavement and alienation that so powerfully characterizes the soldier figure, both during and after the war.

In the official rhetoric of the war, propagated by the General Staff, members of government, official propagandists, and numerous civilian individuals and organizations, there can be no conflict between friendship and comradeship, for the simple reason that group solidarity always takes precedence over individual friendships. This kind of extreme privileging of group over individual was of course not unique to the war, having permeated British culture and dominated the institutions of masculinity for many years before 1914. We have seen that the ideology disseminated by the public schools involved an emphasis on individual submission to group loyalty, privileging the idea of affiliation higher than personal comfort or desire, and insisting that the boys "play up" under the sign of *esprit de corps*. The rhetoric surrounding masculinity – in relation to athleticism, house and school loyalty, patriotism – inevitably relied upon group identification, and this matrix of attitudes about manliness and loyalty to impersonal institutions found its logical culmination in the twin theaters of empire and war. The schools did their part for the war quite spectacularly, supplying not only the lion's share of officers, but also an ideological training ground for generations of young would-be soldiers. For the schools, the war in a sense marked the culmination of their value system, a test and a prism for their creed, and their contribution to the military ethos, including championing comradeship, was everywhere apparent. As one critic explains it, "Whilst few people can have been prepared for the nature of the War, there is no doubt that one section of the community was ready to meet the challenge: the English Public Schools... [E]ducated in a gentlemanly tradition of loyalty, honour, chivalry, Christianity, patriotism, sportsmanship and leadership, public-school boys could be regarded as suitable officer material in any war."[18] In his 1917 poetry collection, Osborn included a section on "School and College," in which we find many exemplifications of the interpenetration of school spirit with military values. Hence the following passage by J. M. Rose-Troup, from a poem entitled "Harrow's Honour":

> The strongest bond of all, the bond of friends
> Made in our youth, o bond that naught can break,
> Binds us to you [Harrow] until our journey ends,
> We live, we fight, we die for Harrow's sake.
> (*Muse in Arms*, 177)

While "Harrow's Honour" may seem to represent an extreme example of the public-school war ethic, its premises about the logical connections among masculinity, school friendships, and the willingness to die in battle formed a critical part of the war's ideological landscape.

In war, however, an ethos of intense group loyalty need not explicitly be connected with civilian organizations such as the public schools, nor even with the idea of the nation, as the diverse units within the British Expeditionary Force (BEF) were themselves offered as substitutes for civilian forms of social cohesion. Like all armies, the BEF was organized in a series of decreasing units, including the division, the regiment, the battalion, the company, and finally the section, and the army naturally valorized the primacy of these organizational units, developing a language to elevate and promote its constituent parts. Several brief examples of the extreme investment in unit identification should serve to convey the war's faith in the ascendancy of these bodies. In "The Spirit of a Division," an editorial essay in the 1918 number of the *Dagger* (a magazine of/for the London 56th Division) the editor writes: "in a division that is for ever fighting, for ever changing, there is something that lives on, is never lost. Rather it grows in strength and character as the years pass by. The soul, the spirit of a division, call it what you will, does not die."[19] The division is imaged as an individual (with a soul, a spirit, its own personality), its corporate nature rendering it superior to any human individual. The writer elides the actual meaning of a division that is "ever changing," substituting the battalion's longevity for the specific existence of any particular soldier. In a 1916 letter home, the soldier Henry Waldo Yoxall explains the power of regimental association: "When you're a member of a great regiment like the Sixtieth you feel yourself in a sense immortal. If the battalion lives the loss of the individual doesn't matter."[20]

In *Goodbye to All That* (1929), a text generally (but not entirely accurately) read for its rejection of war-tainted Victorian values, Robert Graves explains the distinction between regimental loyalty and such sentiments as nationalism: "we [officers] all agreed that regimental pride was the greatest moral force that kept a battalion going as an effective fighting unit, contrasting it particularly with patriotism and religion."[21] Graves adamantly denies that either patriotic fervor or Christianity had any role in trench life, asserting instead a different grid of loyalties, centered around regimental pride and tradition, and expressed at the level of the battalion.[22] At the same time, if Graves repeatedly returns to the battalion as the crucial comradeship unit, he nevertheless accepts that battalions are formed by specific men, and as those individuals die in droves, the corporate body is fundamentally compromised. Thus he approvingly attributes to Sassoon the thought that "there never was such a battalion . . . since 1916, but in six months it would have ceased to exist" (*Goodbye to All That*, 328). For all his assertion of battalion history and corporate personality, Graves acknowledges that after some threshold of decimation, the battalion can lose its coherence as a symbolic entity. Such a concession runs radically counter to the typical rhetoric of war and comradeship, and also conflicts with Graves' own tendency to promote the corporate spirit of the group.

Indeed, Graves' conflicting language helps to underscore one salient point: despite all its self-presentation as the site of male loyalty, the war destroyed friendship. The war assaulted friendship in two ways. Individual friends were killed in the ordinary course of the day, and the concept of friendship was treated with contempt by a bureaucracy that ceaselessly and arbitrarily separated friends from one another. As one officer explained in a letter home, "And as for one's friends, they change more rapidly than anything. Some get killed, and others get sent home to England, and you never hear of them again."[23] Manning's *Her Privates We* focuses directly on this kind of ruthless destruction of intimacies that had been painfully nurtured. For Manning, the crux of the war's tragic irony lies in its creation of intimate ties, many of which transcend barriers of class and region, only to demolish them. As one character has it: "'That's the worst o' the bloody army: as soon as you get a bit pally with a chap summat 'appens'" (*Her Privates We*, 242). With similar insight, Sassoon acidly describes the simultaneous importance and vulnerability of friendship:

All I knew was that I'd lost my faith in [both home life and the war] and there was nothing left to believe in except "the Battalion spirit"...But while exploring my way into the War I had discovered the impermanence of its humanities. One evening we could be all together in a cosy room...A single machine-gun or a few shells might wipe out the whole picture within a week.[24]

As the term "impermanence of its humanities" suggests, and as Sassoon's use of quotation marks around the phrase "Battalion spirit" indicates, the war's very creation of intimacy and group loyalty becomes its most ironic and disorienting trick. Not only did death and injury separate men from their friends, but the inscrutable directives of the war operation regularly and senselessly scattered men apart, even as it thrust them together. Indeed, a sentiment of anger against the war machine for its useless dispersal of friends permeates war texts of all sorts, contributing to a sustained aura of bitterness against authority.

Far from being a site of great intimacy, the war fostered distance and self-protectiveness. In his exegesis of the war's myriad disillusionments, C. E. Montague indicates that both the ceaseless scattering of friends and the sheer scale of the war thwarted intimacy: "Two million men can never be a happy few; nor yet a band of brothers. You have to know a brother first."[25] In an unpublished memoir, W. B. Henderson explains in more detail the problem of the war's disruption of friendship, for which he can find no explanation:

Army life which brings together men of very different types and by forcing them to life [*sic*] in close contact with one another very often causes a feeling of comradeship and friendship to arise, in too many cases breaks up the friendship before it has well begun...To the many men to whom these relationships with their comrades mean much, the feeling comes that it is useless to make friends in the army. They are like travelers coming to an inn for a night, meeting strangers there, spending an evening over the fire in the enjoyment of mutual sympathy and in the discovery of common pleasures and interests, feeling their hearts warming and a kindling desire to know more and to see more of these new found friends. Then the morning comes; each must go his own way; they part.[26]

The war creates friendship – indeed places it at the center of human existence – only to destroy it. Henderson's image of the travelers at the inn indicates the precise dilemma created by the war's mass bureaucracy: at one level, men in the war experience normal emotions of attraction, individual preference, and desire; yet the war's relentless show of authority renders such emotions both futile and dangerous. In a similar mode, David Jones highlights the poignancy of such arbitrary and destructive policies: "For such breaking away and dissolving of comradeship and token of division are cause of great anguish when men sense how they stand so perilous and transitory in this world."[27] If the omnipresence of death leads men increasingly to value their friendships with one another, then the destruction of those intimacies (whether through death or bureaucratic insensitivity) redoubles the sense of looming crisis surrounding the vulnerable individual.

This conjunction of dispersed friendship and foreshadowed death animates a somewhat uncharacteristic poem by Rupert Brooke, the era's icon of romantic heroism and tragic self-sacrifice.[28] Although Brooke is typically remembered for his patriotism and elevation of war – as well as his poster-boy handsomeness – an unfinished poem produced in the last month of his life (1915) suggests that he, too, had begun to view the war's antagonism to friendship as a powerfully disorienting problem related to the ubiquity of death. "Fragment," set on board a military ship, opens by establishing a contrast between the speaker and his "friends": the narrator, "peep[ing] / In at the windows," watches the assembled men, and ruminates on the impending destruction of their handsome bodies. He thus imagines the whole assembly passing into the ghostly realm, "Perishing things and strange ghosts – soon to die / To other ghosts – this one, or that, or I."[29] Despite a certain confusion of identity, as the ghosts merge into one another, the speaker remains firmly outside of this tableau, a moment of war community that both beckons and repels the class-conscious Brooke. Nevertheless, at the center of the poem (literally and metaphorically) is an entwined and gorgeous group of men, whose violent rupture represents the poem's tragedy. Dispersal is the key concept in this narrative of broken community:

> I would have thought of them
> – Heedless, within a week of battle – in pity
> Pride in their strength and in the weight and firmness
> And link'd beauty of bodies, and pity that
> This gay machine of splendour 'ld soon be broken,
> Thought little of, pashed, scattered...
> (*Poems*, 169, ellipses in original)

Clearly, the "broken...pashed, scattered" bodies represent the mutilation to be caused by artillery, bullet, or mine. At the same time, Brooke uses the language of the physical body as a metaphor for the internal state of men whose intimate bonds will soon be "broken...pashed, scattered" by the exigencies of war. The poem's effectiveness derives from this centrifugal motion of bodies, as a moment of complete interdependence – understood as both physical and spiritual/psychological – is blasted apart, and the group fades into a series of flickering ghosts and shadows. Even if Brooke can never quite surmount the barriers of class, he does present the destruction of the men's community as a central tragedy of war. In Brooke's "Fragment," then, the war takes its toll on "bodies of men" in a double sense: it attacks both the flesh of individuals and the corporate existence of the group. The poem thus gives visual form to the central fact that war is hostile to intimacy.

Friendship and comradeship are not allied forms, but antagonists. And it is not surprising that, far from simply accepting the ascendant spirit of the battalion or, like Liddell Hart and Rogerson, assuming a continuum among forms of male fellowship, many war writers describe a deeply troubling irreconcilability between the intimacy of individuals and the imperative to participate in a comradeship that subsumes the individual. On the surface, close relations between men resemble the exalted version of comradeship propagated by conventional rhetoric, and, perhaps for that reason, it is particularly important for the military establishment to contain such ties. Not only does war inevitably break apart the bonds of its participants, but its hierarchic structure and its claims to absolute authority might be threatened by strong friendships between individuals.[30] David Jones' verse war saga *In Parenthesis* (1937), for one, ruminates on the conflict between private experience and the power of the group to construct men in its image. For Jones, such power occurs at the level of the human body, as physical proximity creates new rhythms and sensations among congregated men. The sheer fact of massed bodies moving in formation threatens to overwhelm the individual's capacity for singular thought and to reduce him to a mechanistic cog in a gigantic wheel. In marching at night, for instance, "you only but half-heard words of command, and your body conformed to these bodies about" (*In Parenthesis*, 123). At the same time, such group phenomena reduce the suffering and loneliness of army life, and hence offer sustenance – if at a cost.

Despite this interest in the power of the corporate group to alter individual male bodies, in Jones' poem, interiority and personal desire cannot be eradicated:

Feet plodding in each other's unseen tread. They said no word but to direct their immediate next coming, so close behind to blunder, toe by heel tripping, file-mates; blind on-following, moving with a singular identity.

Half-minds, far away, divergent, own-thought thinking, tucked away unknown thoughts; feet following file friends, each his own thought-maze alone treading; intricate, twist about, own thoughts, all unknown thoughts, to the next so close following on. (*In Parenthesis*, 37)

The narrative here traces a continuous interaction between an individual self that is constituted by the "singular identity" of the massed troops and a self that entirely resists such molding. For all his interest in the way war makes bodies to suit its needs, Jones remains powerfully Cartesian. The word "thought/s," repeated five times in the passage, provides the key to the men's individuality; it is a man's thoughts that are "own" and "unknown," even as the endless file of bodies seems almost to dominate and appropriate the self. In the passage, the terms "file-mate" and "file friend" provocatively describe a form of friendship that is neither entirely personal (because it exists by virtue of its structure, in a particular geographical and bureaucratic space) nor entirely impersonal (the words "mate" and "friend" indicate a potential intimacy that may ultimately conflict with group comradeship).

At a broader cultural level, the idea of the "unknown warrior," a product of the First World War that has become firmly embedded in twentieth-century conceptions of war and mourning, functions for a mass public somewhat like Jones' "file friend." In the years immediately following the armistice, as officials attempted both to accommodate and to allay a vast demand for appropriate public images of the war, the notion of an anonymous body that could represent all the war's casualties, regardless of regiment, rank, or nature of service, provided a resonant symbol of the homogeneity of death in modern war. The anonymity of the unknown soldier points quite directly to the utter destruction of individuality in the name of the nation, yet the symbol worked as a unifying force.[31] What the unknown soldier offered was a touchstone for public mourning, a site where the body became generalized, and hence where universal loss could be engaged as both a personal and a shared experience. The image of the unknown seemed to create a sense of balance, a point of contact between individuality and the enormity of the war ("the still point of the turning world," as Eliot might have it[32]), and this intersection of the deeply personal with the infinitely extended seemed to touch a real chord in post-war culture. Both during and after the war, combatants such as Jones searched for a balancing structure to ward off the eclipse of identity, often turning to friendship as the most elastic and productive category that neither elevated nor obliterated the individual.

One common – if relatively simple – strategy for thwarting the foreclosure of intimacy involved shifting the way relationships were valued, to privilege the transcendent moment of intimacy rather than long-lasting bonds and commitments. War texts of all generic types dwell upon and praise the small-scale, chance encounter, in which intimacy is quickly developed, and the men part as rapidly as they had met. If the war destroys traditional forms of lasting friendship, these texts suggest that the best way to protect personalized intimacy is to proclaim an ironic longevity in fleeting encounters and momentary bursts of emotion. Thus we often find tender descriptions of passing exchanges with strangers, moments of generosity, mutuality, and commonalty that punctuate and transform the torpor of war existence and dispel official platitudes about comradeship.[33] In one among an infinity of such moments: "the three men seated themselves on the parapet of the look-out to yarn and to smoke the pipe of peace and friendship together. This, indeed, was almost the general custom of troops."[34]

In addition to recognizing and valorizing the chance instant of intimacy, war writers often describe heroism and self-sacrifice in terms of a temporary devotion to a particular mate, an emotional bond that passes with the extremity of the situation. In one such passage, W. B. Henderson attributes this form of momentary fellowship to the terrible nature of combat:

in certain conditions this near companionship has the result of bringing men closer together and of developing a spirit of friendship between the most dissimilar natures. In times of danger, particularly, this is the case. Under shell fire; in an attack; when poisonous gases come across; in the presence of death: in all these circumstances the littlenesses of life tend to fall away and the natural man appears, craving for sympathy and companionship in the face of the hideous realities of war. But, these moments are only occasional and they pass. ("Memoir," 18–19)

Here the heroic ideal of valor in war is scaled back and humanized; men crave for "sympathy and companionship," forming bonds out of personal necessity that fade when the necessity subsides. Nevertheless, for Henderson, it is in these moments of friendship, understood as fleeting and circumstantial, that the value of war existence resides. Henderson's language recalls Manning's feelings about how the war constructs an almost formulaic intimacy, yet, for Manning, such reproducibility seemed quite dangerous, a threat to the idea of individuality.

Particularly compelling for its attempt to transform the dispersal and destruction of friendship into a new relational model, in which chance encounters take precedence over lasting bonds, is an unpublished novel by a soldier in an Australian division, Geoff Hawkins. "Ravellings of Red," which takes its very title from the aesthetics of what passes (a fleeting moment of beauty in the sky), is entirely organized by the effort to compensate for the loss of friendship. The novel begins as Robert Hilton, having been arbitrarily transferred to a new battalion, chances upon his original unit, which is almost entirely unrecognizable. Maintaining a powerful attachment to the "mates" and "friends" with whom he originally enlisted, Hilton engages upon an informal hunt for them, only to find that they have gradually been killed, wounded, or otherwise dispersed. Thus the text opens with a futile attempt to return to friendship. After that effort fails, the novel shifts to a series of essentially unconnected vignettes, most of which describe men in states of increasing destitution and loneliness. Even when we witness the instantaneous and poignant development of intimacy between two men, it is only a matter of paragraphs before one is killed in battle or simply removed from the other's vicinity. The narrative time-scheme, like the plot, highlights the ephemeral and transitory nature of fellowship.

The relation between the narrative's fragmentary form and its originary crisis of broken friendship is not coincidental: Hawkins' story represents an attempt to match the formal and thematic structure of a war tale with an overwhelming crisis in shattered friendship. For Hawkins, the idea of impersonal comradeship holds no consolation or truth. He insists instead on an intimacy that develops out of the emotional – indeed almost physical – compatibility of men, arguing that "The camaraderie so much spoken of… was to a large extent superficial. It was only when like met like, with the magnetic consciousness of true affinity, that there was unguarded confidence and complete understanding between men in the trenches" ("Ravellings of Red," 247). Despite Hawkins' strong desire to assert some form of intimate bonding, he recognizes the inadequacy of personal relations in the face of the bureaucratic authority and the extreme horror of the war (which he presents graphically), and his text is thus characterized as much by the complete deterioration of any over-arching ideal of community as by moments of intense personal devotion.

Hawkins' novel lacks a coherent strategy, whether narrative, imagistic, or thematic, for synthesizing its fragmentary parts, yet its very shortcomings illustrate the paradox with which Hawkins struggles: friendship is both everything and nothing in the war, and the challenge for the writer is to find a language and/or form in which to re-invigorate the category of male intimacy. Both popular and canonical war poets took on this challenge of constructing lasting friendship – a goal that the war seems fundamentally to prohibit – and ultimately came to imagine the figure of the shattered friend as a paragon of alienated, suffering masculinity. Although war verse is typically divided along ideological lines – popular poets apologized for the war, canonical poets protested against it – my analysis will operate along a different axis, stressing the ways in which friendship continually confronts comradeship, in a dynamic which emphasizes the internal conflicts of the war-formed subject. If we reject the typical political signposts of alliance or discord among poets, we find remarkable commonalty in both efforts and effects, as "soldier-poets" across the spectrum searched for a form to balance intimacy with comradeship. It is not so much the politics for or against militarism that will occupy me here, that is, but the various strategies for exposing and/or harmonizing discordant forms of male unity.

THE MAJOR WAR POETS: INTIMACY, AUTHORITY, ALIENATION

I begin with Robert Nichols, whose widely read *Ardours and Endurances* (1917) made him one of the most celebrated of the soldier-poets during the years of fighting. Nichols represents a style of poetry that functioned, in part, to convey an understandable idea of the war to non-combatants, and in this sense his work contrasts with the poetry of Sassoon, Graves, Jones, Owen, Isaac Rosenberg, and Ivor Gurney, who are noted today for their ironic, angry, and uncompromising voices. Moreover, most of these poets were suspicious of Nichols as an exponent of the war, not only for the tenor and quality of his poetry, but also because of his extremely limited war service; his emphasis on comradeship seems at times to rely as much on the official language of war as on the experience of combat. Nichols' poems are replete with images of fearless, noble, self-sacrificing comrades, as Osborn's introduction to *The Muse in Arms* might have promised. And Nichols' usage of comradeship – like his treatment of other standard war themes – tends towards an integrative model, where male bonding fits into a relatively conventional narrative of heroic idealism.[35] Yet despite his tendency to sanitize and valorize the war, Nichols asks a series of questions about the relation between intimacy and comradeship in war that cannot easily be aligned with the rhetoric of group identification. In "Fulfilment" (*sic*), Nichols establishes a contrast between heterosexual, romantic love and the superior love of comrades in war.[36] The closing lines of the poem firmly reject the poet's past adoration of a woman, in favor of a de-personalized image of the dying soldier:

> Was there love once? I have forgotten her.
> Was there grief once? grief yet is mine.
> O loved, living, dying, heroic soldier,
> All, all, my joy, my grief, my love, are thine![37]

The contrast between the impoverished status of heterosexual love and the saturated intimacy of men in war provides the crux of the poetic trajectory. In these lines, as in the poem more generally, Nichols establishes what he views to be the most desirable and admirable form of male fellowship to praise: it is comradeship, rather than friendship, since the "loved, living, dying, heroic soldier" is a corporate entity, a composite whose body is both ever-dying and constantly being replenished. As in *Her Privates We*, where the institution of comradeship provided a form for the reproduction of intimacy and heroism, so here Nichols establishes the idea of the soldier as a being who is both individual and abstract. Through the image of the beloved yet de-personalized soldier, Nichols attempts to find a solution to two of the problems that dominate war literature: the paradox of the battalion (its apparent longevity yet continuous decimation), and the desire to achieve an intimacy that will be replaceable when the intimate friend dies.

If "Fulfilment" seems to posit the possibility of a collective being, both individual and abstract, which might reconcile the rift between rival forms of male bonds, at other times Nichols' verse forces this conflict to flare up. His poems must work to accommodate disparate loyalties, attesting to an uneasy sense that competing models of male companionship abut – rather than sustain – one another. The tension between intimacy and impersonality underlies "Boy," for example, a lyric that uses the figure of the killed youth as a vehicle for ruminating on the meaning and value of being a soldier. The poem utilizes the verb "to friend" – a relatively common trope in war poetry – emphasizing the way language is defamiliarized and reconstituted by the intimacies of war. "To friend" indicates at the syntactic level what is also implied thematically: language itself works to address the urgent need to imagine new and untested types of male unity. The poem begins, "In a far field, away from England, lies / A Boy I friended with a care like love," and then goes on to de-personalize the narrative, shifting away from mourning one particular death into an identificatory narrative about soldiering (*AE*, 48). The key turn in the poem comes when Nichols rejects friendship in favor of comradeship:

> Not now as friend, but as a soldier, I
> Salute you fallen; for the Soldier's name
> Our greatest honour is . . .
> The Soldier's is a name none recognize,
> Saving his fellows.   (*AE*, 48–49)

In shifting from friendship to mutual soldiering (and from civilian "boy" to military "soldier"), the men give up their most basic identity, signified by the name, in favor of an impersonal and shared form of identification. Although such a move is clearly connected with a culturally recognized ideal of self-sacrifice (which Nichols highlights in the next stanza, describing the soldier as "the Martyr of a nation" [*AE*, 49]), the poet nevertheless insists that only fellow soldiers can "recognize" one another. Nichols asserts an absolute compatibility among soldiers, a mimetic and complete form of mutual constitution, in comparison with their distance not only from civilians, but also from concepts like "the nation," shared by a wider body. Even in death, the soldier remains cut off from those for whom he allegedly gave his life, so that "Dying, his mangled body, to inter it, / He doth bequeath him into comrade hands" (*AE*, 49).

Despite the soldier's apparent fulfillment in the company of those who form part of his corporate identity, the rejection of friendship has its costs: "Lonely he is: he has nor friend nor lover, / Sith in his body he is dedicate.../ His comrades only share his life..." (*AE*, 49). To subscribe to comradeship over friendship and love is, paradoxically, to accept isolation – a paradox because comradeship is supposed to protect the individual from bereavement. Of course, in invoking the stoic, invincible, yet lonely hero, Nichols recalls a familiar icon in western literature. At the same time, the poem posits a causal connection between loneliness and the loss of friendship, and it is this conjunction that most powerfully marks "Boy" as a partial challenge to much of the war's consolatory rhetoric. Because soldiers are endlessly reproducible, they provide a form of ready-made identity that in war is both necessary and troubling. Nichols utilizes the idea of the soldier in part to function like Jones' "file friend," representing a relational form that provides a measure of identity and solace, at the same time that it remains impersonal and structural, forcing the man precariously in the direction of alienation.

Finally, Nichols' soldier figure, though disdaining self-promotion and perhaps even language ("Deeds are his flower" [*AE*, 49]), is imbued by the poet with an aura of intense moral authority. His superiority over other citizens – signaled by the sacrifice of his individualized name for the name of "Soldier" – marks him as exemplary, a potential voice of the era, whose narrative authority is appropriated by the poet. Thus "Boy" sets in motion a conjunction of themes that will characterize much of the more famous poetry of the period: the substitution of male bonds for civilian models of community and identity; the conflict between friendship and comradeship, whose resolution organizes the poem; the potential for alienation; a consolation, in the form of moral and literary superiority.

One of the ironies of poems like "Fulfilment" and "Boy" is that they simultaneously authorize the lone voice of the bereaved friend and, at the same time, indicate that such a being exists, in some sense, by virtue of his intense relationships with other men. By establishing a figure which arises as a composite being, even as he claims aggressive authority to speak his individual experience, this poetry suggests some uncertainty about the nature of singular identity in war. Another vivid example of such shifting identity, where the sense of corporateness criss-crosses with the individual voice, marks "The Homecoming," a poem by Joseph Lee about soldiers returning home after the war. The conceit of Lee's poem involves the doubling of the returnees: in addition to the actual men whose bodies cross back to England, the dead "also shall return," an irony, since the actual corpses of soldiers were not repatriated after the war (Taylor, *Lads*, 215).[38] Lee provides a visual image for such ghostly shadowing, as each stanza ends with the dead's presence, marked by italics. The last stanza, entirely italicized, projects an ominous and intangible intimacy between the living and the dead, suggesting that the consequences of war friendship (its intensity and destruction) will not simply evaporate after the war: "*A dead man shall stand / At each live man's hand – / For they also have come home*" (*Lads*, 216). Particularly vexing here is the status of the dead in the psychic life of the survivors, who are unable either to terminate or to profit from the intimacies of the war. Not surprisingly, the problem of the ghost is widespread in war literature, and Lee's usage, in which the ghost represents the havoc wreaked on former soldiers by their dead friends, conjoins the persistence of the spirit world with the idea that doubled identity in war presents more of a threat to the soldier than a consolation.

A short, angry lyric by Robert Graves provides a further articulation of war-time doubled identity, where the two-as-one is explicitly produced by friendship. "Two Fusiliers" (1917) radically unites the viewpoint of its eponymous couple against non-combatant identity:

> And have we done with War at last?
> Well, we've been lucky devils both,
> And there's no need of pledge or oath
> To bind our lovely friendship fast,
> By firmer stuff
> Close bound enough.[39]

With an insistence that the intimacy of war supersedes such civilian rituals as pledges and oaths (which themselves often mimic military form and language), the speaker embraces a world-view expressed in military standards, proclaiming absolute self-sufficiency and completeness. In keeping with this war-constituted framework, the poem grounds its interior landscape in the specific landmarks of battle. In the next stanza, a series of place-names – Fricourt, Festubert, Picardy – serve synecdochally to indicate the exclusiveness of a community united by shared experience. Graves' phallic language ("firmer stuff") imbues the poem with an aura of virile

masculinity, even as he creates an image of a mutually constituting and inter-
dependent intimacy. Although Graves' fetishization of virility and military
community might square neatly with domestic propaganda efforts, not to
mention a more general public-school ethos, his representation of the male
individual as completely immersed in the landscape of war – with no ties
or commitments beyond its masculine borders – seems at odds with this
swaggering, imperialist mood. Indeed, the poem's adversarial tone directly
challenges home culture, suggesting that it will tolerate no suspicion of the
profound intimacy it proclaims.

> Show me the two so closely bound
> As we, by the wet bond of blood,
> By friendship blossoming from mud,
> By death . . .

the speaker exhorts, defying the reader to imagine any greater or more
heroic intimacy, even as he heightens the sexuality of his language with
images of wetness and fecundity.

"Two Fusiliers" thus appears to showcase a form of friendship that is both
absolute in its influence over individuals and confident in its assumptions of
superiority. Yet, the poem ultimately commits itself more to a comradeship
model than to a systematic hallowing of intimacy. For one, the title immediately defines the men by their regiment – Graves' beloved Royal Welch [*sic*]
Fusiliers – and hence recalls the standard adherence to group identification.
More importantly, the relentlessness of the "we" voice and the intensity of
the fusiliers' mimetic identity raise doubts about the nature of this relation:
so exactly does the experience and outlook of each fusilier match the other's
as to suggest that they are not so much individuals as aspects of a larger
entity, along the lines of Nichols' "loved, living, dying, heroic soldier." The
men are spatially and historically determined, conjoined into one being
by powerful outside forces, as in Jones' *In Parenthesis*, where congregated
bodies partially created the individual. Indeed, Graves' poem is effective
precisely because it effects a compromise between the total intimacy of
friendship and the impersonal, corporate experience of blind comradeship.
By restricting the power of personal friendships over the individual, "Two
Fusiliers" retains the confident and institutionally oriented outlook that
also characterizes parts of *Goodbye to All That*. In this respect Graves differs
somewhat from Nichols, and markedly from Owen and Sassoon, whose
poetry will encode a recognizable trajectory: the imperative to stabilize,
protect, and claim friendship (over heterosexuality, civilian life, and comradeship) eventually thrusts the poet into a place of alienated marginality.
At the very moment when a particular voice is being solidified as a

representative of modern war, the figure of the shattered friend becomes most troubling as a model of alienated, suffering masculinity.

In Owen's work, the image of the poet is inextricably linked with an ethos of sympathy: "My subject is War, and the pity of War. / The poetry is in the pity."[40] Owen's famous words of preface accurately characterize the tone of his poetry, and, more specifically, his emphasis on pity helps him to mediate the paradoxical and confusing problems surrounding the idea of friendship. I have said that friendship is both everything and nothing in war writing; for Owen, the simultaneous urgency and failure of intimacy create a sense of crisis, and the concept of pity is marshaled to help allay it. Where a poem like Brooke's "Fragment" posits a problematic distance between the speaker and the men he watches, Owen's attitude of intense sympathy towards his subjects works to bridge that distance, to establish a feeling of communion between the poet and the men he poignantly describes. Although Owen at times evinces a patronizing attitude towards the lower ranks – and perhaps the idea of pity embodies this stance of partial separation and superiority – the thrust of his poetry aims towards closing such gaps and creating a spirit of unity.[41] Hence the wrenching closure of a poem like "Disabled," where the voices of the mutilated ex-soldier and the poem's narrator merge into one, produces out of Owen's idea of pity a bond that functions as both a personal testament and a social conscience: "How cold and late it is! Why don't they come / And put him into bed? Why don't they come?" (*PWO*, 153). Through his searing pity for the cold and lonely soldier, Owen sets up a new intimacy to replace the many lost ties that the poem documents. This usage of tonal pathos and shared voice to create an ideal of friendship marks much of Owen's poetry; it is his hallmark.[42]

"Greater Love" presents perhaps the most complete elaboration of the pity ideal, set against impoverished civilian conventions for representing love. The greater love of the title refers to the Biblical dictum "Greater love hath no man than this, that a man lay down his life for his friends" (John 15:13), and this Christian ideal of self-sacrifice is further bolstered by a comparison between soldierly love and the "slender attitude" of traditional romantic discourse:

> Red lips are not so red
> As the stained stones kissed by the English dead.
> Kindness of wooed and wooer
> Seems shame to their love pure.
> O Love, your eyes lose lure
> When I behold eyes blinded in my stead!
>
> (*PWO*, 143)

The theme of greater love, a common one in war verse (as, for instance, in Nichols' "Fulfilment"), recalls the *fin-de-siècle* device, discussed in Chapter 1, of celebrating male intimacy by valorizing its purity, spirituality, and elevated nature, thereby carving out a protected sphere for the beloved body. If such a discourse arises in part to protect the homosexual body from incipient threat, the male body in the trenches is even more precariously situated – consistently and absolutely under siege. To transcend the physical, as propounded by the comradely ideal, might offer an image of masculine desire that escapes the pain, discomfort, dismemberment, and filth that characterized the body's existence at the front.

Yet Owen's "Greater Love" celebrates personal intimacy rather than comradeship, and, perhaps inevitably, friendship returns the body into the actual, mortal world. Further – notwithstanding Owen's own homosexuality – we need to be careful in assessing the poem's homosexual claims, since, syntactically, the text's structure complicates simple binaries. In the above passage, the "love pure" does not refer directly to the love of soldiers for one another, but to the intimacy of the dead body with the land, or, later, the corporeal chest with artillery, "full like hearts made great with shot" (*PWO*, 143). Thus Owen stresses that the pathos of the physical body reaches its apex neither in heterosexual conventions nor in the spirit of comradeship, but at the moment of dismemberment and death. Rather than operate along the axis of homo/hetero, "Greater Love" indicates that the very concept of physical intimacy is shattered by war, and to represent it accurately requires that the poet construct a language that breaks free of standard oppositions. Indeed, at each moment of comparison in the poem, the love that shines brightest derives from the poet's language of scorching sympathy. So far does Owen's horribly exact vocabulary exceed all other forms of language – with lines like "Now earth has stopped their piteous mouths that coughed" (*PWO*, 143) – that we are asked, I think, to question the value of any competing model of romantic discourse, including statements like "greater love hath no man than this, that a man lay down his life for his friends." The only stable division that Owen establishes in the poem is between his own capacity to voice an intimate and explosive pity for war's victims and all who are outside of that relation, including those who tout the "greater love." A sense of despair animates the poem, an intense desire to make permanent the ephemeral intimacy of war, as the poet privileges his own voice of fierce and futile love over other forms that purport to represent desire, intimacy, or male community.

Despite his efforts to create friendship through pity, Owen offers no simple strategy to replace the shattered and broken ideals of either romantic love or heroic comradeship. In "Strange Meeting," for instance, the speaker delineates a number of different possibilities for thinking about appropriate bonds between men, which both entail and surpass the model of transcendent sympathy. The poem begins in the ambiguous, womb-like space of a dream: "It seemed that out of battle I escaped / Down some profound dull tunnel, long since scooped / Through granites which titanic wars had groined" (*PWO*, 125). As the speaker wanders further into the trench-like tunnel, he comes upon a ghost figure whose speech registers the waste of war, "The pity of war, the pity war distilled" (*PWO*, 125).[43] The dead man's voice clearly echoes the speaker/poet's perspective, and this doubling of voice creates a community in suffering. The thrust of the speaker's narrative is to express commonalty of experience and desire with the poet, to become his kindred spirit: "'Whatever hope is yours, / Was my life also'" (*PWO*, 125). The twist, of course, comes when we and the narrator learn the identity of this "strange friend":

> 'I am the enemy you killed, my friend.
> I knew you in this dark: for so you frowned
> Yesterday through me as you jabbed and killed.
> I parried; but my hands were loath and cold.
> Let us sleep now...'
>   (*PWO*, 126, ellipsis in original)

What is dramatized at this moment of recognition – both shocking and expected – is that the normal assumptions about friendship have been radically altered by the war. If "enemy" and "friend" conventionally function as opposites, here they become near-relatives, as the axis of male relations shifts. Combatant men might be structurally opposed (one could not proclaim comradeship across enemy lines), but the possibilities for identification, friendship, and even love proliferate, as the men experience an ambiguous closeness that resists categorization.[44]

Perhaps more than any other of Owen's poems, "Strange Meeting" connects a particular image of male intimacy with the moral authority to speak. The dead German expresses a conscience not just for England, but for the whole of western militaristic culture, as Owen's language, with its jarring pararhymes, its epic imagery, and its simultaneous pathos and anger, sears through the platitudes of popular rhetoric about war and nations. "Strange Meeting" accomplishes a primary goal of much war writing, developing a language for the intimacy of war that relies neither on celebrating impersonal comradeship nor on mourning the endless loss of individual friends. Of course, "Strange Meeting" is remarkable for its liminality, its dreamscape atmosphere and status on the threshold between fantasy and lived reality. In other texts, Owen attempts to find a friendship language within a more recognizably real setting and context.

His most deliberate and straightforward analysis of the bonds of war comes in "Apologia Pro Poemate Meo," a lyric that confidently asserts the enormity and superiority of the intimacy formed by war. The poem's thumping iambs and simple rhyme scheme perhaps conflict with its driving intention to undercut the conventions associated with the love song. Though it opens on a strong note of individuality ("I, too, saw God through mud – " [*PWO*, 101]), "Apologia" quickly moves into a depiction of all-encompassing male community, once again contrasted with a conventionalized and beleaguered heterosexual norm:

> I have made fellowships –
> Untold of happy loves in old song.
> For love is not the binding of fair lips
> With the soft silk of eyes that look and long,
>
> By Joy, whose ribbon slips, –
> But wound with war's hard wire whose stakes are strong;
> Bound with the bandage of the arm that drips;
> Knit in the webbing of the rifle-thong.
>
> I have perceived much beauty
> In the hoarse oaths that kept our courage straight;
> Heard music in the silentness of duty;
> Found peace where shell-storms spouted reddest spate.
>
> (*PWO*, 101)

The language of "Apologia" blurs the distinction between comradeship and friendship, as the depersonalized forms of organized comradeship become infused with a spirit of personal connection and intimacy. Moreover, Owen's confident – even arrogant – portrayal of war-time male bonds does not square easily with my characterization of him as the poet who utilizes pity to effect a genuinely new vision of poetic intimacy. To make sense of this slippage among apparently oppositional images of male fellowship requires an understanding of Owen's treatment of ritual and ceremony.

Clearly, the idea of a formal system for structuring fellowship (oaths, pledges) holds strong appeal in the poem. Owen substitutes the signs of war for conventional romantic imagery, as the domestic tradition of the marital bond is transformed into a virile performance of military duties. However, Owen stops short of reproducing the war's typical apologetics of horror redeemed by comradeship; while his "Apologia" retains a sense of the ritualized spirit that accrues to corporate comradeship, he also insists on the immediacy of individual existence. Owen effects this fusion of the personal with the impersonal through his iconography of the human body. Each element in the fellowship ideal is condensed into an aspect of the physical landscape, and each has a counterpart at the level of the vulnerable male body. The wounded arm wrapped with a bloody bandage; the winding of endless coils of barbed wire; the very throat, tired and hoarse, uttering an oath: these images combine a focus on the body-as-tableau with a stress on the exhaustion of the physical body at work. Owen never allows the reader to lose sight of individual soldiers doing the work of war, as he transforms abstract or ceremonial concepts like loyalty, vulnerability, and comradeship into immediate details of daily, physical existence.[45]

Owen's use of the physical as repository for the institutional can be viewed as a kind of counter-discourse in his poetry.[46] Unwilling to adopt the value-systems associated with such institutions as the church and conventional love poetry, and defiant of their authority over the realms they purport to govern, Owen develops a system for transforming their iconography into his own. Perhaps the most striking tension animating Owen's poetry is the conflict between the intense experience of intimacy, often registered through the idea of pity, and the massive impersonality of war and its structures, including comradeship and other forms of conventional rhetoric. When the poet in "Apologia" proclaims that he has made fellowships more powerful than those in "old song," and that new rituals ensure the longevity of war-time masculine relations, he attempts to freeze the idea of friendship just before it is hijacked by the corporate structure of war. Owen's work moves continuously across the landscape of male relations, as each poem strives to find a Keatsian balance between absolute intimacy, and therefore vulnerability, and the erasure of the individual. By infusing the body itself with the power of culture, Owen hopes to realize male intimacy – to solidify and sanctify it – without relying on the depersonalizing attitudes of the military.

To stabilize friendship is, for Owen, to erect a bulwark against alienation. If we return, for instance, to "Disabled," we can see that the poet's pity, his imaginative merging with the lonely soldier, provides the survivor with his sole hope – however meager – for solace. Owen's poetry teems with figures who exist on the verge of desperate isolation, and it is through the idea of poetic sympathy that Owen effects at least momentary images of community and consolation. There are times, however, when Owen depicts war community as a form of isolation in numbers, producing images of fellowship that also suggest a potential slide into solitary existence. The precarious intimacy of war may represent the soldier's only hope, but such unity also involves a dark foreboding: the very closeness achieved by combatants, set against the edifice of home, portends disastrous consequences for the soldiers, both in terms of their loss of one another and in relation to future civilian life.

"Smile, Smile, Smile," a deeply ironic poem about the criminal ignorance of the press, describes an uneasy community of men that is both entirely self-constituted and perilously situated on the verge of disintegration. The poem opens with a tableau of wounded men reading an inaccurate news story, and it is their ironic smile that the poem elaborates:

> Head to limp head, the sunk-eyed wounded scanned
> Yesterday's *Mail* ...
> ... The half-limbed readers did not chafe
> But smiled at one another curiously
> Like secret men who knew their secret safe.
>
> (*PWO*, 167)[47]

Owen's picture of "the sunk-eyed wounded" leaning together "[h]ead to limp head," and his use of the vocabulary of secrecy has a layered effect. The image of the group of men in a posture of physical inter-dependence provides a visual picture that captures the complexity of war intimacy, indicating the complete attachment of the men to one another, their quiet and elusive bond, but also confounding easy categorization, as they touch one another at an erotically understated location (their heads). Moreover, this tableau, while moving, distances the reader, who is not invited to partake in their strange community. If the text alienates the reader in part by insisting on the impossibility of communication across the military/civilian gap, its persistent language of secrecy hints also at a familiar homosexual iconography. In "Smile," the words "curiously" and "secret" recall a closeted language, but at the same time point to a bond among the men that, once again, has no clear counterpart in civilian life. Their intimacy is formed by their very mutilation, and of course by their marginalization with respect to civilian culture, signified most palpably by their hostility to the *Mail*. If the physical body effects a union among these men, it is a tragic union in dismemberment, a form of mutual dependence and shared incapacity.[48]

Owen's image of men united in an exclusive community of injury and mutual healing finds echoes in other war texts. Edmund Blunden, for instance, suggests similar contradictions in the opening image of *Undertones of War*:

For a fortnight or so I had been in charge of a squad of men nominally recovered from wounds and awaiting their next transmigration. It had been my happiness to march them out to a place at once as sequestered and sunny as I could find, over looking the lazy Adur, and there let them bask on the grass, and tell their tales, and be peaceful. How contentedly they had rested in the lucky sun! Nor was much said among them – their thoughts were their conversation.[49]

Blunden's convalescent men share with the soldiers in "Smile" an unspoken yet absolute form of intimacy, which transpires entirely outside of other forms of community, removed even from the site of war. The narrator himself looks in from the outside, like Brooke watching the men on the ship, and thus sets their enclosed relations apart from the rest of the male landscape. Indeed, one striking element in Blunden's famous memoir is that he never again describes friendship in either visual or narrative terms to match this Owenesque opening, as if to indicate through his silence the precariousness and self-sufficiency of these quiet bonds.

Owen's poetry powerfully suggests the problem of marginalization and isolation, but the poet's commitment to finding a language for structuring the close relationships of combat generally wards off such solipsistic potential. In Sassoon's verse, by contrast, an increasingly close and causal connection develops between war intimacy and the expression of alienation. Sassoon shares with Owen a profound interest in documenting, characterizing, and making permanent the war's masculine ties. Yet, where Owen hopes to sanctify and solidify friendship through a combination of poetic pity and the organization of intimacy, Sassoon's work focuses unflinchingly on the simultaneous over-determination and destruction of friendship, a conflict that tends to resist resolution or domestication. For Sassoon, who rejects the ideal of impersonal comradeship and stresses the war's assault on personal intimacy, the agony of lost friendship becomes the psychic and social centerpiece of male existence and the moral touchstone for the poet's voice.

Offering perhaps the most striking combination of lost friendship, literary authority, and alienation is "The Poet as Hero," a lyric first published in the *Cambridge Magazine*, December 1916, a time of palpable post-Somme embitterment. The text depicts and seeks to explain the poet's rejection of romantic themes and values, in favor of an angry poetry, "Mocking and loathing War" (*WP*, 61). The narrator posits a civilian interlocutor, puzzled and perhaps threatened by the new and jarring tone: "you've asked me why / Of my old, silly sweetness I've repented – / My ecstasies changed to an ugly cry" (*WP*, 61). In defending his own poetic material and style, the speaker at once establishes his version of an appropriate war mentality, places lost friendship at the center of that psychic and cultural position, and connects the condition of bitter friendship-loss with his own poetic mission:

> But now I've said good-bye to Galahad,
> And am no more the knight of dreams and show:
> For lust and senseless hatred make me glad,
> And my killed friends are with me where I go.
> Wound for red wound I burn to smite their wrongs;
> And there is absolution in my songs.   (*WP*, 61)

Like Owen and Nichols, Sassoon sets the relations of war against civilian conventions, both literary and social. The Arthurian model of romantic warrior hero is replaced by a violent, anti-social combatant, who takes pleasure in the very destructiveness that has created him. Nevertheless, as Adrian Caesar argues in his critique of the war poets, Sassoon's poem re-constitutes a number of traditional values associated with both Christianity and militarism. The final couplet's elevation of revenge and religious "absolution" is chilling in part because it recalls the very language of heroic war that Sassoon purports to abhor. However, rather than follow Caesar in condemning Sassoon's ostensibly anti-war poem for its absorption of military values, I want to stress the relation between the poem's violent narrator and his "killed friends," for it is in the conjunction of friendship and alienation that Sassoon locates the crux of his poetic consciousness. The use of the word "killed," in place of the more conventional terms "dead" or "fallen," has several effects: it emphasizes the moment of violent death, the killing itself; it forces the reader to address the issue of responsibility or accountability; and, most important, it maintains a sense of immediacy in the moment of loss. The men who have died are, for the speaker, always being killed, always in the act of crossing the life/death divide that, as Eric Leed has argued, became all too fluid during the war. "The Poet as Hero" takes as a premise the impossibility of mourning during the war; yet instead of attempting to forget his dead mates, the combatant persistently relives the moment of lost friendship, carrying with him an increasing weight of intimacy that cannot be relinquished.[50]

The crisis of lost friendship in the poem becomes the motivation for revenge, the basis for a new psychic organization, and the foundation of the speaker's poetic authority.[51] The poem paints a fearsome picture of a New Man, for whom "lust and senseless hatred" are legitimized by the outrage of wrecked intimacy, and whose passionate desires and "ecstasies" are entirely motivated by war. Moreover, the poem proclaims its own moral legitimacy: if "there is absolution in my songs," it is not solely because the poet has suffered, but also because he has become the mouthpiece for his "killed friends." The speaker's voice thus obtains "absolution," from a continued connection with a host of dead male companions, much as comradeship was often said (in more conventional writing) to "redeem" the suffering of war. If impersonal comradeship had worked to sanctify not only male relations but the war itself, here intimate friendship takes on the mantle of legitimization, but the difference is marked: when personalized male intimacy becomes the centerpiece of emotional existence and poetic justification, the figure who emerges carries with him an unbearable load of pain (since friendship exists in war only to be destroyed), a self-consciously alienated attitude, and a voice of self-justification that will brook no opposition.

"The Poet as Hero" stridently asserts a new poetic consciousness for the soldier who has been remade by the loss of friends; in other poems, this figure seems less an avatar of a confident, new style than a haunted survivor. Sassoon, that is, modulates the image of the bereaved friend to cover various emotional states, all of which render problematic his future assimilation into civilian life. "Sick Leave" provides another extreme picture of the war self as a product of intense personal allegiances to other men, and it suggests, again, that these friendships determine the shape of both the individual and his literary output. Here is the poem in its entirety:

> When I'm asleep, dreaming and lulled and warm, –
> They come, the homeless ones, the noiseless dead.
> While the dim charging breakers of the storm
> Bellow and drone and rumble overhead,
> Out of the gloom they gather about my bed.
>   They whisper to my heart; their thoughts are mine.
>   "Why are you here with all your watches ended?
>   From Ypres to Frise we sought you in the Line?"
> In bitter safety I awake, unfriended;
> And while the dawn begins with slashing rain
> I think of the Battalion in the mud.
> "When are you going out to them again?
> Are they not still your brothers through our blood?"
>   (*WP*, 94)

"Sick Leave" contains a number of elements common to the war's literature: an emphasis on the guilt many officers experienced for abandoning their men while on home leave, a focus on ghosts and ghostly encounters, and a depiction of the continued presence of the war in the combatant's imagination, signified here by the storm, whose bellowing, droning, rumbling, and slashing action echoes the war.[52]

Sassoon posits the dead friends as the very crux of the poet's identity. The poem consists of three entities: the speaker home on sick leave, his dead friends, and the living men who continue to serve in France and whose imagined suffering troubles the narrator. The relations among these groups are entirely intertwined, and, indeed, one question the poem raises is what kind of identity or subjectivity the poet can assert, given the intense power these two groups hold over him and the shifting nature of any individual's placement among them. At the same time, it is precisely the speaker's distance from both sets of men, living and dead, that creates his guilt and turmoil. Paradoxically, the poet finds himself separated from his former companions, alone, "unfriended," even as he has in a sense been constituted by his relations with the men. This inter-mingling of consciousnesses is suggested explicitly by lines like "their thoughts are mine," and less directly by the confusion of voice and pronoun in the final couplet. The line that breaks the poem provides the crucial language to define the narrator's indefinite position: "In bitter safety I awake, unfriended." To awake from sleep into consciousness, which might be understood as a transition into individual self-awareness and the possibility of self-expression, stands here for a moment of emptiness, constituted by the loss of masculine companionship. The speaker, that is, understands his own position as one of isolation, a structural alienation arising from the end of fellowship, even as the power of friendship's commitments continues to hold sway. In "Sick Leave," this status of unfriendedness develops out of the men's blood communion, a form of shared identity at the level of the physical body. If the poem asserts communal blood, and hence permanent attachment, it also ends with a question mark, as if to indicate the poet's extreme detachment from the very beings whose identities influence his own.

Like Jones' *In Parenthesis*, which wrestles with the possibility that assembled bodies might overtake the individual consciousness, Sassoon here identifies the war subject as caught among competing entities, which loosely correspond to the three groups in the poem: the interiorized self, the intimate friend, the spirit of the corporate body. What distinguishes Sassoon's poetry, in part, is that his lyrics refuse to subjugate any of these elements to the others. Rather than allow one form of male identity to triumph over another, he searches for a voice that will represent the soldier's individualized experience, his attachment to intense personal intimacies, and his adherence to a profound – even bodily – battalion loyalty. As both "The Poet as Hero" and "Sick Leave" demonstrate, however, this figure is caught in a conflicted position with respect to civilian social forms, including the idea of the nation, in whose name he is supposed to exist. This basic rupture between identity and peace-time social models, in conjunction with the speaker's intense grief, thrusts him into a solipsism that denies all commitments to existing institutions or conventions.

Sassoon addresses this matrix of problems involving friendship, comradeship, literary authority, and alienation throughout his war poetry. In the later verse, he tends to emphasize the problem of bereavement, and we sense an increasingly desperate imperative to create unity with both dead and living men, however destructive such a process might become for the survivor. "Banishment" provides a fascinating account of Sassoon's famous protest, when he publicly denounced the war effort, and was, for a time, at risk of court martial. Sassoon eventually returned to the front after a medical diagnosis of mental strain (engineered by friends and patrons); in the poem, it is the men of war who recall him to combat. The act of military and social rebellion is presented in the poem as problematic solely for its disruption of war comradeship: "I am banished from the patient men who fight," the poem begins, immediately establishing a gulf between the speaker and the men, created not only by his public anti-war statement, but by the implied intellectual distance between the thoughtful poet and the "patient men who fight" (*WP*, 108). While the poet imagines himself cut off from male fellowship, that corporate state remains one of continued physical and emotional unity:

> They smote my heart to pity, built my pride.
> Shoulder to aching shoulder, side by side,
> They trudged away from life's broad wealds of light.
> Their wrongs were mine.   (*WP*, 108)

So profound is the communion of the battalion that even death cannot separate the inter-twined men, for "they died, – / Not one by one" (*WP*, 108). Typically in the war literature, death is presented as the final category of isolation, and the fear of death as a primary cause of both self-sufficiency and loneliness; hence for Sassoon to present the men's deaths as a moment of community is to assert the power of fellowship in strong terms.[53] At the same time, given the apparent closeness of the fighting men, the poet's own isolation from the scene becomes doubly marked. Sassoon's language oscillates between images of masculine unity that seem to include him and a strong sense of his banishment from the group spirit, the same spirit of male fellowship that in former times had created his pride (an attribute of leadership) and his pity (hence poetic authority). Clearly, his "mutinous" cry is both an assertion of individuality – a moment of moral authority and self-confidence, as against the relentless corporateness of the men – and an attempt to become the voice for that group, to make his language work for their salvation. "Love drove me to rebel" he proclaims, attempting to recapture a spirit of intimacy out of the very act of separation.

It would seem, then, that alienation results from the loss of male comrades, while unity provides the members of the group with identity and solace amid the hellish "pit where they must dwell." Yet Sassoon's language of isolation and solidarity is more complicated than this scheme indicates, as images of darkness and isolation haunt not only the poet but the men. Thus, if he is in "darkness," they have moved "out into the night," and though it is the speaker who is "banished," the men exist "in outcast gloom convulsed and jagged and riven / By grappling guns" (*WP*, 108). Just as Owen in "Smile, Smile, Smile" suggests that the unity of the "sunk-eyed wounded" paradoxically threatens to increase their isolated status, so here, Sassoon's men are only partially enclosed in unity: the other side of that comradeship involves a terrible state of lonely striving, both physical and psychological, a situation that seems to offer little future possibility for comfortable assimilation into civilian life. Thus when the poem ends with a renewed assertion of communion, as the poet is re-integrated into the battalion – "Love drives me back to grope with them through hell; / And in their tortured eyes I stand forgiven" (*WP*, 108) – the image continues to convey a sense of precarious isolation. Of all physical attributes, the men's "tortured eyes" indicate their suffering individuality. If their arms in the first stanza had represented the site of inter-mingling (marching "[s]houlder to aching shoulder, side by side") then their "tortured eyes" provide some resistance to the corporate structure. Moreover, the image of Sassoon literally standing before the men, his body mirrored in their many eyes, suggests, again, his severance from them, even at the moment of forgiveness and re-assimilation. What "Banishment" chronicles, then, is a continuous back-and-forth movement from togetherness to isolation, group to individual; out of this oscillation – central to the speaker's sense of self – comes an unsettled image of the poet endlessly striving for community with men, and finding in this search for male fellowship the motivation for speech.

"Banishment" thus follows "The Poet as Hero" in establishing Sassoon's position with respect to his war friends and comrades as crucially related to his ideal of poetic authority. The theme of "killed friends" and the poet's ever-fresh outrage at this violence remain the core of his war poetry, though the acidic tone of a poem like "The Poet as Hero" becomes modulated and softened in the later lyrics. "Memory," written two years after "Hero" and one year after "Sick Leave," uses more nostalgic and chastened language to make a similar statement about poetic voice and the death of friends. The poem looks back nostalgically to the poet's privileged youth in the countryside (elaborated by Sassoon in the first part of his autobiographical trilogy, *Memoirs of a Fox-Hunting Man*), contrasting those lost pleasures with his current, and presumably permanent, state of sorrow:

> When I was young my heart and head were light,
> And I was gay and feckless as a colt
> Out in the fields, with morning in the may,
> Wind on the grass, wings in the orchard bloom.
> (*WP*, 117)

In a movement that typifies the war's literature, the text shifts dramatically after the first stanza, where youth, innocence, and beauty had found a home in the English countryside, only to be crushed by the suffering and irony of the war. The second stanza thus begins:

> But now my heart is heavy-laden. I sit
> Burning my dreams away beside the fire:
> For death has made me wise and bitter and strong;
> And I am rich in all that I have lost.   (*WP*, 117)

Sassoon's strategy here is conventional, as he contrasts the open, free, outdoor life of youth with an interior (and interiorized) maturity formed by the knowledge of death. In Romantic terms, Sassoon transforms the tragedy of adulthood, Blake's "experience," into the material for poetry. Wisdom, bitterness, and strength combine to create an image of masculinity appropriate to Sassoon's notion not only of war-torn modernity, but also of poetic accomplishment. The poet's authoritative statement, "And I am rich in all that I have lost," establishes his credentials as a speaker and as a man precisely in the loss of the first stanza's innocence.

The last four lines add an even more staggering loss to the demise of idealized home, country, and confident ethos:

> O starshine on the fields of long-ago,
> Bring me the darkness and the nightingale;
> Dim wealds of vanished summer, peace of home,
> And silence; and the faces of my friends.
> (*WP*, 117)

Hailing a Keatsian darkness and nightingale, the poet continues his Romantic troping, and the tone of the last phrase, "the faces of my friends," is much less harsh, aggressive, or immediate than we have seen in other texts. Yet the line, with its evocation of the crisis that has made the poet into a perpetual mourner, nevertheless shakes the edifice so smoothly established. Having taken on the mantle of Romantic poet, the writer now indicates what differentiates this war text from its precursor lyrics in the nineteenth century, as the death of friends becomes the essential material that constitutes the new self. If a modern war aesthetic here defines itself as the heir to Romanticism, it nevertheless asserts its own refusal to be healed by memory, rigidly maintaining its claim of primacy in suffering, and leaving us, like the poet himself, with the permanent echo of intensified and broken intimacy.[54]

POST-WAR ARTICULATIONS: LOST FRIENDS AND THE LOST GENERATION

The paradigm of alienated poet as war-torn friend was to have a lasting impact on post-war culture, and inflects the shape of some of the era's most influential literature. In a 1926 poem entitled "To One Who was With Me in the War," Sassoon provides resonant language to articulate his view of the relation between war friendship and the alienated, post-war consciousness: "It was too long ago – the Company we served with . . . / We call it back in visual fragments, you and I, / Who seem, ourselves, like relics casually preserved" (*WP*, 151, ellipsis in original). Familiar modernist tropes abound here – fragmentation, historical disjunction, the substitution of visual for narrative logic, alienation, a painful awareness of the individual's precariousness in the machine of modern life – and are firmly connected with the problems both of intense personal intimacy ("you and I") and of lost community (the company that cannot be re-assembled). The poem goes on to demonstrate the men's continued immersion in a war mentality that compulsively transfigures the peaceful English landscape into no-man's-land, the calm of home life into the explosiveness of battle. Signs of a psychoanalytic frameworth abound, as the unconscious mind is written onto the physical surroundings. Finally, the poem ends with a typically modernist moment of uncertainty and fracture – "What's that you said?" – as the men's shared consciousness becomes punctured by their post-war surroundings (*WP*, 152).[55]

"To One Who was With Me in the War" follows other war lyrics in simultaneously positing as "relics" of the war both the alienated individual and the mutually sustaining small group, here reduced to a couple. As we have seen, the lone soldier was at times defined in conjunction with images of precarious community, the two forms of isolation not only existing side by side, but also generating one another. In parallel fashion, the post-war literary image of the ever-grieving former soldier will be associated with the idea of the lost generation, a trope which, again, envisions the community of soldiers as simultaneously closely linked and unstable. The notion of the lost generation, it should be noted, functions essentially on a double register. On one hand, the phrase was used to describe the roughly 750,000 British men killed in the war, and tended to carry heavy class overtones: the officer class, groomed for leadership both at home and in the empire, conventionally characterized as the apex of English manhood, was now lamented as all but obliterated. On the other hand, those who returned from the war were also believed to constitute a kind of "lost generation," and this sense that a specific community had emerged from the war held the culture's imagination for many years, in a sense catalyzing an understanding of the society's own failures and responsibilities. As Paul Baümer succinctly declares, "if we go back we will be weary, broken, burnt out, rootless, and without hope... We will be superfluous even to ourselves, we will grow older, a few will adapt themselves, some others will merely submit, and most will be bewildered; – the years will pass by and in the end we shall fall into ruin" (Remarque, *All Quiet*, 294).

In characterizing the idea of the lost generation, we should note the importance of both parts of the conjunction: "lost" (conjuring up images of alienation, solipsism, brokenness) and "generation" (suggesting community, shared identity, intimacy, and perhaps also reproduction, a new generating force). To take just one further articulation of the phenomenon, R. G. Dixon's unpublished memoir composed in the 1980s opens with a rumination on the idea of a war-formed generation. "Once upon a time," he writes, "following the end of the war, we were known as the 'lost generation,' and I suppose that is what we were" ("Wheels of Darkness," 6), and he elaborates his view of what constituted such a community:

war matures young men beyond their years, so that we... become changed, and mature swiftly into the kind of men that are quite different from what we would have grown into had the appalling violences, as well as the companionships and heroisms, of war not taken a hand in our development. Since the Kaiser's War, I have been painfully aware how I am different from many of my compatriots. It has always been difficult for me to be wholly at home with those men who have not been through the experiences of war... as men singled out as subtly different from others. ("Wheels of Darkness," 4)

Dixon's account, which goes on to describe the problem of communicating about the war with non-combatants, synthesizes the core elements in the idea of the lost generation. Above all, he stresses both an ineffable sense of difference between the men who fought and everyone else, and, conversely, a sense of elemental, unspoken mutuality and comfort among those who returned from the war. The intimacy he describes is formed as much by "companionships and heroisms" as by "appalling violences," and, perhaps most importantly, is permanent. If the culture's interest in the group has diminished (hence the "once upon a time" language), for Dixon, their shared identity survives.

The lost generation is a tricky concept – perhaps overly seductive. Casting doubt, for instance, on the historical value of such concepts as the lost generation and the alienated ex-combatant, Joanna Bourke has convincingly argued that the majority of men who fought on the Western Front eagerly returned home with the intention of reconstituting domestic ties. More generally, social historians continue to debate the relevance of the notion of a lost generation, especially in terms of such issues as generational specificity and post-war gender configuration. (In what sense did those who fought constitute a meaningful cohort? Were there really strong and lasting gender imbalances as a result of war deaths?) However, my concern here is not with the historical or statistical accuracy of these lost-generational issues, but rather with their importance for the literary and cultural imagination of the period, what Samuel Hynes calls "the myth of the war." I want to suggest that some of the most influential writers in the two decades following the war – non-combatants whose ambivalence about the war and its survivors is often palpable – hewed closely to the idea of a lost generation, specifically in the sense that they imaged the post-war state as one of alienation, brought on, in part, by the war's assault on male intimacy. I want to close my analysis of war friendship, then, with brief discussions of three texts that provide examples of the diverse ways in which the war's intimacy dilemma powerfully entered civilian discourse: Vera Brittain's *Testament of Youth* (1933), Virginia Woolf's *Mrs. Dalloway* (1925), and T. S. Eliot's "The Hollow Men" (1925). Any number of interesting examples might have been selected, for the paradigm of lost male bonds captured the post-war imagination in vivid and diverse ways. The three examples presented here, however, are especially instructive for several reasons, in addition to their canonicity and influence: each is written from a perspective external to the war; each couples the problem of masculine institutions and intimacies with wider cultural tensions in the decades following the armistice; and each can be said to appropriate the language of lost friendship in service of an explicit modernity.

Vera Brittain's *Testament of Youth* simultaneously chronicles the writer's personal responses to the war, during which she served as a nurse in London,

France, and Malta, and posits a larger phenomenon of cultural transformation through disillusionment. In direct and vigorous prose, the narrative situates its female subject in relation to the overwhelmingly male world of the First World War. It is perhaps ironic that the feminist Brittain, painfully aware of the oppressive mechanisms of patriarchy, offers some of the most famous and empathetic articulations of the lost generation. Despite the diaristic form it often takes, that is, Brittain's enthralling account of the "smashing up of [her] own youth by the War" is not so much a personal testament as a deliberate attempt to speak both for and about a generation.[56] As she explains in the opening line of her "Foreword": "For nearly a decade I have wanted, with a growing sense of urgency, to write something which would show what the whole War and post-war period...has meant to the men and women of my generation" (*Testament*, 11). The narrative she produces, which includes many inserted texts written by other members of that "generation," tells a story of disillusionment, bitterness, and loss, of the way in which "the early ideals of the War were all shattered, trampled into the mud which covered the bodies of those with whom I had shared them" (*Testament*, 446). Like Sassoon's "Memory" and many other war texts, Brittain's narrative is structured according to a Romantic trajectory, where a time of youthful hope and exuberance is smashed by the relentless assault of adult insights and experiences. Like the combatants with whom she so powerfully empathizes, one thing that marks Brittain's Romantic account of experience-as-loss is that she, too, presents the war's disillusionments in terms of devastated male friendship.

From the opening of the narrative, Brittain strongly identifies with her male peers, understanding herself to form part of their elite world, exemplified by the traditions of school and university. Rather than lamenting the exclusive structure of the institutions that perpetuate male power, she expects to win entry into them on the basis of her intellect and ambition. Thus, her feminism takes shape primarily as a matter of women's access to important male institutions. It is a tradition of Great War writing that the immediate pre-war period was a halcyon time, and Brittain's version of this convention involves a sense of enthusiasm for the dawning of female opportunity in academic, professional, and political life. When her male peers are at school and university, Brittain participates vicariously in their lives, as she euphorically works towards her own career at Oxford. Indeed, far from disparaging the exclusivity or sexism of the male communities to which her brother and fiancé belong, Brittain imagines herself as a part of that world, and hence the destruction of that world's perfect wholeness during the war will determine her own experience of fragmentation and isolation. And it is in this spirit of shared disillusionment after the war that Brittain ultimately goes up to Oxford to complete her university degree; once there, she finds herself starkly indifferent, unable to partake in the pleasures of collegiate community, an outcast. At university, Brittain feels entirely disconnected from all forms of conventional fellowship, a figure not unlike the lonely and disoriented soldiers populating much masculine war literature.

What makes Brittain's story of loss and dislocation so remarkable, of course, is that one would expect her to have felt barred by her gender from the very community whose destruction she so tenderly articulates. Instead of presenting the war as a battle between the sexes, as Gilbert and Gubar would have it, Brittain depicts the tragedy as an experience that severs all the war's generation from the rest of society, not so much setting women and men against one another as destroying an extremely close male community that also includes a select group of women. For Brittain, like so many combatant writers of the period, the war's greatest abomination is its shattering of intimacy, an assault on personal ties that occurs in several keys. Most clearly, Brittain describes the terrible trauma when her beloved friends and relatives are killed in combat: "So incredible was our final separation" she writes of the death of her brother, "that it made life itself seem unreal. I had never believed that I could actually go on living without that lovely companionship that had been at my service since childhood, that perfect relation" (*Testament*, 444). For Brittain, the death of her brother means the end of a flawless embodiment of friendship. Her language of perfect community recalls similar moments in the poetry of Owen and Sassoon, where idealized and all-important friendships are shattered by the war, and such killed intimacy provides the key to war alienation.

Even more directly resonant with masculine war literature is Brittain's discussion, in the chapter depicting post-war isolation and trauma ("Survivors Not Wanted"), of the way the war demolished not only her friendship with her brother and fiancé, but also their intimacy with one another. Brittain empathetically registers a crisis of lost male friendship, suggesting that such relations cannot be recaptured and that the survivor will thus remain, in Sassoon's terms, perpetually "unfriended." In describing their deaths, she writes, "The two of them seemed to fuse in my mind into a kind of composite lost companion, an elusive ghost which embodied all intimacy, all comradeship, all joy, which included everything that was the past and should have been the future" (*Testament*, 485). Brittain here conjoins two separate points: the first is a perception of the beloved men as inseparable from one another, a composite being comprising perfect intimacy (and the term "comradeship" invokes the masculine language of war fellowship). The second involves her own relation to the loss of those friends, a position of permanent estrangement that transforms her into a verbal representative for the lost men. Brittain's text echoes much war poetry in connecting the loss of male friends with the compulsion and authority to speak. Even if Brittain never fully belonged either to the overarching institutions that organized male bonds, or to the private intimacy of war, her text powerfully represents that intimacy as the greatest treasure of the war period and its loss as the basis for the fragmented, embittered condition that she believes is the hallmark of the lost generation.

Testament of Youth has consistently found an avid readership, and its depiction of war experience and loss from the perspective of an ambivalently situated female writer perhaps resonated, more than a decade after the cease-fire, for many non-combatants. That is, Brittain's simultaneous attachment and detachment in relation to war community made her an appropriate spokesperson for an experience that was understood in the war and post-war years as both intensely personal and widely shared. For Brittain, the loss of male friendship defines a general sense of historical trauma, and she self-consciously works to capture these war dislocations as a matter of modernity. Her representation of contemporaneity can be said to overlap in certain ways with the cultural enterprise of modernism, even if on formal and generic grounds, her work – conventionally conceived, non-experimental, often sentimental – could not be called modernist. Thus, if shifting from Brittain to Virginia Woolf takes us from the margins into the center, in terms of literary history, in certain respects this movement will suggest homologies and similarities: in their respective areas, the two writers were highly influential, capturing something that has been viewed as exemplary in the response to the war. More important for our purposes, they share a sensibility about lost friendship as a touchstone of war experience, bereavement, and post-war alienation.

Like Brittain, Woolf occupied a vexed position with respect to such powerful masculine establishments as the Cambridge world inhabited by her male friends and relations, and her depiction of traditional male communities is neither consistent nor uniform in her fictional and polemical works.[57] If *A Room of One's Own* (1929) articulates Woolf's frustration (albeit in a spirit of humor and irony) at being excluded from the privileges of Oxbridge, then other texts indicate a more empathetic registering of the beauty of certain forms of male community. As we saw in Chapter 1, Woolf's admiration for the intimate male circle under the softening and invigorating light of Cambridge suggests her adherence to the view that the universities provide an antidote to the detested, enforced community of the public schools. Yet, Woolf does not simply envy male institutions like Cambridge, embittered at her exclusion from the community they engender; nor is her over-riding reaction one of condemnation for their ideological stranglehold on the British middle classes. During and after the war, when Woolf was involved both personally and as a publisher with a number of the war writers discussed here, she came to understand with stunning insight the crucial and devastating role that male friendship played in creating war subjects. In *Mrs. Dalloway*, which is set quite consciously in the aftermath of the war, she shows that male friendship threatens to become an all-devouring category, with the power to disrupt, or even destroy, other institutions such as marriage, love, and friendship between the sexes – institutions that remain valuable for Woolf, despite their clear limitations. *Mrs. Dalloway* suggests that when these over-determined friendships disappear, the individual friend, the survivor, is left in a position of precarious isolation and solitude.

Suspended in time, adrift in London, and incapable of plunging like Clarissa Dalloway into the June day, Septimus Warren Smith not only represents the war, he is a fragment of the war itself. In a novel obsessed with the passing of time, minute by minute, hour by hour, Septimus stands out for his chronic and perpetual stasis. The first words used to describe him accurately characterize his situation throughout the text: "Septimus Warren Smith, who found himself unable to pass."[58] Given that the passage of time – its flowing, circling, perpetual movement – occupies the very core of *Mrs. Dalloway*, both the war and its representative mark a disruption, an impossibility, because, for this novel, to be arrested in time is a death sentence. The language of explosion, fire, and destruction surrounds Septimus from the moment of his introduction in the text until his gruesome death, as if he is himself a bit of shell, a "relic casually preserved" (to borrow Sassoon's phrase) that, like the many unexploded mines imperiling France and Belgium in the years following the armistice, might at any moment detonate and self-destruct. As many critics have noted, Septimus represents the psychic costs of war – not only shell-shock, but a broad sense of historical trauma, with his consciousness holding a residue of the war's unabated pain.[59]

For Septimus, the catastrophic war is internalized as a problem of lost friendship: "He had gone through the whole show... friendship, European war, death" (*MD*, 130–131). At the simplest level, it is the death of Evans that catapults Septimus into his state of numbness. Septimus suffers because he fails to recognize that the end of his war friendship means much more than he had assumed, more indeed than is conventionally conceived, at least outside of a war framework. His shell-shock derives from this massive misrecognition: though the two men "had to be together, share with each other, fight with each other, quarrel with each other," Septimus is unable to contemplate the internal consequence of the cruel fact that "here was the end of a friendship" (*MD*, 130). Septimus has not, in other words, been reading his Owen and Sassoon. It is precisely because friendship is both the most sustaining and the most vulnerable relation in war that it comes quietly to dominate Septimus' psychological organization. The crucial points are, first, that Evans functions as Septimus' whole world, an inter-dependence perhaps compounded by homoerotic desire, *and*, of course, that Evans inevitably dies (as his evanescent name suggests), leaving Septimus utterly alone. Like so many war writers, Woolf demonstrates that, during the war, the friend figure became the centerpiece of the soldier's humanity, and it is thus all the more crushing and ironic that any friend's likelihood of survival was so slim. Lucrezia is quite right to think that "everyone has friends who were killed in the War," but she errs in assuming that for Septimus, whose psychological and emotional landscape has been permanently reconfigured, such losses can be superseded by new ties (*MD*, 99).

On the contrary, the novel powerfully demonstrates that the man formed by friendship and broken by its rupture cannot be re-integrated into civilian life. Marriage, demobilization and the return home, resumption of professional responsibilities: none of these retains any hold over Septimus, who, like the many wracked figures populating the poetry of Owen, Nichols, Sassoon, and others, is haunted consistently by the presence of Evans in the shadows. The sensitive Lucrezia is acutely aware of Septimus' failure to assimilate into the daily routine of London life, and is tortured by his visible appearance of oddity. And for Septimus – "quite alone, condemned, deserted" – such incapacity to shed his war existence or his lost war friendship is experienced as utter alienation: "even Holmes himself could not touch this last relic straying on the edge of the world, this outcast, who gazed back at the inhabited regions, who lay, like a drowned sailor, on the shore of the world" (*MD*, 140). *Mrs. Dalloway* quite directly posits a constitutive link between totalizing male friendship and the terrifying spectacle of alienation. There is no room in this post-war world, the text indicates, for the all-powerful and potentially debilitating investment in male friendship codified by the war. Even characters such as Lady Bexborough, whose maternal loss of beloved son might seem to exemplify the terrific tragedy of war, continue to move forward with the incessant march of time. It is only the figure of the former soldier, the sorrowful male friend, who sees an eternity of isolation, a battle against the tyranny of human nature (as Septimus conceives his struggle), and death.

One might even go so far as to say that Clarissa Dalloway's final tri-umphant moment of human connection at her party requires first that Septimus plunge to his death, eradicating at once a relic of masculine friendship and a visible reminder of the war's destructive power. Clarissa, after all, has been praised by critics for her ability to foster forms of com-munity that reach beyond the domestic family, and she demonstrates this power in part by imaginatively ministering over Septimus' mangled body. In a world scarred by war, Clarissa's model of healing, which depends on empathy and the desire to effect human connections, quite clearly sur-passes the imperious, patriarchal forms of medical treatment embodied by Holmes and Bradshaw. At the same time, Clarissa herself is a figure who has sacrificed one type of exhilarating friendship – her erotic love for Sally – in favor of more conventional relations. If Septimus epitomizes the awesome power of war to re-create the individual through friendship and lost male love, then Clarissa is a figure for civilian modes of community, and the text indicates that, finally, it is her ideal of diffuse social interaction, cleansed of its lesbian possibilities, that prevails.

Given Woolf's attention in novels like *Jacob's Room* (1922) and *The Waves* (1931) to the easy and comfortable traditions available to men for nurturing their friendships, it is ironic, yet entirely characteristic of war literature, that Septimus – such a definitive male friend – can find no hope for mutuality or community. The difference, of course, is class: whereas men like Jacob Flanders are virtually defined by their access to the institutions of male priv-ilege, Septimus could not possibly attend a public school or elite university. We have seen that the rhetoric of comradeship tended to exalt war as a space of class fluidity, yet the complex erosion and reification of class barri-ers during the war was in fact a much more complicated phenomenon, and Septimus finds himself in an interesting middle category: his class position distances him from both the public-school rhetoric of comradeship and the working-class ideal of matey-ness. Indeed, Septimus never once indicates an interest in comradeship, group loyalty, battalion pride, or any form of institution (civilian or military) that might help to sustain or uphold the individual when his intimate friend dies. It is precisely because Septimus is shaped so fully by the extreme intimacy of war, disconnected from any form of safe or nurturing male institutions, including the conventions of comradeship, that he finds himself in the end with no place to go except over the railings.

Septimus offers a striking image of the alienated soldier as bereaved friend. In war literature, this isolated figure at times appears in connection with the self-enclosed group – a precarious form of community, with a lan-guage and sign system of its own, yet insufficient institutional structure to prevent its collapse into fragmentation and solitariness. This second tableau gives shape to another exemplary modernist text, T. S. Eliot's "The Hollow Men," a lyric which directly transforms the simultaneous intransigence and failure of male friendship into the material for modernism. Published in 1925, "The Hollow Men" has consistently been viewed as both characteristic and determinative of modernism: beginning with its Conradian epigraph ("Mistah Kurtz – he dead") the poem depicts experience as a series of utterly fragmented and dissociated shards, where the flotsam and jetsam of religion, history, popular language, and human garbage intermingle to create a consciousness that exists on the boundary between dreaming and waking, death and life.[60] Moreover, the geography and thematics of the war abound in the poem, which is set at once in an abstract landscape of modern reality (or unreality) and in a schematized, distilled version of the Western Front.[61]

Yet one element that makes "The Hollow Men" so accurate as a re-enactment of Great War subjectivity is its emphasis on the hollow men's alienation within their very intimacy. The poem speaks relentlessly in a "we" voice, and its language of intimacy closely echoes images we have seen, for instance, in Owen's verse:

> We are the hollow men
> We are the stuffed men
> Leaning together
> Headpiece filled with straw. Alas!
> Our dried voices, when
> We whisper together
> Are quiet and meaningless
> As wind in dry grass
> Or rats' feet over broken glass
> In our dry cellar
>
>   Shape without form, shade without colour,
> Paralysed force, gesture without motion;
>
>   Those who have crossed
> With direct eyes, to death's other Kingdom
> Remember us – if at all – not as lost
> Violent souls, but only
> As the hollow men
> The stuffed men.   (*Selected Poems*, 77)

The opening image of the men leaning together, with a suggestion both of pathos and of caricature, conjures up familiar pictures of knots of soldiers in postures of careless intimacy. It is an image that necessarily excludes the viewer, who cannot partake of their silent sign system, and it thus establishes a problem of distance not only for the former troops, but also between reader and subject. Relatedly, the crisis of inexpressibility, which has been a major theme in war literature, markedly characterizes the hollow men, whose "dried voices... [a]re quiet and meaningless." Their ineffectual whispers become an expression of sad futility, a symbol both for the particular plight of war combatants, and, at the same time, for the universal inadequacy of language, a familiar modernist fixation.

Eliot captures in these opening lines the paradox of war intimacy, as the men remain both absolutely inter-connected and absolutely alone. If the hollow men cannot be conceived as individuals outside of their corporate existence, they nevertheless radiate an intense self-absorption, represented by the inadequacy of their speech, the failure of their actions ("[p]aralysed force"), and their slow erasure from human memory. Eliot's poem grapples with the complexity of war intimacy, which at times seems purely structural – a by-product of the sheer assembly of bodies – yet is also constitutive of individuality itself. The men in the poem are formed equally by their proximity to one another and by the extreme power of their own depleted interiority. Hence, like Sassoon's "Banishment," the poem's imagery oscillates between eyes, where one expects to find the locus of individual experience ("The eyes are not here / There are no eyes here... Sightless, unless / The eyes reappear" [*Selected Poems*, 79]) and linked bodies ("In this last of meeting places / We grope together / And avoid speech / Gathered on this beach of the tumid river" [*Selected Poems*, 79]). Eliot's text moves back and forth between oppositional states of alienation and intimacy, stressing the impossibility of achieving the kind of stability in friendship for which poets like Owen had striven. At the same time, rather than force the poem to accommodate a transcendent male intimacy, Eliot offers his poetic language as a stand-in for that missed resolution. The voices of the soldiers/friends gradually expire, and the poet provides a new lexicon to recreate and amplify the men's experience of isolation in numbers. Thus as the poem moves towards its close, the voices and visual pictures of the hollow men disappear, giving way to a new series of interspersed and broken narratives.[62] If the status of the bereaved friend provided authority for the war poet, that authority has now been absorbed and appropriated by Eliot's poem itself. Just as Septimus' very existence becomes increasingly untenable in a post-war culture that inevitably moves forward, so the whispered silences of the hollow men are replaced by the patchwork of narrative fragments known as modernism.

"The Hollow Men," *Mrs. Dalloway*, and *Testament of Youth*: each of these works develops a language to capture an idea of the war as exemplary generational event, and in each case a central war image is constituted by the over-determined problem of male intimacy. What Eliot, Woolf, and Brittain each present with a particular valence is the tragic paradoxicality of the problem of friendship, so that at its very moment of ascendancy it reveals its greatest vulnerability. The male friend comes into his own as spokesman or representative for a generation, even as he is destroyed by a profound detachment from sustainable institutions, palpably lacking a cultural vocabulary that can be shared with the non-war world. Even more than Conrad's wanderers whose investment in intimacy outlasts their faith in a Victorian imperial world-view, or Forster's desiring men whose sheer physicality overpowers the consolatory narratives of nineteenth-century Hellenism, the war creates an icon out of the fierce yet defeated male friend. What Eliot, Woolf, and Brittain saw so clearly was the (ironic) exemplarity of this figure: constructed in a world without women, in antagonism against middle-class civilian culture, and in the evaporating embrace of a dying friend. To appropriate and recast that voice, in a sense to adopt the moral legitimacy of the war-torn friend within a new literary context, became a significant strategy in the works of literary modernists, as they forged ahead in rescripting the idea of modernity. It is not so much war as the end of war that finally resonates in these texts, and, with that finality, the status of bereaved and broken friend is dispersed and dissipated into the civilian culture of peace.

CHAPTER 4

"The violence of the nightmare": D. H. Lawrence and the aftermath of war

"Having you, I can live all my life without anybody else, any other sheer intimacy. But to make it complete, really happy, I wanted eternal union with a man too: another kind of love."[1]

D. H. Lawrence, *Women in Love* (Rupert Birkin)

"that is the sum of my whole experience, the search for a friend."[2]

D. H. Lawrence, *Aaron's Rod* (James Argyle)

"But my idea is . . . every man should have a mate – like most of us had in the war."[3]

D. H. Lawrence, *Kangaroo* (Jack Calcott)

Comradeship did not disappear after the war. If the war-scarred friend now became a figure in the civilian landscape, the ideal of transcendent male bonds also found new life in the post-war setting. For many years after 1918, the essential problems of war – loss, injury, mourning, death – would occupy a critical place in British life, and the Victorian history of organizing intimacy, though tarnished, nevertheless retained a foothold as part of the culture's repertory for understanding and processing the trauma of war. No literary figure was more concerned with these shifts and movements than D. H. Lawrence. His is a voice of apotheosis for male intimacy, an unceasing and restless spirit demanding that the social order accommodate and embrace masculine bonds. In Lawrence's writing, the combined effects of the longing for male friendship and its devastating failure are conspicuously derived, and the connection between war and masculine intimacy haunts his work. As with all of his dominant themes, Lawrence's investigation of male fellowship is marked by a quality of excess and extremity, a reiterative mode that bespeaks both insatiable yearning and real despair. Revulsion and desire oscillate endlessly in the Lawrence cosmos, as the goal of male love is repeatedly crisscrossed with violent homophobia, and his texts seem to sag and creak under the burden of unfulfilled friendship. For many of the writers in this study, a sense of urgency and debilitation has permeated the organization of intimacy, mitigated perhaps by the consolations of literary authority; for Lawrence, urgency becomes a wild shout, and the authority to speak a shrieking prophecy.

Lawrence's preoccupation with male bonds forms part of his personal story of misogyny and unresolved homosexual desire, and has generally been understood in these terms. Our conception of his works might expand and deepen, however, if we shift the focus onto a wider cultural panorama, and particularly onto a landscape marked by war. Lawrence always had a vexed relation to the war, an event in which he did not directly participate, but whose psychological dynamics he absorbed in his life and explored in his writing. One might productively ask what Lawrence's obsessive struggles with male bonds and his particular constructions of modernity have in common with the discourses of comradeship and friendship we have been examining, and with other forms of social criticism that evolved from the war. Does the ambivalence swirling around blood brotherhood in his texts have a correlative in the politics of war-time and post-war England, and might such intersections offer new insights into both realms? How does Lawrence's exhaustive attempt to weld friendship with political, psychological, and spiritual goals reflect or challenge elements of the contemporary social order against which he so passionately launched his life-long polemic? Do the formulations of friendship, isolation, and authority that we found in many war texts find echoes or reconstitutions in Lawrence's writing?

In answering these difficult questions, I shall argue that Lawrence took on and rescripted the post-war reckoning with male community and male love. The image I hope to develop is of a civilian society profoundly conflicted on the subject of post-war masculine relations, and of a moment when a variety of thinkers – reformers, activists, and polemicists alongside literary artists – worked both to tackle and to elide the effects of war. The position of the former soldier in civilian life would never be an easy one, and, after the war, one pressing question immediately confronting the culture, and in a sense following from the comradeship ethos of the war, was this: how to comprehend, reabsorb, and assimilate the millions of men returning from the trenches.[4] As the combatants found their way home, social critics confronted the complex challenge of thinking about the war as both present and absent, of its men as both altered and unchanged. The whole notion of a "post-war" culture was an important one for the self-conception of the British in the decade after the war – as Wyndham Lewis wrote in 1937, "Post-war means something quite definite... The War bled the world white. It had to recover... All that was real was in eclipse."[5] The idea that there was something unique and unsettling about the post-war period (which Lewis, for one, dated from 1918 until the General Strike of 1926), involved the returned men in vexed and complex ways, and Lawrence contributed to this phenomenon of reaction and imaginative reintegration. Ultimately, as he struggled in his characteristic style to reaffirm and consolidate a vision of male community, to develop his own theory about the efficacy and power of male bonds, Lawrence transformed the war's intimacy dilemma into a premise for his own literary self-construction.

BODIES OF MEN: THE LANDSCAPE OF POST-WAR ENGLAND

As I have noted, it is a critical commonplace that the Great War acted as a watershed in the early twentieth century, an important dividing line between Victorian England – with its gentility, marked gender differentiation, imperial self-confidence, bourgeois conventionality, and complacency about class stratification – and the modern age of skepticism, radical ambiguity, and the refutation of conventional wisdom. The story should be entirely familiar: men went to war with Rupert Brooke and returned with Siegfried Sassoon; women sent men off with white flowers and welcomed them home with the vote. Or, to use my own terms, the war began in comradeship and ended in killed-friendship. Such changes, though generally celebrated by literary and cultural historians, spelled fear "in a handful of dust," even for those contemporaries who welcomed and helped to usher in the new order. Now, of course, each element in this narrative has been challenged, from the uncomplicated picture of a complacent Victorian culture to the view of moderns as courageous anti-conventionalists. With the heroic model of post-war modernism seeming increasingly insufficient, critics have begun to stress the persistence of the past, rather than a logic of progress, and the fluidity of transitionality rather than its cleanness or clarity. As Samuel Hynes eloquently states it:

It is not true, as is sometimes assumed, that a general wartime enthusiasm for war and its values was overwhelmed and replaced at the war's end by a total disillusionment that informs and defines English culture of the Twenties. Rather, both existed throughout the decade – two cultures, separate and mistrustful of each other, a conservative culture that clung to and asserted traditional values, and a counter-culture, rooted in rejection of the war and its principles. Each culture had its art, its literature, and its monuments; and each denied the other.[6]

In thinking about the problem of male community in the aftermath of the war, this emphasis on contradictory meanings becomes vital. After the armistice was declared in November 1918, England faced a staggering and bewildering array of challenges in almost every area – loosely grouped by contemporaries under the heading of "reconstruction" – including the prominent and immediate problem of demobilizing the forces and addressing the situation of returning servicemen.[7] Enormous numbers of men would now be sent home to join huge numbers of casualties who had been returned over the four years of combat, many of them physically and psychologically wounded. At the signing of the armistice, 3.5 million men were on active duty in the British services, of 6.1 million who had served for Britain in total. Though casualty figures are difficult to specify, a conservative estimate is that in addition to the nearly 750,000 dead, roughly 1.6 million British combatants had serious physical wounds from the war, and another 200,000 suffered from severe mental disorders.[8] Wounds to limbs, hands, head, eyes, and organs; diseases such as tuberculosis, rheumatism, and heart disease; a whole variety of nervous ailments; miscellaneous and unclassified illnesses; disabilities reported to the war pensions office and those that went unreported – the lists multiply in both length and category. The bodies of the dead – such a terrible mass of lost human life – would not be transported back to England, a first in the nation's history, and this controversial decision not surprisingly provoked debate and engendered a host of new memorializing practices.[9] In all parts of the empire, issues of readjustment and "repatriation" (to use another favorite term) pressed upon governments, philanthropic institutions, local communities, parishes, and individuals. Thus British culture, and here I include combatants alongside civilians, had to absorb and make sense of the unique forms of masculine consciousness that had developed during the war – novel configurations of male bodies, terrible new forms of physical debilitation, potentially confusing interpersonal commitments – in the context of a profound spirit of bereavement, shock, and for many former soldiers, the guilt associated with survival. As Winston Churchill declared, "the transition to peace was more violent than the entry into war … it involved a more complete and universal revolution of our minds."[10]

Injury plays a critical part in this story of the war's effects. Elaine Scarry has argued that it is the visible legacy of physical injury on human bodies that distinguishes war from other human enterprises, that the injured remnants constitute a form of shared memory that ensures war's finality at both personal and national levels.[11] Scarry's discussion of the national memory embodied in injured flesh and her argument for the extreme (and overlooked) importance of war-scarred bodies provide a theoretical basis for my own conviction that the returned men hold a key for understanding many aspects of post-war culture.[12] We might describe a process in which war's history is registered on the bodies of its participants, a form of cultural adjustment involving not only the injured themselves, but the body politic in a wider sense (albeit in a rather inchoate and unconscious form). Writing in 1920, one angry war chronicler described the men who fought as those "who had risked their lives and bore on their bodies the scars of war," and this sense of bodily memory ripples through many aspects of the post-war period.[13] The soldier's body came to offer a compelling visual vocabulary for the specific trauma of war, as well as a touchstone for cultural responsibility, and seemed to demand not only unique forms of attention, but also new linguistic practices.[14]

Wilfred Owen's tragic poem "Disabled" (1918) captures with visual force the situation of the wounded body returned from war, cogently prefiguring many of the elements that would characterize the broad cultural response to injured soldiers. In addition to purveying a combination of sympathy and angry disillusionment, as discussed in the last chapter, the poem works to create a poetic space for the incapacitated soldier, a persona who was both ubiquitous and disturbingly silent during the war and in its aftermath. At the center of the poem is a sense of silence and passing over, as the eyes of women drift away from the disabled man in favor of "the strong men who were whole."[15] The suggestion of sexual impotence – an often unspoken yet crucial element in the conception of war debility – haunts the poem. Indeed, the very nature of masculinity is at issue, as the shift from a conventionally defined school- and sport-based masculinity gives way to the helpless, defiant, misogynist, and ultimately mute figure in the chair. The poet speaks for, in lieu of, the silent man, simultaneously representing and eclipsing him. A sense of quiet loneliness swells at the poem's close, a kind of crescendo of loss and desperation. Perhaps most significantly, "Disabled" focuses directly on the injured body, looking with care and nuance at its traumatized surfaces. This is a figure in dire physical straits, marked both literally and figuratively by war, whose homecoming will converge upon many sensitive social issues.

Given the immensity and complexity of the ex-serviceman story, in sheer scale, and in the divergence of experience across class, rank, geography, and nature of combat, historians have addressed the problem in a variety of ways, and it is difficult to generalize about their often conflicting conclusions. The conventional notion, for instance, that the war ushered in a socio-cultural watershed (the literary-historical version of which I have just outlined) has given way in recent years, and many cultural historians now argue that the long-term effects of the war, across a range of categories, were ultimately minimal.[16] Yet what *is* certain is that contemporaries clearly identified dislocations along economic, class, and gender lines as proceeding from the war, that they saw the end of war in terms of inevitable – if uncertain and indefinable – change. As one contemporary social critic posited, "It is difficult... rightly to estimate the effect upon the future of Britain of the gigantic migration which tore men from the fields or from the town and office stool, and sent them out by millions beyond the sea to risk their lives in every corner of the world," because, "at the end they came home also in millions."[17] They came home in millions – but what this would mean was fundamentally unclear.

One phrase, however, captured the contemporary imagination with particular resonance, and will help to define and focus an analysis of male fellowship and masculinity in the context of post-war cultural politics: in a famous speech in November 1918, reprinted in *The Times* and elsewhere, David Lloyd George promised to "make Britain a fit country for heroes to live in." The Prime Minister's language was immediately and endlessly appropriated by reformers and politicians of all persuasions, by former soldiers in formulating grievances and demanding restitution, and by the society at large, as it worked to come to terms with the multiple dislocations embodied by the returned men.[18] "[A] fit country for heroes to live in" is both effective and problematic as a slogan, because it conjoins the idea that the men who fought in the war constitute a particular and specific type (here admiringly called "heroes") with an admission that the culture will have to be altered and improved to accommodate them. The basic structure of "a fit country for heroes to live in" is of a gap between England and its combatant forces, and this disjunctive feature characterizes a great deal of writing about the returned men. The concept of the "fit," with its multiple valences – the metaphor of shape and adjustment, the issue of physical viability (fitness), the active sense of transformation to make something fit – all of this would be suggested by the consistent use of the term across a range of texts and writers.[19] Lloyd George's language is, of course, laudatory, evoking a conventional ethos in which all combatants are heroes, and hence war can itself be conceived as heroic, at the same time that it stresses the inapplicability of such a romantic model to the realities of modern life, suggesting that the idea of the hero might, in fact, be grossly out of tune with prevailing post-war conditions. Overall, when the culture worked to imagine and institute "a fit country for heroes to live in," it acknowledged simultaneously that the war had produced a new individual, with particular loyalties and affiliations, and that such a figure must ultimately be re-absorbed, even at the cost of national self-improvement and painful social change.[20]

The image of the former soldier in a civilian context permeated post-war culture, a figure of pathos, simultaneously alone and associated with (lost) male community. Nearly all of the fictional, non-fictional, and poetic texts explored in the last chapter were published between 1919 and 1930, an outpouring that increased with each year, an incessant rewriting and reconceptualizing of the war that exhaustively exhorted readers to assimilate and internalize an experience that was manifestly inconceivable for non-combatants. Once again, Woolf's *Mrs. Dalloway* (1925) captures the phenomenon, as Septimus, relic and reminder of the war, pierces the fabric of civilian life, highlighting the omnipresence of the war in everyday existence and, equally, its inevitable erasure and obsolescence. Or, in Rebecca West's fascinating novella *The Return of the Soldier* (1918), an upper-class officer's seemingly incurable amnesia, his shell-shock, leads him to discount the privileges of aristocracy, as he returns imaginatively to an adolescent affair with a working-class woman, threatening in the process to overturn the whole operation of the class system. In West's tale, the war's overwhelming power to reshape combatant men, including those of the officer class, profoundly implicates and undermines a pre-war social order that had seemed comfortably fixed in its economic hierarchies. As Enid Bagnold, a former nurse and vivid chronicler of the war, writes in a reminiscence about living next to a convalescent hospital, "Men who have been poured from the battlefield into the hospital are like molten metal, and like molten metal they cool quickly and take strange shapes."[21] Finally, Lawrence's Clifford Chatterly provides another exemplary case, another such "strange shape." Clifford is "shipped home smashed," and his crippled lower half comes to represent not only the direct, physical legacy of the war, but a larger spirit of debility within his social and intellectual milieu.[22] Clifford's injured body becomes a metaphor and catalyst for a psychic and spiritual breakdown among his class, as "slowly, slowly the wound to the soul beg[an] to make itself felt, like a bruise, which only slowly deepens its terrible ache, till it fills the psyche... Now slowly it began to assert itself in a spread of fear, almost paralysis" (*LCL*, 46–47). As these brief examples testify, the return of the soldier – each individual soldier as well as their accumulated returns – became a literary event, in itself a moment of disruption, which also transfixed an array of social changes and uncertainties.[23]

In addition to figuring the return from war in terms of characters and plots, writers developed symbolic language to express and capture the condition of the returned men. Perhaps the most recurrent such image is of "brokenness." It is hard to overstate the ubiquity of the language of brokenness as a dominant metaphor to depict both the physical and psychological condition of former servicemen. *The Times'* 1915 article "For Men Broken in our Wars,"[24] or its 1917 piece entitled "Broken Soldiers,"[25] literally headline the tendency, while writers of all sorts consistently invoke the language of broken (or its corollary, shattered) men: "broken in health and in spirit... broken in the service of king and country";[26] "broken wanderers with curses on their lips";[27] "an army of broken wanderers";[28] "young chaps... broken and useless, with no hope left in life";[29] "England's Broken Dolls"[30] – the list could continue indefinitely. So prevalent was this language that the Director General of the Army Medical Service in 1918 took issue, on behalf of his rehabilitation subjects, with the use of such language to refer to former soldiers. Complaining in particular about Rudyard Kipling's use of the term "broke," in a poem which depicts "old fighting men... broke in the wars," Lt. Gen. Goodwin insists that "A man wounded and partially – even considerably – disabled, is not by any means 'broke'... By practical interpretation of sympathy, and by business-like application, we ought to be able to ensure that the number of men 'broke' in this war is proportionately lower than ever before."[31] What Goodwin's official irritation suggests is that even before the war had ended, the metaphor of brokenness had garnered a kind of cultural currency with real consequences for the perception, and self-perception, of injured men; to combat the image of brokenness was nearly as important to medical officials as was their physical work of rehabilitation. At the same time, of course, the idea of brokenness crossed into a wider conception of intellectual and spiritual debilitation, with a particular resonance for modernism, which famously emphasizes breaks, fragments, disconnection, the shattering of stable constructs. In general, concepts such as "brokenness" operate during the period on the line between direct engagement with the war's effects on human bodies and imaginative constructions of the human condition – spiritual, psychological, and cultural.

Victims of shell-shock offered a particularly powerful challenge, their newly named condition representing a direct and decisive derailment across multiple discourses, ideological as well as medical. From the early years of the war, the increasing presence of soldiers – the very icons of masculinity – in states of mental agony and collapse required medical professionals, military personnel, ordinary soldiers, and lay people to look anew at seemingly settled notions about masculinity, activity and passivity, order and obedience, and the mind/body divide. Beginning as early as 1915, military and civilian organizations were forced to confront the issue of mental breakdown, for cases multiplied on a scale entirely unprecedented in earlier wars. If standard notions of "malingering" or "cowardice" had once sufficed to define and characterize mental breakdown in combat, in the First World War such terms, though still operative (and for some military officials, absolute), became increasingly inadequate. As Sir John Collie, one of the military's top officials on the subject of mental disorders, wrote in 1917, "Neurasthenia is not fraud, it is not malingering, it is not wicked self-deception, and, above all, it is *not* cowardice. It is a real disease"[32] (italics in original). The recognition that pre-war definitions had become insufficient derived not least from the class configuration of mental complaints, with both officers and ranks suffering from mental disorders, and with officers consistently registering a higher percentage of neurasthenic cases. Many early commentators stressed that the officers who suffered from mental breakdowns were "often men who have displayed great bravery," and this problematic welding of notions of virile masculinity with conventional signs of weakness represents a hallmark of shell-shock discourse.[33]

As the war progressed, new theories about mental breakdown were presented and tested. One prominent camp contended that shell-shock was essentially a physical reaction to shelling (a kind of concussion of the brain); others stressed extreme bodily exhaustion; a eugenicist strain can be detected, with some arguing that the men who had nervous reactions to combat were congenitally unfit in the first place; and among those who were friendly to psychoanalysis, a range of explanations and treatments were proposed, focusing on the combatant's unconscious processes. Despite the wide spectrum of medical responses, however, four features can be said to characterize the problem for those required to diagnose and treat shell-shock: first, that the phenomenon had arrived on a huge scale, cutting across lines of class, age, rank, and nature/length of service; second, that a debilitating mental response to war could be both prolonged and delayed, so that the end of combat does not signal the end of shell-shock; third, that there might be a disjunction between an outward appearance of normality and great inward torment, a phenomenon at the center of such texts as West's *Return of the Soldier*, or, conversely, that the psychic trauma of shell-shock might express itself in physical terms, through tics, impaired movement, seizures, mutism, etc.; and fourth, that the primary goal of treatment is to return the shell-shocked soldier to his previous condition, essentially to erase the symptoms and effects of the debility. During the war, this last imperative was pressing, as the object was to re-fit the soldier to return to the front (and, again, the notion of "fitness" and "fitting" was consistently used in this context); after the war, the aim of rehabilitation involved the man's return into family, work, and ordinary civilian life, ensuring as much continuity as possible with his pre-war situation.

At the same time, the figure of the shell-shocked combatant almost immediately provided writers and other artists with a kind of paradigm for the modern condition.[34] Such modernists as Woolf and Eliot emblematized the war not in death or in physical injury, but in psychological wounds, and this conception of the war's human significance continues to hold sway. At the end of the twentieth century, novelists as diverse as Toni Morrison, Graham Swift, and Pat Barker have treated shell-shock as the prototypical injury of the Great War, and, since the 1979 publication of Eric Leed's seminal study of the war's psychological character and consequences, literary critics have demonstrated an equal fascination with the phenomenon. Shell-shock has come to embody a specific image of modernity, defined by disorientation, fragmentation, and radical alienation, by an overall rupture between the individual psyche and the normative culture that surrounds and threatens to engulf the helpless, if defiant, victim. As the mind and body register mutual symptoms and strains, the very notion of dualist borderlines becomes unstable, porousness and ontological confusion replacing strict lines of control. Moreover, because shell-shock so clearly engenders a form of power politics across multiple disciplines, the man suffering from it comes to represent an icon of resistance, and this image of protest – albeit indirect, often silent – contributes to the neurasthenic's status as something of a modernist hero.[35]

Though I shall not address in any detail here these conceptions of shell-shock, many of which I would certainly endorse, I do want to stress that, in several senses, the focus on shell-shock has obscured other, equally prevalent, images of returned men. It is not only that men with physical injuries far outnumbered those in states of serious mental collapse, but also that the visual picture of the injured ex-soldier entailed a kind of ubiquity that has perhaps been lost in our dominant conceptions of the period. The loss of limbs, for instance, carried a particularly vivid visual exemplarity. Douglas McMurtrie, head of the American Red Cross and a prominent voice about disability during the war period, explained in 1919 that "to the public at large the one-legged hero" has come "to typify the toll of warfare in disability" (*DS*, 113). The bulk of contemporary discussion of injury by military medical professionals treated shell-shock as one among a list of prominent disorders, including limblessness, blindness and deafness, and tuberculosis (which actually affected more soldiers than either amputation or debilitating mental breakdown). Equal to the neurasthenic victim, the physically scarred soldier brought home with him a visual and symbolic vocabulary that helped to establish the tone of reconstruction.

It is difficult to overstate the import for civilian contemporaries of the visual markings of extreme physical injury. Soldiers in and out of khaki remained an important part of both urban and rural landscapes, often in forms that called forth a deep sense of outrage, disturbance, and pathos. As one commentator predicted in 1917:

In the aftermath of this grievous war there will be no more lamentable and pathetic figure than the soldier who, by reason of his wounds, is paralysed and left utterly helpless... Indeed, there is no more piteous spectacle of human wreckage than this nerveless body, abject in its impotence and decrepitude, linked with the restless and imperious spirit of sturdy manhood.[36]

What makes the "spectacle" so terrible, for this writer surveying the men at the newly created "Star & Garter," a permanent home for severely disabled soldiers, is the presence of complete physical incapacity in the persons of young men who should, in the writer's view, embody virile, active manhood. In a poem written by an Australian nurse, which depicts wounded men coming home on transport ships, the incapacity of the young and hale engenders complex questions:

> What mean these great white ships at sea, ploughing their eastward
>   tack,
> Bearing their mangled human freight, bringing the spent men back?
> They mean that Australia has been there, they mean she has played
>   the game,
> And her wonderful sons have won their share of everlasting fame.
> Battered, and worn, and war scarred – those who had left their land
> Strong in their glowing manhood, by England to take their stand;
> Those who had sailed, when the war cloud burst, out on a distant
>   foam
> To the tune of "Australia Will Be There" – thus are they coming
>   home.[37]

Despite the conventionally patriotic language here, the writer points to the severe cultural uncertainty surrounding the injured men, as she contrasts their lost "glowing manhood" with the reality of "[b]attered, and worn, and war scarred" bodies, and suggests that their homecoming might be as fraught and troubling as it is joyful (the "thus" of the last phrase unsettling the otherwise happy connotation of "coming home").

For all the effort to reconcile such sights with a rhetoric of heroism, it is the juxtaposition of the wounded with cultural expectations about war that most markedly characterizes these texts. The wounded do not fit the expected picture, and, relatedly, their jarring incompatibility with the romance of war further distances them from much that surrounds them in the civilian sphere. An epigraph to the harrowing memoir from which the above poem is taken, which depicts in poignant terms the struggle of a young Australian soldier who spent over a decade in and out of hospital, maintains that the "torture and suffering" of the badly wounded "cannot even be imagined by those whose bodies have not been torn and hacked in the ghastliness of war and brought again and again to the operating tables" (Tiveychoc, *There and Back*, viii). The sight of maimed soldiers' bodies inevitably evoked strong emotional reaction ("It is pity, pity, pity that I feel," writes Enid Bagnold, in her sad and spare memoir of her time as a nurse[38]), at the same time that it tended to highlight the distance between viewer and subject, as has been suggested by Scarry in *The Body in Pain*. Even Woolf, whose relative indifference to the events of the armistice marks her diaries and letters of the period, records with pathos that "[I]t was a melancholy thing to see the incurable soldiers lying bed at the Star & Garter with their backs to us, smoking cigarettes, & waiting for the noise [of peace celebrations] to be over."[39]

As Woolf's image suggests, the very quietness of these men, from the point of view of the outside observer, is one of their defining qualities, and this issue of silence is at the center of many descriptions of returned men, especially those with grave disabilities. As in Owen's "Smile, Smile, Smile" or Eliot's "The Hollow Men," the men's silence may distance them from civilians, but it works to emphasize their shared consciousness, a kind of distraught fraternity. "The 'Remnant' never forget, they always remember, and are very silent," says the former soldier E. B. Stallard, in one of his "lay sermons" on the subject of the post-war condition.[40] Like the poet who speaks for the helpless soldier in "Disabled," these sermons seem to be offered as surrogates for the voices of the quiet men. In his opening to "The Storyteller," Walter Benjamin suggests that the soldier's emblematic silence, a product of modernity's attack on the human person, resonates as an emblem of the culture's broader narrative disabilities: "Was it not noticeable at the end of the war that men returned from the battlefield grown silent – not richer, but poorer in communicable experience?" Benjamin connects this silence with the extreme embodiment of war, with the unprecedented fact that "in a field of force of destructive torrents and explosions, was the tiny, fragile human body."[41] Like Fussell, who stresses the poignancy of the vulnerable body, at the mercy of the voracious machine of war, Benjamin recognizes that the destruction of the body and the reduction in "communicable experience" go hand in hand.

Hundreds of official photographs of wounded and/or hospitalized men also capture this element of strange and terrible silence. Though it is beyond the scope of this analysis to present and discuss the photographs taken by official war chroniclers and housed in the Imperial War Museum's massive photo archive, I would simply point to two of the most marked stylistic elements in many of the photographs of wounded men. First, in pictures of men on the battlefield, the wounded are often shown in the company of other men, in tender scenes of aid and succor (one man carrying another on his back; two men gently helping a wounded compatriot across a trench; a pair of bandaged soldiers leaning on one another as they make their way to a clearing station; an English, French, or Australian soldier giving a drink or a cigarette to a wounded German or Turk). These pictures of course recall the emphasis on comradeship that was such a central part of official war discourse, and at the same time are infused with the spirit of intimate friendship that we have seen in many cases to undercut the comradely ethos. A second, striking tendency is to emphasize the clean, clear, aesthetic quality of the injured man, against an incongruous background – the incongruity defined by the nature of injury as well as by the often harsh landscape. We might have a picture of a healthy, robust, attractive man, staring comfortably at the camera, yet placed in an extremely bare and rough hospital, his enormously plastered legs hanging from above; or we might be confronted by an image of a young man, impeccably clad and laughing merrily, while standing on one leg, next to an equally hearty legless man in a wheelchair. The point is that in both types of photograph, a strong contrast between a highly formalized and aestheticized surface and the shock of extreme physical wounding produces an aura of uncanniness. It is perhaps difficult for the viewer to know how to reconcile these images of aestheticism and moral/social certainty with the shock of physical injury and the hellish conditions that form the unseen background.

These varied examples bring to the fore what we might think of as an organizing contradiction in the reaction to wounded men: a sense of extreme physical presence, a discomfiting and glaring set of juxtapositions (community and isolation; manhood and incapacity; youth and agedness; beauty and ghastliness; sympathy and distance; the problem of homecoming), alongside a tendency to look away, brought on in part by the men's own eerie silence. As an expert on blinded combatants cautions, "face to face with the blinded soldier, we must forget that he is blind, so that he himself may forget it, and yet we must ever keep it in mind . . . without letting him know"[42] (ellipsis in original). The layers of seeing and not seeing in this advice register a complicated structure of interaction, which the medical establishment seeks to manipulate. In her history of the period, Joanna Bourke has pointed to both sides of the visibility spectrum, the shock for civilians of ubiquitous injury and the tendency to screen out and obscure the disturbing effects of war-time disfigurement. "Throughout Britain – in every town and on every street – someone was affected [by physical injury]," she writes, and "[m]ass-mutilation was there for all to see" (*Dismembering the Male*, 35). Yet, as she also stresses, in relatively short spans of time, "[l]imblessness became normalized," and the sight of "swarms of [limbless] men getting about on crutches...ceased to affect most people" (60).

Or, to give just one further example, Helen Zenna Smith's exceptionally acerbic and disillusioned novel *Women of the Aftermath* (1931) begins by characterizing the civilian scene in the final weeks of the war, when pity for the disabled turns to fatigue:

England is war-sick. Daily the inclination to make little tin gods of the wounded...becomes less...Last week a wounded Tommy with an arm in splints got into a crowded Wimbledon 'bus – it was quite a minute before a man in the corner gave up his seat. He was obviously waiting for someone else to oblige. Six months ago there would have been a concerted rush for the privilege.

A little while back the [servant] turned on my husband and advised him, wounded officer or no wounded officer, to keep his civil tongue in his head... Six months ago she would have wept tears of sugary pity at the wreck of his fine manhood. It is a forerunner of what the disabled heroes are to expect from the hysterical public that cheered them through the city steets [*sic*] to the battlefields, when the war is really finished and done with.[43]

While Smith's language is extreme (here as throughout her novel), she points with rhetorical force to the uncertain place of the disabled in the civilian sphere, as the post-war era begins in earnest – a time marked, in Smith's rendering, by a persistent tendency to want to ignore and forget the war's survivors. For his part, the wounded man in this novel is vengeful and terrifying, refusing to allow any kind of easy assimilation or romanticization of his wrecked state: "[he] has not behaved as the standard blinded hero of fiction behaves"; on the contrary, this is a "morose, bitter-tongued, rebellious" ex-serviceman, who tends to speak in streams of profanity, spitting out his frustrated venom (*Women of the Aftermath*, 16). Overall, the visibility of war-maimed men seems simultaneously to have fascinated and repelled civilians, stunning observers even as it engendered the desire not to see, not to look.

Needless to say, in the years following the armistice, the assimilation of war's injuries was subject to cultural appropriation and diversity. If the extreme debility presented by conditions like mental collapse, limblessness, and blindness paradoxically invited such mixed reactions as outrage, pity, and weary indifference, a slight limp and hardness of expression functioned as tokens of a new ideal of masculinity. The ever-observant Vera Brittain, whose memoir of the war years is marked by an immense parade of disfigured men, nevertheless recognizes in her contemporaries a tendency to valorize the war's scars as signs of desirable maleness. Describing a young, much-decorated officer, she writes:

Since adding the VC to his collection of decorations, the colonel appeared to have become nervously afraid that every young woman he met might want to marry him, and his fears were not altogether unnatural, for with his long row of ribbons, his premature seniority, his painful limp, and his pale, dark-eyed air of a weary Crusader, the tall young man was an attractive and conspicuous figure wherever he went.[44]

Equal to such constructions of injury-as-masculinity was an antithetical portrayal: war injuries understood as physical impotence. I have already mentioned Clifford Chatterly, a figure who is in some ways unusual, thanks to Lawrence's exceptional forthrightness about sexuality. More typically, the problem of sexual impotence was treated indirectly. In *Women of the Aftermath*, the narrator wonders, "Shall I describe the scenes I've been through – describe those horrible nights when Roy has wept like a baby because his manhood was gone," but recognizes that her desire to disrupt the romantic picture of the hero back at home, to "give you an intimate picture of the home life of a physically impotent, wounded hero... isn't worth the fag" (101). Depictions of impotence tended to operate along a delicate line, simultaneously addressing and downplaying the problem. For many soldiers themselves, the terror of being rendered impotent was a driving fear, and various groups distributed literature, directed at servicemen, which attempted to confront these anxieties.[45] Yet, more typically, popular iconography from the period promised the eventual return to sexual potency, stressing the sexuality of recuperation, often by eroticizing the relation of female nurses to their recovering patients. Further, medical and social organizations responsible for rehabilitation produced images of marital harmony and satisfaction for disabled men, simultaneously implying that recovery might be possible, and that sexual intercourse need not be a central part of a fulfilled life.[46] As the editor of a journal for war-injured declared: "a disabled sailor or soldier is not less of a man, but more of a man than he was before the war."[47]

Despite this emphasis on the cheerful prospects for recovery, one of the most resonant, persistent, and troubling visual icons of the period involves the disabled former soldier, typically figured blinded or with lost limbs, begging on the city streets. What this figure poignantly encapsulates is the way war has, at both literal and figurative levels, impoverished the enlisted man. Its political message derives from the attention to the economic impotence of the disabled, a form of downward spiraling that starkly contrasts with the self-congratulatory mythologizing of the trenches as a space of class mobility. John Galsworthy was one prominent figure to take a particular interest in disabled ex-servicemen, and his focus on the potential impoverishment of the ex-combatant is unflinching. Galsworthy conceived and edited a journal for disabled soldiers and interested civilians, entitled *Reveille*, whose modest one-year run included diverse, and often quite rich, fictional, anecdotal, and visual texts, as well as a great deal of practical and ideological input from the rehabilitation establishment. In the opening editorial of *Reveille*'s first installment (August 1918), Galsworthy presents a picture of England as a place overflowing with precariously situated men: "Our eyes look out on a Britain daily more and more peopled by sufferers in this war. In every street, on every road and village green we meet them – crippled, half-crippled, or showing little outward trace, though none the less secretly deprived of health."[48] Galsworthy and his contributors are concerned, firstly, to foreground the economic, physical, and psychic vulnerability of this population, in a sense to compel readers actually to focus on what they cannot help but see. What nearly all commentators on the subject suggest is that in the past, poverty was the lot of disabled ex-soldiers, but a new era in state responsibility towards the disabled is now in the process of being created. The great promise is that, through technological innovation and changes in social attitudes, the disabled can be thoroughly re-assimilated into the solvent, productive population. The great fear, as expressed in text after text, is "drift": "What sort of a Land will it be if, five and ten years hence, tens of thousands of injured in this long tragedy are drifting unhappily amongst us?" asks Galsworthy (*Rev*, 1, 15). "The men who have slipped away – who knows how many? – and the men who are still slipping all the time, will plaster this country a few years hence with human wreckage," fears another concerned official.[49] Yet, as the passages included above from *Women of the Aftermath* suggest, in which a form of sympathy-fatigue is detailed among the war-weary public, it remained an open and volatile question after the war as to how the position of the forlorn and hopeless combatant would play out in both economic and social terms. One former enlisted man wrote with particular vitriol about the injustice of returning from a grisly four years as a German prisoner of war, where he refused to perform work that he felt would aid the German effort, only to find economic doors banged against him:

Since my discharge I am finding it impossible to get any Work owing to my Complaint. They don't seem to want anything to do with anyone who served in the War. This is my experience up to Date [1919], and when I think of all I and Hundreds & Thousands of other men suffered it makes me say to myself was it worth it the Terrible Treatement I Personally Went through simply because I was patriocotic [*sic*].[50]

And, indeed, as returned servicemen did suffer disproportionately from the labor shortages of the post-war decade, it seems accurate to say that the consistently reproduced image of the disabled, despairing, unemployed ex-soldier had at least some degree of statistical truth-value.[51] The figure ironizes the ideal of a fit country for heroes, and enacts a reversal of all conventional myths of war: as masculine adventure; as protection for the cherished homeland; as cleansing, purifying, and ennobling; as the repository of eternal comradeship. Such men risk not only "drift," but dependence, a further form of potential emasculation. Whether such dependence takes the form of traditional Victorian charity, paternalistically conceived, or a more modern form of welfare-state entitlement – either way, the notion of dependence is highly problematic, imaginatively conjoining the soldier with the position of the child.[52] Bagnold, for instance, writes of her patients that "they come in here in uniforms and we put them into pyjamas and nurse them; and they lie in bed or hobble about the ward, watching us as we move, accepting each other with the unquestioning faith of children" (*DD*, 64–65). The process of transformation in the men's status is complex and continuous, as they move from uniform (already an indication of an institutional identity) to the ubiquitous blue pajamas of hospital. Instinctively resisting the emasculating categorization of helpless beings, soldiers often found themselves falling in between seemingly opposed social categories, such as adult and child, patriot and rebel, masculine icon and debilitated relic.

For those whose mission was rehabilitation and reassimilation, there could be no doubt about the appropriate language and conception to apply to the men, the proper side of this binary scheme: disabled ex-soldiers were to be treated not as objects of pity or despair, but as potential wage-earners and productive citizens. The purpose of rehabilitation is to restore the men "as nearly as the nature of their injuries permits, to full participation in, and full enjoyment of, the activities of civil life."[53] An interesting component in the language of self-improvement and positive citizenship involves an undercurrent of antagonism against pity. I have said that the image of the "broken" soldier's body often invoked pity and pathos, and that Wilfred Owen, for one, sought to merge his own language of pity with a defiant and rebellious form of literary authority. Such an effort bumps directly against the bulwark of rehabilitation rhetoric, in which pity – often dismissed as feminine – is portrayed as an obstacle to the real work of physical and psychological rehabilitation: "Pity, like unasked for advice, is very easily given, costs nothing, and is worth next to nothing, unless we mean by it practical sympathy and facilities for useful training and employment."[54] Or, in even more strident terms, "One rule...holds good in every case. One must guard their bedsides from the expression of any debilitating sympathy."[55] What the rehabilitation community wants quite directly to combat is the idea of the ex-serviceman as helpless and adrift. At the same time, other notions of potential threat and disorder abound, and these are less easily contradicted by a rhetoric of active labor, wholesome optimism, and positive citizenship.

Perhaps most significant in the image of the impoverished soldier is the cutting across of visual pathos with the potential for revolt, and here we begin to hear the language of war fellowship amalgamating to the broader problem of the soldier's return. If war has paradoxically created mass impotence (where it promised to re-establish the masculine), nevertheless its subjects ought not to be understood as docile or quiescent. On the contrary, the figure of the disabled ex-serviceman acted as a flashpoint for widespread anxieties about class unrest. The historian Stephen Ward describes 1919 as a moment of simmering radicalism in England, with the former troops in a pivotal position: "Disillusionment settled in quickly for a large portion of returning servicemen," he writes, "Instead of jobs, new opportunities, adequate housing, and other benefits, too many of them found the lines at the local labor exchanges crowded with former comrades...Revolutionary fever was everywhere" (Ward, 22–23). For Galsworthy and his contributors, the question of revolutionary potential was front and center, and its defusing was at the very core of their mission. Galsworthy envisions those maimed in the war as "bitter men and justly bitter; young men with long years of disillusionment and resentfulness before them, the centres of little swirls of discontent and revolution" (*Rev*, 2, 182). Over and over, the civilian world is warned that if the soldiers are not adequately repaid and retrained, "the seeds of a bitter harvest of trouble will have been sown."[56]

Even such an exemplary socialist and reformer as H. G. Wells writes with fear about the war's creation of a new revolutionary type. For Wells, like many of his contemporaries, the culture's failure to provide an adequate social and economic base for returning combatants, a fit country for heroes, inflects his sympathy for the dispossessed with fear of revolution. In his mammoth chronicle of world history, *The Outline of History: Being a Plain*

History of Life and Mankind (1920), Wells draws the following portrait of former soldiers:

In 1913 these masses were living as they had lived since birth; they were habituated to the life they led. The masses of 1919, on the other hand, had been uprooted everywhere, to go into the armies, to go into munitions factories, and so on. They had lost their habits of acquiescence, and they were hardier and more capable of desperate action. Great multitudes of men had gone through such brutalizing training as, for instance, bayonet drill; they had learnt to be ferocious, and to think less either of killing or being killed. Social unrest had become, therefore, much more dangerous.[57]

These lines exemplify a number of observations and anxieties surrounding the working-class soldier: the sense of untold numbers, an almost invariable element in post-war writing, given the scale of the war and the nature of mass conscription; the image of men whose character has been forged by violence, brutality, and desensitization to death; the suggestion that the bonds formed in war might carry over into peace; the overriding notion that the extremity of war produces results that can be neither predicted nor controlled. Taken together, these elements add up to a picture of the working-class ex-combatant as a potential force for destruction, a man who paradoxically threatens the very society he was trained to protect.

In his four-volume study of the Great War, published in 1929, Winston Churchill – as Minister for the War Office in 1919, the official who took charge of demobilization – paints a similar portrait of the dramatic unease surrounding the troops after the cease-fire, vividly portraying the instability embodied by the still-armed, restive forces:

Certainly there were factors which nobody could measure and which no one had ever before seen at work. Armies of nearly four million men had been suddenly and consciously released from the iron discipline of war, from the inexorable compulsions of what they believed to be a righteous cause. All these vast numbers had been taught for years how to kill; how to punch a bayonet into the vital organs; how to smash the brains out with a mace; how to make and throw bombs as if they were no more than snowballs. All of them had been through a mill of prolonged inconceivable pressures and innumerable tearing teeth. To all, sudden and violent death, the woeful spectacle of shattered men and dwellings was, either to see in others or expect and face for oneself, the commonest incident of daily life. If these armies formed a united resolve, if they were seduced from the standards of duty and patriotism, there was no power which could even have attempted to withstand them.[58]

Though Churchill's focus here is more limited than Galsworthy's or Wells', in the sense that his gaze is fixed on a specific moment of potential disorder in the early months of demobilization (a period to which I shall return below), his rhetoric nevertheless closely mirrors the other depictions of ex-soldiers as a potentially destructive force, bred by war, massed in huge numbers, unprecedented and unpredictable. What constitutes this community is specifically their training as killers, their discipline as an army. As one intelligence officer put it in 1920, "In the event of rioting [among ex-servicemen], for the first time in history the rioters will be better trained than the troops."[59] We might note, here, an irony: if comradeship was excessively lauded during the years of combat, it became, in the period immediately following the war, a source of alarm. The government's decision to institute surveillance of former servicemen in the early post-war years, for instance, testifies to its sense of unease surrounding the combatants. Given the near-hysterical fear of Bolshevism that the Russian revolution inspired in many English conservatives, this concern over former soldiers as potential revolutionaries is perhaps not surprising.

It should be noted, however, that for all the historical specificity of the scenarios sketched by Galsworthy, Wells, Churchill, and others, in many ways their language recalls familiar Victorian and Edwardian constructions of the threat posed by revolutionary working-class men. In particular, descriptions of restive former troops evoke a late-Victorian tendency to cast the working-class man as a menacing, unpredictable, rootless outcast, a threat to middle-class comfort and the proper target for reform. Such descriptions hark back to Disraeli's ever-influential notion of "two nations" – the rich and the poor, locked in mutual dependency and potential combat – a configuration which gained conceptual momentum as the nineteenth century progressed. Not only were the poor grossly distinctive, many late-Victorians feared, but they were also dangerously close: "they have streamed across the bridges from the marshes and desolate places beyond the river; they have hurried up in incredible number through tubes sunk in the bowels of the earth, emerging like rats from the drain, blinking in the sunlight."[60] In a 1902 anthology epitomizing the sense of middle-class unease that accompanied the Boer War, C. F. G. Masterman (later an important First World War propagandist) opens with a description of "a new race, hitherto unreckoned and of incalculable action – the 'City type' of the coming years; the 'street-bred' people of the twentieth century; the 'new generation knocking at our doors.'"[61] This figure is "physically, mentally, and spiritually different from the type characteristic of Englishmen during the past two hundred years" (*Heart*, 8). Concerns about masculine viability, a lament about the deterioration of male health, troubling suggestions about the racial and class underpinnings of male degeneration: such rhetoric marks both the First World War and the Boer War, as each war produced its own official military statistics about the deplorable state of British male health, and in each case politicians and reformers repackaged such information for public consumption. Lloyd George, for instance, frequently repeats the phrase "you don't make an 'A1 Empire with a C3 population,'" in a direct reference not only to the conclusions of a 1918 report on the results of war-time medical examinations, but also to a much-publicized survey of army recruiters in 1902 that had found three-fifths of those who volunteered physically unfit for military service.[62]

What I want to stress in the descriptions of working-class ex-soldiers as potential revolutionaries, then, is the way this language simultaneously recalls an earlier moment in social reform theory and insists on something specific and unprecedented about the force of war in constructing new subjects. To resuscitate older conceptions of both threat and containment made sense to many post-war writers, even as they attempted to take stock of what they understood to be a genuinely novel phenomenon, in both scale and character. Masterman, for instance, whose influence remained undiminished after the war, produced in 1923 a study of the condition of England in which he deliberately recalled his own earlier portents about the dangerous fissures in the economic and social fabric. *England After War* operates on the line between exposing what the war has done to British culture and insisting that the new problems in many cases can be understood through an older language.[63] In important respects, the end of the war stunned and startled the culture, and the sense of panic that had swept through the reform community one generation earlier was in a sense replayed on a wider scale and in accordance with the new language of the post-war condition – involving, especially, "fit-ness," "brokenness," attention to group solidarity (comradeship), and the problem of the place for "heroes."

In conceptualizing the return of the soldier, writers and critics almost inevitably indicate that something radical has changed for the former serviceman, that he has become, in effect, a new man. As Bagnold has it, "Something has been born among the armies, something has been made solid in the hospitals...Whatever war is, it separates the combatant from the non-combatant: they do not see alike, nor think alike, nor feel alike."[64] Perhaps the most famous statements of the way war remakes men, who are then fit for nothing but violence, death, and destruction, and whose loyal-ties center entirely around one another, come in *All Quiet on the Western Front*. In one such passage, Paul Baümer declares: "We are burnt up by hard facts; like tradesmen we understand distinctions, and like butchers, necessities. We are no longer untroubled – we are indifferent. We might exist [in the civilian world]; but should we really live there? We are forlorn like children, and experienced like old men, we are crude and sorrowful and superficial – I believe we are lost."[65] Remarque's is an exemplary portrayal of a new species of man, whose primary identifications and associations have been produced by the complex effects of war, including a long-term immersion in an entirely male community. But it is far from unique. As Philip Gibbs wrote in his 1920 exposé of the "realities of war":

But all was not right with the spirit of the men who came back. Something was wrong. They put on civilian clothes again, looked, to their mothers and wives very much like the young men who had gone to business in the peaceful days before the August of 1914. But they had not come back the same men. Something had altered in them. They were subject to queer moods, queer temper, fits of profound depression alternating with a restless desire for pleasure. Many of them were easily moved to passion when they lost control of themselves. Many were bitter in their speech, violent in opinion, frightening. (*RW*, 447)

Gibbs' language points, once again, to various incongruities, including a disparity between surface and depth, as well as past and present. For Helen Smith, a similar spirit of queerness and restlessness is afoot, but, in her account, the transformations wrought by war are even more extreme and absolute, and are shared by women. "Hard-boiled, unbelieving, illusions busted – that's how we emerged," she says of the war's women, "most of us are... strangely stimulated, restless, overcharged with energy, unable to set-tle down quietly" (*Women of the Aftermath*, 123). As a matter of significant social practice, the phenomenon of total estrangement from civilian life – complete radicalization, mental debilitation, total apathy (what Smith calls being "dead inside" [73]) – was naturally rare, and most men undoubt-edly wanted nothing so much as to return to their pre-war domestic and employment situations. However, such easy assimilation was not always possible, and, perhaps more importantly, the *idea* that the social strains of the period could be traced in part to the war's destruction and reconstitu-tion of men on a massive scale and across class lines carried real power in the contemporary imagination.[66] The literature of the period, produced by non-combatants equally with those who fought, is replete with such figures, frozen in time and paralyzed with inaction, unable to return to a pre-war sensibility and equally incapable of reconceiving themselves in a civilian context.

Lawrence's stories are exemplary in this respect, frequently evoking a sense of paralysis, fear, and uncertainty with respect to soldiers returning home. Many of his tales contain returned men – injured and whole, angry and tranquil, sociable and ferocious – and they refract the issue of return in characteristically strange and excessive terms.[67] "Monkey Nuts" (1922) provides an especially interesting example of this kind of reconstructed identity, stressing the way the ex-soldiers' psychic sterility derives from their continued mutual inter-dependence. Feminist critics have noted that the story, like its contemporary "Tickets, Please" (1919), marks an overt and virulent instance of Lawrence's terror of emancipated women.[68] The tale, set in the immediate aftermath of the war, depicts two army men, not yet demobilized, billeted together and engaged in land work. Joe is twenty-three, "a tallish, quiet youth, pleasant looking," devoted to and dependent upon his corporal Albert, "a clean-shaven, shrewd-looking fellow of about forty" (*CSS*, 366). Their harmonious existence is interrupted by the intruding figure of Molly Stokes, an independent, capable, sexually self-confident land girl, dressed in the recognizable uniform of overalls and gaiters. Molly's attempted flirtation with Joe leads eventually to her complete and pitiless humiliation, as the men work together to rebuff her, Joe taking the lead from his corporal, as in war-time. In the end, the status quo is re-established, the adventurous woman is punished, "[a]nd Joe felt more relieved even than he had felt when he heard the firing cease after the news had come that the armistice was signed" (*CSS*, 378). As Hilary Simpson argues in her study of Lawrence's reactions to feminism, the end of "Monkey Nuts" suggests that for Lawrence, as for Joe, even war is preferable to the social changes embodied by Molly's sexual self-sufficiency.

Molly is not the only character in the story whose identity has been remade by the war. Joe and Albert fall equally into the category of reconstituted subjects, and in their case the result is both debilitation and sadism. At the literal level, the men's status is liminal, as they complete their military contract in a civilian capacity; they are neither in nor out of war, and express complete satisfaction with this in-between position. In their personal relations, they clearly follow the military ideal, with Joe consistently and eagerly following his superior's commands. They demonstrate an intimacy born of extended physical proximity (they share a bed, for instance), yet such homoerotic closeness is troublingly transmuted into violence against women. When the utterly passive Joe finally rebukes Molly, he does so in response to Albert's firm hand on his shoulder, a physical or gestural command to counter Molly's domineering directions. Joe's passivity is absolute, the companion to Molly's forthrightness. He will obey one or the other of the characters in the story, and in the end it is the military structure that prevails. Joe is no Lawrentian hero: with no interiorizing or psychologizing whatsoever, the story simply presents as fact Joe's brutality towards Molly and his unthinking obedience to his friend. Handsome savage and mindless servant, yet evincing an easy capacity to inflict harm, Joe is a pure product of war. If the war has created new feminists, it has also formed a totally inassimilable breed of men, capable of functioning only within male communities, dedicated to military notions of leadership and obedience, and betraying a mindset that is neither complacent (witness the harsh treatment of Molly) nor productive (nothing good can be said to come of the story, which ends exactly where it began, in a kind of stasis).

The nihilistic and stagnating relation between Joe and Albert falls quite neatly into Beckett's category of the "pseudo-couple."[69] As we have seen, the pseudo-couple offers a useful title for a particularly desperate place along the spectrum of intimate male relations, especially resonant in terms of the war. In his account, Jameson describes a form of doubled or dialogic identity that hinges on violence and paralysis:

The pseudo-couple is masculine . . . [and] the male pseudo-couple might be understood as a kind of compensation formation, a curious structural halfway house in the history of the subject, between its construction in bourgeois individualism and its disintegration in late capitalism. The partners of the pseudo-couple are neither active, independent subjects in their own right, nor have they succumbed to the schizophrenic fetishization which characterizes contemporary consciousness. They remain legal subjects who nonetheless lack genuine autonomy and find themselves thereby obliged to lean on one another in a simulation of psychic unity which is little better than neurotic dependency. (*Fables*, 59)

This depiction of the pseudo-couple as a compensatory, in-between structure, plagued by a combination of redundancy and marginalization, helps to capture the form of male relation that I have been describing (here and in the last chapter) as a product of war. Lawrence's story, like many of his fictions to be discussed below, envisions a structure of masculine interdependence and intimacy that belongs to its moment: Joe and Albert are like traces of the war lodged in the contemporary imagination, exemplifying its power to destroy and reconstruct. The pseudo-couple is not the only formulation to have developed around the figure of the returned serviceman, but its literary legacy – in the works of Lawrence and Beckett, among others – suggests that it had a particular eloquence in exposing one particular configuration: the simultaneous apotheosis and degeneration of men who have become identified with the community of war.

In the examples I have presented – in "Monkey Nuts," in Woolf's and West's fictions, in various depictions of working-class combatants gathered in menacing numbers – civilian writers develop portraits of men who have been constructed by and for war, whose presence back in England threatens home culture. In all of these cases, class is the central pivot. Whether as a matter of revolutionary masses (Churchill, Wells, Galsworthy), blind, unintelligent obedience (Lawrence), an odd sense of classlessness created by war service (Woolf), or desire that wildly cuts across social barriers (West), the new men envisioned here are marked by a problematic and unstable class situation which directly challenges conventional principles of social order and control. Like the disabled soldier on the street-corner in the popular imagination, they suggest first that the war is responsible for their situation, second that the culture is emphatically falling short of its responsibilities, and third that they are arrested in a state of chronic stasis, an impediment to the idea of progress. A sense of inaction and impotence, as well as scorching isolation and loneliness, hangs over many of these figures. Their situation has been generated in part by the immersion in male community, and has fallen out as a form of intractable separation from the rest of the culture. In some of these portraits, moreover, we glimpse the possibility of organization and mobilization among the volatile former army men. Joe and Albert may not represent any conscious revolutionary force, but they nevertheless have the power, once roused, to inflict a quick and lacerating blow.

What these texts attest is a sense that those returning from the war represent an unpredictable force, and this unpredictability was especially palpable in the months immediately following November 1918. When the armistice was declared, after the initial and shared sense of relief, a period of tense transitionality began, as suggested by the men's situation in "Monkey Nuts," and, during this period, the threatening nature of ex-soldiers seemed particularly tied to their perceived war-time bonds. Demobilization was not an immediate or even swift process; soldiers had signed on for service of three years or the duration of the war, but what this contract legally entailed was uncertain, and many were required to complete a tour of duty before returning to civilian life. (The character of Henry in Lawrence's "The Fox" [1919] provides another example of an ex-soldier in this kind of odd, suspended situation.) Even those whose service had been completed were not instantly discharged, many thousands not reaching home until well into the following year. At the height of demobilization in the early months of 1919, nearly 10,000 men a day were returning home, but, even with such numbers, the process was gradual and, for newer recruits, could take up to a year. Naturally this lengthy time-lag created tensions and frustrations, at times bubbling over into serious unrest. In a study of Australian returned soldiers, many of whom faced an even longer delay than their English counterparts, Stephen Garton writes, "[t]he rootlessness of the soldiers' state...worried those in charge of demobilisation. They noted a 'strange unrest' and an 'unsettling of the mind.' The men seemed 'irregular' and suffered from bouts of lethargy punctuated by 'spasmodic effort.' They feared that these were symptoms of a loss of the 'moral tone' and 'character' that had marked the AIF in battle" (*Cost of War*, 3). Even as upright and soldierly a character as Robert Graves, fed up with delays and eager to return to his family, describes with comic drama his illegal defection in February 1919.[70]

In fact, 1919 saw demonstrations and riots across a range of locations, in England and abroad, initially among angry troops demanding to be demobilized, later among former soldiers with a variety of grievances. The first such demonstrations, which lasted for three days and spread across several towns, began in Folkestone and Dover in early January. As many as 10,000 men were reported to have marched through Folkestone and occupied the town hall, many climbing the portico to declaim against military and civilian authorities and to demand a more equitable demobilization scheme. A wave of similar disturbances followed, and by the third day *The Times* was anxiously admonishing the troops to suspend such "breaches of discipline." "It is realized," *The Times* portentously declared, "...that any general relaxation of discipline throughout the army would be a great disaster and might bring to ruin the victory that has been won at so great a cost."[71] Later in the month, British army forces in France offered similar instances of disobedience. In late January, "a regular mutiny broke out in Calais" as several thousand British troops refused to follow orders regarding movement, and the mêlée was only contained by the engagement of several active army divisions (Churchill, *The Aftermath*, 50). More chaotic and widely reported in the English press was a spate of rioting in the town of Luton on 19 July 1919, concurrent with huge Peace Day ceremonies in London. Although newspapers registered confusion about both causes and responsibility for the rioting, one thing was vividly conveyed: an angry assembly of ex-soldiers had marched to the town hall and burned it to the ground. The Luton riots offered in some ways a more threatening scenario than the earlier demonstrations, in the sense that the rioters were fully demobilized soldiers, men who thus represented a force that might continue indefinitely, its motives and power unknown. Perhaps most shocking, in terms of the level of violence, were events at Epsom on 17 June 1919, when a large group of Canadian soldiers, infuriated at the arrest of two fellow soldiers for drunkenness, marched to the police station demanding the men's release. The assembled mob destroyed most of the station, freed their men, and killed a police officer. Not surprisingly, both the town and the authorities reacted with panic about a general overturning of public order, pubs were closed, and the soldiers were shut out from the town for several days, before legal proceedings were undertaken and events took on a more routine, legalistic flavor. Such scenes were in fact relatively sparse, given the enormous scale and slow pace of the demobilization, yet their public resonance was powerful, perhaps disproportionate to the actual events.[72] The quality of unprecedentedness characterized every aspect of the Great War, and the political ramifications of mass repatriation quite simply could not be gauged. "Who was to know," asks one former combatant, "that this was not the first step towards a social revolution?"[73]

If it seemed that the war was followed by an explosion of undiscipline, this may have been because the war years had witnessed an extraordinary level of voluntary and enforced order, at home as well as abroad. The enormous scale of the war organization was a civilian as well as a military matter, and it called for high doses of discipline and a tolerance of bureaucracy. Civilian existence in the latter half of the war had been characterized by such forms of state control as the giant print propaganda and censorship machine, and the notorious Defence of the Realm Act (DORA), which provided the state with far-reaching powers to survey and control private conduct. Having tolerated and even embraced such a situation during the years of combat, many people in and out of uniform now identified with the unleashing of rebellious energy. Images of soldiers marching, rioting, shouting, breaking the chain of command, demanding to be released from military service, burning down buildings – these images captured with particular effectiveness a certain element in the mood of the moment. At the same time, the sense that soldiers might revolt, that the ubiquitous construct of the good-natured Tommy and the sympathetic officer might dissolve, suggested that the comforting portrayal of what the war had done to men might all along have been simplified and romanticized. Smith's *Women of the Aftermath* focuses unflinchingly on this discrepancy between the image of the heroic soldier and the reality of his violent desire to undermine that very image: "'There's the MC you wanted, mother. I'm blinded and a cripple for life, and I'm sexless – but here's your MC – shove it down the lavatory for me'" (15). With the war over, groups of soldiers in uniform or returning to ordinary life no longer presented a clear or unfailing image of national security.

But the landscape of massed people had other connotations in this period, particularly in the context of public mourning. In *Ulysses*, Leopold Bloom attends a funeral; in *The Waste Land*, thousands of the living dead stream across Westminster Bridge; in *Mrs. Dalloway*, large swaths of people on the street are momentarily galvanized around ambiguous visual forms; *A Passage to India* pivots around the horror and chaos of a crowd in a blinding, deafening cave; riveting mob scenes across the European continent erupt throughout D. H. Lawrence's post-war novels and travel tales – all of these elemental modernist episodes are centrally concerned with the nature of large gatherings of people moving across the landscape of public life. As Michael Tratner argues in his study of modernism's engagement with the "mass mind," even the most erudite artists of the modernist period looked directly and with profound ambivalence at the possibility of representing and realizing the "mass" of mass culture.[74] Modernism, that is, worked vigorously to imagine public space, and is oversimplified when portrayed as primarily an escapist immersion into the individual consciousness. Writers and critics of the period attempted to make sense of new configurations of bodies – particularly male bodies – and the rituals surrounding mourning captured these congregations of war's participants with visual force. Though forms of shared memorializing and pageantry were not, of course, unprecedented in British culture, the frequency and geographical ubiquity of public mourning rituals in this period did offer something genuinely novel.

The years following the war marked a time of terrific, and often shared, public mourning.[75] Large and small, urban and rural, highly organized and relatively informal, memorial gatherings represented types of association based on new terms, since war builds its own forms of community and constructs its own history. Though mourning was often organized around such stabilizing institutions as the family and the local parish, other aggregations complicated and confused the memorializing landscape, especially those which drew together enormous numbers of people in the city centers. A whole language of participation and spectatorship, a way of representing the interconnections between civilians and those who fought, can be said to have taken shape as part of the deluge of memorial activities. Memory and culture constitute two massive and intertwined topics; in recent years, the interest in memorialization and commemoration has blossomed, as artists, historians, social scientists, and literary critics have come to focus on memory as a significant forum for complex cultural work, and an important element in national self-definition. Scholars have come to scrutinize memory's own evolution and its development in and through history. In historicizing the practices of memory, moreover, we can locate particular moments when the notion of memory becomes especially burdened, when it plays a sharp and vital role in community or national consciousness, when its forms seem to tap into very basic and unsettled problems. The period after the First World War represents one such moment. My treatment here of the rich and potentially expansive topic of memorialization remains circumscribed by a particular question: in what ways did the memorializing rituals of the post-war decade – gatherings, processions, moments of silence – intersect with the culture's understanding and treatment of the returned men?

The three most significant, government-sponsored events of the immediate post-war period were the Peace Day victory parade (19 July 1919) at which the original, temporary Cenotaph was unveiled and saluted; the first anniversary of Armistice Day (11 November 1919), which initiated the convention of two minutes of silence at 11.00 a.m.; and the Unknown Warrior ceremony on the second anniversary of the armistice (11 November 1920), which involved the unveiling of the now-permanent Cenotaph and a massive procession of a decorated coffin containing the remains of the unidentified soldier, through the streets of London, to its burial site in Westminster Abbey. Clearly, events such as the Armistice Day moments of silence and the Unknown Warrior procession served multiple and conflicting purposes: providing an outlet for shared grief and a visual spectacle to replace grim images of death in war; helping to fill the gap left by the palpable absence of dead bodies in local cemeteries and churchyards; offering a symbolic system (the unknown soldier, the empty tomb of the cenotaph, the silence in the midst of an otherwise normal workday) adequate to the scope and destruction of modern war; signifying the government's gratitude and attention towards those who fought; and suggesting that the war really was over and could/should be left behind. And it seems that both small-scale memorial events and huge nationalized ceremonies did go a long way towards addressing the desire, on the part of many civilians, for a public response of simultaneous grieving and celebration. Jay Winter has argued that post-war mourning rituals in many of the warring nations did indeed serve their intended purpose of allaying grief and creating a sense of continuity with past traditions and systems of meaning.[76] In the case of the Cenotaph – a huge empty tomb of architectural dimensions, designed by Sir Edward Lutyens, and placed in the central stream of London traffic – the success of the monument is virtually undeniable. At the Cenotaph site, dedicated to "The Glorious Dead," contemporaries demonstrated their need for a place to express private grief in a public form, and the Cenotaph quite wonderfully represents a sophisticated understanding of the war's function in post-war society. Its non-representative structure typifies British memorials of the period, its simplicity and emptiness working to acknowledge grief without purporting to provide heavy doses of religion or other conventional forms of consolation.[77] At the same time, the Cenotaph was deliberately constructed as an ambivalent structure – refusing to offer direct consolation, it requires an imaginative act to make it work; resisting an easy aesthetic appeal, it thrusts itself into the midst of the urban confusion – and hence its message is as much about how war disrupts and complicates the orderly pattern as it is about comfort or healing.

The Cenotaph represents and honors the dead, but it does not directly speak to those who fought and survived, and this brings up an important set of questions about the relation of former soldiers to the discourse of grieving and recovery. The question is whether the returned men have a special role in commemoration, whether they act as a link between dead soldiers and living civilians.[78] Certainly former soldiers, many of them visibly disabled, were given a place in celebration rituals and marches, and this participation worked to emphasize the bonds forged in combat as well as the war's effects on the fighting men. In the last chapter, I pointed to the prominence of the trope of haunting, as combatant men understood themselves to be inextricably connected with their dead war friends. But from the point of view of civilians, the possibility that ex-servicemen might perform a kind of connecting or intermediary function seems to have been overlooked.[79] Instead, both the Unknown Warrior ceremony and the permanent fixture of the Cenotaph seem, ultimately, to express a kind of hesitation with respect to the returned men, to side-step the war's survivors. These conventions utilize an abstract and consciously modern vocabulary to concentrate on the relation between civilians and the dead, a fact that troubled at least some contemporaries.[80] In a poignant 1918 discussion of paralyzed ex-soldiers, Sir John Collie, Director of Medical Services at the Pensions Ministry, writes of the wounded men that "their sacrifice is not less real because it is endured, not in the sudden agony and darkness of the battlefield, but drawn out through unutterable tedium of the wasting years. Along with our illustrious dead, the helplessly maimed must remain in the shadow against which the Light of Victory is set."[81] It is perhaps telling that, even here, the disabled remain in the shadow. In a more combative spirit, Stephen Ward has suggested that the entire concept of the lost generation worked to efface those who returned, to concentrate the society's praise and attention on the glorious dead, at the expense of the millions of troops who survived. He quotes a Labour MP, Jack Jones, shouting in the Commons in 1922, "'You are a dirty lot of dogs slobbering over dead soldiers and starving the living ones,'" and a 1930 article in the *Nation* which recalls that "'we talked of the Lost Generation, and made sure that it was lost... We neglect the survivors as though they did not exist, and keep our pity for the dead who have no need of it'" (Ward, *War Generation*, 30). What these and other such instances indicate is the sense that the relation between the dead and the returned is not a seamless one, and, indeed, that practices of commemoration might bring a certain tension into view. Even aside from direct, politicized competition over resources (emotional as well as material), we can detect the partial occlusion of those who returned in the general practices of remembrance.

The returned troops, and especially the injured, held an equivocal place on the mourning scene. An article that appeared in the *Manchester Guardian* the day after the Unknown Warrior ceremony in 1920, particularly arresting in its descriptive pathos, gives a sense of the disjunctions made visible by the presence of former soldiers in the procession: "Behind the body-guard marches slowly a curious miscellaneous procession – top-hatted, pot-hatted men, some in soft hats, some in caps, some tall, some short, some maimed, some sturdy, some pale and ill, some with many ribbons on their coats, some with only a badge. They are discharged soldiers."[82] The portrait captures a sense of uncertainty on the observer's part, as if the many signs here (hats, decorations, physical impairments, the general miscellany of the group) cannot easily be read. The legibility and coherence of the ceremony itself, by contrast, are never in question. The discharged soldiers, with their striking distinctions from one other and from the rest of the highly synchronized parade, seem to unsettle the writer, and his narrative style seeks to reproduce that sense of surprise for the reader. The piece concludes, after a depiction of the parade, with a second ex-soldier appearance, now an even more harrowing sight:

The official part of the ceremony over, the great crowds that had gathered then began their pilgrimage [to the tomb in Westminster Abbey]; but a more moving sight appeared in six green motor coaches filled with men in hospital blue. In one coach there were men who had lost limbs. In another were blinded soldiers; in another soldiers with terrible injuries who could not rise like the others in their coaches as they came to the Cenotaph . . . Men without legs, in hospital blue, passed along working their hand tricycles. (*Cen*, 27–28)

In addition to the vivid description and the sense of sad pity evoked here, the passage also reminds the reader that these extreme cases of physical disability are not strictly part of the program. They come as something of an after-thought, removed from the lavish, aestheticized event that the writer has just described, segregated and classified by their particular form of debility. Marked out by their hospital blue, the men come to honor rather than to be honored. And this sense of doubleness – the fact that these groups of badly injured men both fix and elude the spectator's gaze – exactly captures what I see as a crucial relation between the returned men and the culture's forms of remembrance.

For the ex-servicemen, finally, are not at the center of the memorial scene. Public memorial ceremonies differ from victory parades, as well as from demonstrations and riots, because they involve civilians as much as combatants, and their ultimate message is that the effects of war are shared, and the uniqueness of war's subjects will, finally, be de-emphasized. Returning to Scarry's notion that the injured flesh of war's victims holds a public memory of combat, it seems particularly important to stress that in the official spectacles of memorialization, like the Armistice Day event described here, the injured bodies were typically not placed at center stage. Indeed, in the Unknown Warrior procession, ex-servicemen were almost entirely overshadowed, first by the civilian preponderance in the presiding hierarchy – with the king in the position of Chief Mourner, followed by the highest military figures, and then religious dignitaries – and second by the sheer mass of civilian participants. With the unnamed body at its center, the ceremony honors the selfless sacrifice of combatants, and, certainly, the visibility of former servicemen in the procession works in that direction; at the same time, the event dramatically features the inevitable erasure of individual soldiers, swamped by mourners and figured by the Unknown. More generally, because the very definition of commemoration involves remembering the dead, the place of those who survived the fighting will inevitably be problematic in mourning events.

But returned men were determined not to be forgotten, and would insist on making the fellowship of war a serious part of post-war civilian life. They realized this goal in several ways, such as sustaining personal, long-lasting ties with former war mates, writing the story of war in terms of male intimacies (as we have seen), and, perhaps most notably, creating new institutions to represent the war's bonds. Indeed, one of the unique features of the political landscape in Britain in the years immediately following the war involved the formation and prominence of old-soldiers' organizations. Although in England these groups never achieved the kind of large-scale political significance that they were to capture in France, Germany, and Italy, where, for instance, former soldiers were often recruited to lend their authority to developing fascist movements, they did contribute to the overall conception of what war would mean in the post-war setting. Organizations of demobilized soldiers were established as early as 1916, their membership reached its apex in 1919, and, by 1921, the most prominent groups amalgamated under the umbrella of the British Legion, a body whose general tone of conservatism and political marginality increased as time passed. Yet in the first years after the war – and even up until the General Strike of 1926 – old soldiers' groups made their presence felt, with each major organization promulgating its own views and holding a place in the national spotlight. Their weekly or biweekly newsletters reached hundreds of thousands of readers, they had considerable parliamentary access, and, most centrally, their public demonstrations and demands were widely reported in the press. In the case of the Luton riots, for instance, the presence of the old-soldiers' associations in the town of Luton was ominously and repeatedly noted in the newspapers, and the groups made strong public statements denying any connection with the rioting. "No one doubted," writes one observer of the action, "that these associations were of great significance and might prove a steadying or seditious influence in the national life" (Carringon, *Soldier*, 257). In general, the old soldiers' associations offer a window into how returned combatants represented themselves in the public arena. As I have already suggested, however, we should not look for a singular, uncomplicated representation of former servicemen; the images constructed by the ex-soldiers' groups, themselves diverse, were neither static nor straightforward.

In England there were two primary old soldiers' groups, corresponding to the ranks of enlisted men and officers. Although fringe groups proliferated, especially around 1919 (the high-point of soldier activism), and though branches were established all over the country and throughout the empire, most notably in Australia, the two major English groups provide the clearest view of the image these organizations would project into the broader culture.[83] By far the largest and most visible, representing all enlisted men and associated primarily with the Labour Party, though consistently denying any political affiliation, was the National Federation of Discharged and Demobilized Sailors and Soldiers, usually called the Federation. The Federation's primary aim was to represent in the appropriate political and economic arenas the demands of its members and their families, including widows. In addition to concerted lobbying work and efforts to disseminate useful information to members, the Federation organized and reported upon a variety of large public gatherings. In 1919, for instance, it helped to stage major unemployment demonstrations, including a rally of 20,000 men in Hyde Park on 5 June. As with the rioting at Luton and the mutiny at Calais – forms of protest from which the Federation distanced itself – these gatherings provided vivid public images of massed ex-soldiers with a clear agenda, a moral imperative, and an uncertain position in the political landscape. As I have indicated, high levels of unemployment and a shortage of affordable housing were chronic in the period, and the contemporary view, fed in part by the Federation's rhetoric, was that former combatants were particularly ill served, and that such a situation represented a biting form of injustice and irony.

Accordingly, the Federation's journal, the *Bulletin*, often adopts an ironic tone, stressing the gulf between military service and post-war rewards, as it covers its central topics of pensions, housing, employment, and land settlement. One typical trope is to use the "fit country for heroes" phrase in some ironized context: as a caption under a sketch of unemployed veterans; as a punch-line in a sarcastic poem; as the heading for an angry editorial. Such a tone of embitterment tends especially to characterize heated subjects like hiring practices, class inequities, political hypocrisy, public ignorance, and profiteering (a theme carried over from war-time combatant literature). Much more disturbing and unpalatable for the modern reader is the *Bulletin*'s anti-feminism. The journal's reiterated targeting of companies and government agencies that hire or maintain women employees over the claims of former soldiers constitutes one of its most direct political messages. The *Bulletin* makes a point of setting needy ex-soldiers against women, and the Federation's strident demand that private enterprise and public agencies develop firm policies of preferment for returned military personnel over women contributed to public consciousness on this volatile issue. Though I would not want to make a claim for the Federation's exact role in influencing hiring and discharge practices, it is clear that the voice of returned servicemen was set loudly, angrily, and extremely publicly against female employment. Such a stance, moreover, can be connected with the biting misogyny expressed by some war writers. As feminist critics have demonstrated, the tendency to present women as collusive in the carnage of the war, to insinuate that civilian women took unfair advantage of the absence of men to thrive and profit, formed an ingredient in war and post-war literature.[84] If a pitched battle between the sexes was raging in some quarters, then, the old-soldiers' groups clearly weighed in as a voice of moral righteousness on the masculine side. It should be noted, however, that much popular rhetoric about women's role in the war was laudatory. Women were loudly and repeatedly honored for their spirit of "courage" and "sacrifice," held up as model citizens for their support of the war, praised for their nurturing of the sick, and approved as setting an exemplary tone in grieving for the dead.

Though women – newly enfranchised and vulnerable to suspicion – provided an easy target for the Federation's venom, the *Bulletin* also expresses a more general sense of vitriol towards the culture at large, which it often presents as cruelly and blindly erasing the war from its shared consciousness. It is here that the Federation is perhaps most interesting, in its portrayal of returned servicemen as a rather unconscious and un-realized force for social change, a group of men who neither fully embrace their own radicalization nor fully accept the existing social order as capable of addressing their pressing demands. The words "seething" or "seething with discontent" are used frequently in the journal, often as a direct threat to public order and complacency. The Federation wants to paint a picture of itself simultaneously as reasonable, thoughtful, politically un-affiliated, anti-Bolshevik (a strident and reiterated stance, reflecting the association's need to distance itself from the socialism with which it was often associated), and, at the same time, as "seething" with rage at the apathy and ungratefulness of the government towards those who fought in the war.

In addition to the *Bulletin*, other journals flourished during the period, catering to somewhat more targeted audiences, and they, too, share this tone of a balancing act between orderliness and protest, acceptance of the status quo and defiance against economic injustice. For instance, in the *"Live-Wire," Official Organ of the National Ex-Service Men's Union of Temporary Civil Servants*, whose primary mission is to increase and improve the employment of former combatants in the civil service, the rhetoric tends to be rowdier than in the *Bulletin*, though the themes, topics, and views are essentially the same. One blistering entry from October 1920, for instance, makes the following demand: "We want the right men in the right places, irrespective of their so-called 'social class' or superficial education. We want our country (and we say 'our country' advisedly, for we bought it with our blood) to be governed properly, not by men whose only recommendation is a spurious class distinction."[85] Or, in an entry entitled "The New War. The Ex-Soldier and the Present State of Things," the writer proclaims that "a great war has left the world in a crippled state," conjoining the condition of the disabled soldier's body with the body politic. He goes on to depict the returning men as bewildered victims of an uncaring nation's excesses, even as his language hints at the potential for revolt:

In the midst of it all the man, who came back, sees a whirl of extravagances and over-eagerness for sensationalism and excitement. He sees men, enjoying in spite of the high prices of everything, a surfeit of the good things of this life, and he sees also that these lucky ones are those *who have not served in any capacity*. The land is flowing with milk and honey for the shirker, while the Ex-Soldier is finding his way to the common lodging house to join the great army of the submerged. (Italics in original)[86]

The writer here evokes a common rhetorical strategy of the war period: to contrast the luxury afforded "the shirker" or profiteer with the hard luck of the man who dutifully served. A sense of injustice and irony reigns. The last phrase is particularly evocative, for the image of "the great army of the submerged" suggests a re-organization of the literal army, now thrown together in disorder and despair, but bubbling with barely submerged rage.[87] What both of these excerpts from the *"Live-Wire"* illustrate is that the voice of ex-soldiers was in part a voice of class defiance, which, falling under the rubric of former military service, now claimed an unprecedented level of legitimacy and moral authority.

If the Federation represents, in part, a form of angry and volatile class disruption, its rival organization, though disseminating much of the same information, adopts a tone of conservative nostalgia. The Comrades of the Great War is the organization for former officers, and the *Comrades' Journal* carries the overwhelming message that what matters now is to appreciate and resuscitate the values and virtues of the war, most centrally comradeship. The *Comrade's Journal* states its goals clearly: first, "To perpetuate the memory and story of the gallant men and women who died for their country," and, second, "To perpetuate the spirit of comradeship, patriotism, and devotion…and to foster these qualities in the rising generation."[88] Celebrations of comradeship abound in every issue, coming in such variety of forms as essay, reminiscence, sketch, and verse. The characteristic cover feature of the May 1919 number, for example, is entitled "Why I Believe in the Comrades!" and includes excerpts from a host of high-ranking officers, lauding comradeship in familiar language: "The good comradeship of our Armies and Navies has been the basis of success in the most terrible war the world has ever been afflicted with"; or "[the] best and most valuable of all [was] the Comradeship of toil and hardship and sacrifice for the supreme cause of humanity"; or "In prosperity equally as in adversity the value of comradeship is incalculable, and it must be an important factor in the work of reconstruction with which we are now confronted."[89]

If such language, reiterated throughout the run of the journal, seems oriented fundamentally towards the past – towards memory – this last passage suggests another important emphasis, also enumerated in the association's goals: to make war-time comradeship a force for change in post-war society. General Sir W. M. Hughes, author of the last of the three excerpts quoted above, makes clear that comradeship is not and ought not to be a relic of war, but rather a living force, and part of the national "reconstruction with which we are now confronted." A June 1919 essay by Clement Edwards, MP, entitled "Why British Comradeship will Beat Bolshevism!"

(anti-bolshevism was a shared feature of the two ex-servicemen's organizations), stresses the relevance of comradeship to civilian conduct: "I am persuaded that there is a new great spirit of comradeship abroad in the nation, bred from the shoulder-to-shoulder sacrifices of all classes in the Great War."[90] The guiding sense here is that the unity of war provides a model and a direct link with the work of post-war reconstruction, a theme often sounded among the more conservative rehabilitation writers. "The struggle," we are told, "has brought home to us the necessity of national co-operation; we shall want that co-operation just as much in the years to come."[91] One final example of the journal's comradeship ethos is a cartoon in the May 1919 number, which gives visual force to the oft-repeated conviction that there might be real potential for war-time bonds to be translated into peace-time work. Under the heading "'Still Carrying On,' the Old Comradeship – And the New," a cartoon shows a double frame. In the background one soldier helps another climb over a parapet; the foreground depicts a parallel image of two strong men working together on a welding project.[92] At one level, the message of all these texts is simple and straightforward: during the war, men developed and perpetuated high levels of virtue through the bonds of comradeship; now that the war is over, such uncomplicated, heroic, masculine forms of community and self-sacrifice should be once again recaptured and redirected towards the public good.

Yet at another level, the moral of the comradeship story is less clear. What would it mean for men to behave as if they remained in an all male, utterly hierarchical, contained sphere, where violence and hardship dominate? Lawrence's "Monkey Nuts," for example, could be read as an enactment of the "Still Carrying On" model: two men, formerly comrades in war, now support one another in parallel fashion in agricultural work. Yet the context has changed drastically – embodied by the figure of the emancipated Molly Stokes – and this form of male community is now distorted by sadism, solipsism, and paralysis. Even the Comrades' own language carries undertones of something a little disruptive, as in the evocation of "a new great spirit of comradeship abroad in the nation, bred from the shoulder-to-shoulder" contact of men from different classes, an image that could interestingly be set alongside such famous modernist visions of trouble as Yeats' "rough beast, its hour come round at last / Slouching toward Bethlehem to be born." What I am suggesting is that both of the major old-soldiers' organizations construct images of association, identification, and affiliation, born of war, that do not sit entirely comfortably within post-war culture. While the Comrades would certainly repudiate the Federation's suggestion of seething rage beneath an orderly surface, of trenches as a site where a rebellious class unity was forged, they nevertheless lay such powerful emphasis on the bonds of war as to raise the question of what role the ex-officer, *qua* ex-officer, might ultimately occupy in civilian life. In the language of the old soldiers' journals, as well as in the visual imagery of mass demonstrations, a picture emerges of the returned soldier as, paradoxically, at both the center and the margins of the post-war world, an object of reverence and pathos as well as an instigator of potential trouble. Thinking back to the last chapter's emphasis on the image and voice of the broken friend, we might say that, even in such public forms as those constructed by the old-soldiers' groups, the former combatant was burdened with too much memory. Defined by war, male community, injury, and the past, his social function was powerfully circumscribed, even suspect, and his role in the nation's reconstruction was profoundly uncertain.

Nevertheless, to project war-time comradeship into civilian modes of cooperation remained an active idea, not only in publications like the *Comrade's Journal*, but also for many civilians and individual ex-soldiers. George Lansbury remarks in his memoirs that "[t]he clergy and many others who supported the war as a war to end war, vainly imagined when the fighting was over that the comradeship of the trenches, the friendship between classes shown during the war, would continue."[93] As late as 1937, a member of an old-soldier's organization, speaking at the dedication of a monument, wistfully remarks: "We might have done more perhaps with the feeling of comradeship which soldiers of all nations have for one another. Perhaps it is not too late even now."[94] Or, to return to a passage examined in the last chapter, R. G. Dixon's unpublished war memoir indicates that perhaps the greatest tragedy of the post-war period is the culture's failure to recuperate the transcendent spirit of comradeship, which Dixon hails as the sole positive element in the war: "I know for myself that I have known no such comradeship as those old years gave to us who fought on the old Western Front. As the years go by... there are fewer and fewer of us left who knew that comradeship... [which] implied a faithfulness even unto death to one's fellows, and this is no empty thing."[95] In these texts, the overwhelming sensibility about male relations is of loss and missed opportunity: if the relations of war had been properly organized, perhaps the culture would have developed and thrived in unaccountable ways.

If a sense of fatality hovers over the musings of those who regret lost comradeship, there were also social critics during the period who attempted to formulate a productive theory of national renewal, based on the power of fellowship. In a sense this is the goal of the old-soldiers' movement. Perhaps most striking for its extreme zeal about comradeship, in the context of the

war, is the work of William Paine. Paine provides an interesting case of
a social theorist schooled in Edwardian urban reform notions, for whom
the war provided a site of reconciliation for his convictions about class
inequities and his romance for masculine bonds. Paine was something of
a dreamer, a reformer who combined practical views about improving the
lives of workers with lavishly utopian ideals about male comradeship and
social transformation. Though Paine has generally been forgotten, and his
reform schemes cannot be said to have belonged to a major movement
or program, he published his work under the aegis of several of the most
prominent leftists of his time, and his efforts form part of a serious and
wide-ranging attempt to reconsider many elements of social justice in the
period around the war.[96] Paine's texts are hymns to male friendship. They
envision a social order centered on homoerotic male bonds – "an England
of friends" – in which the evils of capitalism are overcome by a spirit of
comradely love (*NAC*, 159). The first of Paine's two treatises, *Shop Slavery
and Emancipation* (1912), begins as a relatively straightforward manifesto
for reforming the living-in system that dominated the shop-clerk profession
in the first decades of the century, but shifts quickly into a campaign for
a New Aristocracy of Comradeship, to be based on "the reckless love of
comrades" and organized around the figure of the friend (*SSE*, 106). In a
finale entitled "The Way Out," *Shop Slavery* sings a triumphal paean to the
gospel of male friendship, an appeal to personal enlightenment as a means
of restructuring English culture and attacking capitalist injustice: "With
us it is a question of establishing a new ideal of personal relationship, and
inspiring the whole of the youth of the nation with the same spirit"; or, in
more dramatic terms, "My friend is my God. I know no other God" (*SSE*,
109, 114).

   Shop Slavery was written before the war, and its evocation of a reform
spirit driven by the power of intimate male relations reflects the era of Edward Carpenter and other late-Victorian reformers who, as I have suggested,
imagined that communities of men could be the central engines fueling a
widespread reunification of embattled classes. Paine himself had worked in
London's East End and had been influenced by the University Settlement
Movement, a reform scheme whose motivating force was supposed to be the
bonds of friendship that would develop between university-educated young
gentlemen and working-class men.[97] This legacy of projecting friendship
into the social reform arena, which has marked other texts in this study,
provides Paine with a literary and political antecedent, from which he
feels empowered to launch his own imaginative program: "In Whitman's
'Leaves of Grass,' in Tennyson's 'In Memoriam,' and in Carpenter's 'Toward

Democracy,' we have word of the new spirit as a voice overheard between sleeping and waking; but what we still lack is a concerted plan of action to start 'the friend' on the road of adventure to which he is called" (*NAC*, 54). Invoking the authority of the founding fathers of the fellowship-as-politics ideal, Paine conveys a sense of slumbering masses, ready to be galvanized into concerted action.

If Paine's roots are Victorian and Edwardian, what makes his work interesting for a consideration of post-war masculine comradeship is his striking assertion in his second treatise, *A New Aristocracy of Comradeship* (1920), that the war has fortuitously provided the opportunity for realizing and completing the earlier ideals. *A New Aristocracy* begins by recasting the commitment to male intimacy, a formerly elusive goal, as a product and spoil of war:

> Since then 1914–1918!...
> The New Aristocracy of Comradeship, which I foreshadowed as destined to take shape in the near future, though I dared not say how near, as I could only divine its coming rather than give actual proof of its being already anywhere in existence, came suddenly to life in the Army. That is the glorious fact about the war; what led up to the war is nothing as compared with that. It wanted only an heroic excuse for the spirit out of which this New Aristocracy grew to materialise into a devoted band of brothers ready to die at a moment's notice – preferring almost to die rather than to live – from the very greatness of the inspiration under which it laboured. That heroic excuse was found in the war. (*NAC*, vii–viii)

In these lines, the war's tragedy recedes behind its illustrious success in creating, nurturing, protecting, and elevating male bonds. The passage echoes the discourse of elevated comradeship that dominated during the war years. Moreover, as we have seen in the rhetoric of former servicemen, Paine hopes to disperse the masculine bonds of war into the wider world. If the civilian Paine's plans for the particular uses to which comradeship should be put, as well as his lavish praise for the physical and homoerotic, set him apart from the typical ex-soldier's rendering of comradeship, his basic idea is neither unique nor exotic. For Paine, the potential for male community and social renewal engendered by the war is exhilarating, limitless, and, most importantly, shared.

What Paine anxiously hopes to avoid, however, is the solipsism he feels always stands as a serious pitfall into which men might fall, transforming them from a social force into a paralyzed pair of non-actors, the pseudo-couple. On one hand, Paine believes that individual friendships – like his own all-encompassing relation with an unnamed younger man, depicted in lengthy, erotic, reverential prose – form the basis for a wider program of comradeship. On the other hand, he worries that such engrossing intimacies, "that make and mould a man in white-hot moments of intensity as the glowing iron is beaten out and shaped on the anvil," might become overly seductive in themselves, ultimately diluting and defusing the potential for social reconstruction (*SSE*, 117). Thus, Paine calls for transferring the power of one-to-one relations onto more organized bonds, writing, for instance, that "[the friend] is not one and indivisible, but one and a million times divisible. I find him everywhere because once I found him in a single soul" (*SSE*, 114); or, again, "the pivot of that power [of friendship] should be in ten thousand friendships planted over the whole length and breadth of the land" (*SSE*, 116). The scope of "that power" is meant to be wide, the effects extensive, "a vast new religious ideal of comradeship, whose object is entirely to overthrow the existing form of society and build up a new society in its place" (*NAC*, 52). Paine's plan, with its harnessing of intimacy and desire into a larger political structure, adheres quite closely to the model I have been calling the organization of intimacy – an effort at once to nurture the bonds of individuals and to borrow the authority of traditional masculine institutions. Accordingly, after this invitation to blend individual love with political action, Paine emphasizes the critical importance of constructing forms to organize and realize friendship's potential. Of his own friendship history, he writes:

> We parted, as I have said elsewhere [i.e., in *Shop Slavery*], because there was to be no revolution...
> For a while we lived entirely to ourselves. At last our friendship led us into a cul-de-sac.
> More intense thus than it ever would have been otherwise, it was too intense for the narrow sphere in which we found ourselves. If there had been any great movement ready at hand in which we could have enlisted our sympathies, I still think that the preparation would have been adequate; but we knew of no such movement, and we were jealous of drinking the cup of friendship to the lees. (*NAC*, 44–46)

Ultimately, the concentrated intensity of intimate friendship must be dispersed, in order to rejuvenate the social order. Unless it is channeled into the fight for social revolution, the "white-hot" energy of intimacy always threatens to lead to an implosion *à deux*, in effect to produce the stagnated and unproductive pseudo-couple of works such as "Monkey Nuts."

Paine's religion of comradeship is extreme in both its rhetorical flourish and its ambitions for social change, yet its content – a reform scheme constructed simultaneously out of earlier traditions for idealizing male friendship and out of the imagined bonds of former soldiers – in many ways exemplifies its moment. I have attempted to give a general sense of the urgency that characterized the large-scale imperative to understand, absorb, represent, transform, or simply evade the millions of men returning from the war. Paine's texts make a concerted effort to encourage returned soldiers in effect to lead the nation on a radical program of social reorganization, based on their experiences of intimacy. Yet even in the case of the utopian Paine, several sticking points remain: for one, his language never escapes the logic of the fantastic, in part because he seems to view former soldiers as entirely healthy, able-bodied men, rather than in the more complex state of disability which in fact characterized many of them; and second, the problem of the pseudo-couple cannot be eliminated, for there is no clear way to reconcile the desire to reinvigorate war-time fellowship with the fear that men in such a situation will be helplessly imprisoned in their own destructive world. Do men marching, living, and cooperating together represent the liberation of society or its destruction? Is there any way to recuperate or harness the forces of male association as a permanent part of civilian political or spiritual life, and would such action even be desirable? What about the persistent injury, the "brokenness," of the returned men? These are the questions posed not only by Paine and other writers discussed here, but, perhaps most consistently and prominently, by Lawrence. In his essays and fiction, Lawrence labors to construct a satisfactory, synthetic vision of male friendship, one that will take into account the war's dilemmas of injury, violence, and foreclosed promise; ultimately his pessimism about many of these subjects generates a spirit of intense pain for the would-be prophets who populate his canon.

DESIRE AND DEVASTATION: MALE BONDS IN D. H. LAWRENCE

Lawrence is the poet of the comradeship problem. From early novels like *The White Peacock* (1911), with its rich friendship between Cyril Beardsall and George Saxton, to the fantasies of phallic male community in *The Plumed Serpent* (1926), Lawrence never tired of exploring the attractions and pitfalls of male intimacy, conceived across a spectrum of consciousness, and over a wide geographical landscape. His works tend to unleash, rather than tame or domesticate, masculine desire, which is painted in bright colors and presented with an often feverish intensity. In Lawrence's writing, the male body – a site of both physical essence and cultural power – is always on view, an object of desire, interest, vitality, and precarious mortality. So extensive and exhaustive is Lawrence's preoccupation with male bonds and bodies that it would be impossible here to attempt coverage in any depth.

Instead, I shall look at those texts that most completely, systematically, and provocatively pursue male intimacy as a central feature of male subjectivity, a foundation for social organization, and an important element in the war-riven culture that Lawrence perceived around him.[98] Although some of the literature I shall examine was begun before the war, I hope to suggest that throughout the war period, and especially in its aftermath, Lawrence's exploration of male community overlapped in important ways with the assessments of comradeship that intrigued and troubled his contemporaries. Like Paine and other civilian social critics, Lawrence found in the war an analogue for his previously elusive efforts to organize masculine relations.

Lawrence's absorption in male desire has primarily been understood by critics as a refuge from the feared and detested world of dominating women. Perhaps the most complete articulation of this view is Cornelia Nixon's argument, in *Lawrence's Leadership Politics and the Turn Against Women*, that the shift from *The Rainbow* (1915) to *Women in Love* (1918) marks a transition in Lawrence's schema from a woman-oriented world, in which heterosexual union and female fecundity are celebrated, into a privileging of male relations and an aggressive backlash against female empowerment. Lawrence's shift into the worship of maleness, an anti-feminist sensibility that dominates his later career, is also characterized by an interest in authoritarian politics and a glorification of "the bowels," which Lawrence uses as symbols of male power and rejuvenation, even as they signal his intense anxiety about his own sexuality (in his writing, homosexuality often conjures images of filth and degradation). Nixon's study emphasizes Lawrence's rejection of women as equals and his movement into phallic dominance, and other critics have similarly argued that Lawrence looks to male bonding as a means of resisting female power and authority.[99] While such analyses offer a psychologically convincing picture of Lawrence, helpfully situated within the context of the turbulent women's movement at the beginning of the century, what they obscure is equally important. Discussions of Lawrence the anti-feminist, that is, might lead us to flatten out and homogenize his treatment of male relations, when his portrayals of male community are, in fact, wildly confused, self-conflicted, and disjunctive.

Two assumptions underlie many studies of Lawrence's enthrallment with comradeship, and it will be helpful to begin a discussion of his work by isolating and querying them. First is the notion that there is a smooth and clear relation between what I have called, in the context of war, "friendship" and "comradeship," or, in terms of classicism, "desire and its institutionalization" – that Lawrence's texts establish homologies and continuities among forms of male fellowship. We have seen in war literature, as well as in Forster's and Conrad's works, that conflicts among such forms of male bonding in fact produce rupture, disorientation, bereavement, and anger; for Lawrence, too, no clear continuum can be asserted, and thus it will be best to avoid the assumption that organized comradeship and intimate friendship are parallel and interchangeable conditions. Secondly, though often read as a partial product of his time, insofar as he becomes a spokesman for a certain kind of fascistic masculinism, Lawrence tends to be portrayed essentially as an iconoclast in his renderings of brotherhood, and his many forays into the terrain of male intimacy often seem to represent a purely personal odyssey.[100] This focus on eccentricity is not surprising, given the real strangeness of much of Lawrence's writing, especially on issues of sexuality and desire. And yet, many of Lawrence's contemporaries also believed that social change might follow from the bonds of war, and looked at the male body with a new urgency in light of the war's ravages. Lawrence's experiments with comradeship belong to the chaos of war-time and post-war England, where the fate of the soldier was on many people's minds.

Perhaps the most direct and obvious connection-point of Lawrence with contemporary friendship theorists involves his intellectual and political congruency with Edward Carpenter. We have seen that Carpenter's complete interleaving of homoerotic male friendship into a larger theory of social and economic justice provided a template for social critics and artists in the period, and that Carpenter brought an unusual level of authority, coherence, and completeness to what was typically an anguished and conflicted problem of accommodating male love into stable cultural constructs. In a thorough analysis, Emile Delavenay has unearthed affinities between Carpenter and Lawrence, as a matter of tone, political perspective, objects of interest, and shared intellectual and cultural milieu. Although Delavenay avoids making direct claims of influence – "This study is not meant to be a search for 'sources' of the works of D. H. Lawrence, so much as an attempt to define a mental climate" – nevertheless, he makes the case that Lawrence knew of Carpenter's ideas and had most likely read his work.[101] Delavenay never mentions male friendship, a strange omission; yet Carpenter's utopian ideals of the social power to be harnessed from male intimacy find echoes throughout Lawrence's career. Lawrence shares with Carpenter a serious commitment to the idea that there is, or might be, an important connection between organized male friendship and social change, under the rubric of anti-capitalism and in a spirit of prophecy. Less obvious than his intersections with Carpenter, however, are the ways Lawrence's texts engage with the many rival formulations of masculinity and male community that we have seen to swarm around the figure of the soldier during and after the war. Like Carpenter, Lawrence took on the idea of friendship as a product and a goal of culture; like Paine, he also understood it as a product and goal of war.

I begin with one of Lawrence's lesser-known works, an essay on James Fenimore Cooper's Leatherstocking tales (1919, revised 1924), which speaks quite powerfully to the image of male friends as stark and fearsome survivors. In many respects, the Leatherstocking essay reflects its moment: first published in 1919, and revised over the next several years, the essay engages the wide cultural interest in transforming the strong (and strongly feared) masculine bonds of war into a new social contract for the future. Lawrence finds the high-water mark of Cooper's work, the author's finest achievement and the novels' motivational engine, in the sublime friendship of Chingachgook and Natty Bumppo. Lawrence presents the men's friendship in terms that resonate with his own dreams of perfect male intimacy, as with the period's representations of war-scarred men:

> They are isolated, final instances of their race: two strangers, from opposite ends of the earth, meeting now, beholding each other, and balanced in unspeakable conjunction – a love so profound, or so abstract, that it is unexpressed; it has no word or gesture of intercommunion. It is communicated by pure presence alone, without contact of word or touch. This perfect relationship, this last abstract love, exists between the two isolated instances of opposite race.[102]

This is Lawrence in prophetic mode. The male love depicted here contains a kind of magnetic power, transmitted through the body, yet without "contact of word or touch," in an ambiguous space of an eroticism that denies its own erotic content. In the Leatherstocking essay, Lawrence gestures towards a form of political identity developing out of the men's friendship. In the later version, where the tone of lavish eroticism is somewhat restrained, Lawrence concentrates directly on the social or political ramifications of the men's intimacy:

> What did Cooper dream beyond democracy? Why, in his immortal friendship of Chingachgook and Natty Bumppo he dreamed the nucleus of a new society. That is, he dreamed a new human relationship. A stark, stripped human relationship of two men, deeper than the deeps of sex. Deeper than property, deeper than fatherhood, deeper than marriage, deeper than love. So deep that it is loveless. The stark, loveless, wordless unison of two men who have come to the bottom of themselves. This is the new nucleus of a new society, the clue to a new world-epoch. It asks for a great and cruel sloughing first of all. Then it finds a great release into a new world, a new moral, a new landscape.[103]

Newness is the key here, as Lawrence imagines entirely unprecedented social arrangements following the phoenix-like "sloughing" of outmoded social forms and institutions. Again, this concept mirrors Carpenter's vision of a glorious new world arising from the ashes of dead, bourgeois England, built on a foundation of intimate male friendship. Further, Lawrence's language here is reminiscent of many post-war thinkers who vigorously embraced the notion that the destruction wreaked by the war offered an opportunity to remake and revitalize the nation, and particularly those who hoped that the comradeship of war might play an important role in reconstruction. Yet, Lawrence's racial and sexual politics are always obscure and problematic, and just what such a "new society" or "new world-epoch" might involve remains decidedly vague. Lawrence does not, for instance, envision democracy in Whitman's sense, since in the same collection he attacks Whitman for valorizing a democracy that Lawrence views as fatal to the individual. Nor does he hold out hope for the next generation, for the two heroes of *The Last of the Mohicans* are quite clearly presented as relics, faint traces of a dying history.

In reference to this Leatherstocking novel, it seems, Lawrence can laud the men's friendship precisely because each represents a death, the last of his racial type. For all their mutuality and intimacy, "each of them is alone, abstract, beyond emotion," and such isolation derives in part from the men's final loss of any permanent cultural connections (*SCAL*, 62). In fact, the two men here become another pseudo-couple, a final in-between point of mutual existence before their complete annihilation. Leatherstocking himself, defined and constituted by a last stand in male friendship, eventually comes to look very much like a figure emerging out of the Great War, a man whose place in culture is foreclosed in advance. It is for this reason that he becomes for Lawrence an American Everyman, since "The essential American soul is hard, isolate, stoic, and a killer" (*SCAL*, 66). Lawrence's Leatherstocking is the poster-boy for a subjectivity created by loss and the capacity for violence, and his sublime friendship with Chingachgook represents a moment of unity in isolation, which, for all its vague political significance, cannot prevent his eventual fall into total solitude. Despite the overlay of racial and social significance, then, and notwithstanding the heightened, prophetic quality of Lawrence's language in the Leatherstocking essay, the men's intimacy cannot lead into any new, constructive social arrangement.

I want to suggest, in this vein, that *Women in Love*, which contains the most famous male couple in the Lawrence canon, can also be read as a reflection on war-time intimacies and the dilemmas of recovery. The novel creates an image of the male self as utterly derailed and divided by the in-escapable and unwilled fact that men magnetically attract other men. The project of *Women in Love* – and a host of later texts – is to imagine and develop forms that both formalize and resist this essential feature of men's psychic lives. Like Rickie Elliot in *The Longest Journey* or Paine's activist comrades, Lawrence's protagonists work to organize masculine intimacy into structures that will have a place in the social order and will not in-evitably fall into destruction or bereavement. But, of course, Lawrence's ultimate sensibility features disruption more than unity, and, as with the dying shadows that Lawrence conjures from Cooper's tales, these efforts inescapably lead towards a specific kind of failure. In Lawrence's texts, the bonds of war cannot be harnessed into any kind of lasting structure, and instead produce a form of isolation that proclaims itself a carrier of literary authority and an exemplification of modernity. *Women in Love*, in partic-ular, explores and tests several forms of masculine intimacy, which seem at first to offer the possibility of deep psycho-sexual fulfillment. Yet with the war as the great unspoken event rippling through the text – like the waves disrupting the placid lake in the haunting "Moony" chapter – the novel's interest in structured male bonds results ultimately in a pitiful cry of grief. *Women in Love* transfixes the mood that will come to dominate Lawrence's work, as the desire to organize male intimacy, in the context of the war, is eventually transformed into a sensibility of absolute loss.

Critics have assessed with acuity the homoerotics of *Women in Love*, its attendant violence, and the connection between unresolved homosexual tension and the rising tone of anti-feminism in Lawrence's voice. Christo-pher Craft's analysis of the novel, for instance, shows how Birkin's proposal of eroticized blood-brotherhood with Gerald is violently transposed onto Gudrun's body, in a structure of transmitted blood-letting that offers up a host of victims, culminating in Gerald's frozen corpse. Craft argues "that Lawrence's novel works, with a sometimes psychotic intensity, to produce this loss, this corpse, this murder as its narrative telos, the single defining event toward which the whole creation moves."[104] The novel does seem to move inevitably towards death, and this textual death-drive is perhaps inextricably and tragically connected with the pressing urge to realize male friendship. I want to stress this culmination in violence, disruption, and extreme sadness, even as I hope to demonstrate the great lengths to which Lawrence goes in *Women in Love* to imagine some kind of fulfilling, orga-nized intimacy.

There are two famously homoerotic and over-determined sequences in-volving Birkin and Gerald in the novel, which together comprise the novel's most optimistic statement on the fate of male love. The scene at Birkin's sickbed, which recalls similar occasions of homoerotic tenderness in *Sons and Lovers* (1913), constructs an atmosphere that is both recognizable and slightly unreal. To visit the ill is to enter an equivocal space, made strange by the patient's state of helplessness and immobility. The scene is suffused with eros, as Gerald "look[s] down at Birkin whose throat was exposed, whose tossed hair fell attractively on the warm brow" (*WL*, 210). Despite his vulnerability, a sickbed state of mental and physical liminality agrees with Birkin, who "liked sometimes to be ill enough to take to his bed. For then he got better very quickly, and things came to him clear and sure" (*WL*, 201). For Birkin, Gerald's presence in this atmosphere of uncanny clarity leads him to ruminate on the men's relation both with each other (idealized and eroticized) and with the outside world (held at bay). In this spirit of balance between intimacy and public forms, Birkin makes his famous suggestion of blood-brotherhood: "'You know how the old German knights used to swear a *Blutbruderschaft*,'" he begins, "'That is what we ought to do. No wounds, that is obsolete. But we ought to swear to love each other, you and I, implicitly and perfectly, finally, without any possibility of going back on it'" (*WL*, 206–207). Birkin's suggestion that the men become blood brothers contains many of the elements that have become familiar in this study of male intimacy: an effort to institutionalize and structure what otherwise remains a private and personalized friendship; a connection with a romantic history, here the "old German knights" (*WL*, 206); tension between a spirit of desire and a sense of coercion, as the men come together out of affection, yet with Gerald "deeply bondaged in fascinated attraction" (*WL*, 207); the gesture (the touch of hands) that completes an effort initially framed as linguistic (an oath). In this exquisite enactment of the organization of intimacy, Birkin, or perhaps Lawrence, attempts to solidify and transform the uneasiness surrounding male love by aestheticizing, idealizing, and embodying it, grounding its language in myth and its forms in history. Though Birkin makes several attempts to pinpoint and define his notion of blood-brotherhood – "We will swear to stand by each other – be true to each other – ultimately – infallibly – given to each other, organically – without possibility of taking back," in "[a]n impersonal union that makes one free" (*WL*, 206–207) – it seems clear here, as elsewhere, that the mixture of romantic fantasy and driving desire will ultimately doom the endeavor.

Nevertheless, what is most remarkable is not Birkin's fantasy, but that at this moment midway through the novel, the effort to organize intimacy meets with success, in a scene suffused with warmth, pleasure, and

harmony.[105] If Birkin begins his rumination on blood-brotherhood in response to what he sees as an insoluble problem – "Suddenly he saw himself
confronted with another problem – the problem of love and eternal conjunction between two men" (*WL*, 206) – what follows is a tender sequence,
which ends on a note of mutual satisfaction:

> The eyes of the two men met again. Gerald's, that were keen as a hawk's, were
> suffused now with warm light and with unadmitted love, Birkin looked back as
> out of the darkness, unsounded and unknown, yet with a kind of warmth, that
> seemed to flow over Gerald's brain like a fertile sleep.
> "Goodbye then. There's nothing I can do for you?"
> "Nothing, thanks."
> Birkin watched the black-clothed form of the other man move out of the door,
> the bright head was gone, he turned over to sleep. (*WL*, 210)

This instance of unspoken yet transmitted love contains its troubling aspects, including Gerald's "unadmitted love" and his ultimate departure. Yet
the overall tone is rich and gentle, with sleep representing an encouraging
rest more than a form of death. The comforting image of the happy Birkin
easing into sleep closes a scene that, looking ahead to the Leatherstocking
essay, might have been expected to end in disjunction and bleak isolation.

"Gladiatorial" offers an even more pronounced story of successful masculine bonding, a moment within the confines of the lived world that
nevertheless distills masculine intimacy, both personalized and structured.
The two scenes are linked in obvious ways, perhaps most directly when
the men repeat the hand-holding gesture of the bedside. In the sickroom
scene, a certain hesitancy had marked the touching of hands, until the final
parting, when Gerald takes "the warm hand of his friend in a firm grasp"
(*WL*, 210). This gesture becomes much less tentative and reluctant in the
aftermath of naked wrestling, when "[Birkin] put out his hand to steady
himself. It touched the hand of Gerald, that was lying out on the floor.
And Gerald's hand closed warm and sudden over Birkin's, they remained
exhausted and breathless, the one hand clasped closely over the other" (*WL*,
272). Once again, Lawrence's language emphasizes warmth and mutuality,
with Gerald partially withholding his strength out of consideration for the
weakened Birkin. The holding of hands represents a softened, less invasive
version of the rubbing of bloodied wrists invoked by blood-brotherhood –
a form of violence which, as Craft argues, ultimately gets transposed onto
Gudrun's body in the "Rabbit" sequence. In fact, the entire wrestling match
represents a form of masculine bonding that manages at once to be physical and aestheticized, a way to link male bodies without consigning them

to brutality. The placement of the men's naked bodies within shelves of books – "a tense white knot of flesh gripped in silence between the walls of old brown books" (*WL*, 270) – gives a visual correlative to the notion that this is a moment of extreme masculine unity within, rather than expelled from, the confines of western culture. The men's bodies in this gorgeous scene are exceptionally close, even as they are protected and nurtured in a space marked by wealth, privilege, and the tokens of bourgeois success. The body reaches an apex here, neither brutal (as in Forster's texts) nor entirely destructive of individuality: "So they wrestled swiftly, rapturously, intent and mindless at last, two essential white figures ever working into a tighter, closer oneness of struggle" (*WL*, 270).

Unity in combat, a man visiting his bed-ridden friend: at the center of a novel largely composed between 1914 and 1917, these two moments of supreme male homoeroticism rework familiar war tropes. Indeed, *Women in Love* momentarily transforms the structures of war intimacy – forms of male fellowship that, in the context of combat, generally create sorrow and alienation – into the basis for harmonious, mutual love. If Gerald's visit to the sick Birkin suggests innumerable sickbed scenes in the literature of the war, this bed-side attendance palpably lacks the tragic overtones that inevitably mark such moments in later texts like *All Quiet on the Western Front* (which opens with a devastating hospital visit). The fighting in "Gladiatorial" similarly evokes war language, with Birkin repeatedly stressing the intimacy of battle, at the same time that it remains far away from war's actual horrors. At two rich moments at the center of *Women in Love*, then, Lawrence constructs a space in which structured, eroticized male intimacy develops and thrives. Even after the wrestling match, at the end of "Gladiatorial," both Birkin and Gerald tend towards affirmation ("'Yes, I believe that too. I believe it,'" and "'It is the same'" [*WL*, 276]), in language that will eventually be reversed at the novel's tragic close, where disbelief and disjunction resume their reign.

What happens as the novel progresses is that the forms of structured intimacy that were imagined and nurtured in two poignant interludes are stripped of their standing in the world, reduced to a form of bereavement that closely mirrors (rather than transforming and aestheticizing) the grief of the tortured combatant in war. Indeed, Gerald's death can be viewed, in several senses, as a kind of transmuted war death, and this interpretive context helps to reconfigure a reading of the text. At the simplest level, the production in 1917 of a corpse out of a vital, active male body can hardly be read outside of the scope of war. The novel's final focus on Gerald's excruciatingly dead body confronts the reader with the bald fact of a heavy corpse in place of a living man, and points to the insuperable mass of war dead. The horrific physicality of the dead body, frozen and intact, seems to point outward towards the great heaps of mangled bodies littering the ground of continental Europe. If the frozen North contrasts with the mud of the Somme, and the preserved body differs from the dismemberment that was the hideous result of combat, still, the embalming of this representative corpse, a virtual specimen of the British officer class, seems suggestive of the war's perhaps most definitive feature, the destruction of young men on active duty. More specifically, it is the contrast between Gerald the male friend and Gerald the corpse that partially marks his death with the signs of the war: "Gerald might still have been living in the spirit with Birkin, even after death. He might have lived with his friend, a further life. But now he was dead, like clay, like bluish corruptible ice. Birkin looked at the pale fingers, the inert mass. He remembered a dead stallion he had seen: a dead mass of maleness, repugnant" (*WL*, 480). Gerald's death is mourned and internalized by his male friend, whose voice of protest will now sound the loss heard among so many war writers. At the close of the novel, Birkin takes on the role of the suffering friend, whose subjectivity has been constructed in important ways by male intimacy, and whose position of torment in the aftermath of the friend's death seems both permanent and absolute. The civilian Birkin in a sense takes on the grief of the combatant who has lost his war mate, and the voice that emerges rings with a moral authority similar to that of the grieving soldier.

Women in Love ends with a cry of pain:

"No," [Birkin] said. "You are enough for me, as far as woman is concerned. You are all women to me. But I wanted a male friend, as eternal as you and I are eternal."

"Why aren't I enough?" [Ursula] said. "You are enough for me. I don't want anybody else but you. Why isn't it the same with you?"

"Having you, I can live all my life without anybody else, any other sheer intimacy. But to make it complete, really happy, I wanted eternal union with a man too: another kind of love," he said.

"I don't believe it," she said. "It's an obstinacy, a theory, a perversity."

"Well – " he said.

"You can't have two kinds of love. Why should you!"

"It seems as if I can't," he said. "Yet I wanted it."

"You can't have it, because it's false, impossible," she said.

"I don't believe that," he answered. (*WL*, 481)

These last lines conjoin gender discord with a reversal of the earlier moment of affirmation at the end of "Gladiatorial." Critics have remarked that

Lawrence demonizes Ursula here, transforming her into the representative of narrow conventionality, most ominously with her use of the culturally fraught term "perversity." With domestic ideology on the upswing and the beloved male body eradicated, the organization of intimacy, which seemed in earlier sections to hold out the possibility of fulfillment, has now reached its usual conclusion in loss and futile protest. Birkin's expression of fore-closed desire – "I wanted it" – seems to seal off the hope of institutionalizing male love, leaving in the wake of such a dream a simultaneously broken and defiant male voice.

The war infiltrates and infects the novel, suggesting models for envision-ing male love as well as the language for its failure and loss. In this sense, *Women in Love* actively concerns itself with one of the primary ways in which contemporary culture understood male relations. The text records a profound desire to make the achievement of mutual male desire a central hinge in individual happiness, and to do so by incorporating it into vener-able conventions. And the novel is willing to imagine some fulfillment, as friendship is disengaged from the extremes of either solipsism or group sol-idarity. Perhaps it is the text's ambiguous relation to the war that accounts for its combination of hope and despair with respect to male love. To the ex-tent that men are able to construct forms for their desire, they borrow from the war, without having to succumb to its overwhelming horror. Yet when Gerald's corpse is produced, Birkin is thrust into the position of grieving friend, and this construction, chilling and final, makes for no balancing and no relief. As Lawrence writes elsewhere, "The last great ebullion of friendship and hope was squashed out in mud and blood. Now men are all separate little entities."[106] And, as we have repeatedly seen, out of defeated male love comes the authority to speak, for Birkin's prophetic legitimacy, his status as Lawrentian alter ego, are only heightened by his final position of loss. Nowhere does Birkin's voice command more authority, or his status as heroic social critic reach a higher echelon, than in the closing images of his poignant mourning for his dead friend. Birkin wanted a friend, in the extreme and fraught terms made resonant by the war, and what he got instead was an unassailable, lingering invitation to speak that incessant loss, as Natty Bumppo, in a very different setting, had also seemed a figure for the starkness of friendless survival.

Lawrence himself was crushed by the war. "I am no longer an English-man," he pronounced in 1916, reeling with hatred for humanity, "I am the enemy of mankind."[107] In a thinly veiled autobiographical account of the war years, the chapter of *Kangaroo* entitled "The Nightmare" describes Lawrence's experiences as a civilian during the war: shunted from house to house by suspicious villagers, tormented by the waves of chauvinism that swept the country, consistently maligned as a type of conscientious objector, humiliated by the physical degradation of military medical inspections, fearful and enraged. In the years following the war, when the peripatetic Lawrences permanently turned their backs on England, Lawrence reacted and responded in writing to the after-effects of the war. His interest in male friendship as an organizing structure and a central feature in constructing male subjectivity seems only to have increased in this period. I have suggested that two of the primary images characterizing the returned soldier in the contemporary consciousness involved, first, the grieving, broken outsider, unpredictable, potentially violent, and inassimilable into civilian existence, and second, the man newly formed by male association, identifying with former comrades, whose immersion in masculine community at best provides a locus for helping to reconstruct the culture, at worst threatens to engulf and trouble the social order and/or the combatant himself. In *Aaron's Rod* (1922) and *Kangaroo* (1923), Lawrence explores and develops these two images, with the latter novel most directly suggesting that a displaced Everyman – Lawrence's figure for a kind of tortured modernity – finds both hope and despair in response to the comradeship of the post-war era.

Aaron's Rod is very much a novel about the end of war. The novel portrays a number of former combatants, shattered men who remain utterly incapable of leaving the trenches behind. Most striking in this regard is Captain Herbertson, the former officer who comes to Rawdon Lilly's flat late at night to unburden himself of the unyielding horrors of war: "He had come, unconsciously, for this and this only: to talk war to Lilly: or at Lilly . . . it was a driving instinct – to come and get it off his chest" (*AR*, 113–114). Lilly himself (Lawrence's closest alter ego in the novel) instantly recognizes Herbertson as a type, an icon. Even the officer's class and national markings disappear in the face of war's terrible power, for "underneath it was all the same as in the common men of all the combatant nations: the hot, seared burn of unbearable experience" (*AR*, 114). Not surprisingly, the focal point for this unbearable pain is the wrenching loss of individual friends – in horribly gruesome deaths – the paradigmatic war-time scenario that seems to return in text after text. *Aaron's Rod* is set primarily in Italy, and one of the reiterated ideas in the text is not only that those broken by war will wander far from England, but that the phenomenon of post-war estrangement itself represents an international phenomenon, a broadly European malaise.

If the novel is replete with broken combatants – Angus, too, is instantly recognized as "one of the young officers shattered by the war" (*AR*, 186) – nevertheless, Lawrence in effect transfers their status of depleted, almost ontological uncertainty onto his civilian protagonist. It is as if the actual returned servicemen, like Woolf's Septimus or Eliot's hollow men, have been too completely overridden and devastated by war to function as potential new men, and Lawrence appropriates their state of unpredictable volatility for his hero, a civilian stand-in for the wrecked men of war. Aaron Sisson arguably ranks as one of the least appealing of Lawrence's protagonists, inexplicably desired and courted by nearly every character in the novel. Many social circles galvanize around him, despite his wordless, blank, non-committal, and vaguely antagonistic personality. It seems, indeed, that Aaron becomes an object of desire precisely *because* he lacks all appreciable characteristics or remarkable qualities, and in this sense he carries a certain exemplarity. Aaron is a relic of war-decimated England, whose aimless life follows his rejection of all received social forms, a product of war nearly as problematic as the returned soldiers he both resembles and foils. His character is defined by an extreme rootlessness, a self-willed and consistently perpetuated state abetted only by the promise of male friendship. As early as the novel's opening lines, the mood of post-war uncertainty and unease is established as a universal phenomenon: "There was a large, brilliant evening star in the early twilight, and underfoot the earth was half frozen. It was Christmas Eve. Also the War was over, and there was a sense of relief that was almost a new menace. A man felt the violence of the nightmare released now into the general air" (*AR*, 5). The violence of war has come home, not only in the persons of those who fought, but dispersed in the general atmosphere. Aaron seems to have caught the mood of looming danger, the words "a sense of relief that was almost a new menace" aptly capturing his own psychic state. If it is typically the returned soldier who embodies the "violence of the nightmare" brought back to England, and if *Aaron's Rod* presents a host of "shattered old men" lost to the war, the text nevertheless offers a civilian, ambiguously situated between classes, as a stand-in for the new configurations of men troubling the post-war world.

Aaron is fully identified and associated with resistant, undomesticated masculinity, and with an ethos of exclusive male loyalty. The city of Florence, for example, thrills him – it "seemed to start a new man in him" – because "[it] was a town of men" (*AR*, 212). The novel is populated mostly by men, and seems to surge and flow as a river of masculine, and at times violently misogynist, energy. If the crucial, defining act of the novel is Aaron's abandonment of his family – a sweeping dismissal of the institution of marriage – the primary long-term relation in the text involves his friendship with Lilly. Aaron's quest involves an effort to banish women and conventional structures of commitment (work, marriage, family, nationality) from his life, even as he searches for a male equivalent, the organization of intimacy. His friendship with Lilly, flawed and unsatisfying as it may be, presents the best such possibility, and Aaron grasps at it as at a last straw: "One fact remained unbroken in the débris of his consciousness: that in the town was Lilly: and that when he needed, he could go to Lilly" (*AR*, 264); or, again, "The only thing he felt was the thread of destiny attaching him to Lilly. The rest had all gone as bare and bald as the dead orb of the moon. So he made up his mind, if he could, to make some plan that would bring his life together with that of his evanescent friend" (*AR*, 288–289).

In a study of Lawrence and modernism, Tony Pinkney has argued, following Jameson, that, in *Aaron's Rod*, Lawrence invokes the pseudo-couple as a form of dessicated community.[108] We might say that Aaron's project of making permanent his friendship with Lilly embodies the desperate desire to ward off nihilism under the shelter of this beleaguered relational structure, an image for the depleted remains of civilization and community, as Lawrence understands them after the war. At the same time, however, this friendship needs to be distinguished from such sadistic and static forms of pseudo-couple as we saw, for instance, in "Monkey Nuts." The crucial difference is this: whereas "Monkey Nuts" sketches a portrait of the male couple as a product exclusively of war, an example of comradeship transferred to the ambiguous moment of the armistice, in *Aaron's Rod* the two protagonists have not been constructed directly and entirely by war, even as they exemplify a form of post-war disjunction. The part of their identity that exceeds/precedes the war will essentially combat the brokenness which indelibly marks the former soldier in Lawrence's work. Lilly himself makes a distinction between the "death-courage" of war comrades, who inevitably come home with their hearts broken, and his own ethos of friendship, which he views as life-sustaining and productive (*AR*, 120). Lilly's idea, and Lawrence's behind him, involves the valorization of a form of male fellowship that mirrors the intimacy of war friendship without entailing its inevitable destructiveness. Thus, the friendship between Aaron and Lilly tends to crystallize in moments of beauty that recall Gerald and Birkin more than the paralysis of "Monkey Nuts."

Aaron's halting efforts to secure his friendship with Lilly – generally resisted by the other man – make particular sense in the context of a novel that presents human relations in almost entirely negative and combative terms. Only in the moments of harmony between the two men do we see human companionship in a compelling and arresting state. Even more than in *Women in Love*, that is, *Aaron's Rod* presents a central episode of eroticized male intimacy as a contrast to the conflict-ridden nature of human interaction in general.[109] The domestic and peaceful coexistence of the two men, which pivots on Lilly's erotic rub-down of his friend's sick body, remains brief and imperfect, but its framework of simple, pleasurable companionship resonates throughout the text, above all for Aaron. "Darkness, silence, the firelight in the upper room, and the two men together" (*AR*, 104) – such descriptions suggest an integrity of moment and place, a form of pared-down human companionship that *Aaron's Rod*, like its hero, is willing to valorize. Similarly, the novel's closing chapter sets the men in a moment of clarity and aestheticized simplicity that is never repudiated or corrupted: "The two friends sat in the sun and drank red wine. It was midday... It was one of the most precious hours: the hour of pause, noon, and the sun, and the quiet acceptance of the world. At such a time everything seems to fall into a true relationship, after the strain of work and of urge" (*AR*, 292).

The "true relationship" that emerges here contrasts not only with the novel's portrayal of heterosexual strife, but also with other forms of male association in the text. As I have suggested, we need to be attentive to the differences, as distinct from the continuities, among forms of male community in Lawrence's work. It is of course true that the text celebrates moments of authoritarian, phallic dominance, as when Aaron rediscovers his "black rod of power, blossoming again with red Florentine lilies and fierce thorns" (*AR*, 258). Yet, despite such heavy-handed trumpeting of men's power over women, the novel in no way approves of the forms of masculine political association that it depicts in the Italian landscape. Both the socialists and anarchists presented in *Aaron's Rod* are threatening mobs, rather than embodiments of admirable comradeship. Just as the soldiers who jostle and rob Aaron violate his personal integrity and permanently alter his consciousness, so all groups of men in this text evoke terror. As Lilly has it, "Damn all leagues. Damn all masses and groups, anyhow. All I want is to get *myself* out of their horrible heap... all that mass-consciousness, all that mass-activity – it's the most horrible nightmare to me" (*AR*, 119, italics in original). And it is not only the thoughtless mob that is disavowed, but all groups, for the high-brow English ex-patriates in Florence become most embarrassing when they assemble; in such social settings, their drunken dialogue verges on the imbecilic.

Instead, the text consistently looks for moments of individualized intimacy, those quiet, elemental times when men in twos or threes achieve a form of harmony that is at once acknowledged and unspoken. Yet to pin down such moments of peaceful intimacy seems nearly impossible, an elusive goal that text and characters work earnestly, and often with a premonition of futility, to engender. James Argyle, ardent spokesman for the value of friendship, cannot quite pin down the relation between desire and its institutionalization. Even his strong claim cited as an epigraph to this chapter – "that is the sum of my whole experience. The search for a friend" (*AR*, 239) – suggests the "search" more than the attainment of its goal. The dialogue that follows continues to oscillate between affirming friendship as the most privileged human relationship and submitting to its impermanence and impossibility:

"And will you go on till you die, Argyle?" said Lilly. "Always seeking a friend – and always a new one?"

"If I lose the friend I've got. Ah, my dear fellow, in that case I shall go on seeking. I hope so, I assure you. Something will be very wrong with me, if ever I sit friendless and make no search."

"But Argyle, there is a time to leave off."

"To leave off what, to leave off what?"

"Having friends: or a friend, rather: or seeking to have one."

"Oh no! Not at all, my friend. Not at all! Only death can make an end of that, my friend. Only death. And I should say, not even death. Not even death ends a man's search for a friend. That is my belief. You may hang me for it, but I shall never alter." (*AR*, 239)

Despite the sexual meaning of Argyle's language, I take this dialogue not solely as a credo of homosexual desire, but as another articulation of what both Aaron and Lilly attempt in various ways to theorize. At its core, *Aaron's Rod* epitomizes the male desire to make a world out of friendship, to allow such harmonies to prosper and suffice. Out of the wreckage of the war, the novel seems to suggest, come men whose loyalties and constitutions lead them towards friendship rather than either group comradeship or heterosexual marriage. But such a creed itself cannot be precisely identified, much less realized, and tends to find its affirmation and apotheosis not in institutionalized forms but in temporal moments.

Perhaps it is because such moments cannot be transformed into permanent structures, even though they do carry real weight in the text, that Aaron's hope of organizing his intimacy with Lilly is thwarted and the novel ends on an ambiguous note, neither assuring Aaron's submission to Lilly's coercive ideals nor elevating him to the status of sorrow-filled visionary, along the lines of Rupert Birkin. Aaron is not, let me stress, a prophet, as the narrator's rumination on his musical constitution – linguistically limited, belabored by language – makes clear. Aaron's only real effort to explain and justify his ethos comes in a long and incoherent letter to Sir William Franks, an epistle that Aaron himself recognizes as inadequate, and whose reception is never described. Critics have uniformly noted that

Lilly more than Aaron voices Lawrence's views, and we might recall that Lilly's marriage to Tanny seems generally to be approved in the text, even if it is depicted only in passing. But it is Aaron who takes center stage in the eponymous novel, and it is he who most directly stands in for the broken combatants of war, citizens of the post-war years. The term "broken" is consistently attached to both Aaron and his flute ("The Broken Rod" being the title of the penultimate chapter, to give just one example), and it is his uncertain status at the end, rather than the self-assured future of Lilly the writer, that closes the text. Our last view of Aaron has him looking searchingly into his friend's face, still trying to understand what a program of friendship might entail. Though Lilly expresses confidence that the model must ultimately involve dominance and submission, Aaron's unfinished quest should by no means be taken as an affirmation of Lilly's authoritarian approach.

One of the most distinctive features of *Aaron's Rod* is that it ends neither with the grieving emptiness of Birkin in *Women in Love*, nor with the artist's final apotheosis in solitude that we shall find at the close of *Kangaroo*, two forms of failed intimacy that are clearly connected with literary and moral authority. *Aaron's Rod* concludes, instead, with a question mark, a kind of blankness. Aaron, as I have suggested, functions as a representative figure from the war, in the sense that his dissociation from civilian forms and his dogged commitment to male friendship evoke the image of the returned soldier, but he pointedly escapes both the searing despair and the self-legitimizing voice of the iconic type. Aaron seems destined to continue following friendship as the primary organizing feature of his existence, like Argyle valorizing the search for a friend-as-mate, without either achieving the organization of intimacy (an elusive goal, to say the least) or constructing a voice out of its foreclosure. Perhaps, then, Aaron's essential featurelessness culminates here: in the silence which proclaims neither success nor failure. In this sense, Aaron represents the returned soldier all too well. Like the various ex-soldier movements whose period of national visibility was soon past, Aaron seems destined for fade-out, his equivocal nature ensuring his eventual eclipse (both within the text and in the Lawrence canon).

Aaron's Rod reads as a gasping for breath after the war. Even such Lawrentian institutions as prophecy seem depleted, and the desire to organize friendship into viable social structures remains rather half-hearted, assigned to a passive hero whose agency comes only in fits and starts. It is not surprising, given the overall quality of stunned and hesitant reawakening in the novel, that Aaron's journey produces little by way of either self-authorization or affirmation. In the slightly later *Kangaroo*, by contrast, one gets the sense that the author's belief in vitality is re-emerging, and the novel's vigorous interrogation of masculine association signifies this renewal. The stakes, once again, have increased for male friendship, as the relation of masculine fellowship both to political organizations and to the development of subjectivity comes fraught with desire and resistance. In *Kangaroo*, Lawrence focuses directly on the returned soldiers' movement, at the same time that he revisits the conflicting forms of male intimacy that had marked *Women in Love*. What *Kangaroo* shows, in stark and deliberate terms, is that the war has made male association a viable and powerful new institution, but that the individual artist derives his final stature of authority and integrity precisely by rejecting the mateyness forged in combat and reorganized after the war.

Perhaps more than any other novel, *Kangaroo* directly scrutinizes the possibility of transforming the comradeship of war into the social and political organization of peace. Set in Australia in 1922, the text focuses on the Australian returned soldiers' and sailors' movement, a group whose politics amalgamates elements of the two major English associations, the Federation and the Comrades. The historical Diggers, whose organization later became the Returned Servicemen's League (or RSL), did indeed have many of the characteristics portrayed by Lawrence in the novel: a high level of visibility in the first several years after the war; an uneasy combination of anti-capitalist radicalism with nationalist social politics; a bravura style of masculine, matey, self-sufficiency.[110] Lawrence's choice to focus on Australian returned soldiers makes particular sense in light of the exceptionally important status given to the Diggers in the public imagination. Because the Gallipoli experience was ardently taken up by countless writers, politicians, and military personnel as a founding event of Australian nationhood, the returned men held a special status in post-war civilian culture.[111] The RSL garnered real prestige in the years immediately following the war, at the same time that a (mild) form of backlash against former combatants developed under the tough conditions of a post-war recession. Lawrence's depiction of the organization and its dominant personalities is clearly fictional, yet his portrayal of the Diggers as a viable fulcrum for social renewal speaks to a cultural preoccupation in Australia, perhaps even more than in England: the image of the volatile, returned soldier as a flashpoint for a fractious post-war world.

As if in answer to Rupert Birkin's vision of blood-brotherhood or Paine's call for a New Aristocracy of Comradeship, Lawrence's Diggers closely follow the pattern of organized intimacy. A widespread, highly structured institution, with rituals, forms, ceremonies, and strict rules, the Diggers' movement nevertheless is founded on the intimate friendship pledged by individual pairs of men. As the association's fierce promoter Jack Calcott explains, "'But my idea is, in a job like this, every many should have a mate – like most of us had in the war... Men fight better when they've got a mate. They'll stand anything when they've got a mate'" (*K*, 104–105). Not surprisingly, it is this quality of intimacy, combined with an imperative to revitalize post-war culture, that powerfully attracts Richard Lovatt Somers, the novel's typically Lawrentian protagonist, to the returned soldiers: "What was offered, he wanted so much. To be mates with Jack in this cause. Life and death mates" (*K*, 105). Somers, it should be noted, is neither Australian nor a war combatant, and the double otherness embodied by the Diggers forms an important element in their appeal. Their much-touted mateyness blends a variety of attributes typically associated with the colonial forces in the war, which only increase the men's seductiveness for Somers: rugged masculinity, an embracing of working-class language and style, an attitude of self-assuredness and self-sufficiency, a high level of comfort within all-male communities. The Anzac self-image formed a central feature in nascent nationalist discourse in Australia, and Lawrence taps into this popular image of a national ethos of masculinity formed by comradeship.

Not only is Somers drawn to the Diggers' quality of mateyness, but he also finds in the movement's larger political goals an outlet for his romantic craving for the vibrant, active world of men:

Somers felt drawn towards a strange sweetness – perhaps poisonous. Yet it touched Richard on one of his quivering strings – the latent power that is in man today, to love his near mate with a passionate, absolutely trusting love. Whitman says the love of comrades. We say, the mate love. "He is my mate." A depth of unfathomed, unrealised love can go into that phrase! "My mate is waiting for me," a man says, and turns away from wife, children, mother and all. The love of a man for his mate. (*K*, 197)

As in *Aaron's Rod*, intense male friendship comes into abrupt conflict with heterosexual union and other conventional social commitments. Perhaps most surprising here is Lawrence's assertion that man's "latent power... to love his near mate" can be historicized – the "today" of that sentence places desire for male comradeship deliberately and directly into the post-war consciousness. Whitman is less a prototype than an analogy, the spokesman for male fellowship from one war, while Lawrence focuses on the possibilities that have emerged from another.

"The love of a man for his mate" functions as the watchword for the Digger organization, and its leader, Kangaroo, is consistently presented as a Christ-like figure of infinite, if coercive, love, both giving and demanding passionate affection. Kangaroo is a strange hybrid – a Jewish man evoking Christ; the leader of an insistently masculine group, yet himself highly maternal; a volatile blend of soft compassion and violent rage – and this contradictory constitution suits an organization that Lawrence envisions as both conservative and radical, at once a reactionary political force and the cradle of a "new life-form" (*K*, 98). In a sense, Lawrence's Diggers represent a wonderfully accurate conceptualization of the war's legacy in the political and social arena, for they epitomize the notion that the returned soldier both can and cannot codify the nation's reconstruction: "can" because the sheer power of these reconstituted men is overwhelming, as we see in a potent scene of mob power, when the Diggers "[by] their moral unison annihilat[e]" their opponents (*K*, 313); "cannot" because, ultimately, civilian culture will find a way to absorb or banish their radical potentiality. Even in Australia, which Lawrence presents as fiercely democratic and unconstrained by the old order, the systemization of male love remains a stubbornly temporal force, a structure that may threaten the status quo, but will never achieve its goal of major cultural reorganization.

Indeed, for all our protagonist's powerful attraction to Jack Calcott, Kangaroo, the Diggers, and other forms of masculine political fellowship, Somers rejects the call of mateyness, setting his own integrity against the lure of fellowship. Over and over, in each of the novel's intimate male encounters, we find Somers experiencing an immediate wave of resistance and hostility to the men who so avidly court him. His dilemma is presented by Lawrence with sympathy, and his wrenching yet resolute refusal of friendship could be said to represent a kind of watershed in Lawrence's treatment of the friendship enterprise. Indeed, in his response to male fellowship – as in his more general characterization – Somers is an exemplary Lawrentian figure, a mirror for the author's own struggling ambivalence about male association, a portrait of the artist emerging from war-ravaged England with a host of half-formed, depleted convictions, still holding on, for one last moment, to a faltering ideal of male friendship as an uncompromised institution. In *Kangaroo*, as in *Women in Love*, the text acknowledges a tremendous, undiminished longing among men for intimacy with one another. Yet if *Women in Love* had succumbed to the tragedy of war, the appeal of friendship lingering as an echoing cry, in the later novel, even the desire itself is firmly defeated:

He half wanted to commit himself to this whole affection with a friend, a comrade, a mate. And then, in the last issue, he didn't want it at all. The affection would be deep and genuine enough: that he knew. But – when it came to the point, he didn't want any more affection. All his life he had cherished a beloved ideal of friendship – David and Jonathan. And now, when true and good friends offered, he found he simply could not commit himself, even to simple friendship. The whole trend of this affection, this mingling, this intimacy, this truly beautiful love, he found his soul set against it. He couldn't go along with it. He didn't want a friend, he didn't want loving affection, he didn't want comradeship... He had all his life this craving for an absolute friend, a David to his Jonathan, Pylades to his Orestes: a blood-brother. All his life he had secretly grieved over his friendlessness. And now at last, when it really offered... he didn't want it, and he realised that in his innermost soul he had never wanted it. (*K*, 106–107)

Such language – arresting in both its pathos and its finality – is reiterated with each stage in Somers' involvement with the Diggers, as the text depicts both the powerful claims and the ultimate rejection of organized intimacy. We might note, further, that Lawrence here presents the relation between the textual history of male friendship and the actual function of fellowship in men's lives as contradictory, another rupture in the continuum of masculine friendship. For Lawrence as for his protagonist, there can be no smooth translation from the conventions that bolster and purport to define male love to its embodiment in the world.

Somers' slow discovery of his own disaffection from male comradeship occasions the crucial shift in the novel. Once he has accepted that "in his innermost soul he had never wanted it," a conviction that increases as the novel progresses, the turn to an ethos of complete solitude becomes as inevitable as it is unrestrained. Thus with rising pitch, the narrative refrain becomes a call to solitariness: "That was all he wanted: to get clear. Not to save humanity or to help humanity or to have anything to do with humanity. Now, all he wanted was to cut himself clear. To be clear of humanity altogether, to be alone" (*K*, 265); or "To be alone, mindless and memoryless between the sea, under the sombre wall-front of Australia. To be alone with a long, wide shore and land, heartless, soulless" (*K*, 332). Of course, through all of this, Somers remains entirely dependent upon his wife Harriet, who functions quite conspicuously as a partner to this self-proclaimed solitary. Thus one might point to a degree of disingenuousness in the radical isolation celebrated at the close of the novel. The narrative has never really explored heterosexual marriage, an institution whose dominance and longevity remain unchallenged, even if its qualities are regularly denigrated. Male subjectivity, as Somers would have it, remains an exclusively masculine affair – marriage more a premise than a matter for consideration – and hence Lawrence will insist that the rejection of male community does entail a state of total rupture from "humanity."

I have called Somers "exemplary," but perhaps we can now further refine the term to "distinctive," in the canon of isolated friends. For his story differs in a crucial respect from such predecessors as Rupert Birkin and Aaron Sisson, as well as other figures discussed in previous chapters, all of whom essentially slide unwillingly into a state of desperate friendlessness. Somers, by contrast, avidly constructs his own isolation as an alternative to male friendship. And this willed accession to the separateness that stands as the obverse of male intimacy marks a shift in the paradigm I have been constructing up to now. We have seen that literary authority often develops as a consequence of or compensation for the loss of organized intimacy. Here, however, it seems that Lawrence is ahead of the curve, constructing the literary self out of the requirement to abjure masculine intimacy. To resist male fellowship becomes a form of discipline, a sign of individual integrity, and a guarantee that the artist will continue indefinitely to inhabit the position of lonely outsider – the visible sign of his prophetic legitimacy. One might say that Somers' experimentation with comradeship is always already destined to conclude where it does, for the story of the war, of *Women in Love* and *Aaron's Rod*, and, for that matter, of many other texts we have studied – narratives of friendship turned to isolation – has made the movement from intimacy into solitude nearly axiomatic. To make authority out of rupture, to create a voice out of the refusal to succumb to male intimacy, to renounce once and for all an institution that has always represented an escape from the logic of domesticity – such transformations differ from the fall into alienation that often follows the demise of male friendship.

Lawrence, even more than the other literary figures I have discussed, is looking directly for some kind of artistic apotheosis, a quality of visionary power for both himself and his characters, and in *Kangaroo* he finds such ascension in the willed rejection of male community and male love. Perhaps Somers' approach – a preemptive strike against desired intimacy – has the effect of warding off the peril that accompanied the emphasis on friendship in Forster, Conrad, and in many war texts. As Somers reasons:

If our society is going to develop a new great phase, developing from where we stand now, it must accept this new relationship as the new sacred social bond, beyond the family. You can't make bricks without straw. That is, you can't hold together the friable mixture of modern mankind without a new cohesive principle, a new unifying passion. And this will be the new passion of man's absolute trust in his mate, and his love for his mate.

Richard knew this. But he had learned something else as well. He had learned the great danger of the new passion, which as yet lay only half realised and half-recognised, half effective. (*K*, 198)

Echoing William Paine, Lawrence articulates both the desirability and the danger of creating a social order based on the new bonds of post-war friendship. Fore-warned is fore-armed: Somers makes the move to ward off "the horror we are laying up" (*K*, 198), by refusing in advance the whole project, the creation of "this new relationship as the new sacred social bond, beyond the family." Somers will solidify his status as wandering artist and social critic, as malcontent and truth-teller, by leaping over the crushing problem of developed male intimacy. His alienation – if such a term even applies here – is invited, willed, constructed, self-authored.

One might trace a cycle in the Lawrentian oeuvre as I have constructed it thus far: from *Women in Love* and the Leatherstocking essay, where the tremendous desire to make male intimacy a principle for social organization and personal fulfillment remains unfinished, inducing tragedy and contributing to the image of prophetic hero; to *Aaron's Rod*, a foray into the post-war landscape of all-male community and reconstituted male subjects, in which the only clear assertion seems to be that the quest for organized intimacy remains ongoing and inconclusive; and finally to *Kangaroo*, which presents the high-water mark of male love as political and personal ideal in conjunction with the emphatic rejection of the whole structure. The thrust of *Kangaroo* is to cast suspicion, even contempt, on ideals surrounding male bonds. While it is surprising, for instance, to find Lawrence attributing much credence to a wife figure, Harriet Somers consistently and cogently mocks her husband's adolescent pretensions towards male fellowship, and even Somers cannot help but acknowledge the accuracy of her sharp attacks. It would seem, then, that with the close of *Kangaroo*, Lawrence has reached a concluding point in his analysis of masculine fellowship, a final refusal of the consolations offered by male friendship and a resigned shrug towards the soldiers returned from the war, who may trouble the surface of social existence, but whose power to effect significant change remains circumscribed. Despite a continued – indeed life-long – fascination with the beautiful male body and the appeal of communities of men, Lawrence essentially abandoned the task of organizing intimacy after his post-war explorations.

The Plumed Serpent might seem to present a counter-example, however, since the text lingers over the magnetic communion among men, and the eroticized relation between Ramón and Cipriano plays a central role in the religion of Quexalcoatl. Yet, the novel in fact reflects a quite different set of problems and goals from what we have seen up to now in Lawrence's work; it is not so much a new contract between men as a new contract between the sexes that is sought, and the focus on the desirable masculine god-figure represents a general tone of phallic worship rather than the particular and poignant desire of man for man. *The Plumed Serpent* essentially takes male communion for granted and focuses on men's dominion over women, and this distinguishes it from works like *Women in Love*, *Aaron's Rod*, and *Kangaroo* which directly and seriously address contemporary concerns about male association in the context of the war. Indeed, it is interesting and perhaps ironic to note that insofar as *The Plumed Serpent* moves away from the study of male intimacy, it becomes decidedly more objectionable and problematic for the feminist reader. The organization of intimacy has always been a project for and about western men, and its premises are fatally tied to an ethos of indifference or hostility to women. Yet in *The Plumed Serpent*, the tone becomes much more shrill, as Lawrence shifts his focus from masculine association to a notion of authoritarian heterosexuality, and from white masculinity to the exotic male other. What emerges from these movements is a text rife with primitivism, violent sexism, and the overwhelming fetishization of male dominance. The heroine Kate Leslie is transformed from a self-sufficient, independent, modern woman into a cringing worshipper of male power, and the Mexicans become at times little more than an undifferentiated collection of pre-civilized physicality. Moreover, if the earlier texts had characterized male intimacy in part as a haven where a certain kind of harmonious, aestheticized unity can flourish, here all serious human interactions come fraught with hierarchy and the lust for power or submission. The relations between men are given no real content, since the interiority of the Mexican characters so often seems to verge on caricature. Male bonds are present, of course, part of the Quexalcoatl package, but the sympathetic attempt to balance the desire for intimacy with a social or political agenda is gone, replaced by the impersonal ceremonies of a new religion and the unrestrained worship of male power over women.

The settings for all of these post-war novels seem to invite a fiery masculine interaction. In *The Plumed Serpent*, Lawrence makes much out of the Mexicans' erotic otherness; the novel's entire organization depends upon the trope of the jaded westerner confronted with the unvarnished glory and terror of the primitive, naturalized self, the body before it has been stultified by western civilization. Though less excessively orientalist, *Kangaroo* also relies on the image of the Australian as hyper-masculine, the brusquely self-assured male undaunted by the conventional values of the old world. *Aaron's*

Rod, like all of Lawrence's Italian texts, lingers on Italian men, those dark, sexual figures inevitably presented as both attractive and repellent. And the American frontier of the Leatherstocking essay, despite the foreshadowing of its inevitable disappearance, is almost axiomatically presented as a place of wild, organic plenitude. In all of these cases, the non-English setting contributes to the texts' explorations of experimental communities and new social forms, as Lawrence seems most willing to imagine radical social transformation outside of his home terrain. This move, of course, exemplifies a familiar western tendency to exploit the imaginative geography of the other, as adumbrated by post-colonial theory. The international settings are important, too, as a matter of genre, for these texts (excluding the Cooper essay) at times read more like travel narratives than novels. The 1920s marked a period in Lawrence's career when he published a variety of travel sketches, and he tended throughout his life to conceive of his novels according to their location ("my Australian novel" or "my American novel" are frequent usages in Lawrence's letters).

Yet despite the importance of non-English settings, I want to stress that all of the texts discussed here engage quite pointedly with the home culture of war and its aftermath. We have seen that in the years immediately following the war, England found itself both motivated and frustrated – at times skeptical and resistant – about the imperative to make a fit country for heroes to live in, and Lawrence's experiments with comradeship grow out of this soil. If Lawrence turns his back on England, which he views as utterly unfit for any thoughtful person, let alone a hero, he nevertheless explores different versions of the "fit country" issue in his post-war ruminations. His works, that is, take on the central problem of a gap or disjunction between men formed by war and the civilian culture in which they must be re-acclimated. *Kangaroo* offers the most obvious example, as the returned Australian soldiers epitomize both the problem and the promise of constructing a harmonious relation between the socio-economic climate of the nation and the fractious, volatile men of war. *Aaron's Rod*, too, stresses the incompatibility of home culture with war subjects, especially those civilians who have absorbed the "violence of the nightmare" into their own persons, and the protagonist's fruitless wanderings can be viewed as an escape from the overwhelming challenge of matching society with a war-torn body of men. *Aaron's Rod* suggests that if war has not created heroes, and the country cannot accommodate the men it has produced, then men simply sever one bond after another, holding desperately to what is left, the thin thread of male intimacy. For Lawrence, there is an essential relation between the disruptions in male subjectivity forged by war and the sensibility of loss and prophecy that eventually emerges from the cultural wreckage. The prophetic quality of such figures as Birkin, Leatherstocking, Somers, and to a lesser extent Aaron, derives in part from their stature of friendlessness. Thus, at the level of plot and characters, Lawrence accords the power of language and vision, as well as the quality of representative modernity, to men who have completed the cycle of friendship, isolation, and willed exile. At the same time, his dogmatic male heroes, with their artistic natures and their festering vitriol against conventionality, are offered in part as authorial stand-ins. Hence when he portrays his men as isolated, Nietzschian spokesmen for an uncomfortable new social order, one cannot help but overlay that stance of self-proclaimed clairvoyance with the author's own, and see the final strokes of narrative prophecy as clarion calls from Lawrence himself.

When Lawrence transforms the contemporary infatuation with comradeship and the scarred war victim into a literary investigation of male intimacy and isolation, he constructs out of this dynamic interchange a form of prophetic language that is explicitly cast as a model of truth-telling for a modern moment. And such a public stance is appropriate, for Lawrence's interest in comradeship maps onto a broader cultural conviction that the millions of men returned and remade by war occupy a fundamental place in the story of post-war modernity. The structural impossibility of making a fit country for war's shattered relics becomes an impasse for cultural reformers, but perhaps a resource for literature. With their defining quality of brokenness, these men become a kind of emblem, which in turn helps to give form to a particular spirit or consciousness that Lawrence, for one, wished to appropriate, explore, and continually reconstruct. At the same time, the war's survivors themselves recede – drift away, as many reformers had feared – into a space of amnesia, replaced both by the "glorious dead," as the culture of memorializing found new styles with which to remember and mourn modern mass warfare, and by those civilians who in a sense offered themselves as new voices for the war's pain. Perhaps inevitably, the lost generation seems to be lost again, as writers like Lawrence elaborated their own schemes of modernity, casting a long shadow over the war's actual survivors, and proclaiming themselves perhaps the most apt interpreters of the war's pitiful and painful legacy.

Notes

INTRODUCTION

1. Samuel Beckett, *Waiting for Godot* (New York: Grove, 1982) 58–59.
2. Similar remarks could also be made with reference to Beckett's *Endgame*. Surprisingly, there has been little criticism focusing on male intimacy or homoerotics in these plays. For a series of essays on Beckett and gender, see Linda Ben-Zvi, ed., *Women in Beckett: Performance and Critical Perspectives* (Urbana: University of Illinois Press, 1990). See also Paul Davies, *Beckett and Eros: Death of Humanism* (London: Macmillan, 2000); Mary Bryden, "Gender in Transition: *Waiting for Godot* and *Endgame*," *Waiting for Godot and Endgame: New Casebooks*, ed. Steven Connor (London: Macmillan, 1992) 150–164; John Mowitt, "Queer Resistance: Michel Foucault and Samuel Beckett's *The Unnamable*," *Symploke* 4:1–2 (1996) 135–152.
3. Apsley Cherry-Garrard, *The Worst Journey in the World: Antarctic 1910–1913* (London: Constable, 1922) vii–viii.
4. Another general trend in the critical literature about friendship is to focus on biography, on individual friendships or circles of friends; this kind of work often involves celebrated literary figures and relies on personal correspondence. For those writers who worked together and influenced one another's output in direct ways – Owen and Sassoon, Conrad and Ford, Eliot and Pound – studies of personal relationships prove especially rewarding. For examples of the personalized approach to friendship in the modernist period, see Keith Alldrilt, "Eliot, Pound and 'Burnt Norton,'" *T. S. Eliot: A Voice Descanting*, ed. Shaymal Bagchee (London: Macmillan, 1990) 100–108; Rustom Bharucha, "Forster's Friends," *Raritan* 5:4 (1986) 105–122; Mary Ann Caws, *Bloomsbury and France: Art and Friends* (Oxford: Oxford University Press, 2000); Paul Delaney, *The Neo-Pagans: Friendship and Love in the Rupert Brooke Circle* (London: Macmillan, 1987); Patrick Quinn, *The Great War and the Missing Muse: The Early Writings of Robert Graves and Siegfried Sassoon* (Selinsgrove: Susquehanna University Press, 1994); Peter Dale Scott, "Pound in *The Waste Land*, Eliot in *The Cantos*," *Paideuma* 19:3 (Winter 1990) 99–114. For a study of friendship between the sexes, that generally avoids heavy use of biography, see Victor Luftig, *Seeing Together: Friendship between the Sexes in English Writing from Mill to Woolf* (Stanford: Stanford University Press, 1993). For a reading of the

collaborative text as a kind of homosexual birth, see Wayne Koestenbaum, *Double Talk: The Erotics of Male Literary Collaboration* (New York: Routledge, 1989). For discussion of authorship as a fully collaborative activity, with a focus on the early modern period, see Douglas A. Brooks, *From Playhouse to Printing House: Drama and Authorship in Early Modern England* (Cambridge: Cambridge University Press, 2000).

5. Frederic Jameson, *Fables of Aggression: Wyndham Lewis, the Modernist as Fascist* (Berkeley: University of California Press, 1979) 35–61.

6. Several models that derive from an even wider geographical and temporal framework, such as eighteenth-century German notions of blood brotherhood (invoked by Lawrence in *Women in Love*), the highly visible French ideal of "fraternité," which resonated at least up to the First World War, and the extensive metaphorics of brotherhood in ante-bellum America, are left to different studies. For an account of eighteenth-century friendship conventions, see George Mosse, *Nationalism and Sexuality: Respectability and Abnormal Sexuality in Modern Europe* (New York: Fertig, 1985). For discussion of French Revolutionary discourse, see Lynn Hunt, *The Family Romance of the French Revolution* (Berkeley: University of California Press, 1993). For analysis of ante-bellum America, see Mark C. Carnes, *Secret Ritual and Manhood in Victorian America* (New Haven: Yale University Press, 1989), and Caleb Crain, *American Sympathy: Men, Friendship, and the Literature of the New Nation* (New Haven: Yale University Press, 2001).

7. *Leaves of Grass* was published in three different editions, spanning from 1856 to 1891. For discussion of the text's transformations, with a focus on homo-erotics and the body, see Michael Moon, *Disseminating Whitman: Revision and Corporeality in Leaves of Grass* (Cambridge, MA: Harvard University Press, 1991).

8. Paul Fussell, *The Great War and Modern Memory* (London: Oxford University Press, 1975) 35.

9. Sandra M. Gilbert and Susan Gubar, *No Man's Land: The Place of the Woman Writer in the Twentieth Century, Volume II: Sexchanges* (New Haven: Yale University Press, 1989) 259.

10. Historicizing the war is an ongoing, complex, and multiform process. Several noteworthy cultural and/or social histories are Joanna Bourke, *Dismembering the Male: Men's Bodies, Britain and the Great War* (Chicago: University of Chicago Press, 1996); E. J. Hobsbawm, *The Age of Extremes: A History of the World, 1914–1994* (New York: Pantheon, 1994); Samuel Hynes, *A War Imagined: The First World War and English Culture* (New York: Macmillan, 1991); Trudi Tate, *Modernism, History, and the Great War* (Manchester: Manchester University Press, 1998); and Jay M. Winter, *The Great War and the British People* (London: Macmillan, 1985).

11. Though Fussell's approach to the war has remained generally canonical, one important current of modernist criticism of the 1980s and '90s involved a reassessment of other crux moments (the *fin de siècle*, the thirties), and hence an inevitable downgrading of the war as seminal event. In this work, I hope

to bring together insights about, for instance, gender flux at the turn of the century, with a continued focus on the war's legacy.

12. For a thorough discussion of masculinity and modernism, see Maurizia Boscagli, *Eye on the Flesh: Fashions of Masculinity in the Early Twentieth Century* (Boulder: Westview, 1996). See also Tim Armstrong, *Modernism, Technology, and the Body* (Cambridge: Cambridge University Press, 1998); Gerald N. Izenberg, *Modernism and Masculinity: Mann, Wedekind, Kandinsky through World War One* (Chicago: University of Chicago Press, 2000); and Michael Kane, *Modern Men: Mapping Masculinity in English and German Literature, 1880–1930* (London: Cassell, 1999).

13. For a discussion of the problem of mystifying the body – indeed a lively attack on just the kind of irreducibility I am claiming – see Judith Butler, *Bodies that Matter: On the Discursive Limits of "Sex"* (New York: Routledge, 1993).

14. My language here may echo Elaine Scarry, whose study of the body in pain has strongly influenced my own (Elaine Scarry, *The Body in Pain: The Making and Unmaking of the World* [New York: Oxford University Press, 1985]). I shall discuss Scarry in more detail in Chapter 4.

15. See Michel Foucault, *The History of Sexuality, Volume I: An Introduction*, trans. Robert Hurley (New York: Vintage, 1980). These topics have been thoroughly discussed by diverse queer theorists. See, especially, Joseph Allen Boone, *Tradition Counter Tradition: Love and the Form of Fiction* (Chicago: University of Chicago Press, 1987); Ed Cohen, "Writing Gone Wilde: Homoerotic Desire in the Closet of Representation," *PMLA* 102:5 (October 1987) 801–813; Cohen, "The Double Lives of Man: Narration and Identification in Late Nineteenth-Century Representations of Ec-centric Masculinities," *Cultural Politics at the Fin de Siècle*, ed. Sally Ledger and Scott McCracken (Cambridge: Cambridge University Press, 1995) 85–114; William Cohen, *Sex Scandal: The Private Parts of Victorian Fiction* (Durham: Duke University Press, 1996); Richard Dellamora, *Masculine Desire: The Sexual Politics of Victorian Aestheticism* (Chapel Hill: University of North Carolina Press, 1990); Jonathan Dollimore, *Sexual Dissidence: Augustine to Wilde, Freud to Foucault* (Oxford: Clarendon, 1991); Linda Dowling, *Hellenism and Homosexuality in Victorian Oxford* (Ithaca: Cornell University Press, 1994); and Alan Sinfield, *The Wilde Century: Effeminacy, Oscar Wilde and the Queer Moment* (New York: Columbia University Press, 1994).

16. Tom Stoppard, *The Invention of Love* (New York: Grove, 1998).

17. A word about terminology. Given how much historical specificity has been marshaled by critics in the excavation of sexual rhetorics in the late nineteenth and early twentieth centuries, an attentiveness to language seems warranted. In terms of individual usage, one finds variance: Edward Carpenter preferred the term "Urning," John Addington Symonds "invert," Forster "homosexual," and many others rely on ideas such as "comrade love." While I shall point to such distinctive usage as it arises, for the sake of clarity and coherence, I have generally adhered to today's language. By "homosexuality," I mean sexual relations between people of the same sex; by "homosexual," I refer to a person who identifies and understands him/herself as having a clear and knowable

sexual proclivity in the direction of the same sex; and by "homoerotic" I refer
to a much broader quality of erotic language, imagery, or sentiment organized
around members of the same sex, which need not be connected with specific,
named, or conscious sexuality. In all cases, I hope to set up my readings in such
a way as to obviate questions about the appropriateness of usage; nevertheless,
these terms come fraught with history, and any discussion that repeatedly uses
them necessarily runs linguistic risks.

18. Eve Kosofsky Sedgwick, *Between Men: English Literature and Male Homosocial Desire* (New York: Columbia University Press, 1985). See also Sedgwick,
Epistemology of the Closet (Berkeley: University of California Press, 1990).

19. Kaja Silverman, *Male Subjectivity at the Margins* (New York: Routledge, 1992).
For an account of abjection and the war, see Evelyn Cobley, *Representing
War: Form and Ideology in First World War Narratives* (Toronto: University of
Toronto Press, 1993).

20. See Lawrence Rainey, *Institutions of Modernism: Literary Elites and Public Cul-
ture* (New Haven: Yale University Press, 1998). See also Ian Willison, Warwick
Gould, and Warren Chernaik, eds., *Modernist Writers and the Marketplace*
(New York: St. Martin's Press, 1996); Kevin Dettmar and Stephen Watt,
eds., *Marketing Modernisms: Self-Promotion, Canonization, and Rereading* (Ann
Arbor: University of Michigan Press, 1996); and Joyce Piell Wexler, *Who Paid
for Modernism? Art, Money, and the Fiction of Conrad, Joyce, and Lawrence*
(Fayetteville: University of Arkansas Press, 1997).

21. Virginia Woolf, *The Common Reader: First Series* (New York: Harcourt, 1984)
149.

22. Some typical features that might fall under the rubric of early twentieth-century
"modernity" include: a heightened awareness of the "mass" of mass culture;
new configurations of urban life (including issues of immigration, technologies
of movement, forms/locales of consumption, and suburbanization); a sense
of urgency surrounding the many new forms of women's emancipation; and
intensified experiences of technology, both searing and euphoric.

23. Rita Felski, *The Gender of Modernity* (Cambridge, MA: Harvard University
Press, 1995) 9.

24. Some of the most stimulating work on modernism focuses on connecting recognized literary features with specific elements in the historical and cultural
realities of the period. What these critics have in common is not so much a
specific methodology as an interest in determining how culture – in its most
diverse and politicized sense – contributes to the creation of literary forms
that at times work very hard to obscure that history. Particularly influential
has been a short and dazzling essay by Jameson, in which he claims an intrinsic
connection between modernist forms and central features of early twentieth-
century imperialism. See Terry Eagleton, Frederic Jameson, and Edward
Said, *Nationalism, Colonialism, and Literature* (Minneapolis: University of
Minnesota Press, 1990) 43–66. For other examples, which have strongly influenced my approach to the field, see Michael Tratner, *Modernism and Mass
Politics: Joyce, Woolf, Eliot, Yeats* (Stanford: Stanford University Press, 1995),
which argues that modernists attempted not so much to escape as to engage

notions of mass culture, a claim that moves from a simple notion of modernist elitism and avoidance to a more thick, tense dynamic of ambivalence, absorption, and reciprocity; and Marianne DeKoven, *Rich and Strange: Gender, History, Modernism* (Princeton: Princeton University Press, 1991), which shows that modernism took shape in part as a response to feminism and socialism, two sweeping social movements whose importance with respect to literary form has generally been undervalued.

25. I do not directly or systematically take up the broad issue of the politics of modernism. As a general matter, one question has always been whether modernism represents a radical challenge to the liberal subject and the ideology of capitalism, or, by contrast, an elitist, narcissistic embodiment of those very concepts. For a nice summary of the two critical camps, see the introduction to DeKoven, *Rich and Strange*.

26. Let me mention several other texts that seem fruitful for further study. In T. S. Eliot's *The Waste Land* (1922), the absent, dead friend lurks just beneath the poem's surface. (For the first and most famous example of an argument that *The Waste Land* is a poem of longing for the dead male friend, originally composed in 1952 and immediately suppressed by Eliot, see John Peter, "A New Interpretation of *The Waste Land*," *Essays in Criticism*, 19:2 (April 1969) 140–175. See also James Edwin Miller, *T. S. Eliot's Personal Waste Land: Exorcism of the Demons* (University Park: Pennsylvania University Press, 1977).) Also resonant is Ford Madox Ford's *The Good Soldier* (1915): in an excessively tortured text, in which all human interactions suffer the same devastation as the process of narration itself, it seems significant that the text's crisis point is occupied by the good soldier's helpless body – the male friend reduced to shreds. (For discussion of related issues, see Chris Foss, "Abjection and Appropriation: Male Subjectivity in *The Good Soldier*," *Literature Interpretation Theory* 9:3 [1998] 225–244.) Evelyn Waugh's *Brideshead Revisited* (1944) figures the nature of the empty present largely in terms of the loss of youthful friendship. Lastly, James Joyce's *Ulysses*, which undertakes a search for new configurations of intimate male bonds, might reward an analysis that focuses on Leopold Bloom and Stephen Dedalus as another pair on the road between late-Victorian Britain's idealized male communities and Beckett's striving pseudo-couples. If the text quite clearly borrows from both familial and mythic models for construing the relationship between Bloom and Stephen, it just as clearly rejects and remakes those conventional forms, and it offers extremely rich references for conceptualizing male intimacy. Forms of male fellowship explored over the course of the novel include fathers and sons; images of citizenship and national belonging; the atmosphere of the pub; the university and its friendships; and the classical Greek precedent. (For discussion of homoerotics in *Ulysses*, see Colleen Lamos, *Deviant Modernism: Sexual and Textual Errancy in T. S. Eliot, James Joyce, and Marcel Proust* [Cambridge: Cambridge University Press, 1998].)

27. The simultaneous empowerment and silencing of female voices in the modernist period presents a thicket of problems that have been discussed by a variety of critics. Most important for the present study are works by such

critics as Elaine Showalter and Judith Walkowitz, which have stressed that the thirty-year period flanking the turn of the century marked a moment of palpable gender flux. What Showalter has called "sexual anarchy" refers not only to the sexological revolution – the increasing public consciousness of sexual deviance as a category to recognize, study, classify, treat, punish – but more broadly to a spectrum of social transformations involving, for instance, new conceptions of the separation of spheres; the female empowerment associated with commercial and commodity culture; and the ongoing battles surrounding suffrage, property rights, access to the professions, and anti-prostitution regulation. See Elaine Showalter, *Sexual Anarchy: Gender and Culture at the Fin de Siècle* (London: Bloomsbury, 1991), and Judith Walkowitz, *City of Dreadful Delight: Narratives of Sexual Danger in Late-Victorian London* (Chicago: University of Chicago Press, 1992). See also Bram Dijkstra, *Idols of Perversity: Fantasies of Feminine Evil in Fin-de-Siècle Culture* (New York: Oxford University Press, 1986); Sally Ledger, *The New Woman: Fiction and Feminism at the Fin de Siècle* (Manchester: Manchester University Press, 1997); Sally Ledger and Scott McCracken, eds., *Cultural Politics at the Fin de Siècle* (Cambridge: Cambridge University Press, 1995); Deborah Epstein Nord, *Walking the Victorian Streets: Women, Representation, and the City* (Ithaca: Cornell University Press, 1995); and Elizabeth Wilson, *The Sphinx and the City: Urban Life, the Control of Disorder, and Women* (London: Virago, 1991).

28. See Nina Auerbach, *Communities of Women: An Idea in Fiction* (Cambridge, MA: Harvard University Press, 1978); Shari Benstock, *Women of the Left Bank: Paris, 1900–1940* (Austin: University of Texas Press, 1986); Mary Ann Caws, *Women of Bloomsbury: Virginia, Vanessa, and Carrington* (New York: Routledge, 1990); Lillian Faderman, *Odd Girls and Twilight Lovers: A History of Lesbian Life in Twentieth-Century America* (New York: Columbia University Press, 1991); Faderman, *Surpassing the Love of Men: Romantic Friendship and Love between Women from the Renaissance to the Present* (New York: Morrow, 1981); Caroll Smith-Rosenberg, *Disorderly Conduct: Visions of Gender in Victorian America* (New York: Knopf, 1985); and Martha Vicinus, *Independent Women: Work and Community for Single Women, 1850–1920* (Chicago: University of Chicago Press, 1985).

29. See Virginia Woolf, *A Room of One's Own* (San Diego: Harcourt, 1981).

30. See, for example, Terry Castle, *The Apparitional Lesbian: Female Homosexuality and Modern Culture* (New York: Columbia University Press, 1993).

1 VICTORIAN DREAMS, MODERN REALITIES: FORSTER'S CLASSICAL IMAGINATION

1. E. M. Forster, *The Longest Journey* (New York: Random House, 1993) 69; volume cited hereafter in the text as *LJ*.

2. The elevation of "personal relationships" is developed in Forster's classic essay, "What I Believe." See E. M. Forster, *Two Cheers for Democracy* (New York: Harcourt, 1951) 68.

3. For accounts of Forster's novels that stress the recording of a lived homosexual experience, see Robert K. Martin, "Edward Carpenter and the Double Structure of *Maurice*," *Literary Visions of Homosexuality*, ed. Stuart Kellogg (New York: Haworth, 1983) 35–46; Mark Lilly, *Gay Men's Literature in the Twentieth Century* (New York: New York University Press, 1993) 53–63; and Claude Summers, "The Flesh Educating the Spirit: *Maurice*," *Critical Essays on E. M. Forster*, ed. Alan Wilde (Boston: Hall, 1985) 95–112.

4. T. S. Eliot, from "The Metaphysical Poets" and "Tradition and the Individual Talent," *Selected Prose of T. S. Eliot* (San Diego: Harcourt, 1988) 65, 38.

5. A recent volume of essays seeks to foreground Forster as a queer writer, a welcome move. See Robert K. Martin and George Piggford, eds., *Queer Forster* (Chicago: University of Chicago Press, 1997).

6. An exception to the general rule of excluding Forster from the central modernist pantheon comes in Jameson's "Modernism and Imperialism," which argues that Forster's insight into the relation of empire to metropolitan subjectivity is paradigmatically modernist. Though Jameson's essay has recently become nearly ubiquitous in discussions of modernism and imperialism, his foregrounding of Forster is invariably unnoticed. See Jameson, "Modernism and Imperialism," in Terry Eagleton, Frederic Jameson, and Edward Said, *Nationalism, Colonialism, and Literature* (Minneapolis: University of Minnesota Press, 1990) 43–66.

   Two texts that place Forster as a coda to aestheticism are James Eli Adams, *Dandies and Desert Saints: Styles of Victorian Manhood* (Ithaca: Cornell University Press, 1995), and Richard Dellamora, *Masculine Desire: The Sexual Politics of Victorian Aestheticism* (Chapel Hill: University of North Carolina Press, 1990); for a striking omission of Forster even from this status, see Eve Kosofsky Sedgwick, *Between Men: English Literature and Male Homosocial Desire* (New York: Columbia University Press, 1989). One essay that does analyze Forster's interest in nineteenth-century homoerotic discourse, arguing that Forster produces an aesthetic synthesis by blending the "softness" of Hellenism with a "hardness" associated with modernity, is Robert K. Martin, "The Paterian Mode in Forster's Fiction: *The Longest Journey* to *Pharos and Pharillon*," *E. M. Forster: Centenary Revaluations*, ed. Judith Scherer Herz and Robert K. Martin (Toronto: University of Toronto Press, 1982) 99–112. Joseph Bristow expands on this healthy development of viewing Forster in terms of irrevocable contrast and tension: see Joseph Bristow, *Effeminate England: Homoerotic Writing after 1885* (New York: Columbia University Press, 1995), especially "Against 'Effeminacy': The Sexual Predicament of E. M. Forster's Fiction," 55–99. I shall discuss Bristow's argument in more detail below.

   Accounts of the origins of modernism that entirely (or almost entirely) neglect Forster include Malcolm Bradbury and James McFarlane, eds., *Modernism* (Harmondsworth: Penguin, 1976); Marianne DeKoven, *Rich and Strange: Gender, History, Modernism* (Princeton: Princeton University Press, 1991); Peter Faulkner, ed., *A Modernist Reader: Modernism in England 1910–1930* (London: Batsford, 1986); Hugh Kenner, *The Pound Era* (Berkeley: University of California Press, 1971); Robert Kiely, ed., *Modernism Reconsidered* (Cambridge, MA:

Harvard University Press, 1983); Michael Levenson, *A Genealogy of Modernism* (Cambridge: Cambridge University Press, 1984); James Longenbach, *Modernist Poetics of History: Pound, Eliot, and the Sense of the Past* (Princeton: Princeton University Press, 1987); Louis Menand, *Discovering Modernism: T. S. Eliot and His Context* (Oxford: Oxford University Press, 1987); and Julian Symons, *Makers of the New: The Revolution in Literature, 1912–1939* (London: Deutsch, 1987).

7. For the notion of the "counter-tradition" as a term for strategies that writers adopted to outmaneuver the hegemony of the Victorian marriage ideal, see Joseph Allen Boone, *Tradition Counter Tradition: Love and the Form of Fiction* (Chicago: University of Chicago Press, 1987). The topic of Victorian domestic ideology has been thoroughly treated by diverse critics. To name just three highly variant examples, see Nancy Armstrong, *Desire and Domestic Fiction: A Political History of the Novel* (New York: Oxford University Press, 1987); David Miller, *The Novel and the Police* (Berkeley: University of California Press, 1988); and Mary Poovey, *The Proper Lady and the Woman Writer: Ideology as Style in the Works of Mary Wollestonecraft, Mary Shelley, and Jane Austen* (Chicago: University of Chicago Press, 1984).

8. On bachelors, see Margaret Marsh, *Suburban Lives* (New Brunswick: Rutgers University Press, 1990), and Katherine W. Snyder, *Bachelors, Manhood, and the Novel, 1850–1925* (New York: Cambridge University Press, 1999). On "Clubland," see Brian Harrison, *Separate Spheres: The Opposition to Women's Suffrage in Britain* (London: Croom, 1978), and Elaine Showalter, *Sexual Anarchy: Gender and Culture at the Fin de Siècle* (London: Bloomsbury, 1991).

9. The importance of Hellenism in the Victorian imagination – political, aesthetic, moral, and intellectual – is the subject of two important and exhaustive studies, to which I shall refer periodically: Richard Jenkyns, *The Victorians and Ancient Greece* (Oxford: Blackwell, 1980), and Frank M. Turner, *The Greek Heritage in Victorian Britain* (New Haven: Yale University Press, 1981). More recent works include Richard Jenkyns, *Dignity and Decadence: Victorian Art and the Classical Inheritance* (Cambridge, MA: Harvard University Press, 1992), and Frank M. Turner, *Contesting Cultural Authority: Essays on Victorian Intellectual Life* (Cambridge: Cambridge University Press, 1993). See also David J. DeLaura, *Hebrew and Hellene in Victorian England: Newman, Arnold, and Pater* (Austin: University of Texas Press, 1969). For discussion of Hellenism with a direct focus on masculinity, see Dellamora, *Masculine Desire*, and Linda Dowling, *Hellenism and Homosexuality in Victorian Oxford* (Ithaca: Cornell University Press, 1994).

10. The marbles were purchased and transported to England in 1815, engendering both admiration and debate. The question of where and how to display the marbles was one of many questions, as the era of museum development – the museum functioning as a site of cultural self-definition and imperial justification – was only just beginning in earnest.

11. Matthew Arnold, *Culture and Anarchy* (Cambridge: Cambridge University Press, 1990). Subsequent references appear in the text as *CA*.

12. E. M. Forster, "Terminal Note," *Maurice* (New York: Norton, 1971) 249.
13. In *Sexual Inversion*, Havelock Ellis also suggests a unique social role for "inverts," and, like Carpenter, claims for them an artistic aptitude. See Havelock Ellis and John Addington Symonds, *Sexual Inversion* (London: Wilson and Macmillan, 1897).
14. I am stressing Carpenter's focus on male friendship, because, in my view, it provides a core element in his social vision. Nevertheless, Carpenter should not be flattened out, for his publications were exceptionally diverse and his commitments extensive. In his autobiography, he lists his range of life-goals as "the bringing of the Races of the world together, the gradual evolution of a Non-governmental form of Society, the Communalization of Land and Capital, the freeing of Woman to equality with Man, the extension of the monogamic Marriage into some kind of group-alliance, the restoration and full recognition of the heroic friendships of Greek and primitive times; and again…the sturdy Simplification and debarrassment of daily life by the removal of those things which stand between us and Nature, between ourselves and our fellows – by plain living, friendship with the Animals, open-air habits, fruitarian food, and such degree of Nudity as we can reasonably attain to" (Edward Carpenter, *My Days and Dreams: Being Autobiographical Notes* [London: Allen and Unwin, 1916] 207, 208). In particular, Carpenter is noteworthy for his proto-feminism. He includes women equally in his scheme of the intermediate sexes, he writes passionately on the need for marital reform to free both women and men from sexual and spiritual constraint, and he upbraids middle-class culture for its stifling of female promise.
15. Edward Carpenter, *The Intermediate Sex: A Study of Some Transitional Types of Men and Women* (London: George Allen, 1908, reprint), 89. Volume cited hereafter in text as *IS*.
16. For a thorough chronicle of the Uranian movement, see Timothy d'Arch Smith, *Love in Earnest: Some Notes on the Lives and Writings of English "Uranian" Poets from 1889 to 1930* (London: Routledge, 1970). The word "Uranian" derives from "Uranus," or "Venus," and is meant to convey a sense of purity and spirituality (as distinct from physicality) around the subject of love. It is thus somewhat ironic that the Uranians have come to be read primarily in terms of (encoded) sexuality, an interpretation with which Smith takes issue.
17. Quoted in Smith, *Love in Earnest*, 70. The poem was published in 1918, but, as Smith stresses, belongs very much to the Uranian moment of the 1880s–90s.
18. Quoted in Brian Reade, ed., *Sexual Heretics: Male Homosexuality in English Literature from 1850 to 1900* (New York: Coward-McCann, 1970) 315.
19. Alan Sinfield, *The Wilde Century: Effeminacy, Oscar Wilde and the Queer Moment* (New York: Columbia University Press, 1994).
20. See Showalter, *Sexual Anarchy*.
21. For detailed discussion of the reforms at Cambridge, see Sheldon Rothblatt, *The Revolution of the Dons: Cambridge and Society in Victorian England* (London: Faber, 1968). For Oxford, see Dowling, *Hellenism and Homosexuality*.

Probably the most detailed discussion of the development of public-school ideology during the nineteenth century, with emphasis on the first half of the century, is John Chandos, *Boys Together: English Public Schools 1800–1864* (New Haven: Yale University Press, 1984); another exhaustive treatment can be found in David Newsome, *Godliness and Good Learning: Four Studies on a Victorian Ideal* (London: Murray, 1961); for an excellent summary of "the insufferable ideal" of the public schools, see Noel Annan, *Our Age: Portrait of a Generation* (London: Weidenfeld, 1990) 19–51; the hegemony of the public schools in constructing norms of masculinity is the subject of a number of chapters in J. A. Mangan and James Walvin, eds., *Manliness and Morality: Middle-Class Masculinity in Britain and America: 1800–1940* (Manchester: Manchester University Press, 1984). See also J. A. Mangan, *The Games Ethic and Imperialism: Aspects of the Diffusion of an Ideal* (New York: Viking, 1985). For discussion of the war and the public schools, a subject to which I shall return in Chapter 3, see Peter Parker, *The Old Lie: The Great War and the Public-School Ethos* (London: Constable, 1987).

22. See Parker, *The Old Lie*, 53.
23. E. M. Forster, *Abinger Harvest* (San Diego: Harcourt, 1936) 4.
24. For an interesting discussion of the public schools' determination to create gentlemen – a project rife with irony – see Regenia Gagnier, *Idylls of the Marketplace: Oscar Wilde and the Victorian Public* (Aldershot: Scolar, 1987). Gagnier argues that the burgeoning field of advertising helped to create an atmosphere of self-fashioning that simultaneously reflected and abutted the public-school ideal.
25. Annan, *Our Age*, 43.
26. Kingsley himself preferred the term "manly Christian."
27. E. M. Forster, *A Passage to India* (San Diego: Harcourt, 1984) 257; volume cited hereafter in text as *PI*.
28. J. A. Mangan, "Social Darwinism and Upper-Class Education in late Victorian and Edwardian England," Mangan and Walvin, *Manliness and Morality*, 135–159.
29. The subject of homosexuality in the public schools has been of continuing interest for critics, just as it has troubled the schools throughout their history. For a very personal description, see John Addington Symonds, *The Memoirs of John Addington Symonds*, ed. Phyllis Grosskurth (Chicago: University of Chicago Press, 1984) esp. 94. For a catalogue of homosexual scandals at the public schools during the nineteenth century, see Smith, *Love in Earnest*. See also Noel Annan, "The Cult of Homosexuality in England 1850–1950," *Biography* 13:3 (Summer 1990) 189–202; Alisdaire Hickson, *The Poisoned Bowl: Sex, Repression, and the Public School System* (London: Constable, 1995); and Mangan and Walvin, *Manliness and Morality*.
30. Robert Graves, *Goodbye to All That* (New York: Cape, 1930) 58.
31. Virginia Woolf, *Roger Fry: A Biography* (San Diego: Harcourt, 1940) 43.
32. Virginia Woolf, *Jacob's Room* (London: Penguin, 1992) 37.

33. This language ("the pursuit of knowledge for its own sake") is used frequently by Victorian and Edwardian writers, as well as by contemporary critics describing the ethos of the elite reading groups at both Oxford and Cambridge. Forster's biographer writes that Forster loved Cambridge because "it was a place where things were valued for what they were in themselves" (P. N. Furbank, *E. M. Forster: A Life* [London: Macdonald, 1977] 49–50). See also Peter Allen, *The Cambridge Apostles: The Early Years* (Cambridge: Cambridge University Press, 1978).

34. Dowling, *Hellenism and Homosexuality*, 85.

35. See Dellamora, *Masculine Desire*, and Lesley Higgins, "Jowett and Pater: Trafficking in Platonic Wares," *Victorian Studies* 37:1 (Autumn 1993) 43–72.

36. A number of other critics, in addition to Dowling, discuss the ways in which late-Victorian Hellenists worked with Greek texts and an ideal of Greek culture to construct a legitimate space for male desire. Richard Dellamora (*Masculine Desire*) explores a range of nineteenth-century literary figures, including Tennyson, Hopkins, Swinburne, and Pater, in an effort to understand how a liberatory space for homoerotic desire was created and theorized by these writers, all of whom were associated with Oxford and Cambridge. Dellamora is particularly interested in Pater, and he argues against a critical tradition that has found Pater's late writings to distance themselves from the provocation of the notorious "Conclusion" to *The Renaissance*.

Another more limited discussion of similar themes is Higgins' "Jowett and Pater." Higgins, like Dowling, is interested in the contest over Platonic studies that took place at Oxford over the course of the nineteenth century. Higgins, however, provides a slightly different picture of Jowett, whom he views as a conservative heterosexist, exceedingly careful to rein in any possible homosexual readings of Plato's texts, and tending to favor the more stern and conservative of Plato's writings. Higgins points out that Pater, by contrast, stresses the lover-ideal in Plato, and highlights the purely masculine quality of love in all of Plato's texts.

For accounts of Hellenism that focus on sexuality, and for discussion of male sexuality more generally during the Victorian period, see James Eli Adams, *Dandies and Desert Saints*; Ed Cohen, "Writing Gone Wilde: Homoerotic Desire in the Closet of Representation," *PMLA* 102:5 (October 1987) 801–813; Ed Cohen, "The Double Lives of Man: Narration and Identification in Late Nineteenth-Century Representations of Ec-centric Masculinities," *Cultural Politics at the Fin de Siècle*, ed. Sally Ledger and Scott McCracken (Cambridge: Cambridge University Press, 1995) 85–114; Christopher Craft, *Another Kind of Love: Male Homosexual Desire in English Discourse, 1850–1920* (Berkeley: University of California Press, 1994); Dellamora, *Masculine Desire*; Dowling, *Hellenism and Homosexuality*; Higgins, "Jowett and Pater"; Ruth Robbins, "'A Very Curious Construction': Masculinity and the Poetry of A. E. Housman and Oscar Wilde," Ledger and McCracken, *Cultural Politics*, 137–159; Eve Kosofsky Sedgwick, *Epistemology of the Closet* (Berkeley: University of California Press, 1990); Herbert Sussman, *Victorian Masculinities: Manhood and Masculine Poetics in Early Victorian Literature and Art* (Cambridge: Cambridge University Press, 1995); and Norman Vance, *The Sinews of the Spirit: The Ideal of Christian Manliness in Victorian Literature and Religious Thought* (Cambridge: Cambridge University Press, 1985).

37. Pater revised *The Renaissance* several times, making substantial changes (the most notorious of which involved his suppression of the "Conclusion," later reinstated). I will focus on the 2nd. edition (1877), which contains the Amis and Amile story, as well as an expanded introduction. For discussion of Pater's revisions in the context of homosexuality, homophobia, and Pater's political project, see Dellamora, *Masculine Desire*.

38. Walter Pater, *The Renaissance: Studies in Art and Poetry* (Oxford: Oxford University Press, 1990) 18; volume cited in text hereafter as *Ren.*

39. Walter Pater, *Plato and Platonism: A Series of Lectures* (London: MacMillan, 1893) 203–204; volume cited hereafter in text as *PP.*

40. Walter Pater, *Greek Studies: A Series of Essays* (London: MacMillan, 1928) 24; volume cited hereafter in text as *GS.*

41. For discussion of homosexuality in Pater's life, see Denis Donaghue, *Walter Pater: Lover of Strange Souls* (New York: Knopf, 1995).

42. See Symonds, *Memoirs.*

43. Havelock Ellis and John Addington Symonds, *Sexual Inversion* (London: Wilson and Macmillan, 1897) 173, 172 (cited in text hereafter as *SI*). (For his private draft, see John Addington Symonds, *A Problem in Greek Ethics*, Ten Copies Privately Printed for Author's Use [British Library]).

44. John Addington Symonds, *Studies of the Greek Poets*, 3rd. edition (London: Black, 1893) 361; volume cited hereafter in text as *GP.*

45. Both Turner (*Greek Heritage*) and Jenkyns (*Victorians and Ancient Greece*) point out that the conceit of the Greeks as children was common in the nineteenth century, especially among followers of the highly influential George Grote (of whom Symonds was one). Yet Symonds' particular usage of this metaphor is unique, striking, and probably very far from what Grote would have imagined or condoned.

46. For discussion of the tendency among Victorian intellectuals of all political stripes to compare ancient Greece with contemporary Britain, see Turner, *Greek Heritage*, and Jenkyns, *Victorians and Ancient Greece*. The parallel was generally based on a self-satisfied view of nineteenth-century Britain as the flower of democracy, the heart of a great empire, and the world's center of cultural, technological, and artistic achievement, just as Athens was thought to have been in the age of Pericles.

47. See Christopher Newfield, "Democracy and Male Homoeroticism," *Yale Journal of Criticism* 6:2 (1993) 29–62.

48. See Sedgwick, *Epistemology*, 131–76, and Cohen, "Writing Gone Wilde."

49. John Addington Symonds, *Gabriel: A Poem*, ed. Robert L. Peters and Timothy d'Arch Smith (London: deHartington, 1974). The poem was composed around 1868, first published in part in 1878, and circulated privately after that. It was only published in full posthumously.

50. For discussion of the culture of double-talk, see Thaïs E. Morgan, "Reimagining Masculinity in Victorian Criticism: Swinburne and Pater," *Victorian Studies* 36:3 (1993) 315–332.
51. See Bristow, *Effeminate England*, esp. 55–99.
52. For discussion of Forster's attack on idealism, see S. P. Rosenbaum, "*The Longest Journey*: E. M. Forster's Refutation of Idealism," *E. M. Forster: A Human Exploration: Centenary Essays*, ed. G. K. Das and John Beer (London: MacMillan, 1979) 32–54.
53. The tradition of dismissing *Maurice* begins with Lytton Strachey's reaction in 1915: Strachey, writing to Forster in response to a private copy of the novel, said that he found the second half of the novel improbable, and that he "would have prophesied a rupture after 6 months" between Maurice and Alec. (Quoted in Philip Gardner, ed., *E. M. Forster: The Critical Heritage* [London: Routledge, 1973] 429.) For more contemporary repudiations of the novel's artistic merit, see Jeffrey Meyers, *Homosexuality and Literature 1890–1930* (London: Athlone, 1977); and Judith Scherer Herz, "The Double Nature of Forster's Fiction: *A Room with a View* and *The Longest Journey*," *Critical Essays on E. M. Forster*, ed. Alan Wilde (Boston: Hall, 1985) 84–94.
54. E. M. Forster, *Maurice* (New York: Norton, 1989) 22; volume cited hereafter in text as *M*.
55. Martin, "Edward Carpenter and the Double Structure of *Maurice*," 42.
56. Forster describes his own admiration for Carpenter in "Edward Carpenter" (Forster, *Two Cheers*, 212–215).
57. Two compelling accounts of *Maurice*, both of which focus on the undercurrents and disturbances that characterize sexual intimacy in the novel, are June Perry Levine, "The Tame in Pursuit of the Savage: The Posthumous Fiction of E. M. Forster," *PMLA* 99 (1984) 72–88; and Christopher Lane, *The Ruling Passion: British Colonial Allegory and the Paradox of Homosexual Desire* (Durham: Duke University Press, 1995) 163–166.
58. A first draft of the novel closed with Maurice and Alec, many years later, living close to the land in a state of almost complete anonymity. Forster's revision came as a response to unfavorable reactions from friends.
59. As is well known, Forster's depictions of desirable young men from the working classes and from different racial backgrounds have biographical counterparts in his own life. See P. N. Furbank, *E. M. Forster*, and Martin and Piggford, *Queer Forster*.
60. Quoted in Oliver Stallybrass, Introduction, *The Life to Come and Other Stories*, by E. M. Forster (London: Penguin, 1989) 14.
61. For discussion of sexual and racial politics in several of these stories, see Lane, *Ruling Passion*, 145–175.
62. See, for example, Leo Bersani, "Is the Rectum a Grave?" *October* 43 (1987) 197–222; Judith Butler, *Gender Trouble: Feminism and the Subversion of Identity* (New York: Routledge, 1990); Kaja Silverman, *Male Subjectivity at the Margins* (New York: Routledge, 1992) 299–338.

63. For a detailed treatment of sexual dissidence as a textual, social, and political practice (which, again, omits consideration of Forster), see Jonathan Dollimore, *Sexual Dissidence: Augustine to Wilde, Freud to Foucault* (Oxford: Oxford University Press, 1991).

64. The most direct treatment of the war's role in setting the tone for many of the novel's central events is Allyson Booth, *Postcards from the Trenches: Negotiating the Space between Modernism and the First World War* (New York: Oxford University Press, 1996). For discussion of the Anglo-Indians as wartime chauvinists, see 76–83.

65. Joseph Allen Boone, "Vacation Cruises; or, The Homoerotics of Orientalism," *PMLA* 110:1 (1995) 89–107.

66. In addition to discussing the western orientalist perspective, Boone's essay makes the welcome move of discussing how the position of homosexual lover could be empowering for young Egyptian writers.

67. Sara Suleri, *The Rhetoric of English India* (Chicago: University of Chicago Press, 1992).

68. For an analysis of "rapability" in the novel, see Brenda Silver, "Periphrasis, Power, and Rape in *A Passage to India*," *Novel: A Forum on Fiction* 22:1 (1988) 86–105. For a response that stresses the historicity of gender terms, see Jenny Sharpe, "The Unspeakable Limits of Rape: Colonial Violence and Counter-Insurgency," *Genders* 10 (1991) 25–46.

69. See Lane, *Ruling Passion*, 145–175.

70. For a discussion of Mason's popularity in the first half of the twentieth century, see Roger Lancelyn Green, *A. E. W. Mason* (London: Max Parrish, 1952).

71. A. E. W. Mason, *The Broken Road* (London: Newnes, 1910) 155; volume cited hereafter in text as *BR*.

72. Issues of passing are interesting in this novel. Shere Ali almost passes: "with his straight features, his supple figure, and a colour no darker than many a sunburnt Englishman wears every August, Shere Ali might have passed unnoticed by a stranger" (*BR*, 38). For discussion of passing in the American context, see Susan Gubar, *Racechanges: White Skin, Black Face in American Culture* (New York: Oxford, 1997).

73. Homi K. Bhabha, *The Location of Culture* (London: Routledge, 1994) 85–92.

74. Forster, *Two Cheers*, 68.

75. See John Colmer, "Promise and Withdrawal in *A Passage to India*," *E. M. Forster: A Human Exploration, Centenary Essays*, ed. G. K. Das and John Beer (London: MacMillan, 1979) 117–128; Frederick C. Crews, *E. M. Forster: The Perils of Humanism* (Princeton: Princeton University Press, 1962); Judith Scherer Herz, *A Passage to India: Nation and Narration* (New York: Twayne, 1993); and Benita Parry, "The Politics of Representation in *A Passage to India*," *A Passage to India: Essays in Interpretation*, ed. John Beer (London: MacMillan, 1985) 27–43.

76. For especially strong discussions of Forster's orientalism, see Parry, "Politics"; and Sara Suleri, "The Geography of *A Passage to India*," *Modern Critical*

Interpretations: E. M. Forster's A Passage to India, ed. Harold Bloom (New York: Chelsea, 1987) 107–113.

77. See, for instance, Charu Malik, "To Express the Subject of Friendship: Masculine Desire and Colonialism in *A Passage to India*," Martin and Piggford, *Queer Forster*, 221–235.

2 CONRADIAN ALIENATION AND IMPERIAL INTIMACY

1. For several examples of critics who convincingly link modernism with specific features of imperialism, see Ali Behdad, *Belated Travelers: Orientalism in the Age of Colonial Dissolution* (Durham: Duke University Press, 1994); Chris Bongie, *Exotic Memories: Literature, Colonialism, and the Fin de Siècle* (Stanford: Stanford University Press, 1991); and Frederic Jameson, "Modernism and Imperialism," in Terry Eagleton, Frederic Jameson, and Edward Said, *Nationalism, Colonialism, and Literature* (Minneapolis: University of Minnesota Press, 1990), 43–66.

2. Achebe's famous essay began the process of demystifying Conrad on racial grounds. See Chinua Achebe, "An Image of Africa," *Massachusetts Review* 18 (1977) 782–794, 788. See also Benita Parry, *Conrad and Imperialism: Ideological Boundaries and Visionary Frontiers* (London: MacMillan, 1983).

3. Andrea White, *Joseph Conrad and the Adventure Tradition: Constructing and Deconstructing the Imperial Subject* (Cambridge: Cambridge University Press, 1993).

4. Edward Said, *Culture and Imperialism* (New York: Knopf, 1993) 188.

5. Edward Said, *Orientalism* (New York: Random House, 1979).

6. For especially thorough discussions of the relationship between imperialism and gender, see Anne McClintock, *Imperial Leather: Race, Gender and Sexuality in the Colonial Contest* (New York: Routledge, 1995), and Marianna Torgovnick, *Gone Primitive: Savage Intellects, Modern Lives* (Chicago: University of Chicago Press, 1990). For accounts of imperialism that deliberately refigure a number of critical gender terms, see Joseph Allen Boone, "Vacation Cruises; or, The Homoerotics of Orientalism" *PMLA* 110:1 (1995) 89–107; Christopher Lane, *The Ruling Passion: British Colonial Allegory and the Paradox of Homosexual Desire* (Durham: Duke University Press, 1995); and Sara Suleri, *The Rhetoric of English India* (Chicago: University of Chicago Press, 1992). See also Gayatri Chakravorty Spivak, *In Other Worlds: Essays in Cultural Politics* (New York: Methuen, 1987).

7. Numerous critics have discussed nineteenth-century adventure literature, often in the context of masculinity. See Joseph Allen Boone, *Tradition Counter Tradition: Love and the Form of Fiction* (Chicago: University of Chicago Press, 1984), esp. 226–277; Patrick Brantlinger, "Victorians and Africans: The Genealogy of the Myth of the Dark Continent," *Critical Inquiry* 12 (Autumn 1985) 166–203; Raymond Brebach, *Joseph Conrad, Ford Madox Ford, and the Making of Romance* (Ann Arbor: University of Michigan Research Press, 1985); Joseph Bristow, *Empire Boys: Adventures in a Man's World* (London: Harper, 1991);

Linda Dryden, *Joseph Conrad and the Imperial Romance* (London: MacMillan, 2000); Martin Green, *Dreams of Adventure, Deeds of Empire* (London: Routledge, 1980); Gail Fincham and Myrtle Hooper, eds., *Under Postcolonial Eyes: Joseph Conrad after Empire* (Cape Town: University of Cape Town Press, 1996); John W. Griffith, *Joseph Conrad and the Anthropological Dilemma: "Bewildered Traveller"* (Oxford: Oxford University Press, 1995); Robert H. MacDonald, *The Language of Empire: Myths of Popular Imperialism, 1880–1918* (Manchester: Manchester University Press, 1994); J. A. Mangan, *The Games Ethic and Imperialism: Aspects of the Diffusion of an Ideal* (New York: Viking, 1985); J. A. Mangan and James Walvin, eds., *Manliness and Morality: Middle-Class Masculinity in Britain and America, 1800–1914* (Manchester: Manchester University Press, 1987); Mary Louise Pratt, *Imperial Eyes: Travel Writing and Transculturation* (London: Routledge, 1992); Elaine Showalter, *Sexual Anarchy: Gender and Culture at the Fin de Siècle* (London: Bloomsbury, 1991) esp. "King Romance"; Torgovnick, *Gone Primitive*; and White, *Adventure Tradition*.

8. Green, *Dreams of Adventure*, 3.
9. See Homi K. Bhabha, *The Location of Culture* (London: Routledge, 1994) 85–92.
10. Another prominent convention the text plumbs is the myth of the white god.
11. The Berlin Conference of 1884 is typically understood as the official inauguration of this new phase in European competition over Africa.
12. Quoted in Dryden, *Imperial Romance*, 5.
13. For a discussion of Stanley's text and the discourse(s) of primitivism, see Torgovnick, *Gone Primitive*.
14. Henry M. Stanley, *How I Found Livingstone: Travels, Adventures, and Discoveries in Central Africa* (London: Low, 1872) 583.
15. I do not want to suggest that Conrad in any way admired Stanley himself. On the contrary, while Conrad had a certain nostalgia for explorers such as Livingstone, whose imperial work he felt had been guided by a consistent moral purpose, he abhorred the materialistic and ethically bankrupt activities of Stanley and was disgusted with the Belgian regime's infamous behavior in central Africa.
16. A number of critics have discussed Conrad's relation to the adventure tradition (see White, *Adventure Tradition*; Dryden, *Imperial Romance*; Brebach, *Making of Romance*; and Ian Watt, *Conrad in the Nineteenth Century* [Berkeley: University of California Press, 1979]). Few, however, have connected male intimacy with genre in Conrad's work. An analysis of the relation between genre and masculinity, in the context of *Lord Jim*, is Scott McCracken, "'A Hard and Absolute Condition of Existence': Reading Masculinity in *Lord Jim*," *Conrad and Gender*, ed. Andrew Michael Roberts (Atlanta: Rodopi, 1993) 17–38. For other discussions of Conrad and genre, see Robert Hamson, "Chance and the Secret Life: Conrad, Thackeray, Stevenson," Roberts, *Conrad and Gender*, 105–122; Jefferson Hunter, *Edwardian Fiction* (Cambridge, MA: Harvard University Press, 1982); and Padmini Mongia, "'Ghosts of the Gothic': Spectral Women and Colonized Spaces in *Lord Jim*," Roberts, *Conrad and Gender*, 1–16.

17. For an exemplary case, see Parry, *Conrad and Imperialism*, 20–39.

18. Quoted in White, *Adventure Tradition*, 177.

19. Joseph Conrad, *Heart of Darkness* (New York: Norton, 1988) 7, 8; volume cited hereafter in text as *HD*.

20. For a thorough discussion of issues surrounding liberalism and nationalism in *Heart of Darkness*, see Pericles Lewis, *Modernism, Nationalism, and the Novel* (Cambridge: Cambridge University Press, 2000), especially 97–125.

21. Avrom Fleishman, *Conrad's Politics: Community and Anarchy in the Fiction of Joseph Conrad* (Baltimore: Johns Hopkins University Press, 1967) 99.

22. In this discussion, I focus on encounters between white explorers and describe the representation of Africa as essentially a backdrop against which European masculinity is defined, enhanced, and challenged. *Heart of Darkness* does, of course, stage moments of imperial encounter across the racial divide, most famously in the sequence involving Marlow and his helmsman, whose death-glance could be said to challenge the text's dominant structure of erasure of African subjectivity. However, such moments are presented as provocative and seductive possibilities, foreclosed in advance, entirely subordinate to the text's – and Marlow's – driving urge to move up-river towards Kurtz. *Heart of Darkness* offers only a tenuous glance at inter-racial engagement, which it treats finally as a threatening distraction from the primary urge to create community among white men. This requires that alternative forms of intimacy be foreclosed, in a pattern charted by many post-colonial critics, from Frantz Fanon onwards.

23. For a brilliant discussion of the male protagonists' fundamental urge to be nurtured by a feminine heart of darkness, see Henry Staten, "Conrad's Mortal Word," *Critical Inquiry* 12 (Summer 1986) 720–740. For further discussion of gender and *Heart of Darkness*, see Bette London, *The Appropriated Voice: Narrative Authority in Conrad, Forster, and Woolf* (Ann Arbor: University of Michigan Press, 1990), and Nina Pelikan Straus, "The Exclusion of the In-tended from Secret Sharing in Conrad's *Heart of Darkness*," *Novel: A Forum on Fiction* 20 (1987) 123–137.

24. Christopher Gogwilt, *The Invention of the West: Joseph Conrad and the Double-Mapping of Europe and Empire* (Stanford: Stanford University Press, 1995).

25. See Gogwilt, *Invention of the West*; Nico Israel, *Outlandish: Writing between Exile and Diaspora* (Stanford: Stanford University Press, 2000); Zdzislaw Najder, *Joseph Conrad: A Chronicle* (New Brunswick: Rutgers University Press, 1983) esp. 3–38; Norman Sherry, *Conrad and His World* (London: Thames and Hudson, 1972); and Watt, *Conrad in the Nineteenth Century*.

26. For a particularly thorough discussion of *Under Western Eyes*, see Keith Carabine, *The Life and the Art: A Study of Conrad's "Under Western Eyes"* (Amsterdam: Rodopi, 1996).

27. Joseph Conrad, *Under Western Eyes* (London: Penguin, 1989) 322; volume cited hereafter in text as *UWE*.

28. In Dostoevsky's *Crime and Punishment*, for instance – to name only the most obvious precedent for *Under Western Eyes* – it is a matter of unquestioned inevitability that Raskolnokov's sister and friend will eventually marry.

29. Razumov's position of disconnection in *Under Western Eyes* is related to a persistent tendency among characters to elevate the status of national identity: "'Is not this my country? Have I not got forty million brothers?'" the rootless Razumov rhetorically asks himself, but to little avail (*UWE*, 80). Although the novel periodically attempts to substitute the idea of the nation for other community models, this effort is thwarted for several reasons: first, too many different and oppositional groups can claim the nation for their own, substantially over-determining the concept; and second, Russia is figured in the text as overly vast and illegible to function as the source of personal identity. For discussion of nationalism in *Under Western Eyes*, see Corola Kaplar, "The Spectre of Nationality in Henry James' *The Bostonians* and Joseph Conrad's *Under Western Eyes*," *Literature and Exile*, ed. David Bevan (Amsterdam: Rodopi, 1990), 37–54; and Kaplar, "Conrad's Narrative Occupation of/by Russia in *Under Western Eyes*," *Conradiana: A Journal of Joseph Conrad Studies* 27:2 (Summer 1995) 97–114.

30. In addition to the works discussed here, the imperial encounter organizes such texts as *Victory*, the Lingard tales, and "An Outpost of Progress." For an interesting discussion of male relations in *Victory*, see Lane, *Ruling Passion*, 99–125.

31. "The Secret Sharer" represents something like a test case of this second model. What is perhaps most strange about this extensively over-determined story is the rapidity with which the captain transforms Leggatt into his alter ego. The tale consists of layers of enclosure, from the external world, presented as comfortably whole and detached from the ship; through the ship's interior spaces; into the captain's cuddy; and finally into his secret life. The structure of "The Secret Sharer" – its reduction of social relations into elemental outlines – emphasizes its status as a study in individual psychology, a kind of journey into a thrilling place of otherwise veiled desire, and the captain's return to a leadership position at the tale's conclusion would seem to indicate that a renewed pattern of well-ordered masculine discipline has been reinstated.

32. Joseph Conrad, *Lord Jim* (New York: NAL, 1981) 19; volume cited hereafter in text as *LJ*.

33. For a diverse array of discussions of this dynamic, see Brian Harrison, *Separate Spheres: The Opposition to Women's Suffrage in Britain* (London: Croom, 1978) esp. 91–107; McCracken, "Reading Masculinity"; Showalter, *Sexual Anarchy*; and for a contemporary engagement on the issue of male self-sufficiency, "Why We Men Do Not Marry, by One of Us," *Temple Bar* 84 (1888) 218–223.

34. For a discussion of father/son relations in Conrad's novels, with a psychoanalytic focus, see Catharine Rising, *Darkness at Heart: Fathers and Sons in Conrad* (New York: Greenwood, 1990).

35. This nostalgia for an avuncular presence is even more marked in the Lingard tales, *Almayer's Folly* (1895) and *An Outcast of the Islands* (1896).

36. This tendency to focus upon an elaborate social system, which seems self-justifying but is in fact entirely connected with material or economic conditions, recalls the unspoken relation in the earlier part of the text between

Marlow's "fixed standard of conduct" and a global imperial system. See Frederic Jameson, *The Political Unconscious: Narrative as a Socially Symbolic Act* (Ithaca: Cornell University Press, 1981).

37. I do not treat the theme of collaboration here, and tend to lean towards Conrad as the text's primary guiding spirit. For a thorough discussion of the construction of this collaborative novel, see Brebach, *Making of Romance*. For their own accounts, see Joseph Conrad and Ford Madox Hueffer, *The Nature of a Crime* (London: Duckworth, 1924) prefaces and appendix; and Ford Madox Ford, *Joseph Conrad: A Personal Remembrance* (London: Duckworth, 1924). For an interesting allusion to the pleasures of collaboration within one of their collaborative novels, see Joseph Conrad and Ford Madox Hueffer, *The Inheritors: An Extravagant Story* (London: Heinemann, 1901) 109, 292. For an account of *Romance* that connects the fact of collaboration with the theme of (sublimated) homosexuality, see Wayne Koestenbaum, *Double Talk: The Erotics of Male Literary Collaboration* (New York: Routledge, 1989) 166–173. For simplicity's sake, I shall use the surname "Ford," even though *Romance* was published under the name "Hueffer."

38. Pratt, *Imperial Eyes*.

39. In assessing Kemp's claims to inheritance, we should not overlook his equivocal racial position. Though repeatedly described (and self-described) as "English," Kemp's mother is Scottish, and this undertone of racial difference is never entirely suppressed in the novel. Thus when Kemp will later portray himself as "Saxon" to his enemy's "Celt" (discussed below), the racial self-identification is more willed than inherited. Perhaps it would be most accurate to say that the novel's insistence on subsuming Scottish into English simultaneously conforms to the novel's larger portrayal of the homogenizing nature of modernity and points to the continued remnants of difference that disturb such a totalizing picture.

40. Koestenbaum, *Double Talk*, 169.

41. Joseph Conrad and Ford Madox Hueffer, *Romance* (New York: Doubleday, 1938) 178, 182; volume cited hereafter in text as *R*.

42. Kemp's contempt for labor, as well as the text's larger preoccupation with an aristocracy that produces wealth without work, in some ways conforms to Conrad's life-long dismissal of middle-class bourgeois striving and his infatuation with forms of work that either elude or mask their own productive engines. However, what differentiates *Romance* from such works as *Nostromo* (1904) or *Lord Jim*, in this respect, is the heavy-handedness with which *Romance* presents the contrast between modern capitalism (with its drudgery and alienation) and an old order's imagined exemption from the problems of labor.

43. The tendency to discount any possibility of modernity in the "Orient" – a space defined by its obsolescence – is described by Said in his classic *Orientalism*.

44. The fact that *Romance* was never a popular success is ironic, since Conrad assumed that this novel would be lucrative. On the contrary, it was not until 1913, with *Chance*, that any of Conrad's novels brought him financial solvency.

45. See Benedict Anderson, *Imagined Communities: Reflections on the Origins and Spread of Nationalism* (London: Verso, 1983).

46. Edward Said has provocatively suggested that modernism represents a crisis in filial authority and a shift into what he terms an "affiliative" mode. See Edward Said, *The World, the Text, and the Critic* (Cambridge, MA: Harvard University Press, 1983). For a psychoanalytic discussion of the rise of brotherhood as the dominant political and rhetorical form in the modern world, see Juliet Flower MacCannell, *The Regime of the Brother: After the Patriarchy* (London: Routledge, 1991).

47. For discussion of the development of the pirate image in the British popular imagination over several centuries, see Hans Turley, *Rum, Sodomy, and the Lash: Piracy, Sexuality, and Masculine Identity* (New York: New York University Press, 1999).

48. In its critique of the consolidating power of the imperial state, *Romance* suggests that the liberal concept of a free marketplace belongs with the swashbuckling atmosphere of "Free Traders" and Caribbean adventurers – with romance, in the text's lexicon – rather than in the real world of contemporary legal or trade policy. Without undertaking a disciplined account of economic theory, the text does address the increasing obliteration of individuality (and individual choice) as a category subject to historical movements, and in that sense contributes to a wider turn-of-the-century discussion about the nature and consequences of modern economic forms. Though liberalism remained the dominant conceptual model of economic and political agency in England during this period, a host of competing intellectual currents, which offered real challenges to the centrality of the individualized liberal subject, were also taking shape around Conrad and Ford. For discussion of the fate of liberalism in Conrad's work, in the context of intellectual history, see Lewis, *Modernism*, and Ursula Lord, *Solitude versus Solidarity in the Novels of Joseph Conrad: Political and Epistemological Implications of Narrative Innovation* (Montreal: McGill-Queen's University Press, 1998). For a discussion of Conrad's theorizing of his own labor, see John Marx, "Conrad's Gout," *Modernism/Modernity* 6:1 (1999) 91–114.

49. The status of individualism in modernist literature – triumph or defeat? rise or fall? – is a topic that has interested critics. For thorough treatment, see Michael Levenson, *Modernism and Individuality: Character and Novelistic Form from Conrad to Woolf* (Cambridge: Cambridge University Press, 1991). For an analysis of the complex ways in which modernism both repels and appropriates the "mass mind," see Michael Tratner, *Modernism and Mass Politics: Joyce, Woolf, Eliot, Yeats* (Stanford: Stanford University Press, 1995).

3 "MY KILLED FRIENDS ARE WITH ME WHERE I GO": FRIENDSHIP AND COMRADESHIP AT WAR

1. Erich Maria Remarque, *All Quiet on the Western Front*, trans. A. W. Wheen (New York: Ballantine, 1996) 212.

2. The experience of war was not actually "exclusively male," in the sense that both officers and enlisted men encountered women in a variety of contexts while on service overseas. Prostitution was, of course, extremely widespread, and had

its own hierarchies and practices. Problems of sexual disease were rampant, and the military's awkwardness on the subject was marked, if unsurprising. For discussion of prostitution and the British army, see Craig Gibson, "Sex and Soldiering in France and Flanders: The British Expeditionary Force along the Western Front, 1914–1919," *International History Review* 23:3 (September 2001) 535–579.

3. Critics have long noted that much of the most famous First World War literature was actually composed and published a decade after the armistice. Though most of the canonical British poetry was written during the years of combat, many of the memoirs and novels were not, and, in all cases, the vogue for the disillusioned style of war writing that is now often taken as representative developed about ten years after the war. In this discussion, I will generally not be making a hard-and-fast distinction between those works composed after the war and those written between 1914 and 1918, and am treating the entire discourse as one body of work. The reason for this is partly practical and partly theoretical: many works were begun during the war, perhaps in the form of diaries, only to be completed years later; the war took many years to be interpreted and internalized by both combatants and civilians, and hence whatever story is to be told would not instantly be in place at the end of the war; I consider the war to be a major event in the life of the culture, and its rendering was neither immediate nor unchanging. Nevertheless, I will make some distinctions between "war" and "post-war" perspectives, and the primary point here is to showcase those works which directly and deliberately set the war in the past, often focusing on issues surrounding the passage of time, the end of war, the distinctiveness of peace after combat, and so forth. For both this chapter and the next, then, the dates of writing and publication of the works in question will span several decades; I will mention issues of specific chronology where relevant and, in general, hope to convey the sense that a generalized understanding and assimilation of the war occurred in many registers and over the course of time.

4. The critical tradition surrounding the war can be divided into a relatively neat binary scheme, with Paul Fussell's classic exposition of the war as a series of ironic disjunctions standing at the head of the dominant tradition (Paul Fussell, *The Great War and Modern Memory* [London: Oxford University Press, 1975]), and a diverse array of scholars questioning central Fussellian premises. Many critics have adopted Fussell's claims about such topics as irony, disillusionment, inexpressibility, homoerotics, and the literary legacy of the war. For a near paraphrase of Fussell's points, see Martin Taylor, Introduction, *Lads: Love Poetry of the Trenches* (London: Constable, 1989). Another comprehensive discussion of the war as catalytic event for modernity and modernism is Modris Eksteins, *Rites of Spring: The Great War and the Birth of the Modern Age* (Boston: Houghton Mifflin, 1989). Because Fussell's arguments have been so well incorporated into critical discourse, I will generally assume familiarity with standard themes such as those listed above. I am particularly indebted to Fussell's insights in the "Soldier Boys" chapter, 270–309.

For incisive anti-Fussellian work, see Michael C. C. Adams, *The Great Adventure: Male Desire and the Coming of World War I* (Bloomington: Indiana University Press, 1990); Joanna Bourke, *Dismembering the Male: Men's Bodies, Britain and the Great War* (Chicago: University of Chicago Press, 1996); Adrian Caesar, *Taking it Like a Man: Suffering, Sexuality and the War Poets: Brooke, Sassoon, Owen, Graves* (Manchester: Manchester University Press, 1993); and Jay Winter, *Sites of Memory, Sites of Mourning: The Great War in European Cultural History* (Cambridge: Cambridge University Press, 1995). For an encyclopedic account of the war years that in a sense straddles the Fussellian and anti-Fussellian views, by directly addressing the way writers situated themselves oppositionally as traditionalists or as modern, see Samuel Hynes, *A War Imagined: The First World War and English Culture* (London: Bodley Head, 1990).

For the seminal text on gender politics and the war, see Sandra M. Gilbert and Susan Gubar, *No Man's Land: The Place of the Woman Writer in the Twentieth Century, Volume II: Sexchanges* (New Haven: Yale University Press, 1989). See also Allyson Booth, *Postcards from the Trenches: Negotiating the Space Between Modernism and the First World War* (New York: Oxford University Press, 1996); Dorothy Goldman with Jane Gledhill and Judith Hattaway, *Women Writers and the Great War* (New York: Twayne, 1995); Margaret Randolph Higonnet, Jane Jenson, Sonya Michel, and Margaret Collins Weitz, eds., *Behind the Lines: Gender and the Two World Wars* (New Haven: Yale University Press, 1987); James Longenbach, "The Women and Men of 1914," *Arms and the Woman: War, Gender, and Literary Representation*, ed. Helen M. Cooper, Adrienne Auslander Munich, and Susan Merrill Squier (Chapel Hill: University of North Carolina Press, 1989) 97–123; Jane Marcus, "The Asylums of Antaeus: Women, War, and Madness – Is there a Feminist Fetishism?" *The New Historicism*, ed. H. Aram Veeser (New York: Routledge, 1989) 132–151; Marcus, "Corpus/Corps/Corpse: Writing the Body in/at War," Cooper *et al.*, *Arms and the Woman*, 124–167; Laura Stempel Mumford, "May Sinclair's *The Tree of Heaven*: The Vortex of Feminism, the Community of War," Cooper *et al.*, *Arms and the Woman*, 168–183; Trudi Tate, *Modernism, History and the First World War* (Manchester: University of Manchester Press, 1998); and Claire Tylee, *The Great War and Women's Consciousness: Images of Militarism and Womanhood in Women's Writing, 1914–1964* (London: Macmillan, 1990).

With regard to the psychology of the war, Eric Leed's influential study set the tone. See Eric Leed, *No Man's Land: Combat and Identity in World War I* (Cambridge: Cambridge University Press, 1979). For a highly influential analysis of shell-shock and gender, see Elaine Showalter, *The Female Malady: Women, Madness, and English Culture, 1830–1980* (New York: Pantheon, 1985).

5. Siegfried Sassoon, *The War Poems* (London: Faber, 1983) 61; volume cited in text hereafter as *WP*.

Let me say a few words about my methodology in this chapter. I have limited my research primarily to discussion of the Western Front (France and Belgium), because it was in that arena that the most influential images of the war, from the British perspective, were created. (Gallipoli, too, became a focal point, especially for the Australian and New Zealand contingents.) Among primary sources, I discuss texts from several different categories: widely read poetry and memoirs by writers such as Owen, Sassoon, and Graves; published poetry, fiction, and memoirs that no longer command significant readership; and unpublished manuscript material from the Imperial War Museum, London. The War Museum material will be cited as "IWM", with the name of the collection as it appears in the IWM catalogue.

6. See Judith Butler, *Gender Trouble: Feminism and the Subversion of Identity* (New York: Routledge, 1990). For another example of this kind of critical approach, see Carole-Anne Tyler, "Boys Will be Girls: The Politics of Gay Drag," *Inside/Out: Lesbian Theories, Gay Theories*, ed. Diana Fuss (New York: Routledge, 1991) 32–70.

7. Santanu Das has recently made a similar argument about the difficulty of applying civilian, contemporary categories to the rich erotic terrain of the First World War. Using the "dying kiss" as an exemplory case, he shows the limitations of our conceptions of homoerotics in the context of the physical and emotional conditions of the war. See Santanu Das, "'kiss me, Hardy': Intimacy, Gender, and Gesture in World War I Trench Literature," *Modernism/Modernity* 9:1 (2002) 51–74.

8. B. H. Liddell Hart, Foreword, *Twelve Days*, by Sidney Rogerson (London: Barker, 1933) viii.

9. In *Taking it Like a Man*, Adrian Caesar discusses in depth the problematic idea that suffering in war is redemptive. In a critique of Fussell's reading of the war poets, Caesar argues that, rather than view Sassoon, Owen, and Graves as anti-war poets, we need to re-visit the problematic valorization of violence in their poetry. For Caesar, the idealization of physical and spiritual suffering (which he traces to public-school morality, Christianity, Romanticism, and classicism) is never fully rejected by the war poets, who instead appropriate elements of that history for their own purposes. I shall refer to Caesar's argument throughout my study.

10. Rogerson, *Twelve Days*, 60.

11. For discussion of class hierarchies in both the Allied and German armies, see Leed, *No Man's Land*.

12. Lieutenant R. G. Dixon, "The Wheels of Darkness," 32, 88, IWM.

13. Fussell (among others) has discussed in detail the topic of inexpressibility, and I focus here only on its relation to comradeship.

14. See Chapter 1 for more discussion of standard tropes surrounding the silencing/voicing of male homoerotic language. For the context of war more specifically, see Fussell, *Great War*; Taylor, *Lads*; Caesar, *Taking it Like a Man*; Kaja Silverman, *Male Subjectivity at the Margins* (New York: Routledge, 1992) 299–338, and George Chauncey Jr., "Christian Brotherhood or Sexual Perversion? Homosexual Identities and the Construction of Sexual Boundaries in the World War One Era," *Journal of Social History* (Winter, 1985) 189–206.

15. In an attempt to explain both the popularity and canonicity of First World War poetry (as distinct from fiction or drama), critics have pointed to several factors,

including logistical problems for the writer, the fragmentary and intensive nature of the experience being represented, and long-standing traditions of using the lyric to write about war (in the form of elegy, for instance).

16. E. B. Osborn, Introduction, *The Muse in Arms* (New York: Stokes, 1917) xxii–xxiii.

17. Frederic Manning, *Her Privates We* (London: Davies, 1930) 143–144.

18. Peter Parker, *The Old Lie: The Great War and the Public-School Ethos* (London: Constable, 1987) 17. Parker offers a detailed discussion of the war and the public schools. See also Adams, *Great Adventure*; Caesar, *Taking it Like a Man*; Taylor, *Lads*; and Alan Wilkinson, *The Church of England and the First World War* (London: SPCK, 1978). For an interesting contemporaneous account of how Britain's ruling class essentially killed itself off through its commitment to the war effort, see Charles F. G. Masterman, *England After War* (London: Hodder and Stoughton, 1923) 27–47.

For broader discussions of masculinity and the public schools (a topic discussed at more length in Chapter 1), see James Eli Adams, *Dandies and Desert Saints: Styles of Victorian Manhood* (Ithaca: Cornell University Press, 1995); Maurizia Boscagli, *Eye on the Flesh: Fashions of Masculinity in the Early Twentieth Century* (Boulder: Westview, 1996); Ed Cohen, "The Double Lives of Man: Narration and Identification in Late Nineteenth-Century Representations of Ec-centric Masculinities," *Cultural Politics at the Fin de Siècle*, ed. Sally Ledger and Scott McCracken (Cambridge: Cambridge University Press, 1995) 85–114; Richard Dellamora, *Masculine Desire: The Sexual Politics of Victorian Aestheticism* (Chapel Hill: University of North Carolina Press, 1990); Linda Dowling, *Hellenism and Homosexuality in Victorian Oxford* (Ithaca: Cornell University Press, 1994); Lesley Higgins, "Jowett and Pater: Trafficking in Platonic Wares," *Victorian Studies* 37:1 (1993) 43–72; J. A. Mangan and James Walvin, eds., *Manliness and Morality: Middle-Class Masculinity in Britain and America: 1800–1940* (Manchester: Manchester University Press, 1984); Ruth Robbins, "'A Very Curious Construction': Masculinity and the Poetry of A. E. Housman and Oscar Wilde," Ledger and McCracken, *Cultural Politics*, 137–159; Eve Kosofsky Sedgwick, *Epistemology of the Closet* (Berkeley: University of California Press, 1990); Herbert Sussman, *Victorian Masculinities: Manhood and Masculine Poetics in Early Victorian Literature and Art* (Cambridge: Cambridge University Press, 1995); and Norman Vance, *The Sinews of the Spirit: The Ideal of Christian Manliness in Victorian Literature and Religious Thought* (Cambridge: Cambridge University Press, 1985).

19. A. G. Meacham, *Dagger*, November 1918, 16, IWM.

20. Henry Waldo Yoxall, Letter, 2 September 1916, IWM.

21. Robert Graves, *Goodbye to All That* (New York: Cape, 1930) 229.

22. For biographical discussion of Graves and Sassoon, see Patrick Quinn, *The Great War and the Missing Muse: The Early Writings of Robert Graves and Siegfried Sassoon* (Selinsgrove: Susquehanna University Press, 1994). For a thorough discussion of Graves' homoerotic self-conflict, which impinges on his adherence to traditional male institutions, see Caesar, *Taking it Like a Man*.

23. Edward Frederick Chapman, Letter, October 1916, 32, IWM.
24. Siegfried Sassoon, *The Complete Memoirs of George Sherston* (London: Faber, 1952) 421.
25. C. E. Montague, *Disenchantment* (London: Chatto, 1922) 30.
26. W. B. Henderson, Memoir, XX, IWM.
27. David Jones, *In Parenthesis* (London: Faber, 1937) 137.
28. Brooke's iconic status began almost immediately after his death. For discussion of Brooke in the context of cultural investments in masculinity, see Jonathan Rutherford, *Forever England: Reflections on Race, Masculinity, and Empire* (London: Laurence and Wishant, 1997). See also Paul Delaney, *The Neo-Pagans: Friendship and Love in the Rupert Brooke Circle* (London: Macmillan, 1987).
29. Rupert Brooke, *The Collected Poems of Rupert Brooke* (New York: Dodd, 1932) 169.
30. In an unpublished reminiscence about the war that is unusual for its depiction of one long-lasting friendship, S. Raggett elaborates on the conflict between friendship and military regulation, and fumes against official orders that require men to abandon wounded soldiers during an advance. For Raggett, what this desperate army policy starkly demonstrates is that the war does not tolerate intimacy, even as it creates the conditions for the most extreme personal bonds. "I know one owes a duty to one's country," he writes, "but one also owes a duty to one's friend. I had been wounded and I had been helped a few months earlier. I know what I would have done had I had to choose between going forward or remaining with one wounded pal. Perhaps it was as well that I had not to choose because I would *not* have gone on" (Second Lt. Shallet Heuson Raggett, "Reminiscences of the War (1914–1918)," 28–29, IWM).
31. I shall discuss the subject of memorializing in more detail in Chapter 4. For analysis of memorials and memorializing, see Booth, *Postcards from the Trenches*; Bourke, *Dismembering the Male*; Thomas W. Laqueur, "Memory and Naming in the Great War," *Commemorations: The Politics of National Identity*, ed. John R. Gillis (Princeton: Princeton University Press, 1994) 150–167; and Winter, *Sites*.
32. T. S. Eliot, *Four Quartets* (San Diego: Harvest, 1971) 18.
33. Frank Stewart Flint's poem "Soldiers" (1920) functions along these lines. It dramatizes an agonizing, emotional moment when two old friends encounter one another on a silent march. The friends are forced to pass each other without mutual acknowledgment: "O face of my friend, / alone distinct of all that company, / you went on, you went on, / into the darkness" (Taylor, *Lads*, 107). Although the poet does not valorize such extreme fleetingness, he captures the sense that intimacy in war is often the attribute of a moment's flickering notice.
34. G. O. Hawkins, "Ravellings of Red," 233–234, IWM.
35. Other themes that mark this poetic style include: a romanticization of the outdoor life of war; nostalgia for England and the English countryside; the

continuity between school and war (as we have seen); mourning for dead friends; and the spiritual consolations of self-sacrifice.

36. So common was this theme in Great War poetry that Taylor (*Lads*) includes in his 1989 anthology of homoerotic war poems an entire section entitled "Greater Love." Critics have aligned this motif with a persistent spirit of gender discord in much war literature, along the lines set up by Gilbert and Gubar (*No Man's Land*) in their depiction of the war as a battle between the sexes. If Gilbert and Gubar set the tone for early feminist revisions of the war period, more recent scholars have argued against the thesis of gender conflict. See, especially, Bourke, *Dismembering the Male*, Chapter 3 ("Bonding").

37. Robert Nichols, *Ardours and Endurances* (London: Chatto, 1918) 44; volume cited hereafter in text as *AE*.

38. This problem of lost bodies, most famously memorialized in Brooke's "The Soldier," engendered heated public debate. For discussion of the debates surrounding burial and mourning, see Bourke, *Dismembering the Male*, Chapter 5 ("Re-Membering"), and Winter, *Sites*.

39. Robert Graves, *Poems About War*, ed. William Graves (Mount Kisco, NY: Moyer, 1988) 35.

40. Wilfred Owen, *The Poems of Wilfred Owen*, ed. Jon Stallworthy (London: Chatto, 1990), 192; volume cited hereafter in text as *PWO*.

41. Caesar (*Taking it Like a Man*) argues that Owen shares with Brooke, Graves, and Sassoon a patronizing condescension towards the working-class men, and his critique provides a corrective to an often overly reverent style of criticism with respect to the war poets.

42. A slight departure from this mode comes in "Wild With All Regrets" (in earlier drafts called "A Terre"), a poem dedicated to Sassoon. This agonizing poem is written from the perspective of a dying soldier in hospital, who imagines himself living in/through the life-blood of his friend. Though the image is one of extreme unity and intimacy, it also suggests parasitism, expressing the dying man's anger at the survivor:

> . . . if one chap wasn't bloody
> Or went stone-cold, I'd find another body.
> . . . Which I shan't manage now. Unless it's yours.
> I shall stay in you, friend, for some few hours.
> You'll feel my heavy spirit chill your chest,
> And climb your throat, on sobs, until it's chased
> On sighs, and wiped from off your lips by wind.
> I think on your rich breathing, brother, I'll be weaned
> To do without what blood remained me from my wound.
> (Owen, *PWO*, 188–189)

If Owen's general tendency is towards a fusion of spirits through pity, here that mode is challenged by its own extreme realization. Both speaker and addressee become starkly separated at the moment of imagined unity, for the poem reminds us that there can be no greater moment of individual self-assertion than the moment of death.

43. The conceit of the "strange meeting" with a ghost in a trench-like space is a common one in war literature. Sassoon's "Enemies" provides a particularly interesting version: in a follow-up to "The Poet as Hero," where Sassoon locates his burning desire for revenge in the grief over lost friends (see below), "Enemies" imagines the ghost of his friend David Thomas meeting "in some queer sunless place" with the ghosts of the "hulking Germans that I shot / When for his death my brooding rage was hot" (*WP*, 66). As in "Strange Meeting," the outcome of this poem is a new kind of male communion, which challenges the very terms on which the war is fought: "At last he turned and smiled. One took his hand / Because his face could make them understand" (*WP*, 66). We might also point to T. S. Eliot's incorporation of a similar moment of ghostly encounter in *The Waste Land*, in the episode of the meeting with Stetson, "'you who were with me in the ships at Mylae!'" (T. S. Eliot, *The Waste Land and Other Poems* [San Diego: Harcourt, 1962] 31).

44. Probably the most famous instance of a strong sense of alliance across enemy lines (a theme elaborated by Fussell) comes in *All Quiet on the Western Front*, when Paul Baümer shares a shell-hole with a dying Frenchman, and comes to see the enemy as his likeness, an object of empathy rather than hatred. See Remarque, *All Quiet*, 218–220.

45. For other examples of Owen's tendency to telescope institutional rituals into the human form, see "Song of Songs" and the hauntingly beautiful "Anthem for Doomed Youth."

46. Critics have utilized the concept of the counter-discourse most often with reference to queer theoretical contexts. See Joseph Allen Boone, *Tradition Counter Tradition: Love and the Form of Fiction* (Chicago: University of Chicago Press, 1987).

47. More than any other theme, anger and outrage against the inaccuracy and propagandistic quality of war reporting characterize war texts of all sorts. The reader should also note the ironic reference of Owen's title to a popular war song.

48. As in "Disabled," Owen here looks directly at the injured survivors of the war. I shall discuss issues of disability and the return from war in the next chapter.

49. Edmund Blunden, *Undertones of War* (Garden City: Doubleday, 1929) 1.

50. Many war texts treat the problem of the impossibility of mourning during war and the psychological ramifications for the survivor. As Sassoon explains, in reference to learning about a close friend's death, "This piece of news had stupefied me, but the pain hadn't begun to make itself felt yet, and there was no spare time for personal grief when the Battalion was getting ready to move back to Divisional Rest. To have thought about [him] would have been calamitous" (*Sherston*, 363). Or, in the words of S. B. Abbott, 'We mourned for a few hours and then – forgot them. Callous? Yes – but that was life in France. We lived from day to day and almost every sunset found a grave-digging party putting a comrade into his last bed" (Abbott, Memoir, IWM). Another text that focuses its tragic lens on the problem of inadequate mourning is R. C. Sherriff's drama *Journey's End*, first produced in 1928.

51. In his memoir, Sassoon describes a powerful urge for revenge after the death of his friend David Thomas, an emotional pitch that led him to fight ferociously ("I went up to the trenches with the intention of trying to kill someone. It was my idea of getting a bit of my own back" [*Sherston*, 274–275]). Sassoon was awarded the Military Cross, but he eventually threw the ribbon into the river Mersey as part of his famous protest. See *Sherston*, 508–509.

52. Though I have not discussed the problem of officers' guilt for abandoning their men, the theme pervades war literature. In addition to Owen, Sassoon, Graves, and Blunden, all of whom stress this issue, many unpublished writers describe intense feelings of guilt and strong desires to return to the front as quickly as possible. Thus in his memoir, S. H. Raggett expresses grief at missing the men, and particularly his closest friend, who remain in combat: "It is a natural feeling to want to be 'on the spot' with one's friends; even after I knew war, shorn of its glamour, knew it as it was, I wanted to be there, even when in England and in safety . . . How could one stay away, really? Bodily comfort one had in England, it is true, but not mental comfort. Whilst [on leave], I thought of the life in France, and would have given much to be with my friend, and share his joys and sorrows" ("Reminiscences," 7).

53. The idea of death as the great equalizer is demonstrated with visual poignancy in First World War memorials. The war provided perhaps the greatest challenge in British history – and also a great opportunity – to reconceptualize the nature of memorialization. In general, the war cemeteries tended towards simplicity, austerity, and anonymity. The Imperial War Graves Commission's decision, for instance, that all graves would be identical, regardless of rank or circumstances of death, was at once a practical, ideological, and aesthetic choice. For discussion of First World War memorials, see Fussell, *Great War*; Booth, *Postcards from the Trenches*; Hynes, *War Imagined*; Laqueur, "Memory and Naming"; and Winter, *Sites*.

54. Sassoon was not the only writer to conjoin the problem of the bereaved friend with Romantic iconography. Here are three further examples. First, in Nichols' "Alone," the wounded soldier who narrates the poem performs the role of misunderstood outcast, whose poetic calling further severs him from communication with non-combatants. Conventionally invoking the affective fallacy, the poet allies his own state of grief with the devastation of the larger universe, as he observes a sea-gull, "Wheeling with his reiterant cry / Of loneliness . . . All, all is lone: / Alone . . . / And so am I" (Nichols, *AE*, 60). For Nichols, the isolated state must be experienced as part of a mourning process, whose eventual resolution will involve a satisfactory re-integration into civilian life. His volume of poetry is organized according to a trajectory of healing, and the later poems are meant to provide the uplift that the poet here cannot imagine.

A second example: "An Account of Ill Health," by Edward Shanley, describes the sorrow, guilt, and longing of the invalided soldier thinking of his fellows still in the field. The poem closes with the familiar alienated self, as the speaker imagines himself in a state of permanent isolation: "Then in that new-born world, unfriendly and estranged / I shall be quite alone" (Osborn, *Muse in Arms*, 282).

And finally, perhaps most striking for its synthesis of multiple themes involving intimacy, post-war alienation, and grieving for lost friends is the closing stanza of Herbert Read's "My Company." Having established a strangely excessive image of himself (the officer-poet) in a relation of mutual admiration with his men, the speaker goes on to imagine an eternity of agonizing loneliness:

> But God! I know that I'll stand
> Someday in the loneliest wilderness,
> Someday my heart will cry
> For the soul that has been but that now
> Is scattered with the winds,
> Deceased and devoid
> . . .
> I know that I'll wander with a cry:
> 'O beautiful men, O men I loved
> O wither are you gone, my company?'
> . . .
> This is a hell
> Immortal while I live.
>   (Herbert Read, *Collected Poems*
>   [New York: Horizon, 1966] 38)

55. The notion that modernism can be understood as a kind of aesthetics of trauma has become increasingly compelling for literary critics of the period. This understanding of literary modernism, in turn, follows from the outpouring of studies on memory and trauma with respect to the second half of the twentieth century. For particularly influential studies, see Maurice Hallbwachs, *Collective Memory* (New York: Harper, 1980); Cathy Caruth, *Unclaimed Experience: Trauma, Narrative, and History* (Baltimore: Johns Hopkins University Press, 1996); Shoshana Felman and Dori Laub, *Testimony: Crises of Witnessing in Literature, Psychoanalysis, and History* (New York: Routledge, 1992); Ruth Leys, *Trauma: A Genealogy* (Chicago: University of Chicago Press, 2000); George Lipsitz, *Time Passages: Collective Memory and American Popular Culture* (Minneapolis: University of Minnesota Press, 1990); and James Young, *The Texture of Memory: Holocaust Memorials and Meaning* (New Haven: Yale University Press, 1993).

56. Vera Brittain, *Testament of Youth: An Autobiographical Study of the Years 1900–1925* (New York: Penguin, 1989) 11.

57. Given the prominence in Woolf criticism of the twin topics of feminism and Bloomsbury, it is perhaps surprising that direct and systematic discussions of Woolf's relation to masculinity and its institutions are rather sparse. See Angela Ingram, "'The Sacred Edifices': Virginia Woolf and Some of the Sons of Culture," *Virginia Woolf and Bloomsbury*, ed. Jane Marcus (Bloomington: Indiana University Press, 1987) 125–145; Judy Little, "*Jacob's Room* as Comedy: Woolf's Parodic *Bildungsroman*," *New Feminist Essays on Virginia Woolf*,

ed. Jane Marcus (Lincoln: University of Nebraska Press, 1981) 105–124; and Sara Ruddick, "Private Brother, Public World," Marcus, *New Feminist*, 185–215. For discussion of sisterly community in *A Room of One's Own*, see Jane Marcus, *Virginia Woolf and the Languages of Patriarchy* (Bloomington: Indiana University Press, 1987). See also Merry M. Pawlowski, ed., *Virginia Woolf and Fascism: Resisting the Dictator's Seduction* (New York: Palgrave, 2001).

58. Virginia Woolf, *Mrs. Dalloway* (San Diego: Harcourt, 1985) 20; volume cited in text hereafter as *MD*.

59. For discussion of Septimus and shell-shock, see Showalter, *Female Malady*. See also Elizabeth Abel, *Virginia Woolf and the Fictions of Psychoanalysis* (Chicago: University of Chicago Press, 1989); Thomas C. Caramango, *The Flight of the Mind: Virginia Woolf's Art and Manic Depressive Illness* (Berkeley: University of California Press, 1992); Karen DeMeester, "Trauma and Recovery in Virginia Woolf's *Mrs Dalloway*," *Modern Fiction Studies* 44:3 (Fall 1998) 649–673; Mark Hussey, *Virginia Woolf and War: Fiction, Reality, and Myth* (Syracuse: Syracuse University Press, 1991); Karen L. Leavenback, *Virginia Woolf and the Great War* (Syracuse: Syracuse University Press, 1999); and Sue Thomas, "Virginia Woolf's Septimus Smith and Contemporary Perceptions of Shell Shock," *English Language Notes* 25:2 (December 1987) 49–57.

60. T. S. Eliot, *Selected Poems* (San Diego: Harcourt, 1964) 75.

61. For a thorough and highly compelling analysis of the war in Eliot's poetry, see Vincent Sherry, *The Great War and the Language of Modernism* (Oxford: Oxford University Press, forthcoming). For a brief discussion of the war in "The Hollow Men," see David Roessel, "Guy Fawkes Day and the Versailles Peace in 'The Hollow Men,'" *English Language Review* 28:1 (September 1990) 52–58.

62. Any argument about the shape of "The Hollow Men" needs to be somewhat cautious, of course, given the composition and publication history of the poem. Because the poem was written in parts, and initially published as such, one might question a reading of the overall poem's trajectory. However, Eliot stood behind the whole poem in an unqualified manner, and its music works in a highly unified manner – to argue that there is a movement in the poem from one kind of voice/concern to another seems clearly valid. One might add, too, that *The Waste Land* was also written in piecemeal fashion, and Eliot had originally intended serial publication in parts. It was primarily Pound's firm opposition that kept the poem from being serialized part by part.

4 "THE VIOLENCE OF THE NIGHTMARE": D. H. LAWRENCE AND THE AFTERMATH OF WAR

1. D. H. Lawrence, *Women in Love* (Cambridge: Cambridge University Press, 1987) 481; volume cited hereafter in text as *WL*.

2. D. H. Lawrence, *Aaron's Rod* (Cambridge: Cambridge University Press, 1988) 238–239; volume cited hereafter in text as *AR*.

3. D. H. Lawrence, *Kangaroo* (Cambridge: Cambridge University Press, 1994) 104; volume cited in text hereafter as *K*.

4. My primary concern will be the civilian response to the returned men, rather than an analysis of soldiers' own depictions of their complex and uncertain situation. War writers did, of course, contemplate their position in the post-war world, as, for example, in Sassoon's poem "To One Who Was with me in the War." But a surprisingly large number of war texts follow a structure that essentially concludes with the armistice. Typically, these texts comprise several elements: recruitment and the decision to go to war, training, initial service abroad, the extreme conditions of front-line combat, injury and recovery, return to the front, and finally the armistice.

5. Wyndham Lewis, *Blasting and Bombardiering* (London: Eyre and Spottiswoode, 1937) 18.

6. Samuel Hynes, *A War Imagined: The First World War and English Culture* (New York: Macmillan, 1991) 283.

7. Because the word "veteran" was not used in Britain during the period, I have avoided its usage here. Contemporaries used the prefixes "ex-," "former," "returned," "demobilized," or "discharged," with such nouns as "soldier," "serviceman," and "combatant," and I have followed this practice.

8. In making sense of these numbers, it is useful to note that Britain's pre-war population was 45 million. For extensive documentation, see Jay M. Winter, *The Great War and the British People* (London: Macmillan, 1985). We should note, however, that when it comes to injury, numbers are notoriously uncertain. Pensions and medical reports have clear limitations. In the case of shell-shock, calculating numbers would seem to be practically impossible, and we can assume that the official figure of 200,000 is much too low.

9. The only body officially repatriated after the war was the body of the Unknown Warrior, which was carefully selected by a special government committee. For discussion of public debates surrounding the politics of burial in both England and France, see Jay Winter, *Sites of Memory, Sites of Mourning: The Great War in European Cultural History* (Cambridge: Cambridge University Press, 1995).

10. Winston Churchill, *The Aftermath: The World Crisis – 1918–1928* (New York: Scribner, 1929) 15.

11. Elaine Scarry, *The Body in Pain: The Making and Unmaking of the World* (New York: Oxford University Press, 1985) esp. "The Structure of War," 60–157.

12. Such terms as "shared memory," "cultural memory," and "national memory" have become so widely used in recent years as to have become, arguably, unhelpful. For discussion of the over-abundance of memory language in current historical discourse, see Jay Winter, "The Generation of Memory: Reflections on the 'Memory Boom' in Contemporary Historical Studies," *German Historical Institute Bulletin* 27 (Fall 2000) 69–92, and Kerwin Lee Klein, "On the Emergence of *Memory* in Historical Discourse," *Representations* 69 (Winter 2000) 127–150.

13. Philip Gibbs, *Realities of War* (London: Heinemann, 1920) 448; volume cited hereafter in text as *RW*.

14. It is worth noting that in Germany, the cultural appropriation of the war's martyrs looked markedly different from what we find in England. As George Mosse has shown, the cult of the fallen in post-war Germany became the central element in a new "religion of nationalism," and former soldiers were important contributors to the rise of fascism in Germany, as elsewhere in Europe. However, even in the case of Germany, we should distinguish between the exploitation of the concept of national martyrdom and the actual experience of surviving combatants. See George Mosse, *Fallen Soldiers: Reshaping the Memory of the World Wars* (New York: Oxford University Press, 1990).

    The significance of Christian iconography remains potent in the British as well as German context, particularly in terms of such concepts as physical sacrifice, suffering, martyrdom, and the incarnation of cultural pain in an individual body. For discussion of religion and the war, see Paul Fussell, *The Great War and Modern Memory* (London: Oxford University Press, 1975); Adrian Caesar, *Taking it Like a Man: Suffering, Sexuality and the War Poets: Brooke, Sassoon, Owen, Graves* (Manchester: Manchester University Press, 1993); Alan Wilkinson, *The Church of England and the First World War* (London: SPCK, 1978); and Winter, *Sites*.

15. Wilfred Owen, *The Poems of Wilfred Owen* (London: Chatto, 1996) 153.

16. Among such skeptical cultural historians, I want to mention two scholars who have addressed the issue of post-war reactions to injury and warfare, and have generally concluded that the cultural changes that followed immediately from the war were ultimately short-lived: Joanna Bourke, *Dismembering the Male: Men's Bodies, Britain, and the Great War* (Chicago: University of Chicago Press, 1996), and, with a more limited focus, Seth Koven, "Remembering and Dismemberment: Crippled Children, Wounded Soldiers, and the Great War in Great Britain," *American Historical Review* 99 (October 1994) 1167–1202.

17. Charles F. G. Masterman, *England After War: A Study* (London: Hodder, 1923) 4.

18. *The Times*, 25 November 1918. It is striking to note how persistent the "fit country" language remains in our contemporary discourse, with books and articles frequently borrowing some version of Lloyd George's phrase for their titles. The formulation is often slightly misquoted: frequently the words "fit" and "country" are reversed ("a country fit for heroes to live in"), and often the word "land" is substituted for "country."

19. Earlier in 1918, in a sense anticipating the Prime Minister's stress on "fit," John Galsworthy described the relation between returning troops and civilian life as "a huge jig-saw puzzle [which] confronts us" (John Galsworthy, "The Gist of the Matter," *Reveille* 1 [August 1918] 14).

20. The word "country," too, has rich connotations. With its resonance of the countryside, it calls to mind the pressing problems of accommodation facing many former soldiers, as a housing shortage became one of the central touch-stones in the post-war economic and political turmoil, and as schemes took shape to settle former soldiers in the English countryside or in the

imperium, primarily in Canada and Australia. For thorough discussion of soldier settlement projects in the period, see Kent Fedorowich, *Unfit for Heroes: Reconstruction and Soldier Settlement in the Empire between the Wars* (Manchester: Manchester University Press, 1995). Fedorowich's conclusion is that the government's elaborate efforts to settle ex-servicemen on colonial land – thereby rejuvenating both the men and the imperial agricultural economy – resulted in failure. "In the final analysis," he writes, "soldier settlement neither solved unemployment nor produced untold national wealth. Instead, it created indebtedness, hardship and disappointment" (198).

21. Enid Bagnold, "Outside the Hospital," *Reveille* 1 (August 1918), 96.
22. D. H. Lawrence, *Lady Chatterly's Lover* (New York: New American Library, 1959) 12; volume cited hereafter in text as *LCL*.
23. In American literature, prominent returned and/or injured men can be found, for instance, in William Faulkner's "Soldiers' Pay" (1926), Ernest Hemingway's *A Farewell to Arms* (1929), and Dalton Trumbo's *Johnny Got his Gun* (1939).
24. "For Men Broken in our Wars," *The Times*, 21 July 1915.
25. "Broken Soldiers," *The Times*, 23 April 1917.
26. P. C. Varrier-Jones, "A Plea for the Consumptive Soldier," *Reveille* 2 (November 1918), 242.
27. G. Howson, ed., *Handbook for the Limbless* (London: Disabled Society, *c.* 1921) 69.
28. John Galsworthy, "Looking Ahead," *Reveille* 2 (November 1918), 177.
29. M. Creagh-Henry and D. Marten, *The Unknown Warrior: A Mystical Play* (London: Society for Promoting Christian Knowledge, 1923) 6.
30. A. T. Wilkinson, 78/51/1, IWM.
31. Lt. Gen. Goodwin, "What the War Office is Doing," *Reveille* 2 (November 1918), 229.
32. Sir John Collie, "The Management of Neurasthenia and Allied Disorders Contracted in the Army," *Recalled to Life: A Journal Devoted to the Care, ReEducation, and Return to Civil Life of Disabled Sailors and Soldiers* 2 (September 1917) 237.
33. Douglas McMurtrie, *The Disabled Soldier* (New York: Macmillan, 1919) 154; volume cited hereafter in text as *DS*.
34. The subject of shell-shock is too broad to be considered here. For an early, classic study, see Eric Leed, *No Man's Land: Combat and Identity in World War I* (Cambridge: Cambridge University Press, 1979). A recent collection of essays that spans many of the warring nations is *Journal of Contemporary History, Special Issue: Shell-shock*, guest ed., Jay Winter, vol. 35 (2000). For a more narrowly focused social history of the shell-shock phenomenon in England, see Ted Bogacz, "War Neurosis and Cultural Change in England, 1914–1922: The Work of the War Office Committee of Enquiry into 'Shell-Shock,'" *Journal of Contemporary History* 24 (1989) 227–256. For analysis of shell-shock and gender, in the context of the discourse and treatment surrounding female hysteria in the nineteenth and twentieth centuries, see Elaine Showalter, *The*

Female Malady: Women, Madness, and English Culture, 1830–1980 (New York: Pantheon, 1985). For discussion of shell-shock in the Australian context, see Stephen Garton, *The Cost of War: Australians Return* (Melbourne: Oxford University Press, 1996). For a broader survey of the literature on shell-shock in the period, see Peter Leese, "'Why are they not Cured?': British Shell-shock Treatment during the Great War," *Traumatic Pasts: History, Psychiatry, and Trauma in the Modern Age, 1870–1930*, ed. Mark S. Micale and Paul Lerner (Cambridge: Cambridge University Press, 2001) 206–221.

In addition to literary critical influence, the image of shell-shock as a paradigmatic Great War (and modernist) condition is given rich treatment in Pat Barker's highly acclaimed trilogy of First World War novels, especially *Regeneration* (New York: Penguin, 1992), set in the mental hospital where both Sassoon and Owen were treated. Barker's novels have, in turn, contributed to a heightened attention to the subject of shell-shock treatment in the inter-war period and, especially, to the figure of W. H. R. Rivers.

35. In *The Female Malady*, Showalter characterizes the victims of shell-shock as analogous to nineteenth-century women. Both groups are presented as victims of the patriarchal medical establishment, and both employ resistance strategies that depend, among other things, on indirection and passivity.

36. Miscellanea, *Recalled to Life* 1 (June 1917), 75.

37. Quoted in A. Tiveychoc, *There and Back: The Story of an Australian Soldier, 1915–1935* (Sidney: Returned Sailors and Soldiers Imperial League of Australia, 1935) 218.

38. Enid Bagnold, *A Diary without Dates* (London: Heinemann, 1918) 104.

39. Virginia Woolf, *The Diary of Virginia Woolf, Volume I: 1915–1919*, ed. Anne Olivier Bell (London: Hogarth, 1977) 294.

40. E. B. Stallard, *Remembrance and Reveille or An Ex-Service Man's Sermons out of Church* (London: Stockwell, 1931) 7.

41. Walter Benjamin, *Illuminations*, trans. Harry Zohn (New York: Schocken, 1968) 84.

42. Brieux, "Blinded Soldiers and Our Duty to Them," *Reveille* 2 (November 1918), 195; journal cited hereafter in text as *Rev.*

43. Helen Zenna Smith, *Women of the Aftermath: A Sequel to Not so Quiet* (London: John Long, 1931) 11–12.

44. Vera Brittain, *Testament of Youth: An Autobiographical Study of the Years 1900–1925* (London: Penguin, 1989) 443.

45. For discussion of soldiers' fears of impotence and of cultural responses, see Garton, *Cost of War*, especially "Home Fires."

46. As Douglas McMurtrie, probably the leading voice on rehabilitation, writes in one of many Red Cross pamphlets, "The first responsibility on the part of the family of the injured man is to learn the meaning of disability, and see the hopeful rather than the depressing aspect" (Douglas McMurtrie, *Social Responsibilities in the Rehabilitation of Disabled Soldiers and Sailors* [New York: William Wood, 1918] 1–2).

47. Lord Charnwood, Introduction, *Recalled to Life* 1 (June 1917), 4.

48. I am grateful to Seth Koven's wonderful piece, "Remembering and Dismemberment," for calling my attention to Galsworthy's journal, *Reveille*. Actually, the journal was not entirely Galsworthy's own creation, since it represents a retooling of *Recalled to Life*, a similarly short-run journal dedicated to providing practical/medical advice to disabled former soldiers. Both journals contain a rich mixture of material, and *Reveille* is particularly effective at presenting a broad view of the culture's understanding of war disability in the period around the armistice. I have included many references to articles from the two journals.

49. Colonel Netterville Barron, "Physical Education," *Reveille* 1 (August 1918), 148. It should be noted that this piece forms a rather uneasy entry in *Reveille*, for it is permeated by a eugenicist element, including language about the fear of racial degeneration, which is generally absent from Galsworthy's selections.

50. W. F. West, Diary 7, 92/10/1, IWM.

51. For discussion of the statistics regarding ex-soldiers and unemployment throughout the decade, see Stephen Ward, "Great Britain: Land Fit for Heroes Lost," *The War Generation: Veterans of the First World War*, ed. Ward (Port Washington: Kennikat Press, 1975) 22, 30. For broader discussions of class and labor in the context of the war, see James E. Cronin, *Labour and Society in Britain, 1918–1979* (London: Batsford, 1984); John N. Horne, *Labour at War: France and Britain, 1914–1918* (New York: Oxford University Press, 1991); Arthur Marwick, *Britain in the Century of Total War: War, Peace, and Social Change, 1900–1967* (Boston: Little Brown, 1968); B. A. Waites, "The Effect of the First World War on Class and Status in England, 1910–20," *Journal of Contemporary History* 11 (1976) 27–48; and Waites, *A New Class Society at War, England 1914–1918* (New York: Berg, 1987).

52. See Koven, "Remembering and Dismemberment," and Bourke, *Dismembering the Male*, for discussion of the parallels in the rhetoric and treatment of disabled soldiers and crippled children.

53. Charnwood, Introduction, *Recalled to Life* 1 (June 1917), 1.

54. Lt. Gen. Goodwin, "What the War Office is Doing," *Reveille* 2 (November 1918), 223.

55. Brieux, "Blinded Soldiers," *Reveille* 2 (November 1918), 190.

56. Major Herbert Evans, "Development of the Work," *Reveille* 2 (November 1918), 232.

57. H. G. Wells, *The Outline of History: Being a Plain History of Life and Mankind* (New York: Macmillan, 1921) 1059.

58. Winston Churchill, *The Aftermath: The World Crisis – 1918–1928* (New York: Scribner, 1929) 49.

59. Quoted in Ward, *War Generation*, 27.

60. Quoted in Peter Keating, ed., *Into Unknown England 1866–1913: Selections from the Social Explorers* (Glasgow: Fontana, 1976) 242.

61. C. F. G. Masterman, *The Heart of the Empire: Discussions of Problems of Modern City Life in England* (New York: Harper and Row, 1973) 7.

62. Miles, "Where to Get Men," *Contemporary Review* 81 (January 1902) 78–86.

63. Masterman entitles his chapter on abject poverty "Return of the Abyss," referring to his own earlier study of "The Social Abyss," which warned about a catastrophe of poverty and degeneration that now, once again, threatens to engulf the poor. At the same time, he takes special note of the ironies that attend the condition of returned soldiers. See Masterman, *England After War*.

64. Bagnold, "Outside the Hospital," *Reveille* 1 (August 1918), 96.

65. Erich Maria Remarque, *All Quiet on the Western Front*, trans. A. W. Wheen (New York: Ballantine, 1996) 122–123.

66. For a convincing demystification of the notion that the majority of returning soldiers were fundamentally embittered and alienated, see Bourke, *Dismembering the Male*. For an analysis of the imaginative influence of the notion of the lost generation, despite its historical inaccuracy, see David Cannadine, "War and Death, Grief and Mourning in Modern Britain," *Mirrors of Mortality: Studies in the Social History of Death*, ed. Joachim Whaley (New York: St. Martin's Press, 1981), 187–242, esp. 199–202.

67. Other examples include "You Touched Me" (1920), "The Fox" (1919), and "The Blind Man" (1920). "The Blind Man" is particularly interesting for its focus on the issues surrounding a severely injured returnee and the smoldering, romantic power of male intimacy. The story centers on the psychic and emotional responses of a married couple to the eponymous soldier's return from the war, suggesting both the ease with which his blindness is accommodated and the lingering, terrible power of its transformations. Yet the story ends on a different note, partially echoing *Women in Love* (see below), as the blind man comes to realize his intense and passionate desire for male friendship. That deep desire is not fully returned, and the story ends on an ambiguous note, where friendship seems to disrupt and disturb as much as it comforts and enhances (D. H. Lawrence, *The Complete Short Stories*, Volume II [London: Penguin, 1982] 347–365; volume cited hereafter in text as *CSS*).

68. "Monkey Nuts" was completed in 1919, but was not published for three years. "Tickets, Please" was written in 1918 and published the following year.
    See, in particular, Hilary Simpson, *D. H. Lawrence and Feminism* (London: Croom, 1982).

69. Frederic Jameson, *Fables of Aggression: Wyndham Lewis, the Modernist as Fascist* (Berkeley: University of California Press, 1979) 35–61.

70. Robert Graves, *Goodbye to All That* (New York: Cape, 1930) 349.

71. *The Times*, 8 January 1919.

72. Acknowledgment of mutiny and disobedience was almost non-existent in Britain during the war. Not surprisingly, virtually no reporting of instances of mutiny or defection was allowed in the press. For discussion of the French mutinies, see John Keegan, *The First World War* (New York: Knopf, 1999) 329–331.

73. Charles Carrington, *Soldier from the Wars Returning* (London: Hutchinson, 1965) 257.

74. Michael Tratner, *Modernism and Mass Politics: Joyce, Woolf, Eliot, Yeats* (Stanford: Stanford University Press, 1995).

75. In terms of celebration, the biggest and most lavish victory parade took place on 19 July 1919, after the signing of the Treaty of Versailles. It involved representatives of every regiment in the BEF, including colonial and allied divisions, and it cut across many miles of London. Here was what we might think of as a classic military parade, relying centrally on the aesthetics of symmetry and the image of cohesiveness, at the same time that it highlighted regimental spirit and decoration. Crowds lined the streets and cheered, and many thousands of former soldiers participated.

76. The most thorough and convincing account of the efficacy of both public and private rituals of mourning in the First World War period is Winter, *Sites*. Winter's argument counters the commonplace notion that modernity is characterized by the rejection of conventional forms, such as those which represent death and console grief.

77. In France, where memorials were ubiquitous, the most common approach was to combine a simple geometrical pyramid with a standardized *poilu* (the equivalent of the British Tommy). For discussion of French memorial-making as a complex social product, see Daniel J. Sherman, "Art, Commerce, and the Production of Memory in France after World War I," *Commemorations: The Politics of National Identity*, ed. John R. Gillis (Princeton: Princeton University Press, 1994) 186–211.

78. An interesting case of a work which focuses on the way returned men responded to the memorializing fever is Tiveychoc's *There and Back*, which – as its title suggests – is equally as concerned with the after-effects of war as with the experience of combat. The text closes at an Anzac Day celebration in 1935, where the quality of extreme memory hangs heavy: "They were all there – fallen comrades, veterans and youths. It was one great reunion – a reunion of souls" (Tiveychoc, *There and Back*, 281).

79. On the subject of intercession, it should be noted that the inter-war years marked the high-point in modern history of British interest in spiritualism, as many thousands of civilians sought to reach their dead husbands, sons, fathers, and friends. For discussion of spiritualism during the period, see Winter, *Sites*, and Cannadine, "War and Death."

80. Thomas Laqueur has argued that the Cenotaph and the Unknown Warrior, together with the heightened emphasis on the inscription of names onto graves and monuments, represent a deliberately novel symbolic language of modern war. See Thomas W. Laqueur, "Memory and Naming in the Great War," Gillis, *Commemorations*, 150–167.

81. Sir John Collie, "The Paralysed Pensioner," *Reveille* 2 (November 1918), 230.

82. *Manchester Guardian*, 12 November 1920, quoted in *Cenotaph: A Book of Remembrance in Poetry and Prose for November the Eleventh*, ed. Thomas Moult (London: Cape, 1923) 24; volume cited hereafter in text as *Cen.*

83. Among the more radical ex-servicemen groups, several warrant mention. The Silver Badge party began in 1918 as a political party of conservative ex-servicemen, but never had much impact. In 1919, the National Union of Ex-Servicemen (NUX) and the International Union of Ex-Servicemen (IUX) were

founded on radical, socialist principles. Though comprised of former soldiers, the idea was that these organizations would move beyond the immediate issues of concern to that constituency. Though the NUX and IUX created an initial splash – intersecting as they did with a wave of activism across England – their national visibility never approached that of the more mainstream groups, and they disbanded with the formation of the British Legion in 1921. Finally, in 1931, Oswald Mosely founded the short-lived British Union of Fascists (BUF), which, though not explicitly an ex-servicemen's organization, did lay claim to the legacy of embittered former soldiers, a feature common to fascist movements across Europe in the inter-war period.

84. For the seminal text on the battle between the sexes, see Sandra M. Gilbert and Susan Gubar, *No Man's Land: The Place of the Woman Writer in the Twentieth Century, Volume II: Sexchanges* (New Haven: Yale University Press, 1989).

85. "Official Opposition," *The "Live-Wire," Official Organ of the National Ex-Service Men's Union of Temporary Civil Servants* (October 1920) 3.

86. C. W. White, "The New War. The Ex-Soldier and the Present State of Things," *"Live-Wire"* (July 1920) 20–21.

87. The language here once again harks back to late-Victorian reform literature, with an allusion to Charles Booth's famous image of the "submerged" portion of the population whose utter poverty renders it essentially beyond the purview of social control. See Charles Booth, *Life and Labour of the People of London: Selections* (New York: Pantheon, 1967).

88. The Comrades of the Great War, Leaflet #1, First Series.

89. *Comrade's Journal, Journal of the Comrades of the Great War* (May 1919) 3–4.

90. Clement Edwards, MP, "Why British Comradeship will Beat Bolshevism!" *Comrade's Journal* (June 1919) 5.

91. Evans, "Development," *Reveille* 2 (November 1918), 232.

92. *Comrade's Journal* (May 1919) 4.

93. George Lansbury, *My Life* (London: Constable, 1928) 221.

94. J. L. Hodson, Newsletter for the Old 21st. Association, quoted in R. L. Watson, 93/43/1, IWM.

95. Lieutenant R. G. Dixon, "The Wheels of Darkness," 88, IWM.

96. The first of his two treatises, *Shop Slavery and Emancipation*, came with a foreword, in cautiously laudatory prose, by Wells, while the second, *A New Aristocracy of Comradeship*, forms part of a series of titles, published by Leonard Parsons, others of which were written by such figures as Ramsay MacDonald and Philip Snowden. See William Paine, *Shop Slavery and Emancipation* (London: King, 1912), and Paine, *A New Aristocracy of Comradeship* (London: Leonard Parsons, 1920); cited in text hereafter as *SSE* and *NAC*, respectively.

97. For discussion of the University Settlement Movement, with a special focus on the comradeship ethos, see Standish Meacham, *Toynbee Hall and Social Reform, 1880–1914: The Search for Community* (New Haven: Yale University Press, 1987).

98. Several works with a focus on male intimacy that I shall not discuss are *The White Peacock* (1911), centrally concerned with the friendship of Cyril

Beardsall and George Saxton, presented as rural and organic; *Sons and Lovers* (1913), in which the rivalry of Paul Morel and Baxter Dawes conforms to recognizably Sedgwickian patterns; *Fantasia of the Unconscious* (1922), which shares *Kangaroo*'s interest in male political association; and various Italian sketches, which tend to fetishize the virility of Italian men and the naturalness of their bonds with one another.

Less well known is *David*, a short drama Lawrence wrote in 1925, which focuses on the famous friendship between Jonathan and David. To laud this Biblical friendship – the classic male bond that "surpasses the love of women" – had by the mid-twenties become a commonplace, and one might ask what Lawrence contributes to the well-worn story. I would suggest that the narrative is interesting for its presentation of Jonathan, another entrant into the pantheon of modern male solitaries, defined and destroyed by the unfulfilled desire for organized intimacy. To my reading, the text culminates in the disjunction between David, who is capable of balancing a sexualized marriage with a covenanted brotherhood, and Jonathan, a shattered, bereft figure. David's is a success story, a tale of completion, plenitude, and power. Meanwhile, Jonathan takes on the role of grieving friend, and, notwithstanding the play's title, it is his internal division that becomes a model for a tortured self, and it is his prophetic voice that closes the play. Lawrence thus transforms the David and Jonathan story, the conventional prototype for perfect male friendship, into another narrative of broken friendship as modern prophecy. See D. H. Lawrence, *David: A Play* (London: Martin Secker, 1926).

99. For Hilary Simpson, Lawrence's interest in male bonds is best evaluated in terms of his reactions to the feminist movements of the period. See Simpson, *D. H. Lawrence and Feminism.* Judith Ruderman, in her study of Lawrence's life-long problems with the feared icon of the "devouring mother," writes that "The importance of the relationship between Ramón and Cipriano [in *Plumed*] – as of that between the other blood brothers in Lawrence's works – lies in what it reacts against: the Magna Mater and her smothering love" (Judith Ruderman, *D. H. Lawrence and the Devouring Mother: The Search for a Patriarchal Ideal of Leadership* [Durham: Duke University Press, 1984] 148). And Laura Fasick argues that "male comradeship [in the Italian works] is not a thing sought after from a natural, innate male need, but is a part of a complex reaction to the threat of emasculation perceived as emanating from women and their unwelcome power" (Laura Fasick, "Female Power, Male Comradeship, and the Rejection of the Female in Lawrence's *Twilight in Italy, Sea and Sardinia,* and *Etruscan Places,*" *D. H. Lawrence Review* 21:1 [Spring 1989] 340).

100. For discussion of Lawrence's and other modernists' enthrallment with images of fascistic eroticism, see Laura Frost, *Sex Drives: Fantasies of Fascism in Literary Modernism* (Ithaca: Cornell University Press, 2002).

101. Emile Delavenay, *D. H. Lawrence and Edward Carpenter: A Study in Edwardian Transition* (New York: Taplinger, 1971) 1.

102. D. H. Lawrence, *The Symbolic Meaning*, ed. Armin Arnold (New York: Viking, 1964) 95.
103. D. H. Lawrence, *Studies in Classic American Literature* (London: Heinemann, 1924) 57; volume cited in text hereafter as *SCAL*.
104. Christopher Craft, *Another Kind of Love: Male Homosexual Desire in English Discourse, 1850–1920* (Berkeley: University of California Press, 1994) 189.
105. We might be reminded, here, of the parallel scene when Fielding visits Aziz's sickbed in *A Passage to India*, an equally successful moment in the engendering of structured intimacy, discussed in Chapter 1.
106. D. H. Lawrence, *Phoenix II: Uncollected, Unpublished and Other Prose Works* (New York: Penguin, 1978).
107. D. H. Lawrence, *The Letters of D. H. Lawrence, Volume II, June 1913 – October 1916*, ed. George J. Zytaruk and James T. Boulton (Cambridge: Cambridge University Press, 1981) 648.
108. Tony Pinkney, *D. H. Lawrence and Modernism* (Iowa City: University of Iowa Press, 1990).
109. The marriage of Rawdon and Tanny Lilly poses an interesting possible counter-example, since the text suggests that the couple has developed a form of unity carved out of their own independence, always a central Lawrentian goal. However, as readers, we see very little of this marriage, what we do see generally confirms a spirit of combativeness rather than productive harmony, and Lilly himself indicates that his own marriage falls into the ordinary gender patterns that he and his male friends loudly deplore.
110. For discussion of the Returned Servicemen's League, see G. L. Kristianson, *The Politics of Patriotism: The Pressure Group Activities of the Returned Servicemen's League* (Canberra: Australian National University Press, 1966). For helpful discussion of Lawrence's treatment of the Diggers, see Bruce Steele, Introduction, *Kangaroo*, by D. H. Lawrence (Cambridge: Cambridge University Press, 1994) xxiv–xxxii. For examples of the historical Diggers' self-representation, see C. E. W. Bean's influential *The Anzac Book, Written and Illustrated in Gallipoli by the Men of Anzac* (London: Cassell, 1916), and *The W. A. Digger Book* (Press of West Australian Branch of Returned Sailors' and Soldiers' Imperial League, 1930).
111. For a complete discussion of returned soldiers in Australia, see Garton, *Cost of War*. See also Bill Gammage, *The Broken Years: Australian Soldiers in the Great War* (Canberra: Australian National University Press, 1974); Alistair Thomson, *Anzac Memories: Living with the Legend* (Melbourne: Oxford University Press, 1994); and Marilyn Lake, "Mission Impossible: How Men Gave Birth to the Australian Nation – Nationalism, Gender, and Other Seminal Acts," *Gender and History* 4:3 (Autumn 1992) 305–322.

Index